SEE HOW
THEY RAN

SEE HOW THEY RAN

*The Changing Role of
the Presidential Candidate*

REVISED AND EXPANDED EDITION

————

GIL TROY

HARVARD UNIVERSITY PRESS

Cambridge, Massachusetts

First Harvard University Press paperback edition, 1996

Published by arrangement with The Free Press, a division of Simon & Schuster, Inc.

Library of Congress Cataloging-in-Publication Data
Troy, Gil.
  See how they ran: the changing role of the presidential candidate / Gil Troy. —Rev.
  and expanded ed.
     p. cm.
  Includes bibliographical references and index.
  ISBN 0-674-79680-2
  1. Presidents—United States—Election—History.
2. Electioneering—United States—History. I. Title.
JK524.T76 1996
324.7'0973—dc20   95-50132

This book has been digitally reprinted. The content
remains identical to that of previous printings.

To my parents, Elaine and Bernard Dov Troy,
and my grandparents, Leon and Charlotte Gerson,
for teaching that "wisdom is better than rubies."

Contents

Preface

WHEN I began researching this book, I wanted to study the media's effects on the presidential election campaign as a way of exploring American politics from a long-term, historical perspective. Two discoveries shifted my focus. I found that while thousands of books written about individual campaigns filled library shelves, surprisingly few books analyzed the evolution of the campaign over the past two hundred years. I also learned that searching for media revolutions in the nineteenth-century campaign was anachronistic. Although such technological innovations as the telegraph and railroads transformed both society and politics, traditional attitudes often buffered these changes. In the case of the presidential campaign, therefore, it was necessary to start with the attitudes that governed the campaign. I decided to take one thread from the electoral tapestry—the candidate's role—and unravel it against the backdrop of two centuries of changing expectations.

But these attitudes and expectations were contradictory and unrealistic. I wrote the first six chapters of this book during the first half of the 1988 campaign. Throughout that long winter and spring, commentator after commentator condemned the campaign as lengthy, nasty, and excessively concerned with the "character" question. What, I wondered, would constitute a "good" campaign? Had candidates *ever* focused on the issues? In blaming television, PACs, primaries, or the particular candidates, Americans assumed that the problem of the presidential campaign was a new one. I discovered that in fact the golden age of campaigning never quite existed—that the ideal candidate has remained just out of reach. Little wonder that Americans have been complaining about the presidential campaign, and their choice of candidate, for two centuries.

Seeing how the candidates ran opens a window on not only the campaign but also the presidency, American politics, and American culture. Here is a story of dramatic change, as candidates go from passive to active, from communicating in rare but lengthy statements to telegraphing frequent but ephemeral "sound bites." At the same time, a remarkable continuity emerges: After two hundred years, Americans still complain about the presidential campaign in terms that our ancestors would find strikingly familiar.

————

THE completion of this project marks the end of ten years at Harvard as an undergraduate, graduate student, and lecturer. There and elsewhere I have accumulated many debts that I now happily acknowledge, without of course imposing any of the blame for my work's shortcomings. My undergraduate tutors, Greg Mark and Mina Carson, bear some responsibility for my chosen career, as do two outstanding professors at Cornell University, Richard Polenberg and Cletus Daniel.

I am particularly grateful to Professor David Herbert Donald for his patient and inspiring instruction throughout my graduate school career. His thought-provoking, line-by-line, chapter critiques deepened my argument and lightened my prose style. He continues to be a model mentor—a brilliant scholar, an inspiring teacher, and a good friend. My other adviser, Professor Alan Brinkley, has offered warm friendship, superb advice, and constant encouragement since I took his undergraduate seminar in 1982. Together, Professors Donald and Brinkley saved me from countless errors and propelled me in valuable directions which I only wish I could have pursued more fully. I would also like to thank the historians, along with Professor Donald, who served on my generals committee, Professor Paula Sanders, Professor Isadore Twersky, and especially Professor Bernard Bailyn.

For more recent assistance, I thank my new colleagues at McGill, especially my department chairman Professor Carman Miller, and Dean Michael P. Maxwell, who provided crucial last-minute funding. My students at both Harvard and McGill served as excellent sounding boards for many of my ideas. The deft touch of my editor, Joyce Seltzer, tightened the manuscript while her faith in the project helped exorcise many of my first-time jitters. Others at The Free Press were helpful as well, especially Edith Lewis, Cherie Weitzner, and the book's copy editor, George Rowland.

Harvard College's teaching and research support funds; the Mrs. Giles Whiting Fellowship in the Humanities; the United States Department of Education Jacob Javits Fellowship, formerly the National Graduate Fellowship; the Charles Warren Center for Studies in American History Summer Research Grants; the Harvard University Graduate School of Arts and Sciences Merit Fellowship; and the Harvard University Graduate School of Arts and Sciences helped fund this study.

In examining over 100 manuscript collections in 15 states, many

additional debts accumulated. My travel to various presidential libraries
was made possible by a Gerald Ford Foundation Grant; a Beeke-Levy
Research Fellowship from the Franklin and Eleanor Roosevelt Institute;
a research grant from the Harry S. Truman Library Institute; and a
Moody Grant from the Lyndon Baines Johnson Foundation. In addition
to the ever-gracious archivists at the presidential libraries, the librarians
at the Library of Congress, Harvard University, McGill University, Illinois State Historical Library, Indiana State Library, Lilly Library at Indiana University, New York Public Library, New York State Library, Rush
Rhees Library at the University of Rochester, Rutherford B. Hayes Presidential Center, St. Johns University Library in Queens, New York,
State Historical Society of Wisconsin, Sterling Library of Yale University, University of Chicago Library, and Wright State University Archives deserve thanks. The staff at the Manuscripts Reading Room of
the Library of Congress was especially friendly and accommodating. Permission to quote or reproduce material also came from the Buffalo and
Erie County Historical Society, Historical Society of Pennsylvania, New
Hampshire Historical Society, University of Virginia Library, the Republican National Committee, and the National Broadcasting Company,
Inc.

James Ralph, Jr., read most of my work in its roughest form. I thank
him for his perseverance, insight, and friendship. For various technical
and bibliographical kindnesses I salute Linda Adams, Jean H. Baker,
Barton B. Clark, Marcia Dambry, Matt Gerson, Win Gerson, Steven B.
Greenberg, Donald Levy, Susan Kaplan, Jason Solomon, Thomas A.
Underwood, and Ariel Zwang. Max Mandis graciously gave me the run
of the Max and Elaine Mandis Collection of Political Memorabilia,
while Marvin Silverman provided crucial and skillful photographic assistance. Many friends kindly hosted me during my research travels over
the years. I owe a special debt to Kenneth S. Breuer and Miklos Breuer
of Newton, Massachusetts; Amy R. Sheon and Michele Janis of Washington, D.C.; Tevi Troy and Daniel Troy of Washington, D.C.; Micah
D. Halpern, formerly of New Haven, Connecticut; Michael Mattis and
Judith Hochberg, formerly of Chicago; John Bechhoefer, formerly of
Chicago; the family of Jeffrey and Carol Maisels in Bloomfield Hills,
Michigan; and the Saul and Joan Polasky clan in Cincinnati, Ohio, all
of whom generously allowed me to overstay my welcome at their respective homes.

Of all those friends who helped me keep perspective and offered
pleasant diversions in Boston, New York, Montreal, Jerusalem, Tel Aviv,
Ketura, and Barryville, allow me to single out my three youngest friends,

Oren Lee-Parritz, Lior Avraham Brinn, and Ayelet Rose Brinn, all of Newton, Massachusetts.

Finally, this book is dedicated to my parents, Bernard Dov and Elaine Troy, and to the rest of my family, especially my grandparents, Leon and Charlotte Gerson, my brothers, Tevi Troy and Daniel Troy, and the latest and most welcome addition to our family, Cheryl Horowitz. In these times of domestic strife, I am proud to have a family that reminds bemused friends of the Brady Bunch rather than the Simpsons.

1991

P R O L O G U E

"What Has America Done to Deserve This?"

ON the night of October 13, 1988, one hundred million Americans turned on their television sets to watch the two major party nominees for President of the United States debate in Los Angeles. American voters had been anticipating this clash between Vice President George Bush and Massachusetts Governor Michael Dukakis for weeks. The anchorman for the Cable News Network, Bernard Shaw, moderated the debate and asked the first question. Sounding more like the host of "The Newlywed Game" than a political journalist, Shaw gave Dukakis two minutes to respond to the question, "If Kitty Dukakis were raped and murdered, would you favor an irrevocable death penalty for the killer?" Without challenging Shaw's premise, and claiming that the death penalty did not deter crime, Dukakis advocated an international conference to spearhead the fight on drugs. This passionless response, many believed, sealed Dukakis's presidential fate. After the debate, the Governor quickly left the studio. "Kitty, I just blew it," he told his wife.[1]

This exchange outraged many Americans. Shaw's question was inappropriate and undignified. Rather than calling for a drug summit, Dukakis should have punched Shaw in the nose, some said. Traditionally, aspirants for the highest office in the land had been treated more respectfully. Politicians and people on the street alike pointed to the "Kitty Dukakis question" as further proof that American politics—indeed, America itself—had declined. "What has America done as a nation to deserve an election like this?" *Time* magazine asked, voicing American voters' "collective lament."[2]

1

Symptoms of decline seemed to abound. The 1988 campaign appeared endless, with candidates announcing their intention to run as much as two years in advance. Even before a single primary vote had been cast, Americans groaned, "Is This Any Way to Elect a President?"[3] The long campaigns seemed artificial, an elaborate attempt by candidates to manipulate reporters—who in turn manipulated the people. Pseudo-events, sound bites, and images had replaced rallies, speeches, and issues. George Bush ranted about rapist Willie Horton, the flag, and the dreaded "L-Word," liberalism; Michael Dukakis mumbled about the "Massachusetts Miracle" and his Greek parents. Finally, on Election Day, barely 50 percent of those eligible bothered to vote. Two-thirds of those surveyed disapproved of *both* the candidates *and* the process. "This most dismal of Presidential campaigns . . . has set a new low in modern campaigning," the *New Yorker*'s Elizabeth Drew sighed.[4]

"Who killed the presidential campaign?" many wondered. In 1988 numerous suspects emerged, against whom experts had been amassing cases for years. To some, the problems of the presidential campaign simply reflected the problems of an America in decline. The campaign's "very emptiness suggested its importance," journalist Sidney Blumenthal argued. By "clinging to irrelevant issues," the candidates "postponed [the] crisis of national purpose" provoked by the ending of the Cold War.[5]

Others viewed the modern campaign as the victim of American consumer culture. Electoral politics had been "commodified," historian Robert Westbrook argued, with voting degenerating into yet one more "consumption choice" in the American marketplace. Candidates, it seemed, were trussed up, packaged, and sold to passive, alienated, and gullible consumers. By 1988, many Americans had an almost mystical belief in the power of advertisers to dupe the voters. From 1984 to 1988 the number of people admitting that campaign ads had influenced them doubled, one poll reported.[6] Such potent weapons were blamed for making the campaign superficial, trivial, and negative.

Not only had advertising and broader cultural phenomena transformed presidential campaigns, but great changes had occurred within the American political universe itself. In a few short decades, the century-long reign of American political parties had ended. "The party's over," David Broder of the *Washington Post* quipped. Without parties to control candidates and motivate voters, the presidential campaign had degenerated into a personality contest wherein individual quirks eclipsed policy considerations as voters became spectators who had to be entertained.[7]

As the parties declined, the primaries proliferated. While these state-by-state nominating elections arguably were more democratic, many considered them far less efficient. Primaries favored charismatic candidates like Jesse Jackson and allowed a clique of activists to hold a broad-based party hostage, as George McGovern's youthful "army" had done in 1972 with the Democrats. Primaries also encouraged "retail" campaigns emphasizing personalities over issues.

Changes in the presidential office had similarly affected the campaign. As the presidency became more of what Theodore Roosevelt referred to as a "bully pulpit"—a vantage point for inspiring the people—and more policy-oriented, the presidential campaign became both more populist and more issue-based. Since Theodore Roosevelt, presidents had governed by campaigning and campaigned by governing. Ronald Reagan blurred these two roles masterfully, but so had Franklin Roosevelt and—in 1964 at least—Lyndon Johnson.

This modern "rhetorical" presidency, such as it was, could not reach the public without the press. In the nineteenth century reporters were ciphers, cowed by the men they worked for and the men they covered. By 1988 reporters, especially those on TV, enjoyed professional credibility as well as individual fame. Often, such TV journalists as Walter Cronkite and Dan Rather were better liked, or at least better known, than many candidates. More and more Americans feared the media as a behemoth, even as they relied on it for information, entertainment, and, all too often, companionship. Candidates acknowledged the reporter's role in setting the campaign agenda. Asked why they did not address the issues more often, candidates and their advisers blamed the press, suggesting that if reporters wanted to hear more about issues, they should ask about them more.[8]

Reporters, especially in 1988, in turn blamed the consultants, the new breed of advisers who dominated modern politics. These political hired guns had become so ubiquitous, and the myth of their influence so daunting, that both *Time* and *Newsweek* declared 1988 "The Year of the Handlers." These political consultants emphasized personality traits over party loyalty and political ideals, critics charged. Rival candidates quibbled about who relied more on consultants. Ronald Reagan's speechwriter Peggy Noonan, herself a master puppeteer, simply dismissed all the contenders as "Stepford candidates with prefab epiphanies, inauthentic men for an inauthentic age."[9]

Regardless of who were the most important actors in the quadrennial drama—the handlers, the journalists, the candidates, or the voters—all spoke a common language of sound bites and media markets that had been distorted by television. Again and again in 1988 commentators declared TV the most influential factor in the modern campaign. It, many believed, was the genie that had changed it all—transformed American culture, invigorated advertising, undermined the parties, proliferated the primaries, popularized the presidency, inflated the press, and created the need for expert handlers. And, many feared, 1988 marked the crossing of the Rubicon, the emergence of a fundamentally different, and flawed, presidential campaign. Television had *"become"* the election, numerous commentators concluded.[10]

All these analysts assumed that the campaign had been both revolutionized and trivialized. Most Americans accepted Jimmy Carter's characterization of the 1988 contest as "The worst campaign I've ever seen in my lifetime." Yet these laments were simply the latest in a litany of complaints about presidential campaigning that go back over one hundred years. In 1852, the *New York Mirror* wrote: "In regard to the method pursued by political parties, with reference to electing their respective candidates, there seems to be just one opinion: That 'it is disgraceful to the country'."[11]

Critics of the campaign constantly harked back to a golden age of presidential campaigning that never in fact existed. In 1988, the Kennedy–Nixon debates of 1960 were remembered fondly. In 1960, however, many Americans had found the debates disappointing, especially when judged against the mythic standard of the Lincoln–Douglas debates of a century before. That clash, however, had taken place during the 1858 *state legislature* campaign in Illinois; during his 1860 *presidential* campaign, Abraham Lincoln refused to say anything about any issues. In fact, since the first truly popular presidential campaign in 1840, Americans have found campaigns too lengthy, too costly, too nasty, and too silly.

These persistent complaints reveal that in fifty presidential elections over two hundred years, Americans have failed to develop a legitimate and popular protocol for electing their president. The most elementary act of American democracy remains problematic. The problem is not primarily structural, stemming from flaws in American politics and culture. Nor is it a personnel problem, stemming from shallow candidates or venal consultants. Rather, it is an ideological problem, stemming from fundamental conflicts the Founders themselves failed to resolve. Over two hundred years ago, the men who made our Constitution could not quite decide how much democracy Americans should enjoy, or how popular an office the presidency should be. No wonder that the attempt to select a president democratically has proved so vexing!

Despite all the boasting that the United States is the world's greatest democracy, Americans have yet to make their peace with democratic ideology. In colonial times, "democracy" was a dirty word, associated with mob rule and demagoguery. More Americans considered themselves "republicans," prizing executive humility as an antidote to tyranny, and trusting the virtuous leaders of society to channel the people's passions and avoid "mobocracy." Terrified that ambitious men would subvert the government, republicans placed a premium on presidential character.* They wanted an ideal man, hovering above the people. To demonstrate virtue, a presidential candidate had to remain silent and passive, trusting his peers to choose wisely.

But a competing strain of what we might call "liberal democracy" impelled candidates toward the people. Liberal-democratic thought also fears dictatorship but trusts the people as an effective counterbalance. It advocates majority rule, the supremacy of public opinion, and reliance on the hidden genius of the people. It suspects elites and condemns pockets of privilege. Over the years, liberal democrats have come to view the president as the leader of the people. To demonstrate his leadership abilities, a presidential candidate had to go out among the people and speak to them, preferably about the policies he would pursue as president. Thus, while the president had to be an ideal man, more upright than the people, he also had to be an everyman, able to communicate with them. The presidential campaign was not simply a search for the most virtuous "king," but an opportunity to debate national policy with the future "prime minister."

The struggle to define a proper and effective role for the nominee in the campaign, then, reveals a larger struggle in American culture to advance liberal democracy without abandoning traditional republicanism. Viewed from this perspective, Americans appear tormented. They celebrated successful men while condemning ambitious ones. They championed modernization and progress yet remained traditional. And democracy, their greatest achievement, caused them unending anxiety.

Since 1796, presidential campaigns have attempted to convey a message to the people. Since 1896, the central messenger has been the candidate. For all the transformations in the media and the messages, this fundamental relationship remains unchanged. And the questions "How should the people's representatives communicate with the people?" and "What kind of president do Americans want?" remain unanswered.

*Throughout the text (except where the words begin a sentence) the lower-case form ("republican" or "democrat") refers to the ideology, while where capitalized, the party is meant.

By becoming more active, candidates lost their insulation and were increasingly blamed for the problems of the presidential campaign. Unable to satisfy the competing ideological demands, nominees were damned, regardless of what they did. In 1988, George Bush played the republican man of virtue to Michael Dukakis's democratic leader of substance. Yet to solidify his position as the nation's ideal man, Bush engaged in gutter tactics, while Dukakis's supposedly more democratic, more populist campaign appeared elitist and overly intellectual.

This continuing search for virtuous candidates and a suitable campaign links modern Americans with their forebears. Since the first broad-based presidential campaign in 1840, the complaints have not changed so much, but the target has shifted. Candidates, not parties, now receive most of the abuse. The modern campaign, therefore, has not degenerated; it is not a harbinger of America's decline. Rather, it is the latest chapter in a two-hundred-year-old struggle to come to terms with American democracy and the American presidency.

ONE

Standing for Office
in an Age of Virtue

If a man sollicits you earnestly for your vote, avoid him. . . .
—*The Defense of Injur'd Merit Unmasked, a campaign pamphlet, 1771*

CANDIDATES campaign; presidential candidates campaign for the presidency. To contemporary Americans this notion appears obvious, even redundant. But such was not always so. Originally, presidential candidates were supposed to "stand" for election, not "run." They did not make speeches. They did not shake hands. They did nothing to betray the slightest ambition for office. Candidates were supposed to stay on their farms in dignified silence, awaiting the people's call, as George Washington had done.

I

The demand for passive candidates was rooted in colonial thought and practice. It stemmed from what contemporaries called "republicanism," the complex of attitudes that inspired the American Revolutionary generation.[1] Critics in eighteenth-century England who feared monarchical authority exported their brand of republicanism to the colonies. These pamphleteers and opposition leaders, weaned on the sad example of the Roman Republic, concluded that unchecked governmental power bred political corruption, individual decadence, and—inevitably—communal decline. Restrained candidates symbolically guaranteed against both

7

bloated executives and individual vice. "I never ask'd but one man to vote for me since the last Election," Robert Wormeley Carter of Virginia boasted in April 1776. Although Carter was not reelected to the House of Burgesses, he kept his honor. Campaigning was demeaning and dishonest. "If a man sollicits you earnestly for your vote, avoid him; self-interest and sordid avarice lurk under his forced smiles, hearty shakes by the hand and deceitful . . . enquir[i]es after your wife and family," a 1771 pamphlet warned.[2]

Since the days of ancient Rome, good republicans had yearned for modest leaders, but feared ambitious men. The word "candidate," from the Latin word for white, *candidus*, recalled the Roman politicians, whose white togas suggested their purity and implictly proclaimed "I am no dictator; I am no demagogue." Christianity then bequeathed an ambivalence about worldly success and ambition which made leaders who courted popularity suspect. Eighteenth-century British opposition thought added a fear of power as corrupting and insatiable. Colonists viewed democratic republics as fragile flowers constantly threatened by the whims of the many and the intrigues of the few. Citizens had to be wary of leaders as well as of mobs: Better to be paranoid than complacent.

In such a threatening environment, individual virtue was the key to national success. For republics to prosper, men of character had to sacrifice personal interests for the public good. "Character" was a matter of reputation, the virtuous role individuals assumed in public. While all were supposed to avoid "any Immoralities whatsoever," as the Massachusetts legislature warned, virtuous men were judged more by their public behavior than by their private lives.[3] Demagoguery impeached the candidate's character and undermined the credibility of the electoral victory, even when popular appeals did not end up in dictatorship or mobocracy. Popular campaigning was not only dangerous, it was improper, illegitimate, and unnecessary. Candidates did not have to do anything to get elected, they simply had to allow those who knew them to recognize their virtue.

This campaigning ethos suited colonial society. Most Americans lived in farming communities scattered along the Atlantic coast. Information traveled only as quickly as individuals could: New Yorkers first heard about Lexington and Concord four days after the battles; Georgians waited six weeks. In these self-sufficient polities, people usually knew one another intimately, often making bombast and spectacular campaigning unnecessary. Everyone knew his or her place in society and politics, with commoners expected to defer to their betters.

The code, however, was not inviolate: The American wilderness spawned notions of individual liberty and popular sovereignty. Elections often resembled great "carnivals," the one time when the worthies courted the commoners. In their youth, men like George Washington and Thomas Jefferson let the rum flow on election day—a practice called "swilling the planters with bumbo." Traditionalists denounced these appeals to the masses. Colonel Landon Carter, a proper Virginian, grumbled that during the 1776 election his son Robert "had kissed the —— of the people, and very seriously accommodated himself to others."[4]

The events leading up to the American Revolution realized many of the republicans' greatest fears. Colonists had begun to worry about the loss of "virtue" in England, as "luxury, effeminancy, and venality" mushroomed into "one mass of corruption," according to the Massachusetts lawyer John Adams. More disturbing was what a young Virginian, Thomas Jefferson, called "a long train of abuses," from the Stamp Act to the Standing Army, that revealed the conspiracy of British executive power against American republican prerogatives. In labeling King George III a tyrant, and cataloguing the King's abuses in the Declaration of Independence, Jefferson proved to his countrymen that a corrupt and power-hungry executive threatened their fragile liberties.[5] After the Revolution, it would be up to the American people to fragment, harness, and balance executive power in designing their kingdom of heaven on earth, a democratic republic.

Yet despite this rejection of the King, and despite the revolutionary appeals to the people, Americans feared democracy. The Founders advocated the people's right to choose their leaders, but they doubted the people's ability to choose wisely. Alexander Hamilton declared in *The Federalist* that "the republican principle . . . does not require an unqualified complaisance to every sudden breeze of passion." The people were too susceptible to demagogic appeals; they were slaves to their own emotions. The people's genius, Hamilton explained, lay in recognizing their tendency to "err," and in choosing "guardians . . . to withstand the temporary delusion[s]." The Federalists relied on the traditional deferential politics, bolstered by the Constitution's checks and balances, to protect the people from themselves. Mixing democratic consent and elite rule, faith in the people and fear of the mob, they institutionalized paradox.[6]

Both the presidency and the presidential selection system incorporated these contradictions. The president was to be both king and prime minister, a national figurehead and the people's representative. He was to be a "vigorous" executive, within his limited sphere. He was to be one of the people, but an exceptional man; elected by the people, but not "subservient" to them. Balancing "energy in the Executive" and "safety in the republican sense," the Federalists wanted presidents who were independent yet responsible, decisive yet respectful, and—most important of all—virtuous.[7]

There could be no popular presidential campaign to designate the nation's leading gentleman. As a result, the Constitution gave the people a voice in selecting a president, then drowned them out. Under the original Electoral College, the people chose the state legislators, who chose the electors, who chose the president. Thus, ultimately, the nation's elite decided.[8] According to Hamilton, these "men most capable of analyzing the qualities adapted to the station" would select "characters preeminent for ability and virtue." Demagogues with talents for "low intrigue" would lose; mere popularity would not suffice. All assumed that candidates would stand for the presidency. Their personal characteristics would then be evaluated calmly and rationally.[9] The people and the candidates, therefore, were shunted aside. The elite's inclusion and the candidates' exclusion guaranteed virtue.

Tall and stately, George Washington loomed as the ideal president. "His character, in short, is a TISSUE OF VIRTUES," the *Massachusetts Centinel* proclaimed. After the Constitution was ratified in 1788, and the date set for selecting presidential electors, Washington's election became all but inevitable. Still, Washington played his part in the drama. He refused to lift a finger, or to allow anyone to indulge in speculation, as he awaited the call. The presidency "[has] no fascinating allurements for me," he told his friends. He feared being accused of *"inconsistency and ambition."* Even the slightest discussion could betray some "impropriety of conduct," or "be construed into a vain-glorious desire of pushing myself into notice as a candidate." The old General simply wanted to live and die "in peace and retirement on my own farm." He could then maintain that "most enviable of all titles[,] the character of *an honest man.*"[10]

After the Electoral College chose him unanimously on February 4, 1789, Washington had to wait until Congress convened to count the ballots. During this delay, an impatient Washington worried about the legislators' "stupor and listlessness." Finally, on April 14, 1789, Washington received formal notification of his election. His bags were already packed for the trip to New York, the young nation's capital.[11]

As President, Washington continued to display the desired presidential qualities. He knew he was walking on "untrodden ground" and that almost anything he did created a precedent. He continued juggling virtue and ambition, popularity and demagoguery, admitting that while he prized the "good opinion of my fellow-citizens," he would not seek popularity "at the expense" of his "social duty or moral virtue."[12]

Yet the President served an important psychological function in the young republic. Lacking ancestral traditions or long-dead notables, Americans would always be searching for heroes. Washington recognized this susceptibility to hero worship, and his own responsibilities as the nation's premier celebrity. He established the practice of "going on tour" to unite the nation and gather information firsthand. Washington would not speak during these nonpartisan appearances; they were simply for "seeing and being seen," he said.[13] His trips to New England and the South thrilled Americans, who loved being in the great man's presence.

While such cabinet members as Thomas Jefferson and Alexander Hamilton bickered about policy, Washington remained dignified and aloof. Some observers cheered the fact that, as Secretary of the Treasury, Hamilton played the prime minister to Washington's king. Still others griped about a Hamilton-led cabal subverting the presidency and the republic.

Demoralized by the constant sniping, Washington hoped to retire after his first term. But his close friend Eliza Powel warned that opponents would charge that "ambition has been the moving spring of all your acts," and that, once criticized, "you would take no further risks" for the people.[14] This republican argument to stand for election so as not to appear ambitious helped sway Washington. He did not withdraw his name from consideration. Once again, the electors chose him unanimously.

Twice George Washington had been whisked into the presidential chair, fulfilling all of the Framers' unrealistic expectations. Yet his example misled them. The Federalists' theorizing about presidential selection was flawed, blinded as it was by Washington's stature. None of Washington's successors enjoyed similar universal acclaim among the people or the elites. Never again would one man truly stand for election. After Washington, every candidate had to run, had to advance his own cause somehow. How, then, could candidates gain popular support, if campaigning for support was improper and illegitimate? Answers had to be improvised and then, somehow, legitimized. Thus, by 1800 the Founders' presidential selection system proved unworkable. By 1840 it was abandoned. Conflict, and then democracy, combined to kill it.

II

Republicanism dreamed of a cooperative, nonconfrontational political system wherein civic virtue reigned and elites could solve problems reasonably. While embracing this vision, the Framers prepared for other eventualities. Their system assumed imperfection, it assumed conflict—thus the elaborate checks and balances. Still, the Federalists hoped that the Constitution would be able to control what James Madison called the "dangerous vice" of factions and permanent parties by creating many power centers. Also, having presidents like Washington "who possess the most attractive merit and the most diffusive and established characters" would foster national harmony by transcending policy squabbles.[15]

Yet, even by the end of Washington's term in office, a rudimentary first-party system had developed. Polarized by the growing conflicts over the national debt, manufacturing policy, and French and British machinations, various state organizations aligned loosely as "Federalists" and "Republicans." Campaigning in local politics became respectable as conflict spread and positions crystallized. Feuding Americans expected their representatives to take stands. In 1788 a congressional candidate, James Madison, complained to his fellow Virginian, George Washington, that he was "pressed much in several quarters" to campaign in his district. Madison wanted to win but had "an extreme distaste to steps having an electioneering presence." Increasingly, voting was no longer a personal matter between a citizen and a man of character, but a party matter between groups of citizens and coalitions of politicians. The parties were staking out policy positions, thereby associating candidates with stands on the issues. By the mid–1790s, Madison had become the leader of the fledgling Republican party and a pugnacious campaigner himself.[16]

Parties clouded considerations of individual character with policy questions. They popularized campaigning and institutionalized conflict, forcing candidates to line up on one side of a dispute or the other. Worst of all, party loyalty supplanted the public good. Virtuous leaders were being replaced by corrupt politicians, a phrase which even then seemed redundant. Politicians did not care about "the people as a whole," they only cared about party prerogatives. The party man "must shout huzzas, or whisper calumnies, just as he is bidden," Congressman Gulian C. Verplanck mourned. "His time is not his own. His thoughts are not his own. His soul is not his own."[17]

Parties also steered American politics away from the gentlemanly exchanges the Founding Fathers envisioned. Newspapers aligned with particular parties and became front-line warriors in ever-escalating verbal brawls. During these so-called "Dark Ages of Partisan Journalism," newspapers were always shrill, often dishonest, and increasingly popular. No charge was too extreme, as long as it smeared the opposition. During the 1796 and 1800 election campaigns between Federalist supporters of John Adams and Republican advocates of Thomas Jefferson, the first vice president of the United States was called a monarchist, an egotist, and a traitor, while the primary author of the Declaration of Independence was branded an atheist, a swindler, and a traitor. Republicans accused Adams of conspiring to establish a dynastic succession with his sons, while Federalists accused Jefferson of raping one of his slaves. Jefferson, one Federalist wrote, "[is] a mean-spirited, low-lived fellow, the son of a half-breed Indian squaw, sired by a Virginia mulatto father . . . raised wholly on hoe-cake made of coarse-ground Southern corn, bacon and hominy, with an occasional change of fricaseed bullfrog." The First Lady, Abigail Adams, complained that so much "abuse and scandal" rained down on Americans in 1800, that it could have "ruin[ed] and corrupt[ed] the minds and morals of the best people in the world."[18]

These assaults on character demonstrated the unfortunate effects of party. Such undignified campaigns confirmed the worst fears about politicians and democracy. Parties, it seemed, not only emphasized policy disputes over character considerations, and partisanship over truth, but reduced the campaign to a slugfest.

This political crisis was part of a broader assault on the nation's soul. America's entry into the industrial world of the nineteenth century threatened its republican values as concerns with individual prerogatives weakened the communal vision. Capitalism and commerce converted Americans from farmers to factory workers. The Revolution's egalitarianism, and the rise of cities, undermined the deferential social patterns of the traditional community. New inventions altered Americans' sense of time and space. How could they maintain a virtuous government in this rapidly changing world?

The presidency became a bastion of virtue in the fast-changing republic. With the federal government still distant in fact and function from daily life, state and local contests generated more excitement—and involvement. Americans distinguished between running for the presidency and running for "sheriff."[19] The president was the wise leader representing all Americans; he safeguarded deference, reason, statesmanship. It was not, as later cynics believed, that a statesman was a dead politician. Rather, in the American political universe, a statesman was a politician nominated for president.

Despite the conflict swirling about them, then, presidential candidates strained to remain passive, to appear disinterested. During the 1796 and 1800 campaigns, John Adams and Thomas Jefferson retired from public view to their respective farms. While they corresponded with allies privately, they remained invisible publicly. In 1796, Jefferson became Vice President under Adams. Four years later, Adams told his subordinate and rival, "Well, I understand that you are to beat me in this contest." Jefferson replied that "principle[s]" counted, not the individuals: "Were we both to die today, tomorrow two other names would be put in the place of ours, without any change in the motion of the machinery."[20] Though somewhat disingenuous, Jefferson's response illustrated the growing confusion after barely a decade of presidential campaigning. Virtuous characters remained in demand, but "principles" seemed more important than "men."

Jefferson's victory in 1800 marked the first time under the American Constitution that the opposition came into power. Hoping to return to first principles, Jefferson repudiated parties. "We are all Republicans—we are all Federalists," he declared in his first inaugural address. Jefferson's successors tried to remain on the high road, adhering to the tradition of what one historian calls "The Mute Tribune."[21] Yet all candidates were associated with factions and parties and, unavoidably, policy positions.

Still, most Americans considered parties temporary aberrations. The Federalists gradually dissolved after 1802, and for the next two decades Jeffersonian Republicans dominated American politics. With state legislators choosing most electors, the campaigns electing James Madison and James Monroe were relatively subdued. In 1820, Monroe stood unopposed for reelection. Shortly thereafter, William Lowndes of South Carolina articulated the classic formula that "the Presidency is not an office to be either solicited or declined."[22] During this nonpartisan "Era of Good Feelings," republican harmony and virtue seemed secure.

After 1822 the good feelings ebbed, the conflicts proliferated, and the parties became institutionalized as a democratic whirlwind transformed America. Parties thrived; the suffrage expanded; the citizens of each state, and not the state legislators, began to choose the Electoral College.[23] The Federalist system for insulating the presidency from popular choice was short-circuited.

This emerging liberal democracy counterbalanced traditional republicanism. The patron saint of liberal democrats, Thomas Jefferson, trusted the people: "I am persuaded myself that the good sense of the people will always be found to be the best army," Jefferson wrote while others fretted about mobocracy during Shays' Rebellion in 1787. The people, he declared, "may be led astray for a moment, but will soon correct themselves." European Enlightenment thought and the American experience confirmed both this faith in the people and this emphasis on individual rights. As democracy spread, even old-fashioned democrats like Jefferson and Madison would appear too patrician; these gentlemen were never called "Tom" or "Jemmy." The era of "Old Hickory," Andy Jackson, had begun.[24]

Andrew Jackson symbolized, and fostered, this liberal-democratic revolution. As a presidential candidate in 1824, Jackson promised to declare his opinion "upon any political or national question . . . about which the country feels an interest."[25] In affirming the people's right to know where he stood, Jackson prized principles over character, communication over reputation. Neither Jackson nor his three principal rivals—John Quincy Adams, William H. Crawford, and Henry Clay—openly affiliated with a political party. All were nominally Republicans. After an election characterized by some hesitant popular appeals, Jackson emerged as the favored candidate, winning nearly 40,000 more popular votes than Adams, the runner-up. But without a majority for any candidate in the Electoral College, the House of Representatives decided. Clay's men supported Adams to keep Jackson the vulgarian out of the White House. Jacksonians condemned this "corrupt bargain" for subverting the popular will. In the long run, however, it underscored the undemocratic nature of the traditional electoral system and advanced the steadily mounting democratic revolution.

After being elected in 1828, Jackson declared the president "the direct representative of the people" and appealed to the people directly. In introducing an elaborate system for distributing party patronage, or "spoils," in facing down disgruntled South Carolinians who threatened to nullify 1828's so-called "Tariff of Abominations," and in killing the powerful Second Bank of the United States by vetoing the bill rechartering it, Jackson expanded the presidency and transformed traditional expectations. In addition to being a man of "distinguished character," the president now also had to be a man of "ability and energy," in the words of a New York State nominating committee. Even as Jackson's opponents created a new Whig party to denounce "executive tyranny," millions cheered this popular presidency—Jackson linked the power of the presidency and the power of the people; he expanded both. By 1835,

Alexis de Tocqueville could conclude that "The people reign over the American political world as God rules over the universe." If so, the president stood by as the people's archangel.[26]

Still, even as the people prevailed, their relations with the presidential candidates remained unclear. How could the people rule and perpetuate virtue? With the rise of liberal democracy, the mystery deepened: How could one from among the people lead the people? Politicians and intellectuals could "venerate the masses" and their innate wisdom, as the Jacksonian Democrat George Bancroft did, but they could not quite account for the people's genius. Many celebrated the people as idiot savants who, despite their limitations, eventually found truth. But some wondered whether the people were simply idiots, continually swayed by demagogues. Many still assumed that all popular leaders were demagogues. The decline of deference created the need for popular leadership, but there was no proper way to move the masses. The republic remained imperiled.

Even as the presidency became more prime-ministerial and more active, the presidential candidate remained passive. Jackson himself usually refused to campaign. Like Washington, Jackson longed for "retirement to the peaceful shades of the Hermitage," his Tennessee estate. In contemplating his 1832 reelection campaign, even as he fought his enemies with every popular weapon in his arsenal, Andrew Jackson declared: "I meddle not with elections, I leave the people to make their own President."[27]

III

"I consider it the right of every citizen of the United States to ask and demand and be fully informed of the political principles . . . of those who are candidates for the various offices in the gift of the people," Kentucky Congressman Sherrod Williams announced in April 1836. Each presidential candidate, Williams continued, "has the imperious duty to frankly and fully . . . disclose the opinions which he entertains." Asserting his rights as "a voter, a citizen, and an individual" feeling "an ardent desire to see the perpetuity of our free and happy form of government," the long-winded Congressman posed five pointed political questions to Martin Van Buren, William Henry Harrison, and the other candidates vying to succeed Andrew Jackson as president in 1836.[28]

Four years later, in 1840, some were still smarting from Williams's effrontery. Republican theory frowned upon a candidate who advanced his own cause, as well as a public that breached the candidate's cocoon of dignified silence. "Since the categories of Sherrod Williams set the precedent, every one claims to question the candidate of his life, opinions and general conduct," the venerable lawyer and editor Charles Hammond of Cincinnati complained. "A man has to give up his own self-respect or every hour give some offence to some pedagogue that stands over him with uplifted rod."[29]

Hammond viewed this assault on the candidate's dignity as yet another manifestation of the democratization—and vulgarization—of the republic. Jacksonian Democracy was bad enough. Now, it seemed, Americans craved a dialogue with their nominees: A candidate could no longer await the people's call in republican silence. The Founding Fathers' "well regulated democracy," in which republicanism balanced liberalism, elitism balanced democracy, was upset.[30]

Republicanism remained potent, even if no longer dominant. Nineteenth-century Americans preserved six major elements of traditional political republicanism. First, they continued to fear power as corrupting and continually grasping. Second, as a result, they viewed their democratic republic as fragile; and, third, they considered every chief executive a potential tyrant. Fourth, they distrusted political ambition and yearned for modest and virtuous leaders. Fifth, they suspected popular opinion as easily swayed by demagogues. Finally, many would continue to believe that the elites were the most qualified to select virtuous leaders by withstanding both the mob and the dictator.

The egalitarian countertradition of liberal democracy was rising. But the commitment to republicanism was so strong in early America that Americans would abandon it only hesitantly and haphazardly. Republican vestiges would continue to shape American attitudes long after the ideology became outmoded. When no longer an "ism," a noun, it would continue to function in its adjective form, as Americans preserved their "republican" legacy. For the next half-century, they would cling desperately to the republican taboo. Deep into the twentieth century, amid the technical splendor of mass democratic consumer culture, Americans would continue to cherish the occasional shards from the republican vessel.

By 1840, nominees were confused. Candidates knew what they *were not* supposed to do—neither seek nor decline the office. But no one knew what they *were* supposed to do. There was an initial protocol: The party convention chose a committee to notify the nominee in writing; and the nominee responded with an acceptance letter. Individuals sent personal letters to the candidate, and often received replies. But beyond that the guidelines were contradictory and unworkable. Nominees were associated with party positions defined in platforms and local resolutions. Yet a candidate could not address issues like a good liberal democrat without appearing to be soliciting votes like a bad republican.

Furthermore, the conflicting traditions each had their "corrupt" and "virtuous" sides.[31] The republican tradition, at its best, ennobled both the candidate and the electorate. Candidates carried themselves with dignity and treated the electorate respectfully. The candidates stood by their records and allowed the voters to think without distraction. But if applied halfway, the republican tradition encouraged a false dignity, a posturing which merely substituted the candidate's personal presence and mythologized biography for scrutiny of his principles and the issues. Similarly, the liberal-democratic tradition, at its best, cultivated a dialogue between the candidate and the people. At its worst, melodramatic demagoguery distracted voters and thwarted reason. Unable, perhaps unwilling, to resolve these contradictions, candidates and their advocates justified their own behavior while always criticizing their opponents'.

Such defenders of republicanism as Charles Hammond fretted about the fragile dignity of the candidate, the presidency, the country. This traditional dignity linked Americans with their past; it uncovered—and calmed—Americans' republican insecurities. By defending the dignity of the presidency, Americans could simultaneously pray at their ideological altar, bow toward their ancestors, bless their links with previous republics, curse the ascendant leveling democracy and its politicians, genuflect toward the Constitution's limited presidency, hail the High Public Priest—the president—and look over their shoulders to ensure America's continuing role as an inspiration to the world, especially to Europe.

Simultaneously, Americans like Sherrod Williams demanded frankness from their candidates, upholding the dignity of the democratic dialogue between the people and their leaders. Americans had to avoid the poles of dictatorship and demagoguery, of elite rule and mobocracy. They had to learn to distinguish popular heroes from responsible leaders deserving the people's trust. They had to honor a leader without being seduced by his presence. They had to learn to communicate with their leaders in an increasingly complex society. And they had to keep the president humble as he occupied "the most exalted station in the world."[32] These tasks were imposing. But the insistence on frankness, on the honest articulation by the leader of his views, oriented Americans. With their compasses pointing toward forthrightness, they could master their vexing democracy.

Republicanism and liberal democracy coexisted uncomfortably in nineteenth-century America. Americans were haunted by the ghosts of George Washington and Andrew Jackson. All candidates had to be as aloof, as virtuous, as restrained as Washington, while being as popular, as political, as dynamic as Jackson. Practical Americans ignored the theoretical contradictions and improvised solutions.

By 1840, the presidential selection system would have appalled the Framers. Yet Americans still clutched their traditions. They channeled their discomfort with the improvised system into uncertainty about the presidential candidate's role. By 1840 and then 1844, candidates could have thrown the republican inhibition on candidates out with the other Federalist discards. They did not. Standing by their traditions, they perpetuated confusion.

TWO

To Stand or to Stump?

The Presidency is not an office to be either solicited or declined.
—*William Lowndes, 1821–1822*

"THE greatest excitement prevails," the patrician diarist Philip Hone noted during the 1840 presidential campaign. "Men's minds are wrought up to a pitch of frenzy, and like tinder a spark of opposition sets them on fire." This first truly popular presidential campaign marked a revolution in American politics. From the 1820s through the 1840s, fueled by the revolutions in transportation and communication, flooded by newly enfranchised voters, the elaborate second American party system emerged. As passionate as the religious revivals sweeping the country, as efficient as the new factories sprouting throughout the land, the rival Whig and Democratic parties inspired and organized the masses. Millions of Americans entered the political process not only as voters but as partisans attending caucuses, conventions, committee meetings, and rallies. To win in politics gentlemen no longer had to persuade one another, they had to sway the crowd.[1]

To involve the masses, no novelty was too inane—songs, slogans, floats, coonskin caps, popular newspapers with rough-hewn names like *The Log Cabin*, revival-like "camp" meetings more suitable to the Second Coming than the first Tuesday after the first Monday in November, and a huge canvas ball, ten or twelve feet in diameter, emblazoned with the nominee's name and rolled cross-country, symbolizing, as one journalist recalled, "the great revolutionary ball rolling on with irresistible force over the land." Popular politics became the new American religion, as two and half million men streamed to the polls—ten times the number enrolled in churches.[2]

In part, Americans campaigned so enthusiastically because they were nervous. Martin Van Buren, an effete Easterner, was far less popular than his Indian-fighting Western predecessor, Andrew Jackson. Also, the financial Panic of 1837 had deflated the great Jacksonian boom. Collapses in real estate, and failing state banks, triggered the longest economic depression of the nineteenth century. Americans feared that republican virtue would not survive in this new world of factories, recessions, and political parties. The Whig party itself illustrated the confusion: Although founded as a party of elites opposed to Jackson's monarchical presidency, the party mounted a populist campaign that empowered the people, and the president, even while restraining the candidate.

Roused by Jacksonian Democracy, inspired by increasingly active local candidates, nominees could have plunged into an active dialogue with the people. A commitment to candor could have eclipsed the injunction to be passive. This would have jibed with the president's emerging role as a popular leader and with liberal-democratic theory. But candidates did not, could not, repudiate the republican tradition. Instead, they juggled the conflicting republican and liberal-democratic demands.[3]

Out of this tension emerged four possible options for a presidential candidate. In 1840 and 1844 each of the four major party nominees chose a different path.[4] In the 1840 election the Whig nominee William Henry Harrison was silent but active. Martin Van Buren, his Democratic rival, was forthright but passive. Four years later, the Democratic candidate James K. Polk was silent *and* passive. And Henry Clay, the Whig choice, was forthright *and* active. Yet *none* of the candidates resolved the conflict. All were somewhat inconsistent, and all were criticized. Examining their tactics and the public's reaction thereto reveals the passion amid the confusion. It also illuminates a fault line in the fundamental act of American democracy: electing the President of the United States.

I

On December 19, 1839, William Henry Harrison accepted the Whig party's nomination for president. A Virginia aristocrat who defeated the Indians and the British during the War of 1812, he was often pictured in military regalia atop his white horse. This Western war hero, a cross between Washington and Jackson, offered the Whigs a suitable democratic veneer. Such Whigs as the former president of the Bank of the United States, Nicholas Biddle, recognized that Harrison's appeal was based on "the past, not the future. Let him . . . say nothing—promise nothing," Biddle advised. "Let the use of pen and ink be wholly forbidden as if he were a mad poet in Bedlam." A Democratic newspaper sneered that the retired General would be satisfied to cozy up in his little hut with a barrel of cider and a pension. The Whigs shrewdly appropriated the "Log Cabin and Hard Cider" tag as the central image of their campaign.[5]

Describing himself as "retiring and unpretending," Harrison thanked the National Democratic Whig Convention that had convened in Harrisburg, Pennsylvania, earlier in December. The tone of Harrison's compact acceptance letter fit the traditional republican formula: humble, simple, and not obviously self-serving. If elected, he would serve only one term. Also, he would not "declare the principles upon which the Administration will be conducted," should his friends place him in the presidential chair.[6] These statements were ideologically pleasing and mutually reinforcing. The General offered his restrained candidacy as a guarantee of a limited presidency.

For years Harrison had argued that the Constitution made the President of the United States an "impartial umpire." The leader "of the whole nation—not . . . a particular sect or fragment" had to abjure partisanship.[7] The President virtually represented all the people but remained somewhat removed from them; candidates should also keep their distance. Controversial policy proposals were for legislators, not the chief executive.

Reticence guaranteed national, as well as individual, virtue. Examining "the history of all Republics," Harrison discovered that "as they receded from the purity of Representative Government, the condition of obtaining office was the making of promises." Ambition often made "men of the fairest characters" act like "auctioneers selling . . . linen," advocating anything for "a temporary gain." Since Andrew Jackson's election, Harrison grieved, America had begun to resemble these other, failed republics.[8] Harrison would stave off such corruption and decline.

No man, therefore, should seek out the presidency—one did not beg for "the most exalted station in the world," Harrison explained to Ohio Whigs. The dignity of the presidency and the candidate could tolerate nothing else. Just as Samuel anointed Saul, so should the people seek the man only after a careful "review of his past actions and life."[9] A candidacy had to be genuine and broad-based. Ambitious politicians who curried the people's favor were acting more like stableboys than proper riders of the majestic public horse.

Harrison's blasts against ambition and corruption, his mistrust of the executive branch, and his concern with the virtue and fragility of republican governments, revealed his republican pedigree. Harrison thundered at a rally in Dayton, Ohio: "With my mother's milk did I suck in the principles upon which the Declaration of Independence was founded." For years he had promised to "restore the administration to its republican simplicity and purity."[10] Even if he lost, his candidacy would uphold these values bequeathed by another soldier-farmer, George Washington.

Rooted in a solid ideological foundation, and adorned with the examples of his predecessors, Harrison claimed silence as a proper response to the many inquiries he received. In fact, Whig strategy prescribed Harrison's silence. Simply standing on their opposition to Jacksonian Democracy, the Whigs avoided any "general declaration of . . . views."[11] Harrison's demure republicanism highlighted this approach and quieted Whig doubts about his aptitude. Democratic Senator Thomas Hart Benton teased that only one ability of Harrison's appealed to Whig managers—his "availability." Harrison was an umbrella candidate to unite the disparate Whig elements, a popular figurehead with few enemies and few stated policies. Any statement, no matter how vague, risked party unity. And if the General was the "imbecille" [sic] many Whigs feared, the potential for disaster loomed.[12] With Harrison, silence was proper and politic.

Initially, the Whig strategy worked well. General Harrison spent most of his time in the sixteen-room house in North Bend, Ohio, which party leaders rhetorically shrank into a one-room log cabin. Harrison deferred to his advisers in Ohio and New York, while he answered his many letters. He referred correspondents to his record, in general, and to letters he had written long before the nomination, in particular.

Then the General and his advisers faltered. Whigs announced that Harrison would make no further statements "whilst occupying his present position." A three-man "correspondence committee" began to answer his mail for him. The "General's views" had already "been given to the public," they explained.[13]

Democrats found this rationale for Harrison's silence offensive and unbecoming. It tended toward despotism, not democracy, the *Washington Globe* charged. The candidate "must give direct answers to all . . . reasonable inquiries" concerning his "character and principles." Other-

wise, why bother the people with elections every four years? The controversy revealed the inroads that liberal democracy had made in half a
century. The emerging ethos claimed a candidate's "public course and
opinions" as "public property."[14] More and more people assumed that
American elections required a public dialogue between the candidate
and the people.

The Democrats ridiculed "General Harrison's Thinking Committee."
They dismissed "General Mum" as a "caged" simpleton forced to rely
on his "conscience keepers," a doting old "imbecile" avoiding the public,
an "Old Granny" too feeble to leave his home. These *ad hominem* attacks finally pierced the General's armor. When an allegedly drunk Harrison accosted a Van Buren supporter on the streets of Cincinnati, Democrats cheered that they had at last crippled the General.[15]

The celebration, however, was premature. Harrison responded with
a deft defensive maneuver and a tactical advance combined: He blurred
the target. Distinguishing between opinions and pledges, Harrison argued that he had been forthright about his policy views without mort-
gaging his presidency via a series of pledges. He denied that any of his
public statements contained even one line "that was written or suggested by any other individual." The committee merely was a conve-
nience, keeping him afloat amid the postal deluge. Predictably, these
comments satisfied the Whigs. "There is not a man in the United States
who has more frankly, fearlessly and distinctly expressed his opinions
upon questions involving matters of public policy than General Harrison," Thurlow Weed's *Albany Evening Journal* insisted.[16]

The Democrats were unimpressed. According to them, the few opinions Harrison deigned to express were vague or contradictory. For example, Democrats called Harrison an abolitionist. Harrison refuted the
charge without repudiating abolitionism. He sent private letters standing by "what my *conduct* has been" during the quarter-century he had
lived on the border between a free state, Ohio, and a slave state, Kentucky—a crafty assertion which implied Southern sympathy without
broadcasting it. Frustrated Democrats then accused Harrison of playing
"hide-and-go-seek with the public."[17]

Unable to dodge the Democratic barrage, Harrison decided to bleed
in public. "I am the most persecuted and calumniated individual now
living," he howled.[18] Democratic attacks had put him in an untenable
position. He claimed he was forced to make public appearances to refute
the libels.

In fact, Harrison previously had campaigned without such a justification. In 1835, 1836, and 1838 he made some public appearances in

the Northeast and Midwest to advance his candidacy. But to strengthen his image as the defender of republican tradition, he made no public appearances in 1839 or throughout the first half of 1840. Now, however, he undertook a three-week tour in June, and a month-long trip in September, both ostensibly to demonstrate his vigor.

Harrison's stance was politically comfortable but ideologically slippery. An allegedly silent candidate was now willing to express opinions; a candidate who claimed not to be stumping was now taking to the stump. Harrison stayed within his home states of Indiana and Ohio, two states crucial to Whig success. At informal gatherings along his route, and at mass meetings of tens of thousands, the old warrior sang his plucky song: He campaigned against campaigning as he campaigned.

"I am not with you today, Fellow Citizens, in accordance with my own sense of propriety," Harrison said at Chillicothe, Ohio. "Much more consonant would it be with my feelings to remain at the domestic fireside. . . . Indeed I sometimes fear that upon me will fall the responsibility of establishing a dangerous precedent." But the attacks of his enemies left him no choice. "Appearing among my fellow citizens" was the "*only way* to disprove" the libels. "You must have already perceived," Harrison said to his audience, "that I am *not* CAGED, and that I am *not* the old man on crutches . . . they accuse me of being."[19]

As he knelt in obeisance toward the proprieties and affirmed that he had no interest in electioneering, Harrison did occasionally lapse into a discussion of the issues: "I have certainly refused pledges. . . . My opinions are known upon every subject," he said, clinging to his casuistry. Yet Harrison did make some policy pronouncements: "Methinks I hear a soft voice asking: Are you in favor of paper money? I AM," Harrison shouted to the "ten acres of Whigs" gathered at Dayton, Ohio, on September 10.[20]

Usually, Harrison played coy while campaigning, avoiding the issues. He recounted his battlefield exploits, praised old comrades, indulged in republican rhetoric, and attacked the malicious Democrats. "I do not come here to ask your sympathy or to excite your feelings in my behalf," he said in Cincinnati. "I ask for justice alone."[21]

Harrison recognized that his presence was more important than his rhetoric. In the days before voice amplification, most of the people could not see the candidate clearly, let alone hear him. Harrison's presence drew the crowds, and thrilled them. The military pageantry, the banners, the festive feeling entertained them; his speeches were obligatory adornments.

Whig newspapers followed Harrison's lead. They cheered the candi-

date's tour, emphasizing the size and enthusiasm of the crowd, the spontaneous and deep nature of the popular feeling, and the excitement of
Harrison's presence. "But best of all," one newspaper announced,
"GENERAL HARRISON HIMSELF WILL BE HERE!" The *Detroit
Daily Advertiser* gloried in the General's "classic vigor," his "keen, piercing eye," and his "purely republican" appearance.[22] Whig newspapers
continued to publicize Harrison's opinions on the Bank, the currency,
the presidential veto, while praising his firm refusal to electioneer.

Inevitably the Democrats, like the Whigs, flirted with contradiction.
Having condemned "General Mum's" reticence, they could not now
assail Harrison's stumping tour without highlighting his frankness. Instead, they attacked his speeches as "wretched and vulgar piece[s] of
driveling egotism and point for point . . . [begging] for popularity." The
Harrisburg, Pennsylvania *Magician* first attacked Harrison for not making "a single avowal of principle." Two paragraphs later it quoted Harrison on the impropriety of electioneering, and condemned his behavior
in 1836, "When he travelled over the country, much after the fashion
of a sheriff's candidate, soliciting the suffrages of the people."[23] In effect,
the *Magician* was insisting that the candidate be forthright yet passive—
avow principles *and* avoid electioneering.

The Democratic attacks, however, missed their mark. Harrison's
tour fit into the overall Whig campaign—the military pageantry, the
emphasis on the man rather than his principles, the emotional and patriotic appeals.[24] And, as Whigs serenaded their hero, the Democrats
faced a bigger problem: rehabilitating the battered reputation of Martin
Van Buren.

II

President Van Buren mounted a principled and forthright reelection
battle, but to no avail. His campaign could have been a model for others, balancing liberal-democratic frankness and republican dignity. Yet
his efforts were wasted, his example unheeded. For the Whigs were as
effective in fitting Martin Van Buren into the Republic's demonology
as they were in fitting William Henry Harrison into its pantheon.

Since the 1830s, Whigs had labeled Van Buren a "Magician," a
party "wire worker," a master of "non-committalism"—the latter a word
the Whigs claimed to have coined. In short, Van Buren was a politician.
These appellations tapped into the republic's distaste for politics with
its compromises and demagogic arts. *This* demagogue, however, was no

democrat. Van Buren fancied himself a king, having forgotten that the president was the people's servant. One Whig song, sung to "Allan-a-Dale," contrasted Harrison, the simple hero of Tippecanoe, with the monarchical Van Buren:

> Tippecanoe has no chariot to ride in.
> No palace of marble has he to reside in.
> No bags of gold-eagles, no lots of fine clothes—
> But he has a wealth far better than those;
> The love of a nation, free, happy, and true,
> Are the riches and portion of Tippecanoe.[25]

"Luxury has made fatal inroads upon the frugal habits of our fathers. The principles and examples of WASHINGTON and JEFFERSON have departed," the *Albany Evening Journal* mourned. "Republics have been undermined and overthrown by luxury. This fate awaits our Republic if there be not an immediate and thorough REFORM." Brilliantly, the Whigs wedded fears of parties and politicians, of demagoguery and aristocracy, of luxury and declension, of executive usurpation and monarchical tendencies, to the hapless Van Buren. The republic's bogeyman, a Democratic Caesar, was unleashed.[26]

The object of these fears, the rather benign Van Buren, ignored the slanders and addressed the issues. The President had long appreciated his ironic predicament: If, he sighed, he had "possessed a tithe of the skill . . . so liberally charged upon me," he would not be so reviled. In 1840, Democratic efforts were doomed by economic depression, if nothing else. Still, Van Buren advanced his cause—and the principle that, while a candidate should not stump, he should respond to all "interrogatories from my Fellow Citizens upon public questions." Intimate exchanges between a leader and free citizens were acceptable, even commendable. As he had done in 1836, Van Buren wrote with unprecedented candor; he expected his letters to be published. He penned long, thoughtful responses on dozens of difficult issues, including slavery in Washington, D.C., the federal sub-treasuries he created that were independent of state banks, and the tariff.[27]

According to Van Buren, the contract between the candidate and the voters demanded forthrightness. By replying to questions, a candidate earned "the respect & confidence of the American people." Van Buren distinguished answering questions from soliciting support—the former was a matter of democratic duty, "indispensable to the maintenance of republican government."[28] Also in 1840, Van Buren had a record to defend. Better to explain and elaborate than to try distancing himself from his own administration. And if this candor embarrassed the "caged" Whig candidate, contrasting the experienced leader with the vacuous warrior, all the better.

Van Buren's statements produced no disasters, no embarrassments. Democrats praised their standard-bearer for his eloquence and candor. At the Baltimore nominating convention, Democrats boasted that Martin Van Buren had "nothing to conceal. . . . He presents himself as he is, with but one life, and one set of principles for the North and the South, the East and the West."[29]

The Whig crusaders alternately called Van Buren's "electioneering epistles" too aggressive and too politic. These "self-justificatory effusions" demeaned the presidency by involving the President in "the field of party struggle," the *Albany Evening Journal* said. The President should not be "champion[ing]" his own policies and wrestling in the political mud with his assailants.[30] But then again, the Whigs sniffed, what could be expected from a mere party politician?

Absorbed in his correspondence and in governing, Van Buren remained in Washington for most of the campaign. A few months earlier, fear of Whig criticism had forced him to cancel a visit to Andrew Jackson in Tennessee. Any thoughts he entertained of traveling probably had been eliminated in July 1839, when he visited New York and Pennsylvania. In keeping with George Washington's precedent, Van Buren's tour was professedly nonpartisan. But, unlike most of his predecessors, Van Buren defended his policies, and even mentioned his party, in one of his toasts. Enraged, Whig newspapers called on their subscribers to shun the President, who was "degrading" the office with an "electioneering" tour. New York's Governor, William Henry Seward, subsequently refused to greet his President and neighbor.[31]

The Whigs objected that Van Buren bore himself as "the leader of a party" and not "the President of the nation." The notion of a president politicking was "undignified" and "insulting." He was realizing Alexis de Tocqueville's warning about two-term presidents by converting "the appliances of government . . . into one grand electioneering machine." This politicking was superficial. With all his hand-shaking, the President could not have spent more than half a minute with each person. Could Democrats assume that simply "[the] touch of the great man's hand convinces many a Whig that the sub-Treasury is a panacea"? The very presumption demeaned the people and treated them like idiots. Above all, the Whigs found the pageantry ostentatious. When Thomas Jefferson traveled as President, he "repressed Processions and Pageants as

Anti-Republican." "His Majesty, King Martin the First" had now "thrown off the *disguises* of Republicanism." Van Buren's tour was "the climax of affectation and dandyism,"[32] proof of his monarchical tendencies.

In fact, many Whigs did come out to greet the President, and the crowds were large and enthusiastic. Yet Van Buren returned to Washington sobered by the economic conditions along his route and impressed with Whig preparations for the campaign. He was also chastened by the Whig assaults. After the Northeastern tour, Van Buren stayed close to the White House, pleading engagement in "public duties."[33]

From Washington, Van Buren coordinated the Democratic efforts and professed optimism until election day. But the Whig hullabaloo, Harrison's popularity, frustration with twelve years of Democratic rule, and economic problems defeated the President. "Truth and justice and our sacred Constitution lay prostrate and bleeding at the foot of fraud and falsehood," Van Buren's friend Dillon Jordan wrote. Another Democrat, Thomas Hamer, wondered "Can this people govern themselves?"[34]

Although the losing Democrats sang loudest in the chorus of complaints about the election, the campaign also bothered many Whigs. Henry Clay disliked "appealing to the feelings and passions of our countrymen rather than to their reasons and judgments." John Quincy Adams found stump speeches, mass rallies, and other innovations undignified. By the end of the campaign, Whig diarist George Templeton Strong, and countless others, had "tired of humbug, lying, spouting, swearing, O.K., and the Old Hero."[35] The antics may have been effective, but they seemed illegitimate.

Harrison and Van Buren had resolved their twin dilemmas about stumping and speaking in contrary ways. Each candidate's choice comported with his personality and ideology. Van Buren, as the democratic leader and an experienced politician, addressed political issues, while Harrison, the republican statesman, abstained. Yet Harrison's position was ironic, for despite his rhetoric against politicians and demagoguery, his tactics were the more suspect—making even some allies squirm. Harrison played politics blatantly, but it was a peculiar brand of political antipolitics that appealed to his generation.

In 1840 the candidate provided the central symbol for his campaign—for better *and* for worse. Without William Henry Harrison there would have been no Log Cabin, no Hard Cider, no battlefield celebrations. Similarly—and to the Democrats' sorrow—Van Buren himself, his reputation for wizardry, his intimacy with the Democratic party, gave salience to the Whig attacks. Yet, for all this apparent centrality, candidates remained on the campaign's periphery. In fact, it was not the candidates' campaign; it was the party's campaign with the candidate at the symbolic helm.[36] Voters were preoccupied with local candidates and events. The parties were fragmented into dozens of state and local elements. Indeed, newspapers concentrated on local efforts and neglected the presidential candidates. Van Buren corresponded extensively and shaped strategy, but kept his distance. Harrison sat back and let the professionals manage. Throughout the 1840s, the candidates' activities were sideshows to the party battles.

III

In 1844, having "taught" the Whigs "how to conquer us," the Democrats reclaimed many crowd-pleasing tactics the Whigs had perfected in 1840. "The Whigs complain bitterly that we have stolen all their music," a Democrat would gloat.[37] The Democrats nominated the obscure former Speaker of the House of Representatives, James Knox Polk of Tennessee. "Who is James K. Polk?" Whigs sneered. This time the Whig candidate, Henry Clay, defended his record, while a mysterious Democrat played hide-and-seek with the voters.

Polk would not stump; republican ideology and the Democratic strategy precluded it. He would orchestrate efforts behind the scenes, particularly in Tennessee. But should he speak out? Many urged him to keep quiet. "If you could avoid reading or speaking or writing from now until the election, our success would be certain," his friend Cave Johnson advised. Propriety was prudent. Yet Polk believed that "The constituent has a right to know the opinions of the candidate before he casts his vote."[38]

Polk played it safe in his acceptance. He followed the protocol, waiting for the notification committee's letter apprising him of the nomination. He then accepted in a public letter, invoking the classic formula: "The office of president of the United States should neither be sought nor declined. I have never sought it, nor shall I feel at liberty to decline it."[39] Polk sidestepped his dilemma by addressing his letter only to the Democratic party; with no national audience involved, he could ignore national policy questions.

There remained, however, "but one question which can by any possibility defeat your election," Senator Robert J. Walker, a leading Democrat, warned. "It is the tariff." In such crucial protectionist states as

Pennsylvania, Polk was suspect.[40] During his successful 1843 gubernatorial campaign, Polk had denounced the Whig-backed protective Tariff of 1842. If Polk was silent or repudiated the tariff he would lose Pennsylvania, and probably the election. But if he embraced the tariff he might lose his credibility, his dignity, and the election as well.

Ever cautious, Polk sent two letters to the leading protectionist, John K. Kane. The first letter addressed the issue; the second one authorized Kane to release the original letter only if "absolutely necessary." Polk wanted to avoid appearing before the public "as far as I can do so with propriety." On June 29, Kane wrote to Polk that the Pennsylvania Democrats expected the tariff letter to "do much good," and would release it.[41] A third letter from Polk, discouraging publication of any statement about tariffs, did not reach Kane in time.

"I am opposed to a tariff for protection *merely* and not for revenue," Polk's original letter announced. Tariffs to raise revenue were acceptable, as was the "reasonable incidental protection" they provided. But Polk implied that tariffs solely to protect favored industries were illegitimate. In reviewing his record on earlier tariffs, Polk wisely omitted his opposition to the controversial Tariff of 1842. Relieved Democrats praised Polk's manly and forthright sentiments, while Whigs denounced his straddle.[42]

After the release of what became known as the "Kane Letter," Polk was silent. He declined all speaking invitations, explaining: "In adopting this course I but follow the example of the eminent men who have preceded me as a candidate for that high station." Yet Polk was not idle. He corresponded with Democrats across the nation. He supervised editors of the various fly-by-night campaign newspapers. And he helped organize the Tennessee Democrats, doing all he could to ensure the success of the "Great Nashville Convention." Fifty thousand Democrats, including Polk, overran Nashville in late August of 1844. The candidate greeted thousands individually, but made no major address.[43]

With their respective positions in 1840 not only forgotten but reversed, Whigs and Democrats squabbled over Polk's reticence. The Democrats smugly, and without a hint of irony, stood by their candidate's record and lauded Polk's "frankness." They defended Polk's "course uniformly pursued by all the Presidents." Polk recognized the candidate's "imperative duty" to address "NEW QUESTIONS, or old questions upon which he has not been sufficiently explicit." Having fulfilled that duty, he was now silent.[44]

Meanwhile, the Whigs attacked the Democrats' "mum candidate" for having "too little frankness, too much cunning." Polk's long-time

rival, Tennessee Governor James C. Jones, asked why Polk did not
"speak out like a man." "Why are his lips sealed as with the stillness of
death?" Whigs answered that Polk "DARE NOT ANSWER." How else
could he play the tariff man in Pennsylvania and simultaneously claim
to be "SOUTHERN TO THE BACK-BONE" and thus "anti-Tariff to
the hub"? A constituent, the Whigs now proclaimed, has "A RIGHT
TO KNOW THE OPINION OF THE CANDIDATE BEFORE HE
CASTS HIS VOTE." Horace Greeley's *New York Tribune* mischievously
publicized a prominent citizen's warning that in ancient Rome lazy citizens undermined the republic: "That man deserves to be a slave who
would vote for a mum candidate where his liberty is at stake." The
speaker was Andrew Jackson, commenting not on Polk in 1844 but on
Harrison in 1840.[45] The same journals that defended Harrison's silence
in 1840 attacked Polk's silence in 1844 by resurrecting Democratic attacks on Harrison's silence from 1840.

The Whigs hoped to tease out some statement from the unyielding
Polk with their barrage. They nearly succeeded. The most effective Whig
attempt came toward the end of September. Seven Whigs in neighboring Pulaski, Tennessee, sent Polk five "interrogatories" exploring his tariff stance, and three questions about Texas. They demanded "an early
reply, without reference to his [Polk's] former addresses and speeches."[46]

Polk agonized over a suitable response. A Polk confidant, J. George
Harris, pinpointed the dilemma: "Your *friends* throughout the Union
would be glad to see you *absolutely silent* until the day of the election.
. . . Still, as you truly say, a *refusal* to answer would give . . . [your ene-
mies] something to harp on." Polk penned a half-dozen drafts varying
in specificity of response and pugnacity of tone. "I think any answer
improper," John Catron informed his friend. Polk's running mate
George Dallas recognized the futility of the candidate's position: "No
statement, however explicit, will satisfy your adversaries, and your
friends are content with what they have and know."[47]

Polk eventually decided to remain silent. Perhaps Henry Clay's example swayed him: Clay's candidacy offered a persuasive argument for
discretion. Polk gained political capital by presenting a silent contrast
to his rival's verbosity.

IV

Like Martin Van Buren in 1840, Henry Clay was a political war horse.
The tall, thin Kentuckian's sensitive mien was belied by his exuberance

and his reputation for high living. Clay had been running for president for nearly two decades. He was Andrew Jackson's leading opponent in 1832. In nominating Clay the Whigs chose their natural leader, who boasted tremendous political skills and an enduring popularity among thousands. With these assets, however, came his controversial record, and an equally enduring enmity among countless others.

As one of the great men of the republic, Henry Clay was feted wherever he went. In April 1844, more than a month before the Whig convention, he set off to New Orleans, ostensibly on business. Returning to his Kentucky home, "Harry of the West" visited Georgia, the Carolinas, and Virginia. At every stop hundreds mobbed the "plain farmer," who insisted that he had "come upon no political errand." He had not volunteered to stand for office, and he "never had any taste for these public addresses." Nevertheless, people expected him "to make some exposition of my sentiments and views in respect to public affairs." Henry Clay would not disappoint the crowd. He cleared his throat and, more often than not, plunged into a two-hour disquisition on the leading issues of the day.[48] Whigs, of course, were charmed. Democrats were appalled.

To Democrats, Clay's electioneering and "haranguing" revealed his restless ambition. Just as he was addicted to gambling, he was addicted to campaigning: What better way to gratify his monstrous ego? Democrats who defended Martin Van Buren's precampaign tour in 1839 now attacked the Whig's traveling pilgrim.[49]

Once nominated, Clay announced his intention to retire to his home, Ashland, and await the people's decision in peace. Accepting the nomination bound him to "the duties and obligations" of that station. Choosing a chief magistrate is the people's own business, Clay said. The people "should be free, impartial and wholly unbiased by the conduct of a candidate himself." Clay would return home "as quietly and quickly as possible."[50]

These yearnings for tranquility proved short-lived. After four decades in the public square, Henry Clay could *not* sit silently on his farm. Although he rarely left Ashland, his letters traversed the nation, stirring supporters and enemies alike.

Clay's troubles originated during his Southern tour. For two years Clay confidants had been begging for silence. "[Clay] must be *caged—that's the point, cage him!*" Kentucky Governor Robert Letcher instructed in 1842. But Clay dismissed the warnings, nobly preferring candor: "I entertain no fears from the promulgation of my opinion," he averred. Indeed, while in Raleigh he clarified his stand on the proposed annexation of Texas. In a letter dated April 17, 1844, he warned that annexing Texas would provoke war with Mexico and exacerbate sectional tensions.[51]

This bold "Raleigh Letter" thrilled Northerners and troubled Southerners. "Clay [is] a dead political Duck," Andrew Jackson said. As accusations mounted that Clay was courting the anti-annexationist abolitionists, Southern dissatisfaction festered.[52] In July, Clay tried to mollify his Southern supporters with two letters to Alabamans, shifting the tone, if not the substance, of his stance. Clay said he wanted Texas to join the Union but the price was too steep. In the letters, Clay also tried to separate Texas from the slavery question.[53]

Clay's two "Alabama Letters" fueled the Texas controversy and created a new, more damaging brouhaha. Opponents now accused Clay of reversing himself, of holding "different opinions to suit different latitudes." Clay blows with "every popular breeze in the North and in the South," the Nashville Union cried. Dumbstruck Whig orators initially dismissed one of the Alabama Letters as a forgery. Hundreds of Whigs begged their nominee to lay down his quill. Perversely, Democrats urged him to continue, arguing that Clay was their best ally. "Clay is killing himself," Polk's aide J. George Harris exulted.[54]

These attacks prompted yet another letter from Clay, reconciling the Raleigh Letter with the two Alabama Letters. Clay explained that he had hoped to avoid writing altogether. But he had discovered that silence might mislead people into thinking that Henry Clay was "unwilling frankly and fearlessly to submit my opinions to the public judgment." He then had written the three letters, all of which were misconstrued. This fourth letter, according to Clay, was his last word. A president should enter office unencumbered by pledges and open to all public questions, he argued, belatedly.[55]

Even after the "final" letter, other statements by Clay appeared in the press. Furthermore, with delays in reporting, many newspapers printed accounts of Clay's Southern tour months after his nomination.[56] By the end of the campaign, newspapers had published letters from Clay on the Texas question, the tariff, the Cumberland road, and dueling. Clay never seemed to quiet down. Thus, the public believed that he had mounted a vigorous personal campaign.

This belief framed the debate about the candidates' tactics. It was Polk the silent stay-at-home versus Clay the traveling haranguer. Whigs assailed Polk's reticence and mediocrity, while Democrats assailed Clay's duplicity and breaches of dignity. But Polk's tactics were too similar to Harrison's, and too consistent with contemporary proprieties, to offend many people. If anything, focusing on his silence strengthened Polk's appearance as the ideal "man of spotless morals," the humble person who was "no office-seeker."[57] The attacks also heightened the contrast with Clay, who seemed willing to sacrifice anything for success.

The assaults on Clay's electioneering jibed with the broader Democratic indictment of him as "morally unfit." After decades as the nation's most prominent politician, Clay personified many of the republican fears about politics and its practitioners. And Clay's swearing, gambling, and drinking had long disturbed many. Rather than stilling those concerns, Clay's behavior fed the "private character" issue. The letter-writing debacle bundled all the worries into a single package epitomizing the immoral and self-promoting politician.

Clay underestimated the potency of these attacks: They struck him as nothing new, merely another mark of Democratic despair. Clay "pitied" the Democrats, commenting that, avoiding the great questions of national policy, they took refuge in personal abuse. Accustomed to being charged with "every crime enumerated in the Decalogue," he added that he had lived down these attacks heretofore, and "with the blessing of Providence" hoped to survive them again.[58]

Democrats countered that the issue of private character in a presidential campaign transcended everyday politics. Americans still linked individual and communal virtue. A president's example "[gives] a tone to [the] moral pulse of the nation," the *Albany Argus* explained. But one's public role was no longer the crucial determinant of one's "character." Educators like Horace Mann and Ralph Waldo Emerson preached that individual moral behavior bettered one's "self" and improved society. "Character" now implied ethical conduct. A man "pure and upright in his private character," the *Argus* continued, "is the only safe depository of public trust. . . . The vices and immoralities of private life will be carried into the public administration." Just as a merchant would not select a clerk whose habits were immoral, or parents hire a teacher prone to vice, so should Americans protect themselves from Henry Clay.[59]

In November the republic was protected: Clay lost. Polk's victory was thin enough to attribute it to any one factor—especially Clay's letter-writing. Now, Democrats rejoiced while Whigs mourned. "I am unmanned," Millard Fillmore of Buffalo wrote Clay. "A cloud of gloom hangs over the future. May God save the country, for it is evident the people will not."[60]

The character question in 1844 highlighted the candidate's uncertain role. Americans cared about the character of their leaders, but did not know how to address the issue properly. The campaign no longer took place in statehouses and parlors. But could character be judged on the streets and in the newspapers? Party affiliation now colored most people's character assessments: To Whigs, Clay remained a hero, and the character issue seems hardly to have affected the election returns. It was, like the candidate himself, more important symbolically than actually; and more potentially destructive than constructive.

Candidates were party tools. Whigs in 1840 and Democrats in 1844 learned that a good candidate provided a canvas upon which heroic deeds and noble principles could be painted—providing the candidate was politically obscure. Democrats in 1840 and Whigs in 1844 learned that a well-known and controversial candidate was a curse, casting shadows on the party's idealized campaign portrait. Politicians thus concluded that a candidate was more likely to endanger a campaign than to redeem it; the candidate was a risk to be minimized. No wonder party managers preferred to run their own shows and keep candidates passive and silent.

Clay's defeat left a curious legacy. The legend of Henry Clay, later written into Whig texts and repeated at July Fourth celebrations, attributed Clay's failure to win the presidency to what one eulogist called his "moral courage," his statesmanlike devotion to principle. The lesson was encapsulated in what became the Clay maxim: "I'd rather be right than president." Politicians, on the other hand, learned a less romantic lesson. More than forty years later, a retired Senator and Democratic National Chairman, William H. Barnum, recalled that in 1844 "a clause of less than a dozen words" in one of the Alabama Letters lost Clay the presidency. After that, political managers "made the candidates virtually prisoners."[61] Politicians had learned the value of silence and a different maxim: that, if you'd rather be president—don't write.

The belief that Henry Clay talked himself out of the presidency flourished. Americans concluded, therefore, that frankness was dangerous. But this lesson was wrong. Clay's mistake was not in writing letters; he erred by shifting his position, by currying the favor of too many voters simultaneously. Had Clay written longer, more thoughtful, and more consistent letters, as Van Buren did, he might have suffered less.[62] Clay was defeated neither by principles nor by letter-writing, but by pandering.

Americans, then, misread both the 1840 and 1844 campaigns, disregarding innovations and confirming preconceptions. Amid the confusion and change, they clung to traditional modes of campaigning. Despite Harrison's violation, the republican taboo was still strong. And despite the inclination toward frankness, silence remained golden.

V

In 1844 presidential candidates still did not know how to communicate with their constituents. The major party candidates in 1840 and 1844 each had taken a different path—and faltered. Harrison's strategy, for a time, endangered his candidacy. Van Buren not only lost the election but was forever cast as the hapless victim of Whig tactics. Clay's strategy backfired, seemingly undermining his efforts. And although Polk appeared most successful, his obscurity and silence tainted his campaign with a hint of illegitimacy that grew in retrospect. To whatever degree Polk inspired future candidates, it was with a sheepishness that whispered "I know it is unsporting, but it worked."

With the original system outmoded, the improvised one suspect, democracy at high tide, and even the conservative Whig party appealing to the people, these candidates had unprecedented latitude. In the wake of Jacksonian Democracy, it would have made sense if the ideal of forthrightness had triumphed and if future candidates had been as active as Harrison and as frank as Van Buren. Yet, curiously, the opposite occurred. The contradictory experiences of candidates were puréed into a simple notion that candidates should not, and traditionally had not, run for election. Candidates retreated to passivity and silence.

"I am more and more convinced of the *expediency* as well as the perfect propriety of a Presidential candidate, when once nominated, to abstain entirely from answering all Enquiries regarding public measures," Methodist clergyman Charles Augustus Davis wrote during the 1844 campaign. Troubled by Clay's ordeal, Davis proposed a model letter for a nominee which encapsulated the current wisdom. "I shall enter [the presidency] . . . with no other guide than the Constitution," Davis's candidate would write, endorsing a limited role for a candidate by pointing to the circumscribed presidency itself.[63] Davis thus added ideology to his equation of expediency and propriety, justifying a more complete silence than before.

The criticism heaped upon the candidates bolstered this emerging consensus amidst chaos. There was a perversely pleasing circularity to the pundits' criticism. Partisans damned Polk for what they championed in Harrison, or mocked Clay for what they admired in Van Buren. Democratic newspapers criticized Clay's political pilgrimages in 1839 and in 1844 with the same vehemence that Whig newspapers unleashed on Van Buren's pilgrimages in 1839. Democrats attacked Harrison's mummery and defended Polk's, while Whigs defended Harrison and attacked Polk. Democrats praised Van Buren's letter-writing and ridiculed

Clay's. Whigs accused Van Buren of dissimulating, but the charges eventually boomeranged toward Clay. Clearly, partisanship dictated propriety.

Yet despite all these contradictions, both Whigs and Democrats adhered to similar standards: Statesmen were good; politicians and parties were bad. Republican detachment from the political arena was good and dignified; actively seeking office and soliciting votes was humiliating and bad. Articulating stands on major issues was good and democratic; avoiding questions, and tailoring appeals to particular audiences—especially the different sections—were demagogic and bad. Virtuous men remained in demand.

Jacksonian America brought the people into the electoral process, but it kept the leaders—at least the presidential candidates—out. The myth that the nominee was always passive and silent unified the liberal-democratic and republic traditions, obscuring their contradictions. The myth also linked American ideology, however anachronistic, with political street wisdom, however inaccurate. Party leaders found the republican taboo useful. Just how useful becomes clearer after examining the elections of 1848 through 1856.

THREE

An Age of Parties, 1848–1856

I have no right, as the candidate of the Democratic party . . . to present new and different issues before the people.
—*James Buchanan, 1856*

"MANAGING the Candidate," an 1852 cartoon, shows a nominee standing on the rickety "Baltimore Bridge," the Whigs' convention platform. The candidate, General Winfield Scott, is trying to step over a controversial plank ratifying the Great Compromise of 1850 between the North and the South. Perched on Scott's shoulders, the Whig stalwart William Henry Seward covers the General's mouth and holds the General's right arm, preventing him from speaking or writing. "General," Seward says, "I have been trying to get safely over this Stream for some time, and your Shoulders are broad enough to bear me; never mind your tongue or your pen[,] I'll manage them, but . . . stretch your legs, as I do my Conscience, and you can get over anything."[1]

Seward and Scott, managers and candidates, had to stretch so far in mid-century because as America expanded, it also seemed to be coming apart. From the American Revolution to 1850 population increased tenfold and exports sevenfold, the land mass more than tripled, and the number of states more than doubled. "These United States" were no longer a band of small settlements scattered along the Atlantic; *it* was now a continental power stretching to the Pacific. But fulfilling America's "Manifest Destiny" out West exacerbated tensions between North and South. Many Northerners who tolerated slavery in the South opposed its extension into the new territories. The more America prospered, the brighter her democratic star glowed, the greater was the people's frustration with the sectional problems and with the politicians who failed to solve them.

On a national level, parties tried to avoid sectional issues. But each presidential campaign highlighted the growing sectional incompatibility. Fewer and fewer national figures seemed to transcend the differences. Appeals to party loyalty above all else became at once more desperate and less effective.

"Managing the Candidate" captures the ambiguities surrounding candidacies in the 1840s and 1850s—the tensions between the candidate and the party, and between principles and victory, in an increasingly tumultuous era. Parties wanted an available candidate, broad-shouldered enough to carry the campaign, to attract wavering voters, and to unite the nation. But they also wanted a pliable candidate, sufficiently weak-kneed to defer to the party managers.

I

"A revolution is taking place in public opinion," the *New York Evening Mirror* announced in 1852. "Stumping," first popularized in the 1830s, when speakers spoke while literally standing on tree stumps, was spreading throughout the nation, and especially in the more traditional South. Increasingly, candidates for state legislature, Congress, and various minor offices took to the stump. In the form eventually immortalized in the 1858 Lincoln–Douglas debates, the candidates would crisscross their districts together, addressing the issues face-to-face. The *Mirror* foresaw a day when stumping would promote worthy candidates rather than hucksters; when issues would become more important than family ties or money: "If 'reasons are as plenty as blackberries,' the candidate must give them himself, and orally too, in order to satisfy the voters that he is worthy of their suffrages."[2]

Concurrently, technological advances made many campaign rituals anachronistic. Candidates now operated in a fishbowl. The invention of the telegraph let nominees hear of the convention's decision rapidly and accept it just as quickly. The growth of railroads and cities enabled touring candidates to reach thousands of voters easily. And, with the rise of newspapers, these tours could be reported throughout America, with a correspondingly amplified impact. Surveying these developments, even during the few years from 1846 to 1851, one editor, Samuel Bowles, marveled that "It was something more than progress, it was revolution."[3]

Yet these revolutions in public opinion and technology did not greatly affect the behavior of the presidential candidate. Even when wrenching national crises demanded bold leadership, nominees were mute. The forces propelling candidates toward center stage were offset by the traditional republican sensibilities, the cautionary tales, and, increasingly, party needs.

The party's agenda was simple: Get elected. As electoral contests became closer and closer, both Democrats and Whigs intensified their partisan appeals—Polk's victory depended on barely forty thousand votes of more than four million cast. All questions paled before "one broad, paramount issue," the *Democratic Review* confessed in December 1844: "*Which of the two great leading parties shall be placed in power?*"[4]

The presidential campaign lay at the center of this black-and-white universe. It forged dozens of disparate local groups into one national party, albeit temporarily. Every four years, a dementia swept the country that was both a joyous folk festival and a fratricidal war. During the campaign, America appeared split into two highly organized, politically obsessed, irreconcilable camps. Then, suddenly, Election Day would pass, a party would triumph, the organizations would vanish, public attention would shift, the wounds would heal. The combatants, like good sportsmen, would emerge bloodied but with an enhanced appreciation for the arena itself, the United States of America.

Yet questions lingered. Many remained wary as they plunged into the party game. Even as he accepted a state convention's nomination in 1839, William Henry Harrison acknowledged that this "mode of selecting a candidate for the two highest offices of the Government" offended "many of our fellow-citizens." This chariness would decline with time. Other questions persisted: Was this the best way to elect the president? Wasn't the process unseemly, illegitimate? Every Democratic platform from 1844 through 1856 placed the party's "trust, not in factitious symbols, not in displays and appeals insulting to the judgment and subversive of the intellect of the people, but in a clear reliance upon the intelligence, patriotism and the discriminating justice of the American masses."[5] Confident of their own virtue, Democrats admitted a gnawing discomfort with campaigning. Clearly, the Founders did not have this chaos in mind.

But, to a great extent, parties stifled these challenges. Prizing loyalty above all, partisans defined propriety simply: Everything *we* do is proper, everything *they*—members of the opposing party—do is not. Sim-

ilarly, parties believed that anyone they nominated was acceptable, anyone the opposing party nominated was not. Within each party the belief
in principles, not men, and the voter's commitment to his party, often
regardless of principles or men, reduced the candidates to two-dimen-
sional icons waved before the partisan crowds. The opposing party's
assaults against any nominee who dared assert himself further paralyzed
the candidates.

II

Partisanship bludgeoned presidential candidates into a secondary role,
fortifying the republican taboo's practical and ideological dictates. The
presidential candidate was to remain silent and passive. This neutralized
the individual most identified with the campaign itself. Consequently,
the success of the campaign depended on a party's ability to mobilize
its followers.[6] Yet the party bureaucracy was remarkably fluid: It was
decentralized, autonomous, localized. Every four years, rudimentary national infrastructures appeared—and then vanished. But partisan newspapers mushroomed. And professionals, both behind-the-scenes managers and public leaders, proliferated.

The party model worked best with a mute candidate. The party
machinery selected, the party newspapers promoted, and the party
members elected, the president. Although overlapping, each of these
efforts required different skills. For each of the activities there was a
different archetype—a professional, an editor, a leader. In the 1840s and
1850s, Thurlow Weed was the political maestro of the New York Whigs,
Horace Greeley was the leading partisan editor, and William Henry Seward the consummate leader. The careers of these three masters of the
new politics illustrate how the party system advanced and silenced nominees.

A self-made man, Weed was a printer and editor before becoming
the Whig party "Dictator." He was robust and charming, but slightly
awkward. His political philosophy could be summarized by his only criterion in looking for a candidate in 1840: "Who will poll the most
votes?"[7] Weed exploited the new political realities to win those votes.
With the expansion of American society and government, patronage
ballooned. Weed bestowed positions wisely. With the elaboration of
American communications and politics, costs surged. Weed raised and
distributed money carefully. And, with the emergence of strong parties,

available and loyal politicians were required. Weed chose standard-bearers thoughtfully.

Weed was one of several warlords dominating the local and national parties. With the parties merely a federation of affiliated state machines, local power was the only source of lasting political strength. Before the presidential nominating convention, these warlords roamed the political landscape, seeking viable candidates. Afterwards, they arranged editorial endorsements, orchestrated popular meetings, united warring factions, and funneled money to strategic locales, including neighboring states. Often, they financed their own activities—Weed spent twelve years repaying the $350 he borrowed during the 1824 campaign.[8] Men like Weed, therefore, wanted pliant and popular candidates to avoid trouble, respect local prerogatives, and allow the party operatives free rein.

Weed realized, however, that his machinations could only do so much. He had to broadcast his message through popular party newspapers. Although his own *Albany Evening Journal* dominated Whig politics in New York State, he lacked the skills to inspire the masses. In 1838 he hired a journeyman printer, Horace Greeley, to create a cheap political weekly, the *Jeffersonian*. The baby-faced, seedy-looking Greeley—he was once fired by a boss yelling "Let's have decent-*looking* men around here, at least"—soon became known as the "Adjutant" to Weed the "Dictator." In 1840, Weed backed Greeley's *Log Cabin* and transformed political journalism.[9]

Prior to Greeley's day, party newspapers reflected the sensibilities of some editor who survived on state printing contracts and an occasional discreet party subsidy. The parties sustained these papers but strangled them: The papers could never reach an audience beyond the party. To remedy that, entrepreneurs in the 1830s began "the penny presses." Targeting the urban poor, these one-cent journals earned money from both circulation and advertising. They eschewed partisanship. Instead, they offered a sensational mixture of "licentiousness, no matter how disgusting, lies, however glaring, [and] personal abuse without a shadow of foundation . . . [with which] to gratify the taste of the people," as the patrician diarist Philip Hone shuddered. Catering to the masses in an emerging market economy, these papers proliferated. Circulation soared.[10]

In 1841 Horace Greeley founded the *New York Tribune*, hoping to avoid "servile partnership on the one hand," and "gagged, mincing neutrality on the other." A journalist should "heartily advocate" his party's "principles," yet be free to "frankly dissent . . . on a particular question and even denounce its candidates," Greeley believed. Muting both partisanship and sensationalism, combining popularity and principle, mixing loyalty to Whiggery with Greeley's idiosyncrasies, the *Tribune* flourished. Its weekly edition spread the Greeley–Whig gospel throughout the North and the West to an unprecedented two hundred thousand readers by 1860. The *Tribune* became to many what it was to Clarence Darrow in his childhood, "the political and social Bible of our home."[11]

During campaigns, Greeley and other editors also printed campaign libraries: biographies, lithographs, pamphlets and, eventually, textbooks marshaling all of the relevant material.[12] But the newspaper remained the centerpiece. Having chosen a candidate, the editor would hoist the nominee's name upon the masthead, broadcasting the affiliation.[13] Daily, Greeley and his colleagues printed the usual combination of electoral tidbits, reprints, late-breaking news, thoughtful analyses, and spectacular lies. For all of Greeley's restraint, partisanship still prevailed. The *Tribune*, like all partisan papers, was full of bile.

For the newspapers, campaigning was both serious politics and essential business. Although circulation rose during most campaigns, an unpalatable nominee or an unpopular position could endanger the paper's revenues; protesting readers often canceled subscriptions. Alternatively, papers could profit with a losing candidate popular among partisans. When Henry Clay lost in 1844, Greeley cried. Greeley's business manager, however, grieved less: The *Tribune*'s circulation—and profits— had risen.[14]

Weed and Greeley could mobilize multitudes, but American politics still required a personal touch. Voters no longer delegated their local leaders to select worthy men on only the state and national levels. Now, leaders on *all* levels had to stir the crowd. Managers and editors, therefore, could set the scene and write the script. But they needed actors like William Henry Seward to win the audience.[15]

Weed and Seward collaborated for nearly half a century, from 1824 until Seward's death in 1872. With Weed's backing, Seward rose from the New York State Senate to the Governor's chair to the United States Senate and then to the Cabinet, as Secretary of State. Only the presidency eluded him. Weed considered Seward more refined than himself, and so let him worry about principles and about courting the public. Seward would spearhead the party drive, personifying the party message and inspiring the masses through speeches, parades, and rallies. To adopt the military metaphors of the times, politicians like Seward were on the front lines rallying the troops for their party standard-bearer, leaving strategy to men like Weed.

Seward and his peers were the surrogates for passive presidential candidates. Except in 1840, when his own sense of the gubernatorial proprieties kept him at his desk, Seward stumped during campaigns. In 1848, for instance, he spoke in New York, Massachusetts, Pennsylvania, and Ohio. His prolonged absences infuriated his wife, Frances, who spurned dresses and hats as peace offerings.[16]

In turns instructive and demagogic, inspirational and bellicose, and often with a classical veneer, the stump speeches were in the great tradition of American rhetoric.[17] For some speakers, such as Seward, the prestige of their offices and achievements bolstered their oratory. Others, like the German–American stumpers Carl Schurz and Gustave Koerner, gained their prestige from their oratory. Regardless of their merits or backgrounds, all sought to compensate for the presidential candidate's absence, to translate the excitement of being in a political leader's presence into votes for the unseen candidate. In the eyes of the audience the stump speaker became the candidate himself, even the party itself, energizing principles and party affiliation.

Seward's stumping earned him a national following, enhancing his party power. This success, in turn, fueled his presidential ambitions, complicating his relations with the nominee. As with so many politicians, Seward's strength was his weakness: His outspokenness attracted controversy. Perennial bridesmaids, statesmen-politicians like Seward often cherished their roles as surrogates, enjoying their moment of celebrity on the stump, however fleeting. Sometimes they were content to advise the nominee, sometimes they compensated by championing principles uncompromisingly, sometimes they sulked. Regardless, the quieter the nominee, the more satisfied were the also-rans.

The party reliance on managers, editors, and politicians diminished the candidates.[18] The parties, trusting their professionals, deemed candidates exploitable and interchangeable. The party did not want a candidate to interfere: Parties were enduring; candidacies were fads. Parties secured voters; careless candidates could alienate them. Throughout the 1840s and 1850s, both Democrats and Whigs craved available, pliable candidates. Parties emerged from conventions united behind one candidate, who, respecting republicanism and the platform, kept silent, content to be waved as an icon before partisan crowds. But these unions often were rocky. The Whigs, as the weaker party, found less-submissive candidates, and endured more turmoil during the campaigns.

III

In many ways, Lewis Cass's 1848 candidacy exemplified the ideal party arrangement. Cass had an impressive résumé: war hero in 1812, Governor of the Michigan territory, Secretary of War, Minister to France, and a United States Senator. He was a "doughface," a Northern man with Southern principles—good for unifying the Democratic party amid mounting sectional tensions. And he would keep quiet: "If I am ever elevated to the Presidency," Cass said and would continue to say, "it will be without any efforts of my own."[19]

Once nominated, Cass followed the party script. In accepting the nomination he promised to serve one term, embraced the platform, and pledged silence. If the "conduct" and "opinions" of his forty-year career did not illustrate his intentions, nothing would. "Anything further I might now say, would be a mere delusion, unworthy of myself and justly offensive [to the Democratic party]," Cass said.[20]

Cass then resigned from the Senate. On his way home, he spoke briefly at public receptions. Once in Michigan, he remained relatively passive, taking one major trip to Cleveland. He published some speeches, and his "Nicholson Letter" advocating popular sovereignty— the notion that the people of each new territory should decide the slavery question for themselves. But he shunned controversy and the spotlight.

Whigs sniped about Cass's silence, his character, and his background: "And he who still for Cass can be," one Whig punned, "he is a Cass without the C." On the whole, however, both sides ignored Cass. Most newspapers followed the controversial and popular Whig candidate, Zachary Taylor, more closely—with both praise and damnation.[21] When election day came, Cass had done everything right—except win.

The victor in 1848, Zachary Taylor, proved more troubling to the Whigs: He was *not* an ideal partner. The Whigs were weaker than the Democrats. The Democrats built their party from the bottom up, with a strong foundation throughout America supporting the national party; on the other hand, the Whigs' national party united weaker constituent parts. This weakness undermined the Whigs' relations with the nominees. While Democrats worried only about neutralizing their candidate's potential harm, Whigs needed to exploit their assets—a tall order, given the traditional constraints on the candidate. Democrats, then, could elect a party man, a James Polk. Having learned that statesmen like Clay entailed too many risks, Whigs sought heroes like General Harrison, who offered popularity without controversy.[22] Such candidates, however, often came at a price: Heroes rarely were regular party men. Taylor's candidacy was a case in point.

Commander of the Army of Occupation on the Mexican border, veteran of the War of 1812, known affectionately as "Old Rough and Ready," Major General Zachary Taylor was an ideal candidate—for *either* party. His Mexican War victories in May 1846 catapulted him into contention for the nomination. For the next two years, both Whigs and Democrats would nominate the General. "Convention be damned," an impatient Kentuckian yelled shortly after Taylor's victory at Buena Vista in February 1847, "I tell ye General Taylor is going to be elected by *spontaneous combustion.*"[23] Yet the mating dance between Taylor and the Whig party was complicated, and the resulting marriage was strained.

Questions about politics besieged Taylor for two years. For most of this time he was in the field, first fighting the Mexican War and then supervising the occupation. From his military tent-turned-campaign headquarters, the General responded. At first, the pleas to run shocked him: "Such an idea never entered my head, nor is it likely to enter the head of any sane person," he sputtered. Taylor was tired, his wife was ill, and he felt unqualified. He boasted that he had "never . . . so much as . . . voted for one of our chief magistrates," and belonged to no party. He knew that people were skeptical of his demurrals—proof that many viewed the republican inhibition as an affectation—but insisted he was sincere.[24]

As the pressure increased, Taylor shifted—a little. A "sense of duty to the country" forced him to overcome his "repugnance" and permit people to advance his name, he explained. He might defer to the "spontaneous move of the people," but "without pledges." He would only accept a nomination to be "President of the nation, and not of a party." Exploiting the continuing discomfort with American politics, Taylor placed himself above the "trading politicians . . . on both sides."[25]

Taylor's shuffling alarmed Whig professionals. Thurlow Weed, who after meeting the General's brother on a steamboat in 1846 became satisfied with Taylor's party fidelity, advised against letter-writing. But Taylor responded to letters out of "courtesy." More and more variations on the Taylor waltz, stressing his reluctance and independence, appeared in newspapers. By late 1847 his letters had alienated many regulars: "Why should he wish to occupy grounds . . . more elevated than [that of] all others who have aspired to that high office?" one Virginia Whig asked. Others wondered if a Taylor victory could ever be a Whig victory. Being "in favor of a Whig candidate only," Weed could no longer support Taylor. Whigs, it seemed, had to choose between party regularity and a popular candidate, between principles and success. Henry Clay sighed: "I wish I could slay a Mexican."[26]

Taylor had his own choice to make, and yielded to the party and to success. Wary of making "pledges," and conscious of his ignorance of political "details," Taylor embraced the Whig party more firmly in his first "Allison Letter" of April 22, 1848: "I AM A WHIG, *but not an ultra Whig*," he said, distancing himself from "party domination."[27] This profession of loyalty to the bosses, along with his popularity among the masses, clinched the nomination. The slaveholding General was hailed North and South. Taylor claimed he won on his own nonpartisan terms, without promises of any kind. This victory signaled "confidence in my honesty, truthfulness & integrity never surpassed & rarely equalled [since George Washington]," Taylor rejoiced.[28]

Many Whig regulars, however, remained distressed. Henry Clay, the symbol of Whig virtue, sulked. Promising to sit this contest out, Clay complained that "The Whig party has been overthrown by a mere personal party. . . . Can I say that in his [Taylor's] hands Whig measures will be safe and secure, when he refused to pledge himself to their support?" Clay mourned in June. The *Jonesborough Whig* did not know "which most to d[e]spise, the *vanity* and *insolence* of Gen. Taylor, or the *creeping servility* [of the Whig convention]" that nominated him.[29]

After his nomination, Taylor tried to keep a low profile. Still, he remained in the public eye, and the campaign suffered for it. His letters continued to appear in newspapers, offering new cautionary tales on the perils of candor. And he continued to oscillate between partisanship and nonpartisanship. When renegade South Carolina Democrats nominated him, Taylor alternately reaffirmed his commitment to the Whig party *and* said he would have accepted the Democratic nomination in his quest to be "President of the whole nation."[30] Democrats pounced on this contradiction. Was Taylor the Whig candidate, or the people's candidate, they asked.

Democrats knew that this question irritated the Whigs. But they themselves seemed unsure of the answer, attacking Taylor for misleading both the party and the people. In their scattershot criticisms of Taylor and the Whigs, Democrats upheld the new politics and the old, both democracy and republicanism.

As the candidate of "no avowed principle," this new "General Mum" undermined both the democratic dialogue and the party system, Democrats charged. How can a silent candidate be "[sent] into the executive chair of a nation founded, as is ours, upon the very rock of *public opinion* itself," editor Thomas Ritchie asked.[31] The Founding Fathers would have been surprised to hear that "public opinion" had replaced virtue as the foundation of American politics. Similarly, the Founders would have been surprised by Howell Cobb's characterization of Taylor's "no party" candidacy as "a blow at the corner-stone of our whole political system." In his widely reprinted speech "The Necessity of Party Organization," the Georgia Congressman reminded straying Democrats that party identity mattered more than a particular candidate. In so doing, Cobb and his fellow Democrats deemed the new party system essential for "self-government."[32]

When they tired of defending democracy, Democrats offered more traditional critiques. Overlooking their supposed faith in the people, they accused the Whigs of "address[ing] the senses by the most disgraceful humbugs." Such demagoguery was the handiwork of a cabal, for Zachary Taylor could no more produce many of the statements attributed to him than "extemporize another 'Paradise Lost'!" the Washington, D.C., *Daily Union* charged. By signing Taylor's name to speeches which were too eloquent, letters which were too literary, or documents too partisan for the "no party" man, these Whig manipulators humiliated their candidate and threatened the republic.[33]

By September, Henry Clay had endorsed Taylor, yet many Whigs still fumed. Taylor's second Allison Letter, on September 4, attempted to heal those wounds. Complaining that he had been misunderstood, Taylor again embraced the Whigs. He claimed that in keeping with "good Whig doctrine" he "would not be a *partisan* president, and hence should not be a party candidate."[34] Taylor then closed the subject, again.

Democrats called the letter fraudulent and ghostwritten by Whig politicos, but the letter worked. The Monroe, Pennsylvania *Democrat* called Taylor "the most inconsistent, contradictory, and two-faced man that has ever figured before the American public." Still, the second Allison Letter "awakened the zeal of the now united Whig party," Weed recalled. What Taylor said was secondary; the letter was an excuse for Whigs to return. Seward captured the Whig sentiment when he supported Taylor "on precisely the same grounds on which I have hitherto voted for Whig candidates—because they are commended to me by the Whig party." In a close election, with New York again the swing state, Taylor triumphed.[35]

To hacks like Weed, the election results "vindicated the wisdom of General Taylor's nomination." But to purists like Greeley, Taylor triumphed, rather than "our principles." Clay's 1844 loss, Greeley explained, had strengthened Whig convictions: The 1848 election "demoralized" Whigs and undermined the faith of "the masses" in the party. It was a pyrrhic victory, Greeley believed; Whigs were "at once triumphant and undone."[36]

Taylor's erratic waltz illuminated the dilemmas facing both the candidates and the parties. In his myriad contradictions, Taylor covered the ground of all four candidates from 1840 and 1844. At times he justified candor; at times, silence. At times he was active; at times he professed passivity. Ultimately, however, Taylor's position affirmed passivity. He fancied himself the new George Washington and often appeared to be awaiting coronation, not election. Along with his Democratic counterpart, Lewis Cass, Taylor, once nominated, upheld the status quo.

Ironically, the Whig party sellout marked a party triumph. Except for the second Allison Letter, which itself was a party victory, Taylor avoided the limelight after the nomination, deferring to advisers like Weed, Greeley, and Seward. Weed tried to unite the Whigs and to widen the division between antislavery "Free Soil" Democrats and Democratic regulars.[37] Greeley, after pining for Henry Clay, held his nose and endorsed Taylor in late September. And Seward eventually stumped. Whigs showed their loyalty to the party, not the man, as did the many Southern Democrats who stuck with Cass. The party machine worked.

IV

In 1852, Whigs again needed a military hero. The party, like the nation, seemed to be splintering. The divisive forces of economic sectionalism, cultural conflict, and political strife were focused on one narrow issue: the expansion of slavery into new territories. In 1848, both Taylor and Cass had tried to downplay the strife, unsuccessfully. In his brief stint as President, Taylor's attempts at evenhandedness enraged his Southern brethren. Increasingly, partisans on both sides viewed compromisers as traitors. When they convened in Baltimore, the Whigs were so divided that they found an acceptable standard-bearer only on the fifty-third ballot. Still, their bid for unity failed. General Winfield Scott erred. He deviated from the party model and violated the republican taboo—he stumped.

Lieutenant General Winfield Scott enjoyed a more illustrious military career than Zachary Taylor, and better civil qualifications. Erect, regal, Virginia-born, a genuine hero against the British in 1812 and the Mexicans thirty-six years later, Scott fancied himself a military grandee. He loved parading around wearing his cocked hat and displaying his sword. Also he often referred to himself in the third person. As a long-time Whig, he had been a presidential possibility for over a decade. Scott's candidacy, unlike Taylor's, was identified with a party faction and a particular policy—the antislavery sentiments of William Seward's Northern Whigs. The Baltimore platform appeased Southerners by endorsing states' rights and the elaborate Compromise of 1850. Scott telegraphed his approval, becoming the first nominee to address a convention directly. Antislavery Whigs supported their candidate while "spitting upon the platform," in Horace Greeley's memorable phrase.[38]

Scott's nomination was another Whig bid for popularity: "I defy anyone to sit down & read . . . a life of the General . . . without being moved," the Whig A. W. Bradford wrote. But Bradford also regretted Whig reliance on that life, anticipating a day when the Whig party would be strong enough "that we may afford to do without Generals."[39]

General Scott was supposed to follow the party script with a dignified silence. For the first few months after the convention, he was quiet. During the preconvention struggle, Scott had avoided letter-writing: How could "covering a half sheet or a whole sheet of foolscap" add to a forty-year career, a supporter had asked. Scott avoided a celebration of his War of 1812 heroics in late July, citing the proprieties.[40] The partisan newspapers, as usual, traded charges and fabrications, but mostly overlooked Scott and his Democratic opponent, Franklin Pierce.

During the summer, however, Scott became restless. He began to write letters, exhibiting the traits that later prompted one Democrat's offer to "furnish" Scott "liberally with stationery." Democrats hoped, and Whigs feared, that Scott's "vanity & letter writing" would harm his campaign. Whigs also worried that active candidates became independent—and ungrateful—presidents. "I know you made him and we've got him and it's better Scott than any body else . . . ," one New Yorker confided to Seward in August, "but I am a little afraid that . . . if elected he may be apt to say 'my own right arm hath gotten me the victory.'"[41] Strong parties gorged on passive candidates and a weakened presidency.

In mid-September, Scott decided to do something more daring than writing the occasional letter. He concluded that, as one supporter said, "A live lion in good voice, will produce . . . a far greater and more lasting effect by being *seen* and *heard*, than all the . . . [campaign biographies] which can be written." Encouraged by some advisers and emboldened by egotism, Scott took to the stump.[42] Using an inspection of a military hospital site in Blue Lick, Kentucky, as an excuse, the General left Washington for a five-week tour of the Northeast and the Old Northwest.

Unfortunately for Scott, the tour aggravated his Achilles heel: It proved to his critics that "Old Fuss and Feathers" was indeed vain and pompous. Scott's verbal slips during the Mexican War—"[a] hasty *plate* of soup" and "firing *on* the rear"—were well known, and remembered by pranksters who distributed soup bowls at rallies. His transparent attempt to circumvent the republican taboo made him appear garrulous and silly as well. Again and again Scott protested: "I left Washington . . . not dreaming that I should be called upon to open my lips at any public meeting whatever. I went upon a journey of professional duty." But as Scott stretched a one-week journey into five, the artifice wore thin; his solicitude began to grate. To charm Catholics and Protestants, Scott attended a Catholic mass one Sunday morning and an Episcopal service that evening. To prove that he was not anti-immigrant, Scott cheered, when he heard an Irish voice during a speech, "I hear that rich brogue."[43]

Democrats called the denials and the posturing "the best joke[s] of the season." "If Scott is not stumping it and electioneering for the presidency, what is he doing?" the *Louisville Democrat* wondered. He certainly was not going about on "public business." Democrats waved copies of telegrams which said "*General Scott leaves here this morning, via Harrisburg.* HE WILL CONSENT TO PUBLIC RECEPTIONS ON HIS ROUTE." Nevertheless, loyal Whigs continued to deny that General Scott was "on the stump."[44] Whigs and Democrats agreed that the tour's legitimacy hinged on its spontaneity and its nonpolitical nature.

Even without his blunders, Scott would have been caught in the thicket of contradictory attitudes toward oratory and democracy. American oratorical standards were shifting from a grand classical style too refined for democrats to a "middling" style too vulgar for republicans. Still, oratory remained the prized currency of American politics. Speakers like Daniel Webster enjoyed great fame; children memorized so many speeches that "American history began to seem a series of events connecting famous orations," historian Daniel Boorstin has noted. Scott's inanities on the stump devalued this oratorical tradition. He confined himself to war stories and empty tributes—gushing, for example, that Kentucky was "great in the growth of horses, great in the growth of cattle, and greater still in the growth of men and women." Avoiding the sectional imbroglio, he flattered both slaveholders and abolitionists. If

Scott were going to speak, shouldn't he address the issues? "He has not given utterance to a single political idea," critics complained.[45]

Yet Scott peddled such nonsense because he knew that nominees were not supposed to orate. Simply by speaking, Scott "level[ed] himself . . . to equality with demagogues," one Whig complained. The very popularity of oratory—its effectiveness and its function as entertainment—undermined its legitimacy in the eyes of contemporaries. Rhetoric was demagogic and thus unsuitable for men with Scott's reputation for "delicacy, refinement and martial honor."[46] Great stump speakers such as Webster became celebrities, not presidents. Oratory, like democracy itself, was both prized and feared.

Scott had been neither silent nor eloquent, failing to soothe concerns about either oratory or democracy. In going to the people he was too democratic; yet his appeals to them were antidemocratic and insulting. By avoiding the issues he encouraged *"man-worship* . . . that unmistakable relic of king-craft" anathema to a rational, issue-based democracy. But the very people who attacked Scott for assuming "[that] the people are stupid" and trying to sway emotions revealed their own lack of faith in the people's ability to withstand the demagogue's charms.[47]

Whatever its democratic merits, Scott's tour offered an unambiguous and unprecedented affront to republican government. "Here, for the first time in the history of our republic, is a presidential candidate, seen taking the stump," Whigs and Democrats fumed. The "wise and patriotic FATHERS" did not "beg . . . for votes." The *Nashville Union* viewed Scott's action as "one of the most dangerous crises of our institutions"; such unvirtuous behavior humiliated the candidate as well as the nation. Scott was prostituting himself for "base purposes of party," the *Daily Union* charged. Not only did he lack the decency to resign his commission when nominated, but he was exploiting his military position. A candidate who "forgets propriety so often," the *Daily Union* warned, would do the same as president.[48]

Even while bickering about the tour, however, Whigs and Democrats alike reflected common values. Both parties used images of fluctuation and of flight. Whigs rejoiced that the "lofty" Scott uplifted them and the nation; Democrats feared decline, saying that Scott stooped to the level of the masses, degraded the electoral process, and demeaned the presidency and the army.[49] These opposing images revealed a common insecurity about the republic, a worry about the legitimacy of the electoral enterprise, and a desire for the candidate to help Americans transcend the political realities of partisanship and demagoguery.

Hoping the results would reinforce the proprieties, Democrats dutifully labeled the trip a disaster. Scott's defeat during the October elections in Pennsylvania, Indiana, and Ohio thus "vindicated the intelligence of the people." The *Nashville Union* offered an epitaph for *all* stumping efforts: "May every innovation upon the received usages of our fathers, in so important a matter as the Presidential election, be equally signally rebuked!"[50]

Predictably, most Whigs defended "General Scott's tour of duty" as successful and as the people's "heartfelt demonstrations" to a hero. "[Scott] seems to have awakened zeal in Ohio," Thurlow Weed told Seward. Whig newspapers stressed the "intense" excitement of each welcome. These accounts, emphasizing the greetings' spontaneity, enthusiasm, and nonpartisan nature, as well as the candidate's surprise, popularity, humility, and greatness, became formulaic.[51] First used to describe Harrison's jaunts in 1840, the formula was perfected in 1852 and used for the next half-century.

––––––––

After the election, most politicians adopted the Democrats' position: Scott's tour was a disaster. During the campaign, the Whig diarist George Templeton Strong observed that "Scott's stumping tour may have done good among the masses, but I'm sure it has lost him respect with sensible people everywhere."[52] After the campaign, the "sensible" people and the party regulars discounted the gains from the tour. Unfairly, they blamed Scott for the Whig debacle. Divided and disintegrating, the Whigs were probably doomed from the start anyway. This repudiation of the tour, accompanied as it was with forebodings of apocalypse and the breaking of party discipline, reflected the potency of the republican taboo. It also illustrated that history is written not only by the winners, but by the "sensible" people.

This near-universal condemnation of Scott's stumping in 1852 forces a reconsideration of William Henry Harrison's efforts in 1840. Why was one generally condemned and the other generally ignored? The answer reveals both some of the peculiarities of Scott's situation and some of the changes in American society and politics in the dozen intervening years. Harrison's nomination avoided major divisions among the Whigs; Scott's did not. Harrison's justification for stumping—a defense against slander—was more plausible and poignant than Scott's ruse. Finally, Harrison's tour played to his strengths, while Scott's underlined an already existing vulnerability: his vanity and clumsiness. On the stump, statements that might have been excused in others damaged Scott.

The extraordinary developments in transportation and communication between 1840 and 1852 also colored Scott's tour. Whereas Harrison had traveled throughout Indiana and Ohio on an improvised series of carts, wagons, and ferries, Scott used the railroad.[53] Traveling in greater comfort to larger towns, the up-to-date general let the railroad map dictate his itinerary.

This high-speed tour received more attention than Harrison's simpler efforts—to Scott's delight *and* frustration. In the interim the number of newspapers had increased, circulation had soared, the time lag in reporting events had declined, and journalistic methods had improved. Now editors could not overlook an assault on the republican taboo. Scott's every action was reported; his remarks were transcribed. The telegraph, which heralded Scott's arrival in each town, also circulated accounts of his speeches throughout the United States.

The reproduction of these talks hurt the General: Stump speeches were meant to be heard, not read. Pleasantries that sounded good at a railroad station looked foolish in the morning paper, especially when repeated from place to place. Back in 1840, stumpers could afford to repeat themselves; speeches were ignored, or doctored before publication. The swift transformation of public utterances into campaign documents caught Scott by surprise—and made him appear shallow and tiresome. Eventually, politicians would learn to keep one eye on the listening local audience and the other on the reading national newspaper audience.

Scott enjoyed less ideological latitude than had Harrison. Electoral practices were uniquely fluid in 1840. Harrison might have been able to destroy the republican code; Scott could not. By 1852 the republican taboo had solidified: Scott's failure marked the taboo's success.

The Democrats contrasted Scott with their model of republican modesty, Franklin Pierce. Of good patriotic stock, a Mexican War volunteer who had served under Scott, Pierce had been both a Congressman and a Senator. Twice in his career he had resigned from high office, each time opting for the simple life of a New Hampshire farmer.[54] Democrats hoped that this unexpected compromise candidate would help unite their party and the Union. The virus of sectionalism had infected the Democrats' Baltimore convention. Cass, Stephen A. Douglas, and James Buchanan led the balloting at various points, but none could get a majority, let alone the required two-thirds. On the forty-ninth ballot, Southern Democrats pleased by Pierce's attacks on abolitionists joined with his New Hampshire cronies and engineered the nomination.

Pierce was the ideal party candidate, an obliging party tool. Keeping to a proper course, he further linked party regularity and the republican taboo. For the first time, the notification committee visited a candidate to offer the nomination officially in person. Subsequent candidates would make a short acceptance speech at this notification ceremony, but Pierce kept quiet.

Party professionals begged Pierce not to write letters, pointing to precedent and warning that, as his friend Gideon Welles said, letters alienate ten to the one they attract. When asked his opinion, Pierce said he stood on the platform without presuming "to enlarge or narrow it." Interested in avoiding the embrace of controversial leaders, Pierce limited his travels. "Be the candidate of all," Welles had urged. The handsome, innocuous, compromise candidate did just that, championing the nation's Compromise measures. He was "our modern Cincinnatus," the *Mirror* observed, "waiting the will of the nation."[55]

Despite the consensus of the professionals, the party rank and file wanted to hear the candidate. "Recognizing the right of all constituencies to know the views and sentiments of their candidates, I hope you will not think it presumption in me, if I ask you a few plain questions," a typical letter from a Georgia Democrat began.[56] But Pierce shrugged off this democratic dilemma. He did not yield.

"Pierce has a talent for silence that will serve far better than his antagonist's electioneering," George Templeton Strong sighed. The Whig diarist was right. Pierce sent out surrogates to make speeches. He worked quietly with an old Bowdoin College classmate, Nathaniel Hawthorne, on a campaign biography. The demure Democrat greeted visitors warmly, wrote private letters to supporters, and spoke at some local functions. Willing to clarify "history," he even defended his conduct during the Mexican War in a few strong public letters. Still, overall he maintained a dignified contrast with the voluble Scott. The strategy worked: In November, Pierce triumphed, further vindicating the republican taboo.[57]

Pierce's silent and passive course unified the party. Antagonistic personal and sectional forces had made whatever peace they could in nominating him; any more statements would threaten that harmony. Also, in such a divided party, the leaders of different factions vied for the candidate's ear. Any visit, anywhere, would favor one leader at another's expense. With Pierce keeping a low profile, the Democratic politicians he had defeated for the nomination could lick their wounds. Scott's strutting across America did not salve any bruised egos; Pierce's silence did. Democrats united behind the party and its muted figurehead.

The 1852 campaign was particularly nasty. Such Whig papers as the *Detroit Advertiser* called Pierce "[a] dwarfish abortion of a statesman," while Democrats portrayed Scott, one Whig complained, as "one of the most dishonest men in the world." But, even while slinging mud, most editors agreed that such vituperation disgraced America. Some editors repudiated *all* slanders: Parties consist of so many "capable, honest, deserving patriots" unlikely to be fooled by a corrupt nominee, Horace Greeley reasoned in the *Tribune*, that, unless incontrovertible, libels should be ignored.[58] While Greeley seemed about to replace the outmoded right of kings with the divine insight of parties, most editors agreed that the party was more important than the man.

The 1852 campaign, then, further allied the republican inhibition with the party ideal. Both Whigs and Democrats wanted a passive and silent candidate because it was proper, it was safe, and it was best for the party. In Cass and Pierce, Democrats had two candidates who deferred to party; in 1848 and 1852 the Whigs lacked that luxury. Policy disagreements festered and other factors swayed elections, but the party consensus on candidate proprieties solidified.

V

By 1856, both major candidates deferred to the party; the Whig party, however, had died of sectionalism and nativism. The Whig bequest to the new Republican party included antislavery Northerners and the demand for passivity. At its first presidential convention the two-year-old party nominated the dashing John C. Frémont, a forty-three-year-old explorer. "That must be a very dark and squat log cabin into which the fame of Colonel Frémont has not penetrated ere this," Greeley observed, stressing Frémont's availability.[59]

"It is difficult to sit still with such excitement in the air," wrote Henry Wadsworth Longfellow about the first Republican campaign in 1856. Repelled by slavery, and trying to compensate for their rudimentary organization, Republicans crusaded. "It was a struggle between two civilizations," abolitionist George W. Julian recalled. Paramilitary "Wide-Awake" companies drilled in the streets. People serenaded the popular "Pathfinder" and his equally popular wife, Jesse Benton Frémont. A newcomer to the United States, E. L. Godkin, was appalled by the "little arts" used to woo the "uneducated," yet impressed by the serious "themes . . . under popular discussion." Thousands of campaign documents clogged the mails. Circulation of crucial journals like Greeley's *Tribune* soared.[60]

Colonel Frémont watched the frenzied campaign from the relative quiet of his Manhattan brownstone. As befitted the leader of what he called "a great movement of the people," Frémont's acceptance letter was the longest and most substantive to date. He gave the Republican platform a bear hug. He condemned the extension of slavery and called for the admission of Kansas as a free state. After the acceptance, Frémont greeted delegations, huddled with advisers, and kept up his correspondence. He attended a New York City rally just before the election, but did not speak: "My nerves seem to preserve their usual tranquility," the candidate reported.[61]

To the South the pace was more frenetic at Wheatland, James Buchanan's Pennsylvania estate. But the Democratic nominee also shunned the public. The sixty-five-year-old Buchanan was weary, and wary of assuming the presidential "crown of thorns." Born in 1791, first elected to Congress in 1820, Buchanan had served as Minister to Russia and Secretary of State. In 1852 he had wanted the presidency, and expected the nomination, but was thwarted. Thereafter, he had sailed off to England as Minister to Great Britain, drowning his presidential aspirations.[62] Four years later, the Louisiana political operator John Slidell secured the nomination for "Old Buck," who now found himself in the middle of the sectional brawl.

Throughout his career Buchanan had wooed the South; even though Southern extremists were disgruntled, his nomination indicated a Democratic tilt toward their section. The mounting violence—exemplified by the outbreak of guerilla warfare in "bleeding Kansas" and the caning of Senator Charles Sumner in the Capitol itself—made bisectional appeals useless. The Democrats decided that Congress should not interfere with slavery in the territories.

Buchanan dutifully filled his role as chief cog in the Democratic machine. Except for a brief trip within Pennsylvania he stayed home, greeting callers and sending out advice. He refused to deviate "one jot or tittle" from the convention's compromise platform. "I have no right, as the candidate of the Democratic party, by answering interrogatories, to present new and different issues before the people," he said in his acceptance letter. "If I begin now to explain, there would be no end to explanations," Buchanan added privately. Ignoring pleas to travel and clarify the issues, Buchanan supervised efforts in Pennsylvania and conciliated Democrats, from national leaders to town officials. The powerful Mississippi Democrat Robert J. Walker is "very sore," John Slidell told Buchanan. "Do not fail to write immediately." And Buchanan dutifully wrote.[63]

Although Buchanan and Frémont followed parallel courses, hewing to party wishes, partisan invective reminded everyone that candidates could be damned, regardless of their actions. "There is no such person running as James Buchanan," Pennsylvania Republican Thaddeus Stevens thundered; "*He is dead of lockjaw.* Nothing remains but a platform and a bloated mass of political putridity." The *National Era* and other Republican newspapers attacked Buchanan's devotion to the Democratic platform, calling it "meek and submissive demagoguism."[64]

The election became a question of "*party* strength," as Illinois Republican Lyman Trumbull noted. The Democratic organization raised twice as much money as the Republicans, blanketed the country with documents, and organized each precinct. In November, Buchanan's victory was a Democratic victory—and a sectional one.[65] The Republicans still had much to learn; the Democratic machinery still worked.

America in the 1850s needed a strong leader. "The experience of the last fifteen or twenty years," E. L. Godkin said in 1859, "has convinced everybody that the man is of far greater importance than his creed." But party prerogatives and the republican taboo insulated candidates from political strife and, in 1856, produced a pensioner and an explorer. "A candidate must have a slim record in these times," Horace Greeley admitted.[66]

As sectionalism intensified, compromise became difficult, and national coalitions dissolved. The nominees could not unite disparate factions because there were no acceptable compromises. Candidates, then, could only unite through indirection or insignificance. They could be Northern men with Southern principles like Cass, or Southern men with Northern principles like Taylor, forcing people into trusting either the beliefs or the background but not both. They could be soldiers who transcended politics, nobodies whose records eluded detection, or tired politicians like Buchanan who soothed passions. They had to preserve whatever balance the party struck. Maintaining this balance required silence. Candidates, then, hid behind the platforms. An American tradition of leadership that celebrated obfuscation flourished. A Webster or a Seward could be bold, but he could not be president.

Opponents' attacks, as well as his own party's agenda, subdued the nominee. A candidate knew that no matter what he did, partisan newspapers would howl. Although most attacks would be dismissed as partisan smears, a nominee had to avoid attacks that might sway his own supporters. The Taylor and Scott experiences proved that inaction was expected, action was dangerous.

Candidates, then, became figureheads, icons drained of reality and relevance. Any action they took was condemned by a worried adviser, an offended party faction, or a sanctimonious opposition. Checked internally and externally, the browbeaten candidates retreated into silence.

————

For all their differences, Whigs and Democrats agreed about the role of the nominee. It seemed that party needs, republican sensibilities, and political caution resolved the debate about candidate proprieties. Voters were to consider the platform, but not the personality, the principles, not the man. The democratic and republican dilemmas were solved by making the parties democratic and the candidates republican. The parties embodied democracy, making popular appeals, mobilizing the masses, addressing the issues. Candidates, on the other hand, maintained the traditional republican silence. Ironically, the party autocrats and operators, such as Weed, Greeley, and Seward, heralded the new democratic era, while the people's only national representatives, the nominees, heeded the ancient republican tenets.

This party primacy checked the growing tendencies toward stumping. The 1848 campaign marked the party triumphant. The 1852 campaign showed the republican taboo at its peak. And 1856 illustrated the continuing demand for innocuous candidates. But as the sectional conflict escalated, the institutional crisis deepened, parties dissolved, and the nation lurched toward civil war, the republican taboo—along with so many other American traditions—would be challenged.

FOUR

Passive Winners
and Active Losers

I am no speaker and I don't want to be beaten.
—*President Ulysses S. Grant, 1872*

THE slavery debate raged for over twenty years, shattering one national institution after another. In the 1840s, the General Convention of the Methodist Church divided, unable to accommodate proslavery and abolitionist sentiments under one steeple. The Baptist Missionary groups soon followed. In the 1850s, when the Supreme Court tried to settle the question, the outcry was so great that fears of another Dred Scott debacle paralyzed many future Justices well into the twentieth century. Even the paradigmatic vehicles of American accommodation, the political parties, choked on this issue: Sectionalism helped strangle the Whig party after the 1852 election, and the Democrats finally succumbed in April 1860 when convention delegates in Charleston, South Carolina, failed to agree on a nominee.

Amid impending apocalypse, as four candidates vied for the presidency in 1860, the republican taboo persevered, bolstered by party demands and cautionary tales about Clay's letters and Scott's travels. "The candidates who are most cautious of committing themselves to any course of policy, save themselves . . . a great deal of trouble. . . . The people have nominated you without any pledges or engagements on your part, and they want you to do nothing but allow yourself to be elected," a wise editor told one nominee. "Make no speeches, write no letters as a candidate, enter into no pledges, make no promises." Abra-

61

ham Lincoln welcomed William Cullen Bryant's insight: "I appreciate the danger against which you would guard me," he replied.[1]

Yet Americans *solicited* speeches, letters, pledges, and promises from their candidates. One Philadelphian informed Lincoln that he had become "public property," and "I do not feel as though I were committing a breach of etiquette by addressing you." "I am a voter and I want to know exactly every inch of ground you stand upon," a Mississippian wrote. "If you suit me I'll go for you. If not away with you!"[2]

As it turned out, every candidate from 1860 through 1876 would have to balance the cautious demands of tradition against the democratic demands of the people. Each nominee began his campaign expecting to maintain a traditional silence. But for many, the popular pressure and the national and party crises would undermine their plans. The weaker candidates found it hardest to resist the growing demands for active campaigns. In the world's greatest democracy, would only losers take to the stump?

I

The four candidates in 1860 began their unusual campaign routinely—with vows of silence. The nominee of the fledging Republican party, one-time Whig congressman Abraham Lincoln, followed Bryant's advice. The Constitutional Union candidate, the long-time Whig Senator John Bell, endorsed his party's desire to stand on no platform but "the Constitution, the Union, and the Laws." The Southern Democrats' candidate, Vice President John C. Breckinridge, swore that he had "written to nobody . . . intrigued with nobody; . . . promised nobody." And the regular Democratic candidate, Senator Stephen A. Douglas, said that if the people did not know his opinions, it was too late "to explain them now." By far the most famous of the candidates, the squat Illinoisan had long crusaded for compromise. For the first time in his life, the voluble Senator said, he expected "to look on and see a fight without taking a hand in it."[3]

Many voters, however, ignored these vows. Some demanded to see the candidate as a simple matter of democratic rights. Most stressed the tactical gains to be made. And some insisted that the impending civil war required unprecedented efforts. With the party weakened and the need for a strong president apparent, how could candidates remain passive?

A new generation had arisen in America that knew not the Framers' republicanism. Most voters in 1860 had been born between 1810 and 1839. "The genius of the United States is . . . in the common people," Walt Whitman, born in 1819, chanted. From the 1830s through the 1860s, as this new generation matured, America witnessed a flowering of liberal democracy. Educational institutions—common schools, public libraries, newspapers, voluntary associations, lyceum bureaus, universities—proliferated. Literacy rates and circulation of reading material soared. Property barriers to suffrage crumbled, allowing millions of adult white men to vote as mass political parties flourished. In the established Eastern cities egalitarianism undermined deference, while out West pioneers mastered self-sufficiency and self-government. Intellectuals embraced individualism and self-reliance.[4] Simultaneously, industrialization and a sustained economic boom further boosted the autonomy and confidence of the common man. Curmudgeons grumbled about the common man's inability to govern, and the decline of American civilization, but they were increasingly ignored. "In a system like ours, where almost every man has a vote and votes as he chooses, public opinion is really the government," the editor and lecturer George W. Curtis declared in 1862.[5]

The presidency was popularized as well. "The President is up there in the White House for you. . . . It is not you who are here for him," Walt Whitman wrote. The public now demanded *active* nominees. The "people [want to] see you face to face and hear your views," a Georgian told Stephen Douglas. A nominee came from the people, belonged to the people, and should go out among the people to get elected. The president no longer *virtually* represented the nation; now he was *literally* a representative, elected directly and accountable to the voters.[6]

Some simply wanted to honor their candidate. Many in 1860 wished, in particular, to see Senator Douglas, their hero. "Your . . . manly and straightforward patriotism, make[s] us so desirous of shaking you by the hand," some Massachusetts Democrats wrote. Although the tradition of hailing the conquering hero reached back to at least ancient times, Americans were particularly susceptible to the magic of a celebrity's presence. Ritualized greetings for prominent men evolved in American towns, featuring torchlight processions, serenades, and a brief acknowledgment by the honoree. These ceremonies affirmed the power of the people while celebrating the American faith that a new generation of heroes could arise to succeed the Founding Fathers, the last of whom had died relatively recently. With the growth of the railroad and the rise of stumping on local levels, Americans wanted to hail their presidential nominees as well.[7]

Party activists had less sentimental motives. North and South, they assured Douglas that his presence would "very materially change . . . things" in their state. Douglas did not even have to campaign. Simply visiting would provide a "pretext" for a "great state meeting." News of a "friendly call" would spread, and the magic of his presence, *if* he "did not say one word, would tend more to overcome prejudice . . . than your friends could do during the campaign," one Ohioan slyly suggested.[8]

If simply appearing would be helpful, the correspondents believed, actually speaking was a godsend. At minimum, Douglas could then "correct" the many "misrepresentations" circulating. But he could accomplish much more. The people were lazy but educable. "I have never known the people in a better frame of mind to hear & be convinced," Alabama editor John J. Seibels wrote.[9] The emerging liberal-democratic ethos had gained ground: It had checked traditional concerns with demagoguery and given the nominee an educational function. Democratic leaders now were *obliged* to address the issues.

Douglas's visit was as important to the leaders as to the masses; his arrival puffed up the local Democrats. He could charm leaders and editors, inspire workers and speakers. He could raise money or, failing that, compensate for the "cash deficit" with his "electric presence."[10]

These entreaties to visit were routine by now. They had often been advanced in previous contests and often been ignored. But the crisis of 1860 was singular. Douglas believed that only his party could "save the country from Abolitionism and Disunion."[11] Yet the Democrats themselves were split. Twice, Southerners had stormed out of party conventions—first at Charleston in April, then at Baltimore in June. Eventually, these seceders nominated their own candidate, John C. Breckinridge.

After his own nomination, Douglas had promised to avoid political discussion, trusting the people to "take the matter into their own hands." He arranged to spend the summer in Newport, Rhode Island. But he could not stand still. Anxious about the country's future, frustrated by his party's failure, and certain of his own forensic skills, Douglas decided to stump—surreptitiously. So it was that in mid-July he left New York City, ostensibly to see his mother in upstate New York, attend his brother-in-law's graduation from Harvard, and visit his father's grave in Vermont.[12]

To Douglas's "surprise," wherever he went crowds greeted him and demanded a speech. For nearly a month he traversed New England, protesting too much his surprise and then "lapsing" into supposedly nonpartisan speeches—often for over an hour. And the more he stumped, the more invitations he received. In fact, "As you have been in all the other New England states," a Maine Democrat explained, "our people would feel hurt if you did not come."[13] After resting in Newport, Douglas did visit Maine. Then he went down to the border states, to settle the estate of his first wife's late mother in North Carolina. Douglas's "lapses" became more frequent, more thorough, and more partisan, with the seceding Southern Democrats his favorite target. His campaign was becoming a crusade for the Union.

Unfortunately for Douglas, his "crusade" was also becoming a laughingstock. By September, Douglas had yet to visit his mother. His opponents circulated an "ADVERTISEMENT FOR A LOST BOY," wandering in the Northeast, with a penchant for clambakes: "Talks a great deal and very loud—always about himself. Has an idea that he is a candidate for the Presidency."[14]

More seriously, opponents indicted Douglas on the usual charges of breaching republican etiquette. Douglas, the *Charleston Courier* sneered, "has not even the common honesty . . . to admit that he is on an electioneering tour for the presidency!" And inevitably, on July 24, 1860, the Republican *Illinois State Journal* branded Douglas's tactic unprecedented: "This is the first time in history . . . that any candidate for that exalted position has ventured to electioneer for it. It has heretofore been regarded as an office no man should seek by direct means, let alone by partisan stump speeches." The *Journal* hoped that "Mr. Douglas . . . [would] be the last as he is the first."[15]

Responding to the critics, Douglas did not stop stumping; he stopped pretending. He finally found his now-famous mother on September 15. He then headed home to Illinois. His speeches became bolder, more eloquent, more acute. They were longer, less frivolous, and lacked the posturing of his summer speeches. Douglas was now trying to save the Union "by burying Northern Abolitionism and Southern Disunionism in a common grave."[16]

Douglas avoided personalities, refused to temporize, and addressed the issues, thereby advancing a series of liberal-democratic proprieties. Dismissing the warnings about making speeches "off-hand to fifty thousand people at a time," Douglas cried: "What a pity it would be if a man, by the honest expression of an honest sentiment, should lose anybody's vote." He said he did not want a "padlock" on his lips: He would answer all questions boldly. He would make the same statements North and South.[17]

The cross-country tour took its toll—on Republicans and on Douglas himself. The "Little Giant" spoke tirelessly to "acres of people" at rallies and at railroad stations. Lincoln's campaign manager, David Davis, considered his rival's rallies "much larger than I liked to see," but he also distinguished between a "high pitch of excitement" and victory at the polls. Davis noticed that Douglas looked "worn and very much dissipated." Rumors of heavy drinking abounded.[18]

In October the Republicans swept the bellwether state elections in Pennsylvania, Ohio, and Indiana. Douglas's slim chance had vanished. "Mr. Lincoln is the next President," he said. "We must try to save the Union. I will go South."[19]

Douglas's Southern swing was noble, but futile. Wherever he went he drew large crowds, but much hostility. While he was boarding a boat in Montgomery a dock collapsed, toppling Douglas and his wife—a fitting metaphor for the collapse of Douglas's candidacy, and his beloved Union. On Election Day, after visiting twenty-three states in three-and-a-half months, Douglas won only twelve electoral votes. The entire experience proved enervating: Within a year the forty-eight-year-old candidate was dead.

With Douglas's stumping tour, presidential campaigning had crossed a divide. Democracy's growth and the party crisis had propelled an ambitious nominee onto the stump. The republican taboo had been weakened—although rumors of its death would be greatly exaggerated for the next thirty years. After 1860, *all* candidates considered stumping. Nominees were now "public property" with an important educational role. Douglas had offered a powerful model of what would become more familiar: a leader of a democracy talking to the people.

———

"There is a modest mansion in . . . Springfield," orator Isaac Hazelhurst declared. "Its occupant . . . is surrounded now with the simple comforts of domestic life." Celebrating this indifference to a "post of honor too high to be sought," Hazelhurst cried: "What a beautiful illustration is thus presented of the working of our free institutions . . . making virtue and wisdom the only qualification for government."[20]

Abraham Lincoln's silence was motivated less by virtue than by hard-nosed political wisdom. Months before his nomination he had devised his strategy of passivity and party regularity, a pragmatic approach he would follow throughout his presidency. As a relatively obscure politician pursuing first the Republican nomination, and then election, he determined to "give no offense to others, leav[ing] them in a mood to come to us if they shall be compelled to give up their first love." He made his acceptance letter "sufficiently brief to do no harm." Lincoln asked one question of each contemplated move: "Will it help or hurt?" As a result, he limited his correspondence and his public appearances.[21]

Lincoln's caution was not novel; his brazenness about it was. Traditional protestations of innocence seemed less necessary in a culture increasingly priding itself on its ambitiousness and its practicality. As Lincoln passed the campaign in dignified silence, opponents assailed his "abject cowardice" and his contempt for the people and democracy. Occasionally, Lincoln contemplated responding or even stumping, but his aides dissuaded him. Little wonder that early in the campaign, according to his friend William H. Herndon, Lincoln was "bored—bored badly."[22]

Lincoln's slim victory seemed to vindicate his strategy; the taboo endured. Winning less than 40 percent of the popular vote suggested that *any* statement could have backfired. Yet two important shifts had occurred. First, Lincoln's brazen refusal to stump weakened the ideological foundations of the inhibition. "Propriety" in campaigning was now less a question of taste than of tactics.[23] Second, Douglas's bold crusade placed the people's liberal-democratic demands to see their candidate on a par with the republican concerns about campaign virtue. Whether active candidates would make campaigns more serious or more frivolous remained to be seen. And just what campaigning—by nominees or their surrogates—accomplished remained unclear.

II

The abbreviated 1864 campaign was "altogether exceptional," according to the diplomat and author Charles Francis Adams, Jr. In a nation convulsed by civil war, parties sought to universalize their appeals. The Republican party convened in a "National Union" Convention, renominating President Lincoln and giving him a Southern Democratic slaveholder, Andrew Johnson, as a running mate. The Democratic party waited until September before nominating General George B. McClellan to run with the antiwar "Copperhead" George Pendleton.[24] Yet, for all the campaign's peculiarities, the candidates themselves played familiar roles.

In his brief campaign, McClellan discovered the challenges vexing a nominee in mid–nineteenth-century America. He first had to clarify his relation to the party and its platform. The Democrats' rancorous convention in Chicago called for an immediate end to the fighting before restoring the Union through negotiations. Many of the "War Democrats" opposed this "Peace Plank" and urged McClellan to repudiate the platform. Echoing Zachary Taylor's 1848 struggle with the Whigs, former Brigadier General Isaac J. Wistar argued that McClellan had not sought the nomination and was not "bound" by the platform. McClellan was "the candidate of the people, against the politicians" and should follow his own "convictions."[25] This republican idea, applied to a more democratic era, strengthened the candidate at the party's expense. While Taylor could ignore the issues, more or less, McClellan had to address them. In becoming the parties' primary salesmen, candidates began to study the pitch more carefully. No longer merely standing on the party platform, candidates like McClellan began adapting it to their own dimensions.

After a suspenseful week-and-a-half, McClellan released his acceptance letter. "The Union is the one condition of peace," he declared, reversing the Chicago convention's priorities. Pendleton and other Copperheads were furious. The vice-presidential nominee refused to appear with his running mate throughout the campaign. The New York *Daily News* called for a new convention, "either to remodel the platform to suit the nominee, or nominate a candidate to suit the platform."[26] McClellan had chosen candidate autonomy over party loyalty, but many leading "Peace Democrats" stood by their principles and repudiated the man.

McClellan's assertion of independence stemmed partly from conviction, partly from calculation. He needed "disaffected Republicans." Also, after being serenaded for months, McClellan believed his appeal transcended mere partisanship. He forgot the expert warnings not to overestimate "the net value of popular applause."[27] Popularity, he would soon learn, did not guarantee election.

McClellan also learned that while the people and local leaders clamored for the nominees, the national leaders often ignored them. Democratic editor Manton Marble drew up an elaborate campaign plan in October, mentioning McClellan only once in passing. Still, Marble encouraged McClellan to write personal, nonpolitical letters to his former military comrades. Also, prominent Democrats consulted with McClellan in his New Jersey home. And when McClellan visited New York, he was serenaded. Some of the more activist Democrats urged a stumping tour, arguing that this "momentous campaign" invalidated the "cultivated proprieties heretofore justly accorded to Democratic Candidates."[28] But McClellan had grasped the central lesson. Except for a short trip to Pennsylvania, he accepted the candidate's silent destiny.

President Lincoln also accepted the candidate's lot, publicly. He had, he said, neither the time nor the inclination to campaign—although he took frequent readings of the political barometer. Lincoln's strategy was summarized in the aphorism he bequeathed to American politics: "Don't swap horses while crossing the stream." But as he struck the pose of statesmanlike disinterest, he worked behind the scenes. "The President is too busy looking after the election to think of anything else," Secretary of the Treasury William Pitt Fessenden grumbled.[29]

Lincoln's campaign, however, ultimately relied on neither party nor personality, but the battlefield. "I am a beaten man," Lincoln said, "unless we can have some great victory." On September 1, General William T. Sherman conquered Atlanta. Bullets swayed the ballots in this election.[30] McClellan captured only twenty-one electoral votes. Lincoln's victory, then, raised a new question: Did campaigning matter?

III

To the 1868 Republican nominee, Ulysses S. Grant, campaigning did not seem to matter much at all. The slovenly clerk turned Civil War hero simply would not court the public. The Union's great martyr, Abraham Lincoln, had been dead since 1865. The new President, Andrew Johnson, was despised from North to South. Grant's unrivaled popularity qualified him for the presidency—both in his mind and in the minds of others. Both parties, therefore, tried to draft him even though, as one Republican Senator admitted, "We do not exactly know where he stands."[31]

Grant accepted the nomination as a "duty," but rather than hitting the campaign trail he went on vacation. His passivity stemmed from neither the traditional republican sensibilities nor Lincoln's brazen pragmatism. Uninterested in politics, Grant wanted the electoral victory as proof of the people's affection. When notified of the nomination, he said "Gentlemen, being entirely unaccustomed to public speaking, and without the desire to cultivate the power, it is impossible for me to find appropriate language to thank you." After writing a brief acceptance letter, he went off to the Rocky Mountains. Along the way, a witness reported, Grant was "as dumb as a mute" and "had to be told to take off his hat" when the people hailed him.[32]

Grant then retired to his farm in Galena, Illinois, to avoid the people and the politicians alike. Although still the Army's Commanding General, he relaxed, presuming that "Military affairs get on as well with-

out me, as they would with me in Washington." Yet he did take time
to teach his aide Adam Badeau his theory on correspondence: "If you
do not answer, the letter will answer itself." Frustrated Republicans anxious to communicate paid Badeau to relay information between Galena
and party headquarters. "A person would not know there was a canvass
going on if it were not for the accounts we read in the papers," the
serene General observed. His "summer vacation" was "very pleasant."[33]

Initially, the Democratic nominee Horatio Seymour mirrored Grant's
mixture of disinterest and passivity—although in reality Seymour was
not quite that lazy. A stirring orator whose lengthy sideburns framed
his bald dome and bulging eyes, Seymour did not want to run. Once
nominated, he said he could no longer take "an active part" in the
campaign.[34] Seymour's candidacy was riddled with problems. The Democratic party was in shambles. It was bankrupt. Both Seymour and his
running mate, Frank Blair, were ideal targets for the Republicans, who
relished waving the "Bloody Shirt" of civil war. As the wartime governor of New York, Seymour both had opposed Lincoln and was tainted
by the 1863 New York City draft riots. And although Frank Blair had
been a Union General, he had called for the "overthrow of reconstruction." An observer sighed that "one party had nominated a Rebel and
the other a man without brains."[35] After losing the October elections in
Ohio, Indiana, and Pennsylvania, Democrats *begged* Seymour to stump.

The taboo "has no foundation in reason," the *New York World* said,
and "ought not to weigh a feather" in this hour of need. The Democrats
lacked money, manpower, organization, and newspapers. Should Seymour, their one asset, "the most powerful and impressive speaker in the
United States," be silenced? And had not Stephen Douglas established
a precedent? Journalist William Cassidy noted that "In England, all the
ministers & half the higher clergy are on the stump. Napoleon is on the
stump & King Wilhelm of Prussia. Even the Pope lets fly on 'allocation'
every now & then." If autocrats could do it, democrats should, too.
"When you cannot trust your cause or your candidate," Cassidy explained, "a policy of reserve is commendable; but we need discussion."[36]

Seymour caved in to this "universal sentiment" among his friends.
He claimed he was campaigning as a good democrat should, but he
seemed haunted by his republican ancestors. Again and again he embraced liberal democracy while acknowledging the traditional proprieties. "I go to speak to this people," he said, "not because I wish to do so,
but because you have called upon me to go into this contest along side
of you." Acknowledging the traditional concerns with oratory, Seymour

called for "calm, fair, dispassionate, and patriotic" talk, not demagoguery. Although clearly worried about offending sensibilities, he did not see how a candidate could remain passive in a participatory democracy: "It is said that I am an interested man, and so I am, and so is every man who pays taxes and helps to support this Government," he declared in Erie, Pennsylvania. "How would it be if none of those who had an interest in this contest were to take part in it?"[37]

Seymour's whirlwind two-week tour bolstered his cause. From his home in Western New York, Seymour crossed Pennsylvania, Ohio, Indiana, and Illinois. Democratic newspapers, predictably, reported renewed zeal and wholesale conversions. President Andrew Johnson, despite his own failure on the stump in the 1866 elections, approved of a tour.[14] "The present position of public affairs . . . demands it," he wrote. "The mass of the people should be aroused."[38]

Of course, traditionalists warned that Seymour "[would] lose both respect and voters by his presence on the stump." The pro-Republican *Cincinnati Gazette* objected to this "most strange . . . departure from former precedents." But to the Republican charge that "Grant takes his cigar—Seymour takes the stump," Democrats responded: "Seymour for President—No Dummy for Us."[39]

This partisan squabble about tactics bespoke a more fundamental conflict. Contrasting conceptions of the presidency clashed in 1868. Each candidate's tactics reflected his vision of the presidency and his perspective on the institutional brawl that Reconstruction provoked. Unhappy with President Andrew Johnson's moderate plan for reconstructing the South, Radicals in Congress attacked the presidency. They dictated terms to the South and limited the President's appointive and military powers. They assailed him for trying to rouse the people with his electioneering "swing around the circle" during the 1866 congressional election. Finally, they impeached him in March 1868. Grant would defer to this Radical Congress; Seymour would not.

Grant's passivity as a candidate signaled his beliefs in a limited presidency. His letter of acceptance echoed General Harrison's republican views. Grant refused to "lay down a policy to be adhered to, right or wrong, through an administration of four years. New political issues, not foreseen, are constantly arising," he explained. As a "purely administrative officer," the president "should always be left free to execute the will of the people."[40] In essence, Grant was saying "Trust me—issues change; my character won't."

Grant and his party envisioned a caretaker president, deferential to the people and the Congress, who responded rather than initiated, who enforced laws rather than made them. Under the American system the people ruled through their representatives in Congress. When Republicans dominated, the president should "execute Republican laws"; with a Democratic Congress, he should "[execute] Democratic policies with equal readiness"—the remoteness of the latter possibility emboldening Republicans to make this theoretical concession. The president should be "merely a good Executive, not a mighty champion of our favorite ideas," the *Tribune* insisted.[41] Oratorical skills for such a leader were not only unnecessary, but often dangerous—an invitation to demagoguery. Americans wanted noble actors, not smooth talkers. The presidency, then, was not the forum for popular leadership that Andrew Jackson had conceived and Andrew Johnson desired. Rather, it offered republican ballast in an ever-changing political system.

Democrats tried to defend the presidency against the Radical onslaught and against the threat of "such personified negations" as Grant. "The Presidency is no place for a man without ideas and destitute of a policy," the *World* cried. With his lengthy acceptance letter and his energetic stumping tour, Seymour personified this vision of an active president. While respecting the people's will, Democrats saw the need for a president to balance off the majority's "fitful impulses." In fact, the presidency anchored the American system, guarding the people's "deliberate settled will as expressed in the Constitution."[42] Ironically, the Radicals' vision of a republican presidency revealed more faith in the masses but stifled a dialogue between the American people and their president; the democratic model distrusted the people but encouraged the dialogue.

This scrimmage over the president's role reflected the postwar growth of nationalism and liberal democracy. The "General government" was now "the supreme and exclusive national government," and the state governments were "subordinate," not "coordinate," the thinker Orestes A. Brownson noted. Industrial and technological developments facilitated this centralization as homogeneous mass-produced products, growing national corporations, telegraph wires, and railroad tracks bonded the country.[43]

Despite fleeting congressional maneuvers to the contrary, these twin forces of nationalism and liberal democracy boosted the presidency. As always, when the national government's powers and purview grew, so did the president's. Increasingly, the people viewed the president as their champion. U. S. Grant won his battle against the activist presidency—twice.[44] But *this* war would eventually be lost.

IV

In 1872 President Grant would not switch campaign tactics, just as he hoped the nation would not swap presidential horses in midstream. After his renomination, Grant retired to Long Branch, New Jersey, for most of the campaign. In October, New York lawyer Edwards Pierrepont reported that the President was "just as easy as tho' he were driving horses on a smooth road with a good cigar in his mouth." This insouciance frustrated William E. Chandler, the Republican National Committee's industrious secretary, who saw "no reason why, if Grant can stay at Long Branch . . . I should not come to New Hampshire for a little rest." For months Chandler and others begged the President to "coddle" one politician, to "smooth . . . down" another. Grant "is a Soldier, and knows better how to deal with his enemies than his friends—I mean, of course, his political friends," the poet and Minister to Turkey George H. Boker sighed.[45]

Grant did make some efforts, however. He conferred with visitors at Long Branch. He redistributed some federal jobs in important states at Chandler's request. In the press, he occasionally jabbed his opponents. But he refused to stump. "It has been done, so far as I remember, by but two presidential candidates heretofore, and both of them were public speakers and both of them were beaten," Grant explained. "I am no speaker and I don't want to be beaten."[46]

Despite their superiority in manpower, money, and organization, Republicans worried about this presidential passivity because their party was divided. Many of the "best men," genteel political reformers, were disgusted with corrupt "Grantism," epitomized, they believed, by the President's forty-two relatives on government payrolls. A founder of the Republican party, George W. Julian, recalled: "I could not aid in the reelection of Grant without sinning against decency and my own self-respect." The reformers launched the Liberal Republican party in Cincinnati during May. Angling for popular support, the convention nominated Horace Greeley.[47]

Greeley was famous but controversial. In his long career he had embraced many ideas, had made many enemies. He opposed many of the reformers' proposals, including civil service reform and tariff reduction. And he was hostile to the Democrats, who held the key to victory. "Why, the honest, thinking mass of Democrats could no more vote [for Greeley] than a Jew be persuaded to eat pork!" the *New York World* sputtered.[48]

When the Democratic national convention nominated Greeley, the election became "a choice of two evils" for many, a Republican told William E. Chandler. "Has the country no choice for ruler," the *New York World* asked, "between a scheming, sordid despot and a good-natured, hare-brained dreamer?" But Greeley made peace with his foes. His campaign theme was "National Reunion"—which, loosely translated, meant "Anyone but Grant." Without satisfactory alternatives, many stood by their respective parties. Republican Henry Lee expressed his party loyalty crudely: "We shall 'return to our vomit' and not try the new purge." Many Republicans and Democrats were unhappy and would choose not to vote at all: The voter turnout of 71.3 percent was the lowest in the half-century from 1852 until 1904.[49]

Greeley was not quite comfortable in his new role. He tried to respect the proprieties, repairing to his farm in Chappaqua, New York, resigning from the *Tribune*, and refusing to solicit either interviews or support. Yet Greeley continued his "habit of 40 years standing" and answered every letter sent him. The *Chicago Tribune*'s editor, Horace White, begged him to stop, remembering that in 1844 Henry Clay "killed himself & almost broke Mr. Greeley's heart by writing one letter," about the annexation of Texas. Alfred Cowles, White's publisher, warned Greeley's successor at the *New York Tribune*, Whitelaw Reid, that if Greeley signed any more letters, "I will swing the *Chicago Tribune* around for Grant so fast it will make your head swim." Reid explained to Greeley and others that no one had written letters or made speeches while a candidate for the presidency "save to his own hurt." The danger of distortion was great.[50] Pragmatism eclipsed courtesy; Greeley was silenced.

In August, Greeley combined a vacation to his New Hampshire birthplace with a modest campaign swing through New England. Initially, the *New York Tribune* treated its founder's trip as entirely "private." When greeted, Greeley tried to be benign. A nominee "stands in a peculiar light," he explained, parroting Reid. "Whatever he says is liable to be misinterpreted." Also, the "people" should contemplate the issues "without regard to the aspirations or hopes of either of the candidates."[51]

While Greeley campaigned, Republicans drenched him in "a shower of mud," *The Nation* noted. Grant men pilloried Greeley's speeches, his disparate passions, and his trademark chin whiskers, white coat, and white hat. They laughed that Greeley the protectionist called for tariff reduction; Greeley the abolitionist supported the South; Greeley the Republican ran with Democrats. After the election, Greeley moaned that he had been "so bitterly assailed that I hardly know whether I was running for President or the penitentiary."[52]

Aroused, Greeley made his first partisan stump speech, in Portland on August 14. He acknowledged "the unwritten law of our country that a candidate for President may not make speeches." Yet, he insisted, "There is a truth to be uttered in behalf of those who have placed me before the American people." Greeley swore that he had made no deals, promised no offices, to win Southern and Democratic support. Having said that, he hoped to return to his farm and his dignified repose.[53]

But supporters, frustrated with Greeley's "silk glove treatment" of his opponents, lobbied for action. Just as Seymour's nomination neutralized the Democrats' leading orator in 1868, the leading editor, Greeley, was neutralized in 1872. Greeley should either return to the *Tribune* or take to the stump. "Things are proper now & this year that never were before," Democratic Congressman Michael Kerr argued.[54] Greeley loyalists who had first pressured the candidate not to write now pressured him to stump. Expediency eclipsed dignity. Letters were dignified but dangerous, for the written word was less flexible, more powerful. Stumping, on the other hand, was safer but undignified. The nominee's exciting presence compensated for his cautious and colorless words. Also, the complaints about correspondence came at the start of the campaign, when Greeley had something to lose; stumping was a desperate alternative when he had nothing left.

By agreeing to stump, Greeley conceded defeat: "If I thought I could be elected, I would never make this trip, but I want to leave a good record behind me," he confessed. On September 18 he began an exhausting swing through New Jersey, Pennsylvania, Ohio, and Indiana, never sleeping more than four hours at a time. Reports of the deterioration of his wife's health further depressed him. In Cincinnati he was forced to clarify his Pittsburgh remarks. At Louisville a brick just missed him; at Cleveland a rock shattered a nearby window. Often, when he thought he was alone, Greeley "would put his hands to his head and cry out: 'Oh!' as though suffering intense pain," the *New York Sun* reported after the campaign.[55]

Greeley addressed the issues while professing personal disinterest. Wherever he went, he preached "peace and reconciliation." "We have no purposes that we wish to conceal," he said, jabbing Grant discreetly; "We have no principles . . . that we don't desire the people to know." He appealed for votes boldly, but indirectly. "I know your generous hearts are with me," he said. "I believe your votes will testify that your hearts are sound and true."[56]

Many Liberals like Henry Watterson, the editor of the *Louisville Courier-Journal*, were pleasantly surprised by Greeley's "marvels of impromptu oratory." Reid said that Greeley's "perfect" speeches had done "immense good." Grant's men, the *Tribune* claimed, were in despair. In Indiana, however, exasperated Democratic managers cut short Greeley's tour.[57]

Again traditionalists attacked the tour as unprecedented, repugnant, and ineffectual: "For the first time in the history of the country a prominent candidate for the presidency has found it necessary to take the stump in his own behalf," the *Hartford Courant* moaned, adding that Greeley was the "great American office beggar," a "demagogue" who believed that the "man should seek the office rather than the office the man." Greeley would discover that stumping produced no political capital, the *Cincinnati Gazette* added. People merely crowded to see traveling candidates "as they would to view a procession of wild animals."[58]

By 1872 these old-fashioned voices were drowned out by recitals of precedents for stumping. "Such speeches have been more or less the practice of Presidential candidates for the last twenty years," the *World* claimed. Yet just what the nominee was to do remained unclear. Some people, such as Manton Marble of the *World*, justified being both passive *and* active. Marble, like most Americans, still "incline[d] to deprecate speech-making and letter-writing by a presidential candidate." But, having urged Seymour's tour and blessed Greeley's, Marble no longer believed that stumping "goes against public proprieties."[59]

Increasingly, then, stumping was accepted, but considered a trial by fire, a "perilous ordeal" to be endured. All agreed, however, at minimum, that "propriety" and "individual self-respect" should restrain the candidates. The campaign may be, as one political writer said, "a discussion with sticks," but the candidates should not club each other.[60]

The political debate, then, centered less on the propriety of the stumping than on the characteristics a candidate's behavior revealed. Greeley, the "Gabbing Philosopher," the "garrulous old woman," made some Republicans question "whether he ever has any definite beliefs on any subject." The silent Grant, on the other hand, struck Darwinian Democrats as being "of the inanimate or lower formation, and . . . condemned to be dumb."[61]

This focus on personal characteristics raised a difficult question for nominees and democratic theorists: Which is more important, the party and its principles or the individual leader? Partisans and the reformers agreed with the *Hartford Courant* that, against the larger questions of the country's "destiny" and party principles, "Grant is nothing and Greeley is nothing."[62] Party leaders realized that an obsession with candidate personality would come at their expense, while many reformers wanted to see more substantive questions discussed in the campaign. In a liberal-democratic polity, virtuous politicians addressed the issues while personality was an illegitimate, albeit all-too-popular, consideration.

Yet, many did not see how personal discussions could be excluded from politics. It was not just that the "heads of the ticket incarnate the issues," as the *New York World* had cried in 1868. Rather, the president continued to epitomize American virtue. Questions about a nominee's honesty, ability, and loyalty to the Constitution, though "personal," were essential. The Emersonian emphasis on moral conduct had strengthened the connection between public and private virtue. A public character "is often an artificial one," George Washington's hagiographer Parson Weems wrote in 1858, dismissing the traditional distinction. "It is not, then, in the glare of public, but in the shade of private life, that we are to look for the man."[63] This notion pushed nineteenth-century Americans into ever closer scrutiny of the individuals striving to lead the country. As nominees became more active, debates about the relevance of personalities would become more heated.

During the tour, Greeley sensed impending doom—for both his candidacy and his life. He seemed to be running not only for the presidency, but for his place in history. In June, Greeley wrote what could have been his epitaph: "If I should die before election, or be beaten therein," he wrote to a friend, "please testify for me that I do not regret having braved public opinion, when I thought it wrong and knew it to be merciless."[64]

On October 30, Greeley's wife died. After that, he was increasingly listless. Grant's triumph did not seem to surprise Greeley; he received the news with "perfect indifference," the *Sun* reported. "I am used up," Greeley sighed. By the end of the month, he was dead. The *New York Times*, noting that the campaign shattered his health and spirit, claimed that "Mr. GREELEY died of 'Liberal Republicanism'."[65]

Americans in 1872, Ohio Governor Rutherford B. Hayes said, were "sick of politics." They were sick of parties and personalities, of unattractive candidates and venomous campaigns, of electioneering and the electoral process itself. "To elect their own rulers is, indeed, a great privilege of free citizens," the *New York Evening Post* said. "But the principles and methods by which they have come to select them for election are execrable."[66]

The Liberal Republican movement had promised redemption. The movement's collapse shattered hopes for reform and made the American political system at once stronger and more objectionable. Yet the move-

ment did not die. It rejuvenated republican sensibilities, just when democracy appeared triumphant. It helped redefine electoral "virtue,"
pointing to the day when addressing the issues would replace maintaining silence. The genteel reformers would now push for campaigns of
education, not inspiration. Also, the focus on personality, regardless of
its legitimacy, suggested a role for the candidate and a purpose for the
campaign: a forum for scrutinizing potential presidents.

V

The 1876 campaign was the most evenly balanced in nearly three decades. *Neither* candidate was *ever* desperate enough to attempt a bold
move. The contest between Democrat Samuel J. Tilden and Republican
Rutherford B. Hayes thus offers a guided tour of the conventional political wisdom in the 1870s, and of the changes since 1860.

Governor Hayes employed the same cautious strategy before and
after his nomination. His aloofness prior to the convention secured his
"surprise" nomination as the available candidate. Though he was not
well known, Hayes remained "cool," even "indifferent" during the campaign, refusing to stump or to "interfere" in National Committee matters. He would not refute any slanders. On Election Day, he would not
even vote for himself. He followed the advice he gave his campaign
biographer, William Dean Howells, that "Silence is the only safety."[67]

Hayes tried to forestall attacks on his obscurity and circumspection
by releasing "a bold . . . letter of acceptance." The letter, nearly six times
longer than either of Grant's efforts, affirmed the party platform and
advocated civil service reform, hard-money policy, and reconciliation
with the South. Hayes also made occasional nonpartisan appearances,
including a well-publicized trip to the Philadelphia Centennial Exhibition. He "managed to shake some four thousand people by the hand
and to make half a dozen speeches" while avoiding the dangers facing
candidates in their new public roles. He spoke "without saying anything
I regret . . . without 'slobbing over,'" avoiding the Scylla of substance
and the Charybdis of fatuousness.[68]

Hayes's modest, patrician bearing "lived up to the strictest requirements of the code," *The Nation* noted after the election. But by 1876
such passivity was problematic. The publication mocked Hayes for saying nothing in the campaign beyond acknowledging that "ours was a
republican form of government and this was the hundredth year of the
national existence." Demands for policy clarifications and more personal

appearances arrived in Fremont daily. When it seemed that Hayes had
lost, many blamed his silence for his defeat. The Republicans
"blunder[ed] . . . in making too much of the party and too little of the
candidate and his principles," the *New York Tribune* concluded.[69]

The Democratic nominee, New York Governor Samuel J. Tilden,
received more attention. A millionaire railroad lawyer turned reformer,
Tilden was hailed—and cursed—as the greatest political tactician since
Van Buren. Tilden actively sought the nomination. He corresponded
with party leaders, sent out emissaries such as his friend Abram S. Hewitt, and established a literary bureau to circulate documents. Many
Democrats resented this "shameless expenditure of money and . . . unprecedented advertisement."[70] But they respected his ingenuity.

After his nomination, Tilden professed a disinterest which those
conscious of his tactical virtuosity dismissed as a pose. The sixty-two-
year-old Tilden was frail. He had suffered a mild paralytic stroke and
was, in the historical novelist Gore Vidal's acid terms, "a martyr to
dyspepsia." Republicans overlooked Tilden's weariness and wrongly
charged him with seeking the presidency "by the same kind of personal
activity and management that a man in a country village displays in
seeking votes as constable." With Tilden, then, Democrats had the
worst of all possible worlds. Their great tactician was idle, but he was
still condemned for politicking.[71] Similarly, donors withheld their contributions, assuming that the wealthy Tilden could and would bankroll
his campaign alone. But he did not, and the Democratic effort faltered.

Tilden's every move was filtered through this public assumption of
political Machiavellianism. In what at the time was considered a novel
move, he withheld his acceptance letter until he had consulted with his
running mate, Thomas Hendricks. The 4,400-word acceptance dwarfed
Hayes's own considerable effort. Democrats praised Tilden's bold calls
for reform in government expenditures, civil service, and currency as a
departure from the traditional acceptance letter "of fine phrase and loyalty to the platform." Still, Republicans attacked Tilden's duplicity and
mocked his "uncommon slowness."[72]

Nevertheless, Tilden helped rationalize the presidential campaign—
if only by example. The liberal reformers of 1872 had spearheaded the
drive against the "unreasoning enthusiasm" of the American presidential campaign. They longed for a quiet campaign of issues. At the same
time, what historian Alfred D. Chandler, Jr., calls the "visible hand of
management" had begun to systematize American business. Using Tilden's New York State campaigns as models, Democratic campaign chairman Abram Hewitt launched a sophisticated campaign of organization

and education. To improve coordination, the Democratic National
Committee was divided into various departments, including a literary
bureau and a speakers' bureau. To understand the political "market,"
voters were carefully canvassed. Campaign literature flooded the nation,
including, fittingly enough, pamphlets resembling pocket-size railroad
timetables. None of these techniques may have swayed the outcome,
but they all anticipated the shift in American campaigning from inspiring and mobilizing voters to educating and then merely counting
them.[73]

Despite the Republican claim that Tilden was overanxious for the
presidency, he refused to refute the damning allegation that he evaded
his income taxes during the Civil War. Democrat William C. Whitney
urged Tilden to "sacrifice . . . personal feeling & delicacy for the sake of
the party." To fight, "You must yourself personally *come before the scenes
and make a sensation.*" Annoyed and humiliated, as he put it, Tilden
would not dignify the charges with an answer. He would eventually
release a statement promising to block the South's payment of the Confederate war debt, but he would not respond to the income-tax libel.
Democrats were miffed. Some wondered whether Hayes's son Webb and
other Republicans were right—that "Tilden's denying nothing because
he can not."[74]

This presumption that Tilden's discretion signified guilt revealed the
shift in assumptions from the 1850s to the 1870s. By 1876, after the
democratic ethos had spread and some candidates had taken to the
stump, silence was only occasionally golden. The public had become
accustomed to public statements and appearances from the candidates.
Active candidates were increasingly important to party success. Frankness now prevailed—within limits, of course. Acceptance letters were
becoming lengthy policy statements. Candidates could make occasional
public appearances without public censure, as both Tilden and Hayes
did. Tilden's silence, therefore, was seen as guilty and wily.

The rising tensions between the candidate and the party organization reflected the nominee's increasing importance. Hayes squabbled
with Zachariah Chandler, Tilden with Hewitt. Anxious about losing
power, party loyalists insisted that, as the *Enquirer* argued, "Principles
are longer-lived than men, and . . . measures . . . are greater than candidates."[75]

But the people did consider personal reputation, and a growing
chorus deemed the question unavoidable. "The careful scrutiny of candidates . . . reveals their view of vital and fundamental questions," *Harper's* argued, blurring the line between concerns with character and with

issues. The *Courant* added: "Nothing sifts a man's character like a presidential canvass."[76]

New answers were emerging, then, to the perennial question "What's a campaign for?" A campaign tested candidates, searching for flaws before they emerged in the presidency. A campaign promoted the candidate's and the party's ideas through education. A campaign then, was a showcase for both the party and the candidate.

Still, as various newspapers suggested in the fall of 1876, the "customary" reserve remained the "highest wisdom." Hayes's and Tilden's inaction showed that stumping remained a novelty justified only by national crisis—the rationale that Douglas, Seymour, and Greeley had used. Of course, "We always believe that vital interests are involved in Presidential elections," Thurlow Weed admitted.[77] The 1876 campaign proved that nominees stumped only if their candidacy, and not the nation, was endangered; personal—not national—interest prevailed.

The period from 1860 through 1876 solidified the roles of both the people and the candidates in the campaign. The spread of liberal democracy, the rise of nationalism, the strengthening of the presidency, the crisis of the Democratic party, and the continuing transformations in technology and the press all thrust the candidates toward the people. Had any of these factors been the determining one, if the republican taboo had not been as strong as it was, even U. S. Grant might have felt compelled to stump. But while liberal democracy had expanded, republican dignity remained a concern. For all their love of the "go-getter" spirit and innovation, when they elected their presidents, Americans remained remarkably traditional.

Questions proliferated. The growing spotlight on the candidate undermined the party: Would party leaders realize this and inhibit candidates, or would they push the nominees on the stump when short-term gains beckoned? The limits on the candidate were undefined: How could a candidate appeal to the people without appearing overanxious? It remained unclear when modesty became antidemocratic, and openness demagogic. Candidates were also unsure of how to be frank but not careless, modest yet not reclusive. For the next twenty years, American politicians would experiment with various solutions—elaborate notification ceremonies, front-porch campaigns, and rear-platform stumping tours—searching for a balance.

FIVE

The Front Porch or the
Stump? 1880–1896

I know no reason why I should not face the American people.
                                        —*James G. Blaine, 1884*

THE post–Civil War economic boom spawned a new kind of hero.
The yeoman farmer and the Yankee trader no longer served as ideal
economic types in a world of industrial conglomerates and transcontinental mass-marketing networks. All of a sudden everyone wanted to
be a millionaire. In 1816 there were barely half-a-dozen Americans worthy of that designation in all eighteen states, yet by 1876 there were at
least that many in the Congress alone. When such eponymous figures
as Carnegie, Rockefeller, and Guggenheim created family dynasties in
steel, oil, and copper, ambition stopped being a dirty word. Rather, it
became the key to the American dream that Horatio Alger celebrated
in his best-selling, rags-to-riches novels. Still, both ambition and wealth
remained somewhat suspect. While Americans envied the luxuries that
"captains of industry" enjoyed, these same "robber barons" appeared
greedy and ruthless. In calling this era the Gilded Age, Americans simultaneously celebrated their nation's rise to great wealth and mourned the
republic's decline.

Gilded Age politics reflected these contradictions. With the end of
Reconstruction in 1876 a burst of patriotism swept the land, as Americans sought to bury their differences in a red-white-and-blue Centennial celebration. At the same time, instead of honoring politicians as
public servants nobly serving democracy, Americans viewed politicians
as pigs feeding at the public trough. In one 1880 cartoon surveying "The

Two Rival Political Huckster Shops," where Republicans and Democrats had "Nominations for Sale," the "Spirit of Washington" said to the "Spirit of Jefferson": "Behold the result of our sacrifices and labors!"[1]

Some hoped that presidential candidates could offer an alternative to the sleazy politicians preying on the local parties. In 1880, *The Nation* demanded that presidential candidates "take the stump on their own behalf." Such direct communication would improve both the nomination and the platforms, E. L. Godkin's influential journal believed. The party position could not be so vague; the candidate could not be so obscure and mediocre; and the public would have valuable memoranda to be used in "watching and criticising" the eventual winner's presidential career.[2] More and more Americans were willing to repudiate the republican taboo to preserve some vestige of virtue in an increasingly vulgar republic.

In demanding more democracy while mourning the decline of republican virtue, contradictions abounded. In the 1880s, expectations of the presidential candidates were more fluid than at any other time since the 1840s. Candidates were supposed to be active, but not overanxious; forthright, but not gabby. *No* candidate could be passive and silent. *All* candidates now at least acknowledged some serenades, and released substantive acceptance letters. But beyond that, *no one* knew what was proper or practical. Presidential candidates were poised to become the educational leaders of their campaigns. For better or for worse, however, this effort would fail, an ironic victim of the traditional demand for dignity.

I

One by one, the restraints on a presidential candidate had been cut. Since the 1850s, America's transportation and communication networks had been sophisticated enough to make a stumping campaign viable. Since the Civil War, liberal democracy had spread to the point where people demanded direct communication with their leaders. Now, in the 1880s, the party shackles on the candidate were loosening.

Parties still dominated American politics. With each campaign the national committees became more centralized, more thorough, more efficient. Throughout the 1880s the Democratic and Republican parties were balanced nationally, producing record voter turnouts of almost 80 percent.[3] Yet the party grip was slipping: By 1880 the press had grown in influence and autonomy; fewer newspapers were mere party organs

advancing political interests. Now they were businesses peddling a product—the news. Horace Greeley's successor at the *New York Tribune*,
Whitelaw Reid, pioneered the use of the Mergenthaler linotype for easier typesetting. He hired professional staffers committed to accurate reporting. He followed his conscience, not his party.

Reid's rival, Joseph Pulitzer, also considered party secondary. "[We]
serve no party but the people," the Hungarian immigrant declared. Pulitzer desired truth, but he kept his eye on circulation. He wanted a
paper "more powerful than the President." He took over the *New York
World* in 1883 and created a mass medium with bold headlines, "human
interest" stories, front-page cartoons, and illustrations. In the process
he helped shift the focus from party matters to personalities. By 1890,
according to one rival, Pulitzer had "transformed the best-written and
least-read newspaper in New York into the worst-written and most-read
newspaper in New York."[4]

Although both the Republican-leaning *Tribune* and the Democratic-
leaning *World* were fiercely political, party leaders could not either rely
on them or guide them. If charmed by the opposing candidate—or, more
likely, repelled by their own—the papers bolted. Ever more reliant on
objective accounts telegraphed from across the nation, and interested
in attracting both Republican and Democratic customers, they covered
the news. Concerned with personalities and not parties, idiosyncrasies
and not abstractions, they focused on the candidate and his actions.
The press was still overwhelmingly partisan, with two out of three newspapers in 1880 claiming party affiliations, but individual papers were
covering candidates more thoroughly and accurately.[5]

Just as newspapers found their economic interests diverging from
their partisan ones, party bosses found local interests diverging from
national ones. Elaborate local machines emerged, especially in the cities.
Resting on a solid foundation of immigrant votes, fueled by patronage
and graft, the machines bored into the expanding city bureaucracies.
The men running these machines concentrated on the power and the
spoils extracted from their own locales. They mobilized voters for the
party, as long as the nominee paid homage. Beyond that, they often
ignored presidential politics.

State leaders, on the other hand, took a special interest in the presidential campaign. Supported by local bosses, men like the two titans of
New York state politics, Republican Roscoe Conkling and Democrat
David B. Hill, were free of national party discipline. They did not support a candidate unless they were assured of receiving their patronage
rewards. Their tenacity, in the long run, was self-defeating. Their in-

trigues during the campaign often forced the nominee into a more central, even independent, position. And their lust for patronage fostered a reaction against boss rule.

Similarly, party bosses' success in mobilizing votes prompted a backlash against popular politics. Their gluttony tarnished the parties. Repelled by party greed, disturbed by the unseemly spectacle of American campaigns, influenced by American business practices, and inspired by Samuel J. Tilden's success in New York, many politicians in the 1880s and 1890s tried to make American politics more rational. A Republican editor from Iowa, James S. Clarkson, realized that "the brass band, the red light, and the mass meeting" were losing their power. Political discussion was going from "the open field, as in Lincoln's day, to the private homes," where each family searched for the party whose policy offered the most benefits. The time had come for education, not exhortation; documents, not parades.[6]

Clarkson and others initiated campaigns of education, subdued and rational appeals to prudent voters. Clarkson noted the growing emphasis on such economic issues as the currency and the tariff. "[In this] age of telegraphs and fast mails the people think, and know what they want," Congressman C. A. Boutelle of Maine said. The people were more educated, and more educable.[7]

This faith in the American voter was the bedrock of liberal democracy. Many assumed that as democracy and its institutions grew, so did the popular intelligence. Yet Americans had always been ambivalent about their own abilities. Republican theory hoped for popular virtue, but did not rely on it. Americans were still not sure they could trust themselves. The danger to democratic institutions comes "when vital questions . . . [requiring] tension of thought to understand and some self denial . . . are submitted to popular decision," Congressman William L. Wilson of West Virginia observed. "The mob," Richard Croker of Tammany Hall said, "is fickle, bold, and timid by turns. . . . a mere creature of emotion."[8]

Americans wanted to believe with *Harper's Weekly* that a campaign was a discussion of the principles that would shape the policy of the administration, and that ultimately, as the 1884 Republican nominee James G. Blaine claimed, it was a search for truth. Too often, however, the campaign became a "discussion with sticks." Modern democratized republicans now accepted that "to give all men a due degree of influence in the government is the surest way to promote the welfare of all." But they still believed that "The government of the best men is really the best government," and that the basis of popular government was "virtue." By now, virtue was part morality, part education.[9] Addressing issues became a mark of substance, not of demagoguery. The republican discomfort with democracy was thus sublimated into calls for serious campaigns.

Hoping the people were fit to rule, but fearing otherwise, partisans often charged their opponents with appealing to "the ignorant and gullible classes." "Our" men made rational appeals to worthy voters, while "they" made demagogic appeals to the unenlightened. Of course, if the voters were properly informed, they would choose properly. Every election thus became what the *New York Times* would call the 1884 election, "A Test of the People."[10]

The decline of the parties and of popular politics forced the nominees into more direct and more democratic relations with the people. The *New York Tribune* pronounced in 1880 that candidates whose opinions were wholly unknown could no longer win. The *New York World* reported that most people did not "hold a candidate responsible" for fatuous party compromises; the candidate made his own platform in his letter of acceptance. As acceptance letters eclipsed party platforms, they "shape[d] . . . the contest," Carl Schurz insisted, and the people learned more about the candidates.[11]

But candidates were still restrained; the republican taboo lingered. Traditionalists bristled at signs of ambition. Politicians remained wary of substantive appeals, preferring exciting but silent appearances by the nominee. Americans wondered: How should a democratic leader address the people?

II

The two major party nominees in 1880 offered contrasting answers. The Democratic nominee, General Winfield Scott Hancock, was a professional soldier and a political novice, an available candidate more suited to the era of the warrior after whom he was named. He deferred to his party and its platform. His opponent, James A. Garfield, was an amateur soldier and a professional politician. Nominated by a divided Republican party, Garfield was on his own. His acceptance letter was long but evasive. After the acceptance Garfield ran an active campaign but continued to avoid the issues; any elaborations threatened party harmony. Hancock, on the other hand, ran a dignified campaign. His acceptance letter was shorter than Garfield's, and innocuous. But, as the election approached, the General felt compelled to clarify the Democratic position in letters and interviews.

Democrats admitted that Hancock's chief qualification for the presidency was his acceptability to both the North and South. A Union war hero, Hancock had won friends in the South after the war as a conscientious military governor of Louisiana and Texas. He stayed at his post at Governors Island in New York as head of the Army's Atlantic Division. There, in full uniform, he received delegations three days a week. Initially he avoided issues, preferring to "let well enough alone." Turgidly he explained: "I have no right to mar the present situation of the party by a set of expressions, superfluous to its adopted platform of principles, with which I am in full accord."[12]

Republicans called the tactics of the "padlocked" candidate outmoded and dishonest. They acknowledged Hancock's heroism, but they complained that he represented "no policy, no principle, no issue, nothing but the party which has nominated him." Mischievously, they circulated a pamphlet entitled, and presumably detailing, *Hancock's Record*, all of whose pages were blank. After Hancock's vapid acceptance letter, the *Albany Evening Journal* wondered just where the "proper" place was for the General to "divulge his precious notions." Once, according to the satirist Petroleum V. Nasby, when rival Democratic factions visited simultaneously, Hancock pretended to faint. Nasby imagined that Hancock later sighed: "There must be a new plan fixed. . . . I can't keep on faintin' in this way till the first uv November."[13]

The new "plan" involved more frankness. In late September, Hancock released a letter promising to block payment of any Southern war claims. Most Republicans doubted the reliability of a "candidate's letter intended to affect votes during a campaign." But some, like the stump speaker William M. Evarts, doubted the party, not the candidate: "If there is anything that the country can rely upon as true in purpose and in fact, it is in a candidate's letters," Evarts said.[14] Statements from candidates had become common enough to no longer automatically be suspect, yet remained infrequent enough to command respect.

In October, Hancock addressed the tariff problem. Republicans had gained in manufacturing states by claiming that the Democrats' "free trade policy" would not protect American industry. In an interview with the *Paterson Daily Guardian*, Hancock explained that even with a tariff for revenue only, Democratic tariff rates would still protect industry. Besides, he said, "The tariff is a local question." Though economically sound, these remarks were politically disastrous. "That," Republican Edwin Cowles chuckled, "is one interview too many."[15]

Democrats blamed the interview for their subsequent defeat. Democratic National Chairman William H. Barnum said that Hancock had defeated himself and his party, just as Henry Clay had in 1844. On Election Day, the General went to sleep early. At 5 A.M. his wife awakened him, saying "It has been a complete Waterloo for you." "That's all right," Hancock replied, "I can stand it." He quickly fell asleep again.[16]

In blaming Hancock, Barnum and others clung to their anachronistic beliefs that nominees could only damage a campaign, and that silence was golden. They concentrated on the fact that Hancock had spoken, rather than the imprudence of his actual remarks. Yet remaining silent amid the tariff debate and the doubts about his abilities could arguably have been just as crippling to Hancock. Much as they disliked it, party leaders had to learn this lesson. Never again would Democrats nominate a soldier with no proven abilities to communicate with the people.[17] After Hancock, party leaders would encourage the nominee to stump.

The victor in 1880, James A. Garfield, was a dark horse of sorts in the contest for the Republican nomination. A nine-term Congressman and Senator-elect from Ohio, he was familiar to Republicans but lacked a national reputation. The Republicans were divided, with Carl Schurz's Independents advocating a thorough civil service reform; James G. Blaine's Half-Breeds tolerating some changes; and Roscoe Conkling's Stalwarts rejecting all reforms. When the Stalwarts' third-term "boom" for U.S. Grant collapsed, Garfield—a Blaine ally—won unexpectedly.[18]

Garfield's nomination did not bring peace. Garfield often had to choose between allowing his enemies to undermine his efforts and alienating them further. For example, when the Stalwarts tried to dictate the choice of national chairman, Garfield's ally William E. Chandler thwarted them. As a result, the nominee had unprecedented input in the selection of Marshall Jewell as chairman. But now Garfield's actions, not just the company he kept, angered the Stalwarts. Rather than begging Garfield to retire, as most had done with previous candidates, party leaders invited Garfield to visit New York to appease the regulars.

Garfield was "very anxious to avoid the visit." He assumed that the Stalwarts, with nowhere else to turn, would eventually fall into line. He did not want to appear to be surrendering to them. Other Garfield advisers, concerned with the candidate's dignity and autonomy, agreed. But Garfield's men in New York insisted, characterizing the visit as a consultation with activists, not a capitulation to Roscoe Conkling. Hancock, stationed in New York, confers with party men daily, they reasoned. Why could not Garfield consult with his allies? The dependable

Chandler urged: "On such a momentous question as the Presidency no mere matter of etiquette should stand in the way."[19]

Unwilling to "rebel unreasonably," Garfield agreed to the trip. Despite his advisers' pleas for "no letters and no speeches," Garfield *had* to respond to serenades as he traveled through Ohio and New York. "Certainly you are no coy maiden to be shut out from the gaze of the ungodly," one National Committee member told Garfield. "Trust to your own good sense of propriety and the necessities of the occasion." Such experienced politicians as Chandler—and Garfield himself—held their breath.[20]

Surprisingly, Garfield's public efforts were more successful than his private ones. Conkling did not even attend the Fifth Avenue Hotel summit. Other New York leaders were soothed and impressed by the enthusiasm that greeted Garfield's train: At most stations to and from New York, Garfield said but little "beyond thanks & an occasional remark on the localities through which we passed." The ovations surprised both Republicans and Democrats. Garfield was delighted. He had mastered this ordeal and showcased his appeal. Many now doubted "the foolish custom which seals a presidential candidate's lips." To *Harper's Weekly* and others, stumping had become a "question of expediency."[21]

Garfield's success activated demands for more stumping. Americans liked a candidate who could stand up and talk sense and "who ain't afraid to open his mouth for fear he makes an ass of himself," his aide Thomas M. Nichol reported. An accomplished orator, accustomed to electioneering and thrilled by his successful trip, Garfield was tempted. "[If] I could take the stump," he sighed, "I should feel happier." Echoing *The Nation*, Garfield thought that if stumping were "the custom it would insure better nominations." But many Republicans feared novelty and warned him that he would be compelled to repeat himself if he spoke many times, and that this "would finally look to the public like trimming." President Hayes cautioned: "Sit cross legged and look wise until after the election."[22]

Garfield did mostly remain at home after August, but he could not remain silent. Almost every day politicians, family friends, and delegations of devotees converged on his farm near Mentor, Ohio. Most of these swarming visitors were uninvited—and unwelcome—but the Garfield family had to host them anyway. Thus Garfield's sons and campaign secretary often slept in the attic, or even the barn. With his yard "filled with voters from all parts of the country hurling speeches at me on all subjects," Garfield "could not play dummy on my own doorsteps." If he said nothing, he endorsed a visitor's statements implicitly. But if he responded, he risked blundering. Instead he spoke briefly about unrelated topics. Often, relieved, he wrote in his diary: "I think no harm has been done."[23]

This pioneering "front-porch" campaign—the phrase was not used until 1896—was impromptu, but useful. It linked the nominee with the people without enmeshing him in controversy. Even though he evaded the issues, Garfield appeared candid. He offered an articulate, confident, engaging contrast to his at first reclusive, then bumbling, opponent. At the same time, remaining at home protected the candidate from allegations of excess ambition. He adhered to the form of the republican taboo. This exercise ritualized contradiction: The nominee played the good democrat, addressing the people as equals in his own home, while the people expressed their fealty to their virtuous and modest republican leader.

Throughout the nasty campaign, Garfield refused to refute the many allegations made against him. But when the Democrats released the "Morey Letter" in late October, a missive allegedly in Garfield's hand and expressing antilabor, pro-Chinese sentiments, Jewell begged Garfield to denounce it. After five days, convinced that "No one else could reply but me," Garfield denounced the allegations. The Democratic *Cincinnati Enquirer* wondered why Garfield "maintained a dogged silence until he was forced to make a disavowal."[24] As with Samuel Tilden's tax problem in 1876, silence appeared tantamount to guilt.

The campaign revealed that forthrightness was not yet an unmitigated virtue, but accessibility was. It was better to be active than passive—even while avoiding the issues. Ironically, although crippled by his gaffes, Hancock looked like the candidate of "concealment," while the cautious Garfield appeared as the candidate of "candor."[25] Democrats attacked Garfield's New York tour, and Republicans condemned Hancock's silence while ridiculing his pronouncements, but few in either party attacked Garfield's homey greetings to his guests. For an orator confident of his ability to greet people without being controversial or cloying, the front porch offered a reasonable solution.

III

In 1884 most candidates and party leaders still preferred passivity and silence. Both Democrat Grover Cleveland and Republican James G. Blaine intended to be quiet. Both hoped for a serious, educational campaign. But whereas Cleveland more or less adhered to his original plan, Blaine could not.

One issue dominated the 1884 campaign: James G. Blaine. Former Speaker of the House and Secretary of State, chronicler of his twenty years in Congress, a charming man with piercing black eyes and a General Grant beard, Blaine was the model American statesman. He had, however, one minor flaw. Somehow, on a yearly salary rarely exceeding five thousand dollars, he had become a millionaire. As his fortune grew, so did the accusations of influence peddling, bribery, cover-ups. The *New York Sun* would attack "Blaine, the beggar at the feet of the railroad jobbers, the prostitute in the Speaker's chair, the lawmaking broker in land grabs, the representative and agent of the corruptionists, monopolists and enemies of the Republic."[26]

Even among Republicans, "Men went insane over him in pairs, one for, one against."[27] The rank and file loved Blaine, and the Stalwarts hated him. The Independents considered him proof of the evils of party as organization. Upon his nomination at Chicago in 1884, the Independents, called Mugwumps, bolted. As in 1872, personalities more than policies spurred the reformers.

Conscious of this Republican split and of New York's importance in the election, Democrats nominated the state's upright, reforming Governor Grover Cleveland. Previously a sheriff and mayor of Buffalo, Cleveland lacked Blaine's experience, reputation, and charisma—the New Yorker had never even visited Washington, D.C. Still the *New York World* recognized Cleveland's assets: "He is an Honest Man. He is an Honest Man. He is an Honest Man."[28]

The campaign pivoted on this clash between the trustworthy reformer and the political prostitute—until Cleveland's honor was itself tainted. On July 21, the Buffalo *Evening Telegraph* uncovered "A Terrible Tale": that Cleveland had sired an illegitimate son. The child's paternity was unclear, but Cleveland had nobly accepted responsibility. Rather than denying the scandal, Cleveland ordered his staff: "Tell the truth."[29]

Cleveland's case challenged the republic's moralists. His public character remained unblemished. By eighteenth-century standards, then, his crime was relatively minor—Benjamin Franklin, among others, was known as a rake. Furthermore, this affair was clearly in the past; Democrats wondered how many bachelors could "conscientiously cast the first stone." And yet, this kind of conduct did not befit the nation's "ideal man." Wasn't private virtue a prerequisite for public virtue? No one doubted the purity of Cleveland's public life or of Blaine's private life, a Mugwump elegantly·reasoned: "We should [therefore] elect Mr. Cleveland to the public office which he is so admirably qualified to fill and remand Mr. Blaine to the private life which he is so eminently qualified to adorn."[30]

Cleveland's stoic response to the scandals further indicted the unrepentant Blaine, who had been dodging allegations since 1876. The most damning evidence against Blaine was his clumsy cover-up attempt. On September 15, the *Boston Journal* published Blaine's 1876 correspondence with a businessman, Warren Fisher, Jr., supplied by James Mulligan, once Fisher's clerk. Fisher had helped Blaine sell some near-worthless railroad bonds in a series of questionable but profitable transactions. In one of these "Mulligan Letters," Blaine ghostwrote a letter for Fisher exonerating himself. In the accompanying cover letter, Blaine explained the ruse and instructed: "Burn this letter."[31]

The derisive shouts of "Burn this letter" underlined the quandary of the slandered candidates. Should they ignore all libels, as Tilden did in 1876, or should they address only the most damaging one, as Garfield did in 1880? With an increasingly sensational press and an increasingly active candidate, attacks would proliferate. The strategy of silence would become more difficult. When a candidate did respond, he rarely convinced opponents. Even in 1880, many Democrats went to the polls believing that Garfield had written the forged Morey Letter.

Blaine was unsure of just how to respond to the charges. When rumors circulated questioning his marriage date and the legitimacy of his dead infant son, Blaine exploded. He filed a libel suit and published a letter explaining the confusing details. "You can imagine how inexpressibly painful it must be to discuss one's domestic life in the press," Blaine wrote. Although his heartfelt response quashed these calumnies, Blaine could not however squelch the other charges. He yearned for a month-long "experiment" during which the press would ignore the scandals.[32] The campaign was faltering. Party leaders clamored for action.

Blaine decided to stump. Although some still doubted that "any intelligent men" would change their minds "after gazing at Mr. Blaine a few minutes," many believed that enthusiastic receptions proved a nominee's popularity and induced zeal into the campaign. Blaine offered a frank and modern rationale for his tour: He was not scouting a military site, searching for his mother, or even making, as Garfield had made, incidental speeches on his way to party consultations. He had a doubtful state, Ohio, and an issue, the tariff. "I am a profound believer in a popular government," he explained, "and I know no reason why I should not face the American people."[33]

From mid-August until Election Day, Blaine stumped and his people responded. At first he limited himself to pleasantries, often leaving before other speakers launched fuller arguments. But as the state campaign in Ohio heated up, Blaine began to champion the protective tariff. Most accounts attributed the eventual Republican victory in Ohio to Blaine's four hundred speeches. "No American statesman has ever done anything so bold or so brilliant," John Hay wrote.[34]

The New York Times and other Blaine opponents condemned the speeches as monotonous and barren diversions from the character issue. "There never was furnished so gigantic and prolonged a spectacle of vote-begging," a Democratic paper claimed. Cleveland, on the other hand, made few campaign appearances and "[did] nothing which lowered his dignity," The Nation said. He did not try to "snatch an office which it was the people's privilege to bestow unasked."[35] Stumping might be acceptable, but modesty was preferred.

On October 19, the exhausted Blaine considered returning home to Maine. But party officials begged him to visit New York City. Blaine gave in. Ten days later, he met with Republican clergymen. The soon-to-be-infamous Reverend Samuel D. Burchard greeted Blaine by denouncing the Democrats as "the party whose antecedents have been Rum, Romanism and Rebellion." Blaine missed the offending remark, but an alert Democratic National Committee member, Senator Arthur P. Gorman, did not. Realizing that the more visible nominees were also more vulnerable, Gorman had underlings transcribe all public remarks made at Republican functions. By the next morning, thousands of Irish Catholic votes and, many believe, the election itself, had been lost.[36]

Politicians again drew the wrong conclusions, ignoring the gains that Blaine made in Ohio and punishing him for his candid stumping campaign, even when the Burchard blunder could have happened in the candidate's backyard. Many concluded that, as one Republican said, "the best thing would be to send . . . [the nominee] to Europe." For the next fifty years, managers and candidates feared being "Burchardized."[37]

In 1880 and 1884 passivity was newly untenable, but activity was not yet respectable. When candidates gave political speeches supporters worried, and when they confined themselves to pleasantries, opponents snickered. "I would not make a single political speech," President Hayes had advised Garfield in 1880, suggesting instead that he "Give them a chunk of wisdom in every talk." No wonder many agreed with the Buf-

falo Commercial Advertiser that it was the habit of candidates "to equivo-
cate, to trim, to mouth meaningless phrases, to write glittering generalities, in short, to dodge every point at which opposition is likely to be
encountered."[38]

The candidates, then, were caught between ideology and expedience. Theoretically, as an aspiring democratic leader, the nominee was
supposed to inform people about his positions and his record. Without
chasing after the people, but without avoiding them either, the candidate was to strike the keynote in the educational campaign. But the
success of appearances rather than substance, the fear of blundering,
and the growing concern with personality militated against a serious
confrontation with the issues. As a result the candidate became more
active, but not necessarily more forthright. Cynicism about the process
festered.

IV

The 1888 and 1892 campaigns were more subdued than their predecessors. "Old time methods of campaigning are obsolete," the *Washington
Post* pronounced in 1888. "[This] will be a campaign of argument, not
of brag and bluster."[39] But as campaigns moved away from spectacle, the
nominees were thrust toward it.

The two combatants in both campaigns, Republican Benjamin Harrison and Democrat Grover Cleveland, tried to avoid campaigning.
Each hid behind presidential dignity when running for reelection,
Cleveland in 1888 and Harrison in 1892. But, as challengers, each was
forced into the spotlight. In 1888 the people sought out Harrison—literally. In 1892 Cleveland was forced to seek the people. Both learned that
nominees now had to campaign, despite the hazards.

President Cleveland began the 1888 campaign handicapped: Democratic leaders resented his independence. "He is above all a Cleveland
man and he has no use for any who are not like himself, Cleveland
men," the *Newport Observer* said. His call for tariff reduction had alienated many Northern Democrats. Warned that his attack on protectionism would benefit Republicans, Cleveland nobly but recklessly inquired:
"What is the use of being elected or reelected, unless you stand for something?"[40]

To Cleveland, this principled and educational approach limited
even his own role. "[The] campaign is one of information and organization," the President said. "Every citizen should be regarded as a thought-

ful, responsible voter, and he should be furnished the means of examining the issues involved in the pending canvass for himself."[41] Invited to address a national farmers' organization, Cleveland refused; he was vacationing. Also, he barred Cabinet members from the stump. And when "Frankie Clubs," named in honor of his young bride Frances, sprang up, the President forbade them as undignified.

Benjamin Harrison, on the other hand, cooperated with party leaders, enjoyed a popular issue in protectionism, and was less restrained. Chastened by the 1884 defeat, Republicans united in 1888. Matthew S. Quay, "the greatest political general" of the century according to the New York boss Thomas Platt, became national chairman. The nominee, a former Indiana Senator, was accommodating and available. "Some men," a Republican newspaper admitted, "are born great, some achieve greatness, some have greatness thrust upon them, and others live in pivotal states."[42] At first many considered Harrison just such a geographical accident. But by November, impressed Republicans reconsidered.

Harrison wanted "a Republican campaign, and not a personal one." He would "encamp on the high plains of principles, and not in the low swamps of personal defamation or detraction." And he would not stump: "I have a great risk of meeting a fool at home," he conceded, "but the candidate who travels cannot escape him."[43]

Harrison did not realize quite how many fools might come to his home. Within days of his nomination, his aide Louis Michener recalled, "Delegations from the neighboring towns began visiting him to express their joy." Haunted by Burchard's specter, Harrison tried to control these "spontaneous pilgrimages."[44] A committee arranged the visits and reviewed proposed introductory speeches—twice. Two to three times a day, at the appointed hour, Harrison would stride from his house in Indianapolis to nearby University Park, listen to the greetings, and respond. Afterward, Harrison edited these speeches and sent them out on the Associated Press wires for publication the next day.

To compensate for Harrison's icy demeanor, his managers supplemented these speeches by publicizing personal tidbits about their candidate. These speeches and stories, the growth of the human-interest angle in the press, and the increased interest in a candidate's personality, exposed the nominee as never before. Americans learned about Harrison's hat size ($7\frac{1}{2}$) and shoe size ($6\frac{1}{2}$), the price of his shirts ($27 per dozen) and suits ($45 to $55), and his favorite sports (fishing and baseball).[45] Like the home visits, these tidbits maximized exposure while minimizing the risks.

Still, Harrison's exposure worried many Republicans. Quay was reputed to have one word of advice for candidates who spoke: "Don't." "[Harrison] is daily in as much danger as if he passed through pestilence and death," former Postmaster General James N. Tyner said. In fact, Harrison's style fit this type of campaigning—familiar yet dignified, epigrammatic but not demagogic. In ninety-four speeches to 300,000 people in 110 delegations, Harrison made no major blunder. He made no bold or memorable statements either, though he did defend the high tariff, civil service reform, and increased veterans' pensions.[46]

As autumn progressed, Harrison's energy flagged. He nearly collapsed from exhaustion. He joked, halfheartedly, that "Even at home, when I sit down at the table with my family, I have some apprehensions lest someone may propose a toast and insist that I shall respond." Harrison's trouble stemmed from "the exhausting effort to say nothing," *Harper's Weekly* claimed. Of course, it followed, "The danger is that he may happen to say something." This daily handshaking and speechmaking was, it concluded, "a wholly unnecessary torture for a Presidential candidate, not to mention the risk to his health, his election, and his reputation."[47]

For the second time in three campaigns, visitors descended on a candidate's home and, in effect, forced a homebound campaign. Though some questioned its wisdom, few questioned the dignity of the exercise. No one doubted the propriety of the people seeking out the candidate. This practice suited the rural Midwest of Garfield and Harrison more than the urbanized East of Hancock and Cleveland. It appealed to a population which would travel for a day to a state fair, and had no downtowns to visit for diversions.[48]

The front-porch phenomenon, then, grafted modern practices onto traditional ones. The candidate's purview was now national, not local. Railroad tracks, not dirt roads, linked the candidate with his neighbors. The desire for personal contact with the nominee grew, and could now be satisfied tastefully. Also, in a crowning modern touch, delegations were organized not just by locale, but by profession.

Although Cleveland nosed out Harrison in the popular vote, he lost in the Electoral College. Many observers blamed Cleveland for failing to inspire the voters: Documents and principles did not win elections. Charles Dana's *New York Sun* first asked who beat the Democrats, then rejoiced in answering: Grover Cleveland. "Perhaps I made a mistake from the party standpoint," Cleveland admitted, "but damn it I was right. I have at least that satisfaction."[49]

The victorious Harrison somewhat presumptuously thanked a higher authority. "Providence has given us the victory," he exclaimed.

Matt Quay, aware of "how close a number of men were compelled to approach the gates of the penitentiary" to ensure victory, snapped: "Providence hadn't a damned thing to do with it."[50] Therein lay the seeds of Harrison's 1892 defeat.

V

Harrison's aloof folksiness, so effective at his Indianapolis home, failed at the White House. "The President's personality [is] his most unfortunate possession," one reporter wrote. To make matters worse, the "White House iceberg" froze partisans out of patronage jobs. As disgruntled Republicans attacked, Harrison grumbled that Washingtonians appeared to think that "the President of the United States has nothing else to do but fill the offices." This party split compelled Harrison to run for reelection—"A Harrison never runs from a fight," he said. Unable to find an alternative, the Republican convention renominated Harrison, who promptly installed his own puppet as party chairman. The leaders of the party were "tremendously unfriendly" to him, he explained. "If I am to be elected I must elect myself."[51]

Such self-sufficiency made Harrison vulnerable to republican criticism that he was neglecting his official duties and risking his credibility. Incumbents were more constrained than challengers. The president was supposed to stand as the "embodiment of principles," not run as an office-seeker. Active campaigning from the White House would pollute the public interest and threaten democracy, many believed. The thought of a president campaigning "disgusts the people," the New York Times pronounced. Balancing ambition and tradition, Harrison planned an active but cautious campaign. He would take to the stump. He would, eventually, placate the bosses. But he would not "talk politics" when he received the "non-partisan attention" due the president. Harrison planned to make bland statements and avoid "any phrase . . . that was susceptible to a twist."[52] Practical fears of sticking his foot in his mouth shaped Harrison's strategy more than traditional sensibilities did. This kind of calculus inevitably would spawn a campaign emphasizing appearance over substance.

Harrison's notification ceremony illustrated the tone he sought for the campaign. Previous White House ceremonies informing the incumbent of his renomination had been simple and small. This notification, the New York Times reported, was a big "family affair." Harrison danced his baby grandson in the air. Cabinet members took turns passing out lemonade and salad. "It was exactly as they do in Indiana," said a Hoosier witness.[53]

Unfortunately for Harrison, he could not follow his novel campaign plan: By midsummer his wife was dying. "It is hard for me to feel or take much interest in public matters," he told a friend. In mid-September he cancelled his proposed tour; a "decided set-back," all agreed, to his campaign.[54] It would be twenty years before a president stumped for his own reelection.

———————

Like Harrison, Grover Cleveland had two major problems—his personality and his party. "The two candidates were singular persons," Henry Adams noted, "of whom it was the common saying that one of them had no friends; the other, only enemies." Each was, to an extent, running against his own party. Never a friend of the bosses, Cleveland had offended the regulars with his self-righteous independence as a president *and* as a candidate. Both parties, therefore, found themselves "organized for business and . . . afraid they will be successful," one Democrat remarked.[55]

Cleveland knew that this time, to succeed, he had to be more accessible than he had been in 1888. But he would not stump. "I have never been a stump speaker," he said in 1891, "and do not think I should be a success in that role."[56] Concerned with his dignity and bothered by gout, Cleveland hoped to pass the summer fishing off the Massachusetts coast.

But Cleveland's energetic ally, William C. Whitney, disagreed. Whitney wanted to extract Cleveland from Buzzard's Bay. He engineered a public notification ceremony to link Cleveland with the people. By 1892 the notification ceremony was a quaint remainder from the times when candidates did not learn about their nominations for days, and a reminder of the ideal republican relationship between the candidate and his nominators that never quite existed. Since Franklin Pierce's notification in 1852, the ceremony had included the nominee's close friends, neighbors, and party allies. It usually took place at the candidate's home, and featured a brief speech. Whitney remembered the many frustrated Democrats in 1876 unable to "at least look on" at Samuel Tilden's notification. Why not rent Madison Square Garden and invite 15,000 witnesses, Whitney thought. A public ceremony could unite and inspire the party. He reasoned, somewhat tautologically: "The more people who can witness the notification the more popular will the event be."[57]

Predictably, Cleveland was wary, but most Democrats were thrilled. "I am opposed to making the notification too much of a public demonstration but shall defer to your judgment," Cleveland told Whitney. Former Congressman R. J. Vance found it fitting "that the Democratic party, which is the party of the people, should be the first to do away with the exclusive idea."[58]

On the night of July 20, thousands filled Madison Square Garden. It was hot. And it was noisy: Few could hear Cleveland's speech, or that of his running mate, Adlai Stevenson. New York Governor David B. Hill did not appear, underscoring party disunity. But Democrats loved the demonstration. National Chairman William F. Harrity rejoiced that it united the party and "indicated that the candidates were in touch with the people." It also attracted attention, as hundreds of voters read reports of the ceremony "where only one would ordinarily have read them." This innovation, the *Indianapolis News* said, marked a change "in the temper of our institutions. . . . To do this thing openly and amidst the unchecked presence of the multitude smacks of pure democracy."[59]

"Is Mr. Whitney feverish?" horrified Republicans asked. The intimate reserve of notification ceremonies, the *Washington Sentinel* explained, had preserved the republican "propriety and dignity appropriate to the occasion." Now, Democrats paraded candidates for the highest honors in a place devoted to "dog shows" and "horse exhibitions." And, the *Commercial Advertiser* added, in keeping with the spectacle, Cleveland acted like "a hired orator before a district meeting." The venerable Republican journalist Murat Halstead exclaimed: "No Presidential candidate in the course of American history ever before made a speech so unworthy of his dignity" as did Cleveland.[60]

In questioning the Democratic claim that the ceremony proved Cleveland's popularity, Republicans showed that there were various ways to attract popular attention, with varying degrees of legitimacy and significance. Men did not always vote as they shouted. Spectacle was the most base—Cleveland was decried as "Jumbo," the notification ceremony resembled "Coney Island." Today's eye-catching fad could be forgotten tomorrow. More impressive, but still not meaningful or dignified, was celebrity. Cleveland, a former president, was well-known, and bound to attract a crowd. But so, too, were prize-fighters like John L. Sullivan and James J. Corbett. That people cheered a spectacle or greeted a celebrity merely showed the "peculiarity of human curiosity," nothing more. True popularity emerged from a longer, continual relation between the leader and the people. But even popularity could be misleading and temporary. Ultimately, voters had to be influenced "through their intellects rather than through their emotions."[61]

The novel ceremony illustrated the spread of democracy and the changing relations between the nominee and the people. The traditional notification emphasized the candidate's local ties, his debt to the elites who nominated him, his distance from the tumult of campaigning, and his intention to remain at home. Over the years, the notification committee grew to represent the party, in all its diversity. In the public notification, the active candidate embraced the people and the nation. To an extent he circumvented the party and transcended both his home and his intimates. It was no longer Samuel informally anointing Saul, but an ambitious representative man publicly hailed as the people's choice.

The notification also highlighted the tensions surrounding the candidate's emergence into the spotlight. The form of the ceremony was educational—the two running mates read long and substantive speeches. But the impact stemmed from the spectacle. With so few able to hear the speeches, Cleveland's presence, not his oratory, excited the participants.

After this bold opening, Cleveland quickly returned to Buzzard's Bay. The number of visitors increased; many were going to Fall River, where Lizzie Borden had just axed her father and stepmother. Cleveland hoped to carry on an active correspondence while remaining at his summer retreat, while Whitney recommended no letters and much traveling—a candidate had to be deployed carefully. When Cleveland wrote letters, even on innocuous topics, they often appeared in print. He risked becoming "common" in the campaign, Whitney feared. At the same time, by staying at home, Cleveland's personal influence would be lost. Cleveland could "heal lots of sores by patting a fellow on the back & saying ' . . . we are all friends now'"; in public, he could strike dramatic blows.[62] Whitney's inversion of the traditional etiquette anticipated the modern campaign in which personal ties with individual voters took a back seat to public politicking and peacemaking.

Eventually, Cleveland stirred—he knew that passivity could be suicidal. He made peace with the regulars. He visited New York City regularly. However, especially after Mrs. Harrison's illness and death, he refused to stump. Finally, toward the end of the campaign, he appeared at some rallies. Still, his appearances did not rouse voters from their lethargy. Neither candidate inspired much passion, and many found the canvass surprisingly subdued.

Many commentators hailed this listlessness as a sign that "The rawhead-and-bloody-bones style of electioneering has passed away from us for good." Popular politics was declining. The *New York Herald* welcomed this "new era in American politics," in which intelligent and well-read Americans thought for themselves and ignored the "appeals to passion and ignorance" typical of earlier campaigns. Yet as the educational campaign arose, so, too, did an interest in personalities. In 1892 the *North American Review* printed a symposium: "The Man, or The Platform?" Fifty years earlier, the question had been unthinkable; all then agreed that "principles" were more important than "men." But much had changed. Now, party bonds were weaker and, as Senator G. G. Vest of Missouri said, the personality of candidates was becoming more "potent." Congressman William L. Wilson justified this concern with personality in the contemporary rhetoric of substantive politics: "In the education of the masses, the life of the teacher is more catching than his tenets."[63]

Candidates, then, were more prominent, more independent, more active—and more confused. From party workers they received contradictory messages. On September 21, B. L. Wade, an Ohio Democrat, told Grover Cleveland that voters preferred to "quietly come and vote their views." Organization and education were sufficient, Wade said, implying that the candidate was superfluous. Two days later, F. H. Busbee of North Carolina urged Cleveland to visit his state, where the population was especially subject to personal influence. "We do not ask for speeches," Busbee said, "but we do beg for the personal compliment of a visit." "Take my advice," Cleveland sighed to a friend, "and never run for President."[64]

Candidates also learned contradictory lessons. Thrust forward by party travails, nominees learned that their presence *could* spark the campaign. But they also learned about the dangers of stumping. Fearing controversy, let alone blunders, nominees filled an inspirational rather than an educational function. In effect, they switched roles with the parties. As parties devoted themselves to education, candidates began to generate the emotional appeals—a shift which endangered the candidate's traditional stance as the bulwark of republican virtue.

Active candidates perplexed both regulars and reformers. Regulars needed active candidates, but still did not want them. Active candidates presented a competing power base and could cripple a campaign. But the Democratic failures of 1880 and 1888 seemed to indicate that without active candidates parties would lose. Reformers, on the other hand, hoped for an educational millennium hastened by the candidates. When that failed to arrive, the reformers would launch increasingly bitter attacks against the electoral process itself.

VI

The 1896 campaign furthered the revolution in the candidate's role. The Democratic party collapsed and William Jennings Bryan emerged center stage. For the Republicans, William McKinley mounted a vigorous front-porch campaign which, by the new standards, seemed natural, even subdued. Instinctively, as they campaigned, both candidates resorted to emotional appeals rather than substantive ones.

In 1896 Americans feared apocalypse. The Panic of 1893 had depleted America's gold reserves and bankrupted over 15,000 businesses, including 491 banks. The following winter, Jacob Coxey's ragtag "Army" of unemployed had marched on Washington, begging for relief. Down South and out West, desperate farmers turned to the Populist Movement to redistribute money and power away from the Eastern financial interests. As sectional tensions weakened party unity, such Republicans as Henry Cabot Lodge fought to save the country from "a disaster which would be second only to 1861." Similarly, Democrats like E. C. Wall of Wisconsin fought about whether there should be a republic or not: "Whether a few men of wealth shall govern this land or the people." The myriad disagreements were reduced to the Battle of the Standards—whether American currency should continue to be anchored in gold, or expanded and cheapened by being redeemed for silver too. "The whole country has been set to talking about coinage—a matter utterly unfit for public discussion," John Hay moaned.[65]

All recognized that this campaign would be exceptional. The sober appeals of 1888 and 1892 would not work in 1896. The *New York Times* expected that both parties would rely on speakers rather than on "millions of dreary documents." The primary speaker and "naturally the central figure of the campaign" now would be the nominee, Whitelaw Reid of the *Tribune* predicted.[66]

Although the Republican party had some "silverites," the Democrats were hopelessly torn. The intraparty showdown came at the Democrats' Chicago convention. In constructing the platform, the majority advocated the free and unlimited coinage of both silver and gold; the minority upheld the gold standard. The debate climaxed when a thirty-six-year-old, two-term Congressman, not well known beyond the silverite forces and his native Nebraska, spoke. William Jennings Bryan's defense of the common man instantly became a classic: "We will answer their demands for a gold standard by saying to them: You shall not press down upon the brow of labor this crown of thorns, you shall not crucify mankind upon a cross of gold." With those words, Bryan became the

Democratic nominee and, eventually, also the nominee of the National Silver Republicans and the insurgent Populist party. With those words, Bryan came to personify the silver crusade—for better *and* worse. "No man in civil life had succeeded in inspiring so much terror, without taking life," as did Bryan, *The Nation* would conclude.[67]

Overnight, Bryan became a national figure. When he returned home from Chicago, he and his wife Mary recalled, "Our very house had altered its appearance. . . . Streamers of bunting festooned it from porch to eaves; . . . the crowd which filled the front yard overflowed into the house. . . . It was a symbolic atmosphere. The public had invaded our lives."[68]

Bryan's campaign began conventionally enough, with warnings from Democratic National Chairman James K. Jones of telegrams "asking all sorts of question all intended to injure you. . . . Your record and opinions are well known and ought to be sufficient." But Bryan did not have the luxury of following that advice. Many powerful Democrats had abandoned him. "I am a Democrat still, very still," David B. Hill of New York said. Bryan also had few newspapers, little money, and not much organization. But he did have a marvelous voice, immeasurable energy, an enviable ability to sleep almost anywhere, and a Jeffersonian faith that the masses would respond to his appeal. "I make no apology for presenting myself before those who are called upon to vote," he declared, "because they have a right to know where I stand on public questions."[69]

Bryan could serve as "his own committee, his own manager, his own document," the *New York Times* would report. Overwhelmed by correspondence, he inverted the traditional etiquette, as Whitney had done. "As time will not permit a full discussion of political questions in so large a number of private letters," he wrote, "I shall, in order to avoid discrimination, reserve all such discussions for public occasions."[70] The mass audience took precedence over the individual citizen. Bryan's first public occasion was at Madison Square Garden, where he accepted the nomination, as Cleveland had four years before.

Thousands mobbed the Garden on August 12 for what may have been the worst speech in Bryan's career. Somewhat insecure about his claims to the people's minds, if not their hearts, and disturbed by the accusations that he lacked presidential stature, a subdued Bryan *read* the two-hour-long speech. Most listeners thought it a disaster. The *New York Times* cruelly thanked Bryan for tranquilizing the masses. Faced with a kind of Hobson's choice, Bryan had decided to "disappoint" the few thousands in the hall "to reach the hundreds of thousands who would read the speech in print."[71] In fact, his address was no worse than most acceptance speeches, including McKinley's.

For the remainder of the campaign, however, no one would accuse Bryan of being too intellectual. In twenty-seven states, over 18,009 miles, in 600 speeches, averaging 80,000 words each day, the barrel-chested Bryan played on his audience's emotions. The tour was extraordinary, and exhausting. Consuming up to six meals per day, sleeping in snatches, and taking periodic alcohol rubdowns to preserve his strength—though never imbibing—Bryan sang his silvery song. So many people crowded his train that he simply spoke from the rear platform of the last car, and a campaign tradition was born.

Ever conscious of the newspaper audience reading his speeches daily, Bryan varied his tune. At every stop the baggage handler on his train ran back to hear each rendition. In celebrating this "Unprecedented Campaign," the St. Louis Post Dispatch swept aside all questions of dignity: "We have not selected you for a master to obey . . . but as a representative—an advocate before the highest of all earthly tribunals . . . the American people. You cannot be lowered in appealing to them unless you show yourself unworthy of their dignity and greatness."[72] The heretofore pristine republican notion of "dignity" now had a *democratic* meaning. The people and their leaders were peers!

If he intended to attract attention, Bryan fulfilled his goal; his impact on the election, however, was less clear. A record five million Americans heard his booming voice. He received continual press coverage; even hostile newspapers reprinted more of his speeches than those of McKinley. But many editors claimed that mere curiosity attracted the crowds, a charge Bryan resented. There certainly was a difference between curiosity, even popularity, and electoral victory. "I have ridden fifty miles to hear you speak tonight," one Westerner told Bryan. "And, by gum, if I wasn't a Republican I'd vote for you." In later years, Bryan himself would tell this story, having discovered that in his presidential campaigns he was better at attracting crowds than votes.[73]

Bryan's stumping also attracted much abuse. Many opponents stunned by the scale of the tour, forgot all of Bryan's predecessors on the stump and condemned this unheard-of assault on dignity. "He is begging for the Presidency," John Hay said of Bryan, "as a tramp might beg for a pie, with no idea that it is a matter of any more importance." Others, while acknowledging the precedents, deemed the intensity of the effort uniquely undignified. Still others attacked Bryan's "flippant and reckless speeches," his demagoguery. He eschewed "logical argument"—he was, they shuddered, "The Emotional Candidate."[74]

Bryan's approach had an appealing and unprecedented directness. He had none of the traditional intermediaries. He had few organizational trappings, and used none of the traditional justifications for stumping. It was just William Jennings Bryan and the people.

———

William McKinley offered a safe, traditional, solidly Midwestern contrast to the fire-breathing Bryan. A "great politician," according to Senator Charles Dick, McKinley had built his career on the protective tariff crusade. Early in the great currency battle, Speaker of the House Thomas B. Reed observed, "McKinley isn't a silver-bug, McKinley isn't a gold-bug, McKinley is a straddle-bug."[75] Shrewdly, albeit belatedly and halfheartedly, McKinley embraced the gold standard.

Under Mark Hanna's direction the Republicans combined inspiration, organization, and education. Furthering the bureaucratic revolution in politics, different bureaus appealed to different constituencies—Germans, blacks, wheelmen, even women. Hundreds of speakers were deployed; hundreds of millions of pamphlets were distributed. The campaign was systematically organized along "business principles," as Hanna put it. All these efforts required vast sums—no party would spend so much money again until 1920.[76]

The Republican campaign, however, started slowly. Many believed that if the election had been held during the summer, Bryan would have won. Unnerved by Bryan's campaign, many Republicans, including Hanna, urged McKinley to stump. McKinley refused, unwilling to risk his dignity or leave his invalid wife. His 12,000-mile tour to sixteen states in 1894, in anticipation of this campaign, had been sufficient. A tour now, he feared, "would be an acknowledgment of weakness." McKinley also recognized that no matter what he did on the stump, Bryan would upstage him: "If I took a whole train, Bryan would take a sleeper; if I took a sleeper, Bryan would take a chair car; if I took a chair car, he would ride a freight train."[77]

Respectful of the traditional taboo, ever-fearful of being "Burchardized," and impressed by Harrison's 1888 campaign, McKinley decided to greet delegations at his home in Canton. Leery of spontaneity, he and Hanna choreographed the appearances. Delegations were carefully chosen. The speeches of introduction and McKinley's replies were scrutinized.[78]

McKinley captured the nation's attention: "The desire to come to Canton has reached the point of mania," Francis Loomis reported. Eight hundred to one thousand letters a day poured into McKinley's home. From mid-June through November he spoke over 300 times to 750,000 visitors from thirty states. The visitors scavenged souvenirs from all of Canton—bits of twigs, clumps of grass, and parts of the famous front porch itself. But people also showered McKinley with gifts. Loomis found the house "painfully overstocked with campaign curios [ranging] all the way, in size, from ink stands to bath tubs."[79] These gifts attested to the increased centrality of the candidate and the desire of individuals to cement their bond with him. Tributes from followers to leaders signified that the follower belonged to the leader, and simultaneously made the follower feel that the leader belonged to him.

In greeting the visitors, McKinley had a formidable task—to say something without saying nothing, and nothing that he would regret. Whitelaw Reid considered the efforts "the best series of speeches" a candidate ever gave. But many disagreed. The partisan *St. Louis Post Dispatch* claimed that McKinley's oratory was forgettable because "No heart is moved, no brain is inspired, no lips are touched with the sacred fare of eloquence when the battle is for Mammon."[80]

No one, however, questioned the dignity of McKinley's position. His desire to be President was obvious. Mark Hanna wrapped the nominee in the American flag and, according to Republican Theodore Roosevelt, "advertised McKinley as if he were a patent medicine."[81] But this level of interest and activity was becoming routine. That by stumping in place in 1896 McKinley seemed passive and mindful of the taboo indicated how much the revolution in presidential campaigning had accomplished; the attacks on Bryan showed that the revolution was not quite complete.

———

The party crises of the 1880s and 1890s catapulted the candidates into the campaign. Americans experimented with the nominee's role in the campaign, hoping to further the liberal-democratic revolution while quelling the republican rebellion. These experiments transformed the canvass. The front-porch campaign, the public notification ceremony, and the stumping tour linked the candidates with the people and placed them on an equal footing symbolically.

These innovations helped obliterate the ideological and actual distance between the candidate and the people that buttressed the republican taboo. No longer mere icons, candidates now appealed directly to the people, who learned much about each candidate—from his shoe size to his world view. Public communication with large audiences became more important than informal letters to individual voters. The gentleman was no longer speaking to his neighbor privately; rather, the leader was exhorting his followers publicly.

Each innovation appeared to enhance the candidate's educational role. Candidates could now, if they chose, spearhead the educational efforts in print as well as in person. Some reformers hoped that a new taboo on spectacle would replace the traditional ban on all participation. But, in fact, the innovations expanded the nominee's inspirational role. Active nominees appealed to the people's hearts, not their minds.

The taboo itself was partly to blame for this twist. For decades, considerations of pragmatism and propriety restricted a nominee's educational role. When candidates dared to stump, they often relied on mere presence rather than on substantive speeches. Pleasantries were safer. They also fed the modern interest in "personality" in the traditional guise of "character." Increasingly the nominees became the inspirational leaders of the campaign, and the parties the educational leaders. Passive qualities no longer helped candidates—positive qualities and energetic efforts did. The contrast between Hancock the dignified but inarticulate figurehead of 1880 and Bryan the strident orator of 1896 illustrates the change.

Fittingly, two contradictory ways for democratic leaders to address the people flourished side-by-side. The party documents and the lengthy candidate acceptances were substantive appeals that made the interaction an intellectual exchange. The continuing party spectacles and the impassioned candidate appeals made the interaction an emotional one. In the twentieth century, therefore, candidates' actions would threaten the dignity of the campaign, and, in an ironic twist, parties would appear to later generations as bastions of substance and purity. It may not have been what the reformers desired, but it was closer to what the people demanded. Whenever Americans mobbed a candidate at home or on the stump, they ratified this new role.

SIX

The "Old-Fashioned" Campaign Trail

'Tis Tiddy alone that's r-runnin', an' he ain't runnin', he's gallopin.'
—*Finley Peter Dunne's "Mr. Dooley,"* 1900

WILLIAM Jennings Bryan's rear-platform campaign trumpeted the arrival of a new generation of political leaders. The first generation of lingering republicans, most born before 1810, had sought to uphold the Founders' ideals in theory even as they undermined them in practice. They wanted a silent and bland nominee, deferential to party. The second generation of emerging liberal democrats, born between 1810 and 1850, tried to balance the conflicting streams. Weaned on democracy, they accepted a greater role for the candidate but were unsure of just what constituted legitimate participation. The new generation of imperial democrats, born after 1850, grew up in an increasingly united nation committed to an expansive democracy. Many of these men were less wary than their fathers had been of executive power and of powerful executives. Their energetic stumping campaigns became so widespread as to appear old-fashioned overnight.

Theodore Roosevelt was the representative man of this generation. He propelled the presidential campaign and the presidency into the twentieth century. He dominated every campaign from 1900 through 1912; each becoming a referendum on Roosevelt. In each campaign he filled a different role—vice-presidential nominee in 1900, incumbent in 1904, retiring President in 1908, insurgent in 1912. And to each role he gave a new dimension. By 1912, along with William Jennings Bryan, William Howard Taft, Woodrow Wilson, and others, he had recast the

108

campaign.¹ Personality, not party, now counted the most. The nominee shouldered a larger part of the campaign. The candidate's rhetoric shifted. And the candidate's coveted prize, the presidency, expanded.

I

When Theodore Roosevelt charged into national politics liberal democracy had triumphed over republicanism, and the proprieties were being redefined to tolerate an active but substantive campaign. Having been wooed by the candidates in 1896, millions expected even more aggressive courting when Democrat William Jennings Bryan and Republican William McKinley were renominated in 1900. With Bryan at the helm, the Democrats would not disappoint. President McKinley, however, did not consider the front porch of the Executive Mansion a suitable forum for campaigning. No longer a "private citizen," McKinley felt "that the proprieties demand that the President should refrain from making a political canvass in his own behalf." In anticipation of the campaign, McKinley made a two-week, eighty-speech, Midwestern tour in 1899. But some even questioned the propriety of this "electioneering enterprise." McKinley spurned all subsequent invitations.²

McKinley's passivity accentuated his image as an effective and dignified chief executive guiding the nation. The country was prosperous, the dinner pail was full. "There is only one issue in this campaign," McKinley's "boss" Mark Hanna said, "and that is, let well enough alone."³ McKinley's aloofness was proper and practical.

Passivity, once demanded and still expected of incumbents, could now be considered exceptional. Forgetting tradition, the *Ohio State Journal* gushed: "There is no parallel to it in the history of American politics—this faithful, patient adherence to public business in the midst of a campaign."⁴ This twist reflected the new expectations imposed on *all* nominees.

With McKinley at rest, his running mate Theodore Roosevelt became "the central figure of the active campaign," Senator Henry Cabot Lodge exulted. This prominence would advance the prospects of a Roosevelt presidency in 1904. But too much attention could prove dangerous. Lodge feared that his gregarious, emphatic friend would overshadow the staid McKinley and alienate the President's men. Roosevelt perceived the dangers. The rough-riding war hero and popular Governor of New York had been imposed on a noncommittal McKinley and a hostile Mark Hanna, who screamed during the convention: "Don't any of you realize that there's only one life between this madman and the Presidency?"[5]

Roosevelt sought to limit his campaign role and respect the proprieties. He tried to abort plans for Rough Rider marching units and refused to "canvass from the rear end of a railway train, as a . . . second-class Bryan." Such behavior was "undignified," the Harvard-educated governor demurred, preferring the quiet of banquet halls. But Roosevelt was too potent to remain bottled, and could no more resist the lure of the campaign trail than Republicans could resist sending him. "No candidate for Vice President in the whole history of the Republic ever made such a canvass in a national campaign," the New York boss Thomas Platt noted. Then again, "No Theodore Roosevelt was ever before nominated." Roosevelt gave 673 speeches to an estimated three million people, while Bryan delivered 546 speeches to approximately 2.5 million voters. Roosevelt did not just outdo Bryan in volume; he buried him in rhetoric. Roosevelt excoriated Bryan and the Democrats for appealing "to every foul and evil passion of mankind," resorting to "every expedient of mendacity and invective." "'Tis Tiddy alone that's r-running'," a satirist's fictional bartender, the sagacious "Mr. Dooley," observed, "an' he ain't runnin', he's gallopin'."[6]

Roosevelt's rhetoric illustrated his curious code of candidate honor. He insisted on running more as a governor than as a colonel, and demanded discretion in private discourse. But *public* debate should be uninhibited, he believed. And he did not consider vehemence undignified, especially when firing at such a target as Bryan. As the push for educational campaigns cooled American political culture, Roosevelt and Bryan made the nominees the campaign firebrands.

Students of rhetoric would note that Bryan was more of an orator, favoring a refined and formal style, while Roosevelt was more of a "spellbinder," a word first coined in 1888 and connoting a more spasmodic and colloquial approach. Bryan, who relied more heavily on rhetorical appeals, attracted more criticism. The nation wanted "a calm, safe business-like man," not an "orator" and "agitator" for president, Republicans insisted. Summoning atavistic fears of demagoguery and autocracy, they made a virtue out of McKinley's inability to "arouse popular enthusiasm." Popular appeal did not qualify someone for the presidency and could be dangerous. Passive traits, like "being modest and unassuming," deferring to Congress, and not being a "dictator," were still prized. Americans want a quiet doer, not a flamboyant talker for president, the *New York Herald* explained. "Mr. Bryan believes the highest expression of statesmanship is found in rhetoric; Mr. McKinley believes it is in the rumble of wheels and blowing of whistles."[7]

The logic of this position forced some Republicans to condemn Roosevelt's exertions as well. The *Times* accused him of shirking his gubernatorial duties to engage in an unnecessary and "unseemly" frivolity. The whole stumping "business" was "undignified"—witness Bryan—and "obsolete": Why bother traveling when all Americans could be reached by telegraph?[8]

While the cry of impropriety was as old as the republic, the charge of obsolescence was startling. But many of the trappings of the stumping campaign did seem archaic. With more and more Americans receiving their political news at home, the itinerant candidate soliciting the people's favor seemed old-fashioned. The spectacle accompanying the visit—the bands, the revelry, the parades—further tied stumping to the nineteenth century.

Still, most partisans approved of stumping, and strained to prove that their nominee had outshone his rival. They discounted their opponent's efforts and exaggerated their hero's accomplishments. The Democratic *St. Louis Post-Dispatch* claimed that 1.6 million people heard Roosevelt, half of the more objective estimates. On the other hand, Republicans publicized the number of speeches Roosevelt delivered, the miles covered, hands shaken, even railroad systems used. Each statistic was a badge of legitimacy quantifying the candidate's ties with the people.[9]

With these record-breaking efforts, Roosevelt eclipsed McKinley. Roosevelt rejoiced that he was "an important factor" in this "great campaign." The vice-presidency might be a gilded cage, but the campaign had established Roosevelt even more firmly in the public mind. One cartoonist even portrayed him as the tail wagging McKinley the dog. But the President tolerated his running mate's grandstanding; the election results were compensation enough: "I can no longer be called the President of a Party," McKinley proclaimed. "I am the President of the whole people."[10] By allowing Roosevelt to upstage him, McKinley profited from the republican taboo. Standing in his majestic role as President, he let Roosevelt run for Prime Minister.

In 1900, clashing ideologically and personally, Roosevelt and Bryan helped bury a century-old tradition of candidate passivity. They more than doubled the number of speeches made by all previous candidates. Despite Roosevelt's determination not to ape Bryan, the two ran similar campaigns. Relying more on the politics of charisma than of party, both men converted their popularity into political capital. Bryan pioneered the form of the rear-platform campaign; Roosevelt helped legitimize it. To many in 1896, Bryan's novel campaign mirrored his radical politics: Both were rejected. In 1900, with both Bryan and Roosevelt campaigning actively, the lines were blurred. The question of proprieties transcended partisan preference.

This joint accomplishment was a triumph both of temperaments and of a generation. Both Roosevelt and Bryan were charismatic extroverts. Born nearly twenty years after McKinley, they grew up in a political culture increasingly skeptical of parties and cordial to bold democratic leadership.[11] They excited the people, not merely the partisans. They loved to stump. With their popularity, they could circumvent the traditional party leadership, as Bryan did in 1896 and Roosevelt would in 1904. But Bryan was learning, and Roosevelt would soon learn, that strength on the stump does not always translate into success at the polls.

II

The assassination of President McKinley barely six months into his second term brought this new generation to power abruptly. "We are too old to heal of such a wound," the sixty-four-year-old John Hay wrote to Whitelaw Reid ten months later.[12] To further accentuate this changing of the generational guard, Theodore Roosevelt, only forty-three-years-old, became the youngest President in American history.

By 1904, few doubted that Roosevelt would run for a full term and win. Roosevelt loved being President. His politics of exuberance had helped Americans cope with McKinley's murder. All agreed that the campaign would be a referendum on Roosevelt. "Your personality has been the Administration," Secretary of War Elihu Root told the President. Roosevelt's brand of charismatic medicine treated America's turn-of-the-century ills. Americans were no longer isolated in what historian Robert Wiebe has called "island communities." They were aware of new, complex national and international problems. The "plain people" needed a national focal point; Roosevelt offered them his presidency. They worried about the perplexing new challenges; he offered them cures.[13]

The President had long been a national icon, America's "ideal man"; Roosevelt gave this symbolism political bite and relevance: The ideal man accomplished real things. Utilizing the growing communications and transportation systems, the President now went to the people, literally, and they turned to him. To do his job, to advance his policies, the President, in effect, was campaigning constantly. An active campaign would enhance his power and his stature. Yet, after his nomination, Roosevelt was uncharacteristically passive, unusually silent. The traditional taboo against presidential campaigning would neutralize his greatest asset—his personality.

Roosevelt wanted to campaign actively. With what John Morton Blum calls Roosevelt's "characteristic lack of confidence," he feared that he had alienated too many Republican partisans and that his Democratic fans would not vote for him. Even when crowds roared during his 1903 tour preparing for the campaign, Roosevelt worried that the cheers were not "for T.R." but "for the flag." Lacking an independent political organization, he dreaded relying on the hostile Republican regulars.[14]

Roosevelt bulldozed precedent to secure the Republican nomination. Trying to forge his own organization, he chose the officers of the Republican convention and dictated the platform. His secretary, George B. Cortelyou, became Republican National Chairman. The President "threw pretense aside," journalist William Allen White gleefully recalled. "He assumed full responsibility. . . . Of course, over-nice people objected," preferring "the punctilios of hypocrisy which certain other Presidents had felt constrained to use."[15]

Rather than trying to match the bold Roosevelt, the Democrats in 1904 offered a dark horse to woo alienated Republicans. The Democratic Convention in July nominated the obscure Alton B. Parker, Chief Justice of the New York Court of Appeals. Neither a Bryan nor a Roosevelt, this bland nominee suited gold-standard, conservative Democrats. He personified an old-fashioned campaign strategy and was precisely what Roosevelt feared: "I am a very positive man and Parker is a very negative man," the President complained, "and in consequence I both attract supporters and make enemies that he does not in a way that he cannot. He can be painted any color to please any audience; but it is impossible to make two different pictures of any side of my character."[16] This assessment, and Parker's nomination, overlooked the revolution in electoral expectations that rendered this strategy obsolete.

The dynamic President and the sedate Judge clashed. Republicans hailed Roosevelt with their traditional litany of superlatives—honest, just, competent, patriotic, Lincolnesque. They added a host of hosannas that testified to the conception of the presidency Roosevelt pioneered. Words like "vitality," "strength," "energy," and "moral courage" abounded. The Democrats countered, assailing the "spasmodic, erratic,

sensational, spectacular and arbitrary" Roosevelt administration. Their
man, Judge Parker, embodied "reverence," "obedience to the law," and
"judicious conduct." Further contrasting himself with the power-hungry
Roosevelt, Parker promised that he would retire after one term. An old-
fashioned republican, he would be an "independent" executive, freed
from the pressures of courting the public.[17]

As Parker familiarized himself with the issues and rituals of the push
for the presidency, Roosevelt squirmed in his presidential straitjacket.
"There is little active part I can take in the campaign," he mourned, as
he did as much as he could. He released the longest acceptance letter
ever written by a presidential candidate, then retreated into public silence. Privately, he bombarded Cortelyou and others with advice. He
ghostwrote speeches about himself. Somewhat wistfully, he reminded
Cortelyou that, if necessary, he was "perfectly willing . . . to appear in
the campaign myself, either by speech or letter." "I think it depresses
you a little," Senator Lodge wrote the President, "to be the only man in
the country who cannot take part in the campaign for the presidency."[18]

As partial consolation, Roosevelt continued to make headlines
throughout the nation. The President enjoyed a symbiotic relation with
the press. He considered reporters the most influential people in the
country; they made him the most famous man in America. If the presidency was his bully pulpit, the newspapers were his megaphones. His
motto, one favored reporter wrote, was "Let me have free access to the
channels of publicity and I care not who makes my country's laws—or
what the other fellow does."[19] He opened the White House to the press
and to the nation. He always welcomed photographers. His children,
especially the spirited Alice, became public figures.

This focus on White House trivia disturbed staid Republicans.
Whitelaw Reid of the *New York Tribune* tried to "stop the gush of the
correspondents about the Roosevelt children." Reid wanted fewer descriptions of their "pranks. . . . The themes we need to present now are
[for] grown men; and children have little place in a Presidential campaign."[20] But it was hard to tame the junior Roosevelts, their father, or
the press.

In those days of the sensational press, Roosevelt understood that a
public figure had to entertain as well as educate. He pandered to the
growing focus on personality. "Character" was concerned with internal
strength; "personality," with popular appeal. As contemporary manuals
preached, character was good or bad; personality, famous or infamous.[21]
Personal details became entertaining fragments to grab public attention,

rather than miniature tests of character. Publicizing a candidate's shoe size, daily schedule, or family life entertained but did not illuminate—it simply created an illusion of intimacy, of openness, between the nominee and the mass newspaper audience.

Still, Roosevelt suffered through this public silence and private coaching. He felt "as if I were lying still under shell fire just as on the afternoon of the first of July at Santiago. I have continually wished that I could be on the stump myself." He became unduly pessimistic, even desperate, about the outcome, leading to what the crusading editor Oswald G. Villard would call "the most pitiful if not contemptible act" of Roosevelt's career—his surrender to the trusts.[22]

Recognizing the limits of his maneuvering, Roosevelt concluded that only one thing could guarantee victory. This same ingredient, money, had long nourished the Republican party. But Roosevelt's "trust-busting" had alienated the traditional donors. Corporations would not bankroll their self-proclaimed nemesis. Roosevelt and Cortelyou strove to reconquer the corporate hearts: While Cortelyou solicited corporations individually, Roosevelt wooed the Wall Street moguls. He lobbied railroad baron E. H. Harriman for $250,000.[23] This appeal to the fat cats reflected Roosevelt's frustration with his anomalous position. He was more willing to flirt with corruption privately than to repudiate the traditional etiquette publicly.[24]

Ironically, Roosevelt's staid opponent ended up mounting the more energetic campaign. Parker had been "loath to accept the nomination," his wife recalled, and wanted to maintain a judicious silence throughout the campaign. To Parker, the tranquility of the law was more appealing than the hurly-burly of politics. Stumping was "undignified"; "personalities and innuendoes" were irrelevant.[25] He hoped to conduct a front-porch campaign from Rosemount, his Hudson River estate in Esopus, New York, greeting visitors and speaking occasionally.

These expectations were outmoded. Parker began paying what the *New York Sun* called "the penalty of prominence." Photographers invaded Rosemount, dogging the Judge everywhere—even down to the Hudson River for his morning skinny-dip. Parker banned all photographs, except by special permission: "I reserve the right," he said good-naturedly, "to put my hands in my pockets . . . without being everlastingly afraid that I shall be snapped by some fellow with a camera." The *Sun*, while praising his modesty, explained that in this new age of publicity "A candidate can have no privacy and a photographer no mercy. . . . A candidate is public property and estopped from putting up signs of 'No Trespassing'." Here, at least, Parker could learn something from his rival, who "satisfies the affectionate solicitude of his fellow citizens" by accommodating the press.[26]

In claiming the candidates as "public property" the *Sun* boldly invaded the nominee's personal life. In 1840, Democrats and Whigs had squabbled about whether a candidate's "public course and opinions" could be considered "public property"—his private life remained private.[27] In the ensuing six decades the rise of the press, the growing interest in "personality," and the invention of photography blurred the line between public and private. Photographs were harder to control and harder to refute. No one could force General Harrison to speak, but whenever Judge Parker left his house he was at the photographers' mercy. Similarly, when Democrats in 1840 charged that Harrison's "log cabin" actually was a mansion, Whigs could dismiss such "libels"; a photograph of Parker "in the flesh" carried much more weight.

Once he was nominated, Parker also found it difficult to remain silent. The Democratic platform ignored the troublesome currency question. Parker telegraphed the convention, upholding the gold standard and inviting the delegates to nominate someone else if they disapproved. The move thrilled conservative Democrats, who exulted: "The Sphinx became a man."[28]

With his acceptance speech, Parker discovered the perils of frankness. His obscurity made this speech of particular interest. The "public will for the first time hear him speak in his unrestricted role as candidate," the *Globe* said, implying that judges were constrained by dignity but candidates now were not. In his speech, Parker proposed relying on the common law as a "complete legal remedy against monopolies." But the common law did not apply on the federal level. "Every time he opens his mouth, his stock perceptibly drops," one Democrat moaned.[29] The Judge's inexperience in national affairs made him particularly vulnerable. A minor slip became a major gaffe.

At first, Democrats applauded Parker's decision to avoid stumping. The *Norfolk Landmark* voiced the traditional sentiment that the "presidential candidate who stumps in his own behalf cheapens himself." Others treated the practice as old-fashioned and tiresome. The *Boston Advertiser* declared stumping obsolete, because "Votes are made and lost now through the newspapers." "Our politics has been over-talked by candidates," the *Brooklyn Daily Eagle* said. Better to ponder both candidates' "deliberate utterances" without distraction.[30]

The Republicans contended that Parker the "Mummy" was obliged to speak because he had no record. "Haven't the People a Right to

PATRIÆ PATER

Americans have always wanted a president who was one of the people, yet also above the people. George Washington epitomized the traditional republican ideal of a candidate who stood apart from the masses. His dignified silence during the first two presidential campaigns set unrealistic standards for all subsequent nominees. Rembrandt Peale's portrait (*above*) shows the common perception of this ordinary-looking Virginian as a republican demigod. The scene *below* from April 14, 1789, illustrates the ideal in action—the candidate, tucked away on his Virginia farm, is pleasantly surprised to hear from his gentlemanly peers that he has been chosen to lead the republic. (*Library of Congress*)

William Henry Harrison, the "Washington of the West," sought to embody the republican ideal for a generation that was already embracing more democratic notions. This lithograph from the 1840 campaign portrays Harrison as a well-rounded candidate—a soldier, a statesman, a farmer, and, in the lower right-hand corner, a producer of plebian "hard Cider." (*Library of Congress*)

Nominees in the 1840s functioned as icons, political symbols to be bent to the party's will. The Democrats' Polk–Dallas poster from 1844 exemplifies the not-quite-human portrayal of these icons. (*Library of Congress*)

"I ask no favors, and shun no responsibilities."

Z. Taylor

The Zachary Taylor etching on a silk badge from the Whigs' 1848 campaign echoes the republican dictum that one should neither seek nor decline the office. (*Library of Congress*)

MANAGING A CANDIDATE.

In an 1852 cartoon, party managers use the republican taboo on campaigning to stifle a candidate. The scheming politician William Henry Seward hopes he and the Whig party will be carried into the White House by their muted presidential nominee, General Winfield Scott. (*Library of Congress*)

"TAKING THE STUMP" OR STEPHEN IN SEARCH OF HIS MOTHER.

When a candidate did take to the stump to campaign actively, as Democrat Stephen A. Douglas did in 1860, he could expect to be ridiculed for demeaning the office to which he aspired. To maintain the fiction that he respected the republican taboo on campaigning, Douglas claimed to be on his way to visit his mother. (*Library of Congress*)

Although he had clashed with Douglas in the famous debates two years earlier, when nominated in 1860 Abraham Lincoln retreated into republican silence, maintaining a dignified contrast with his active rival. In this Lincoln–Hamlin poster from the Republicans' 1860 campaign, the candidates appear more lifelike than their predecessors of the 1840s, but still seem somewhat remote. (*Library of Congress*)

Like the earlier Democratic long-shot Stephen Douglas, Horace Greeley felt com-pelled to campaign energetically dur-ing his losing effort in 1872. Increasingly, only probable losers took to the stump. (*Smithsonian Institution*)

HORACE GREELEY ON HIS WESTERN TOUR ADDRESSES CITIZENS OF PITTSBURGH IN THE RAIN

By the time the nation celebrated its centennial, candidates were depicted in posters as more fully human. Still, neither Democrat Samuel Tilden (*left*) nor his opponent, Republican Rutherford B. Hayes, felt desperate enough in 1876 to take to the stump—proof that the taboo against mingling with the people endured. (*Library of Congress*) To accommodate increasing democratic demands in the 1880s, candidates began hosting delegations of voters. *Below*, William McKinley accepts the Republican nomination in 1896 from his soon-to-be-famous front porch in Canton, Ohio. (*Smithsonian Institution*)

Although the republican taboo was violated half a dozen times from 1840 to 1896, only after William Jennings Bryan's three election campaigns would traditionalists stop condemning stumping as "unprecedented." As seen here, in 1908, during his third campaign as the Democratic nominee, Bryan campaigned actively (as did his rival William Howard Taft). This marked the first time that both major-party nominees took to the stump. (*Library of Congress*)

Know?" the *New York Tribune* asked. Having introduced the front-porch campaign, Republicans now dismissed it as undemocratic. In one cartoon Uncle Sam asked: "Why don't you come out on the platform, Alton?" And Parker responded: "Thanks, I prefer the front porch." The caption sneered, "IT'S SAFER!"[31]

The front-porch campaign rose and fell swiftly. Originated in 1880 and 1888, perfected and properly named in 1896, by 1904 the tactic was suspect. Subsequently, any challenger who attempted it would be dragged onto the stump.[32] Devised to accommodate the people, the front-porch campaign was now deemed a way of hiding from them. This shift stemmed from the rise of stumping and the transformation of politics from street theatre to newspaper fare. By 1904, Americans were more mobile but less willing to travel for political purposes. Rather than seeking out the nominee, the people wanted the nominee to seek them out.

By September, worries about a narcotized campaign overshadowed the Democrats' concerns with dignity. Parker's scruples were earning him respect, but not votes. Many Democrats now expected their candidate to stump. Party leaders told Parker that "The one thing more than anything else that the people of the country want to see is the candidate." The people did not want lengthy policy speeches, the *Review of Reviews* said. They "wanted to see, hear, and know the man, not the rhetorician or debater."[33] This equation implied that candidates stumped to showcase their personalities rather than address the issues.

Parker escalated his efforts too late. In September he began dividing his time between Esopus and New York City, to be more accessible. His speeches became more vigorous. Eventually he stumped in New York, New Jersey, and Connecticut. When he "awoke to the necessity of impressing upon the country by pen and by tongue the importance of the great issues he represents the people awoke" too, the *St. Louis Post-Dispatch* asserted in November. Finally, it had become "A Real Campaign."[34]

Parker's decision to stump was partly motivated by rumors he heard of Roosevelt's capitulation to the financiers. In late October, Daniel Lamont visited Parker. "Well, you are going to be licked, old fellow," Lamont, who had been Grover Cleveland's aide before working on Wall Street, said. "How do you know?" Parker asked. "Why," Lamont replied, "the large corporations . . . have underwritten Roosevelt's election just as they would underwrite the construction of a railroad to San Francisco."[35] Lamont allowed Parker to publicize the charges, but demanded anonymity.

Parker pounced. If he could not win, he "could at least start a fight against contributions to campaign funds that would insure cleaner elections in [the] future." In late October the Judge attacked Roosevelt's "shameless . . . willingness to make compromise with decency." Democrats chimed in, assailing this selling of the presidency. But the hapless Judge had no proof which he could publicize. His vague accusations came late enough to appear to be a roorback, a last-minute attempt to embarrass the President, but left enough time for a counterattack. Republicans huffed: "Does he [Parker] think the American people will permit their President to be slandered like that?"[36]

Furious, Roosevelt exploited Parker's mistake. "I should feel an intolerable humiliation if I were beaten because infamous charges had been made against me and good people regarded my silence as acquiescence in them," he seethed. Armed with this excuse, Roosevelt made his first political statement since his acceptance. He released a public letter on November 4, explaining that he spoke "lest the silence of self-respect be misunderstood." Roosevelt dismissed Parker's charges and denounced the Democrat's descent into "personalities." Simultaneously, he affirmed his own campaign message: "If elected I shall go into the Presidency unhampered by any pledge . . . save my promise . . . [to] see to it that every man has a square deal, no less and no more."[37]

Roosevelt's superb timing and rhetoric only furthered his electoral victory. The landslide "stunned" him. To his wife he crowed, "My dear, I am no longer an accident!"[38]

Violated but still potent, the republican taboo affected the election in contradictory ways. Roosevelt knew that a president "can't indulge in personalities, and so I have to sit still and abide the result." This restraint offered an anachronistic respite from his hyperkinetic presidency. Having expanded the presidency, he was not about to undermine either it or his own popularity. There was only so much change he could impose on the American people. Even more telling, he suffered the damning accusation of excessive ambition in silence. Immediately after the election, Roosevelt promised to retire in 1909. "I did not wish to say anything that could be construed into a promise offered as a consideration in order to secure votes," he said in explaining his delay.[39] Deference to a supposedly obsolete tradition from a politician as shrewd as Roosevelt reveals that Americans in the early 1900s still hoped to keep their President somewhat insulated from politics.

Still, despite his official silence, Roosevelt dominated the campaign. First his action, then his inaction, highlighted the taboo's growing irrelevance. His precampaign activities, his bold statements, and his looming presence changed the presidential equation. He made it acceptable, almost necessary, for a candidate to be a "very positive man." His landslide affirmed his conception of the presidency as well as his personal appeal. And by doing everything but stumping during the short period from convention to election, he exposed the increasing obsolescence of the taboo.

Similarly, Parker's belated stumping campaign reveals both the extent and the limitations of Roosevelt's impact. To a degree, Roosevelt wrecked Parker's front-porch strategy. To match the President, the challenger had to outdo him. Parker was continually compared to Roosevelt, be it regarding accessibility to photographers or frankness on the issues. Yet Roosevelt was not alone in propelling Parker toward the stump. An intrusive press, the democratic demand for candid nominees, even the stumping campaign itself, all had emerged by 1896, let alone 1900. Democrats did not need the spectre of Theodore Roosevelt to mobilize their nominee—but it helped.

Fittingly, as the twentieth century's first great publicist, Roosevelt's signal contribution to the 1904 campaign was to advertise new behaviors rather than create them. Even while maintaining official silence, Roosevelt legitimized, popularized, and fed public demand for the active nominee. In his strained and clamorous silence Roosevelt deferred to tradition even as he subverted it.

III

Roosevelt's decision to retire in 1909 stemmed from his vision of the presidency and the continuing American fear of power. Although he had been elected only once, he was President for over seven years and did not want to appear to violate George Washington's two-term precedent. The vast power a president wielded obligated him to keep it only for "a limited time," Roosevelt explained. By retiring, Roosevelt distinguished between expanding presidential power and usurping it. He also prevented anyone from wondering whether "self-interest" motivated him. As the "president" of "the plain people," Roosevelt refused "to destroy their ideal of me." Clearly, American politics remained tied to the republican conception of "self-abnegation" as virtuous, and power as dangerous.[40]

By 1908 Roosevelt regretted his promise not to run again. He continued to have "an exceedingly good time" as President. He still had much to accomplish, and remained "the most popular man in the coun-

try," Senator Lodge observed. But his characteristically unequivocal retirement promise immobilized him. He found an heir in his genial and
portly Secretary of War, William Howard Taft. The two had worked
closely together throughout the second term, and Roosevelt exploited
all his patronage powers to force Taft's nomination at the Republican
convention. Taft hated politics. It "is awful to be made afraid of one's
shadow," as most campaigners are, Taft thought. Never having run for
office, he viewed a national election campaign as a "nightmare."[41] Taft's
inexperience guaranteed a continuing campaign role for Roosevelt. It
also made conflict inevitable. Roosevelt wished he could run but could
not; he wanted a vigorous campaign. Taft dreaded running and wished
he need not; he wanted a quiet campaign.

Roosevelt was Taft's greatest asset as well as his greatest liability.
Roosevelt's anointment boosted Taft. It also assured continual carica-
tures of Taft, the Roosevelt lackey. Pundits joked that T.A.F.T. stood for
"Take Advice from Theodore." In directing Taft to limit the "number of
times my name is used" in the acceptance speech, the President said:
"My name should be used only enough thoroughly to convince people
of the identity and continuity of our policies."[42] Therein was the challenge: How to link the two men without allowing the public to forget
Roosevelt or ignore Taft? How to create an illusion belied by both public
and private realities—by Roosevelt's popularity and his continuous
stream of advice? Rather than letting Taft be Taft, Roosevelt tried to
make him into another Roosevelt.

Taft's principles and temperament dictated a quiet, traditional,
front-porch campaign. "I have never thought that it was profitable for a
candidate for office to make fifteen or twenty speeches a day from the
rear of a Pullman car," Taft explained. "It is impossible in any such
speeches to get one's ideas clearly before the public." Initially, Roosevelt
liked this strategy. "I believe you will be elected," the President told Taft
in mid-July, "*if we can keep things as they are*; so be *very* careful to say
nothing, not one sentence, that can be misconstrued." Taft, with his
mentor's blessing, went off to play golf in Virginia. "The beauty of golf
to me," Taft explained, "is that you cannot play if you permit yourself
to think of anything else."[43]

Yet other things soon intruded. The Democratic convention nominated William Jennings Bryan once again. This time, Bryan considered
changing his tactics. In his notification speech he would introduce the
"over-shadowing" question of the campaign, "Shall the People Rule?"
He would then address "the various economic questions, the tariffs, the
trusts, railroads, labor, banking, etc." in a few major speeches. After

that, he would write articles and give interviews. But he would stay at home. "I believe I can do more good in this way than I can by traveling and making brief speeches," he explained.[44]

Bryan, however, could not abide the calm, nor could his devotees. The new expectations he helped to create imprisoned him. By mid-September he was stumping. "I am endeavoring to meet the exactions of the campaign," he told a crowd in Buffalo. As always, these enthusiastic throngs misled Bryan—but then, his curse always was to attract people, not votes. A story, perhaps apocryphal, was told of Bryan's daughter just making a trolley, and panting, "I seem to be the only member of the Bryan family that ever ran for anything and caught it."[45]

The Republicans, too, were misled by Bryan's crowds. By mid-August, Roosevelt decided that "We must put more ginger in the campaign." He led a chorus of demands insisting that Taft take the stump. Republicans were worried, especially out West where the cowboy president was more popular than either his party or his judicious heir. Also, "pilgrims" were not flocking to Taft's front porch in Cincinnati. New legislation banned railway passes, and few were willing to pay two to twenty dollars to see the nominee. He now had to seek the people. The *Washington Times* said: "It is not undignified, it is not improper. The people want to see and listen to the men asking their votes."[46]

All of a sudden, Taft could not abide being "denied participation in an active campaign," or "depending wholly upon necessarily fragmentary reports as to what is going on." *The Nation* welcomed Taft's "change of mind" and his rationale for the tour. "As he travels," Taft "will get a clearer idea than a thousand delegations could give him of the temper of the people and of their desires in the way of political changes."[47]

Bryan gloated over Taft's turnabout. Having branded Taft's initial silence as cowardice, he now sensed Republican "panic." Bryan reminded "the Republican papers" that in 1896 and 1900 "They said it was demagogic to run around the country hunting for votes. Now it is eminently proper since Mr. Taft is going to do it," he smirked. "My greatest sin is to be made a virtue by imitation."[48]

Taft faltered at the start of his 18,000 mile, 400-speech tour. The lawyerly Republican read lengthy manuscripts. He confessed his misgivings: "I am from time to time oppressed with the sense that I am not the man who ought to have been selected."[49] This rhetoric went beyond the formulaic assertions of humility. It was so self-effacing as to undermine confidence. It was not what Theodore Roosevelt had in mind.

The President set out to give his friend, a man of resolute if plodding character, some "personality." Roosevelt peppered Taft with advice, offering a crash course on campaigning and spellbinding: Be bold, be colorful, attack, act, enjoy, "Professor" Roosevelt urged. He told Taft to avoid delicate issues and to fortify his speeches: "Hit them hard, old man!" He asked Taft to stop citing his court decisions, for "People . . . think it is impossible for them to understand and they . . . promptly begin to nod." Treat the "political audience," Roosevelt taught, "as one coming not to see an etching, but a poster." The successful political artist uses "streaks of blue, yellow, and red to catch the eye, and eliminate[s] all fine lines and soft colours." Above all, Roosevelt stressed, "Smile, *always*"—years before such advice made Dale Carnegie famous.[50]

Taft eventually mastered these techniques. The skills were essential to the powerful "rhetorical" presidency Roosevelt had fashioned. Taft began to greet his audiences more confidently. "It is a great pleasure for me to speak," he declared in Newark. He also spoke more forcefully and, following the Roosevelt method, more colorfully. He equated Bryan's plan to use tariffs to destroy trusts with "burning down the house, as the Chinaman did, to get roast pig." Roosevelt boasted that his pupil was "at last catching the attention of the crowd."[51]

The increasingly bold candidate conformed to the Republicans' rhetorical specifications. Although Judge Taft was temperamentally more like Judge Parker, Republicans packaged him as the next President Roosevelt. They praised his "literally dauntless courage" and his "limitless capacity for hard work." They balanced all references to Taft's judicial experience with affirmations of his zeal. Taft appeared as "a combative altruist" ready to complete Roosevelt's mission.[52]

Republicans also cast Taft as "The Candidate of the People and for the People." Traditional campaign literature portrayed the nominee as a humble tribune and praised his common touch. The nascent art of public relations taught that these qualities had to be dramatized, not just described. Three years after the founding of the nation's first public relations firm, Parker & Lee, and under constant scrutiny by the press, the traveling candidate's campaign became a protracted demonstration of these attributes.

In amusing, humanizing, and often trivializing publicity, the Republican National Committee billed Taft as "the best natured" presidential candidate "of them all." He "knows how to hold a baby." In one town, Taft continued speaking in the rain, saying "I can stand it if you can."[53] The fact that Taft's ample proportions had to be squeezed into this Rooseveltian mold testified to the growing entertainment value of the candidate's personality.

This trivialization could be nonpartisan as well: As the candidate became a popular product, his likeness could be harnessed for commercial ventures. The Goldman Brothers ran an advertisement in the *St. Louis Post–Dispatch* with portraits of Bryan and Taft. Headlined "What the Two 'Bills' Say," the ad bragged that "Moore's Air Tight Heater Is the Stove that's elected 'President' by the 'People' year in and year out."[54] "Dignity" was rapidly becoming a mere partisan brickbat.

Despite Taft's success on the stump, many Republicans still hoped that Roosevelt would "stir things up." "Give us Roosevelt," Western Republicans pleaded. "It is useless to try to fetter him," a Republican newspaper observed. Roosevelt's opportunity to plunge into public battle came in mid-September, when the "yellow journalist" William Randolph Hearst accused Standard Oil of bribing Republican Senator Joseph B. Foraker, Democratic National Committee Treasurer C. N. Haskell, and others. Long hostile to Foraker, and anxious to "put a little vim into the campaign," the President repudiated Foraker and attacked Bryan for not firing Haskell. This prompted a clash between Bryan and Roosevelt in public letters and interviews. "The American people are disgusted by the unseemly exhibition of the President of the United States and a Presidential candidate quarrelling like angry fishwives," the *New York Herald* exclaimed.[55]

One reporter, H. L. West, doubted that voters resented this unprecedented move. A president should "make known his views, especially if he can present them in such forceful manner as to win votes for his party," he argued, accepting the new presidential protocols. The President was not supposed to be some silent "Buddha." The "majority of people want a flesh-and-blood President. They want him dignified . . . but the divinity that doth hedge a king has no place in the White House."[56]

West stumbled on a growing dilemma for the modern presidency. Traditional American ideas of presidential dignity and passivity combined notions of kingly "divinity" with republican simplicity. The growth of the office required a more majestic protocol; the days of informal strolls and talks with citizens were numbered. But as the flesh-and-blood leader of the plain people, a president needed a democratic protocol as well. Complaints about affronts to dignity multiplied while definitions of dignity blurred.

Though successful, Roosevelt's actions and instruction during the campaign unsettled both pupil *and* teacher: Roosevelt disliked shadow-boxing behind Taft. Mrs. Taft, among others, resented Roosevelt's condescension. For Taft, the campaign was "one of the most uncomfortable four months of my life." Still, Taft's victory temporarily erased these frustrations. Roosevelt exulted "We have beaten them to a frazzle." Taft told his mentor, "It is your administration that the victory approves."[57] During the campaign, the struggle between Taft's need for Roosevelt and his desire for independence proved merely inconvenient. It sowed, however, the deeper conflict that in 1912 shattered their friendship and the Republican party.

———

The 1908 campaign marked a milestone in campaign history: For the first time, both major party candidates stumped actively and openly. But most contemporaries—and subsequent historians—ignored this watershed, the "oversight" illustrating the wide acceptance that stumping enjoyed after a decade of Bryan and Roosevelt. This neglect also epitomized the degeneration of the taboo. Its demise was not only unmourned but unnoticed. The debate about stumping no longer centered on tradition and proprieties but on tactics and partisanship. Anxious candidates no longer had to pretend they were disinterested. In fact, Taft had to prove that he really wanted the presidency by working for it. Passivity was dangerous. In America's consumer culture, ambition was no longer a dirty word, and was in fact required. Neither Taft nor Bryan wanted to stump in 1908—but they had no choice.

To win in the twentieth century, candidates had to run. At the Republican convention, a Republican rival unintentionally paid tribute to Roosevelt's impact on the campaign and the presidency. Henry S. Boutell of Illinois nominated the leader of the Republican Old Guard, House Speaker Joseph Cannon, for President against Taft. In his speech, Boutell articulated the criteria for the modern presidency in which charismatic men dominated parties. "The head of our ticket is the leader of our party," Boutell declared. "He should, therefore, be a man who will give the ticket its greatest possible strength and character. His personality should be an inspiration in every congressional district; his name a talisman in every election precinct; his public record expressive of the glorious history of our party."[58]

A campaign of personalities had become not only acceptable but respectable. When Bryan's running mate, John W. Kern, charged the Republicans with "Trying to make issues of men," the Republican National Committee asked: "Why not? Are the Bryanites afraid 'to make issues of men'?" More and more observers, Democrats and Republicans, mythical bartenders and eminent scholars, agreed. "Th' issues are clearly marked. There ar're none," Finley Peter Dunne's Mr. Dooley reported in 1904. The campaign "is largely a mere question of candidates," political scientist Moissei Ostrogorski said in 1908.[59]

Yet as the candidate became more active, public skepticism about both the candidate and the campaign grew—in 1908, observers were still proclaiming the triumph of the educational campaign. The *National Magazine* made the by-now-routine announcement hailing "the inauguration of a new era in political campaigning." Hereafter, the campaign would be brought "quietly and directly to the homes of the people," where "they can think clearly." Democratic officials boasted that 1908 marked "the Dullest Campaign in [a] Quarter Century." Echoing James S. Clarkson's 1880s rhetoric, one official explained: "With less red fire and less music," the voters would learn that "a National campaign is not a circus performance . . . but serious business involving education of the voters . . . and a thorough discussion of the issues."[60]

The aspirations for a campaign of substance had been reduced to a ritualistic heralding of a day that would never come. The virtuous campaign of issues was pitted against the pedestrian campaign of personalities. Still hoping for a dignified campaign, many Americans became increasingly disillusioned. Objecting in 1908 that all the campaign speeches were "ignoble in substance and petty in spirit," the *New York Times* sniffed: "The speakers of the campaign are wrong if they suppose the people no longer care for serious political debate." In 1904 the *St. Louis Post-Dispatch* had observed: "There is a loud complaint against quadrennial elections."[61]

IV

In 1912 the grumbling about "the intolerable burdens of [the] 'Presidential year'" continued, *The Nation* reported.[62] Expectations remained unrealistic and contradictory. The people demanded excitement and substance; the politicians, involvement and caution. To many, the triangular battle among Woodrow Wilson, William Howard Taft, and Theodore Roosevelt was undignified, excessively personal, disruptive, and destructive. The chorus of complaints grew ever louder.

Taft proved not to be the president Roosevelt wanted. In 1910, when Roosevelt returned from hunting in Africa and hobnobbing in Europe, the friendship crumbled. Roosevelt claimed that Taft had sold out to the Republican Old Guard. The Republican party was deciding, Roosevelt believed, whether to be "the party of the plain people" or "the party of privilege."[63] He embraced Progressive reforms expanding popular power, including the direct primary to nominate presidential candidates.

Fed up with the manipulation of nominations by the party bosses, many people felt shut out from their own government. The feelings of impotence that impelled the Populist and Progressive movements also spawned the direct primary crusade. "Go back to the first principles of democracy; go back to the people," the Wisconsin Progressive Robert M. La Follette insisted in 1897. Although some thinkers like Arthur George Sedgwick warned that trusting to popular election was "the democratic mistake," others like Richard S. Child said it was "lese majeste to allege that there are any limitations to the people in either morals or learning."[64]

The direct primaries offered the one opportunity for Roosevelt to seize the Republican party from his protégé. By 1912 a dozen states allowed voters to choose delegates to the national convention directly. For the first time in American history, a popular preconvention campaign was possible. Unconsciously echoing Bryan, Roosevelt proclaimed: The major issue is "the right of the people to rule."[65]

Taft himself was probably the last person in America to believe that Roosevelt would run against him, observers half-joked. The President found it "hard, very hard . . . to see a devoted friendship going to pieces like a rope of sand." In February 1912, borrowing a phrase cowboys used when they were ready to fight, Roosevelt announced "My hat is in the ring."[66]

Roosevelt ripped into Taft and the Republican Old Guard, the defenders of "privilege and injustice." The fury of these attacks pulled Taft into the campaign. Ironically, the languid Taft now became the first President to stump for his own renomination. Throughout the spring, the two friends battled in the Republican primaries. Bitter, they fought like schoolboys. "Puzzlewit," "fathead," "egotist," "demagogue," they called each other. Taft felt "humiliated" that he was "the first one that has had to depart from the tradition that keeps the President at home during political controversies." But Roosevelt had given him no choice. "I represent a safe and saner view of our government and its Constitution than does Theodore Roosevelt," Taft said.[67]

Arbiters of taste in the nation were appalled. This "spectacle . . . should bring a blush of shame to the cheek of every American," the New York Times declared in April. Some critics attributed this violation of presidential dignity to Roosevelt's demagoguery, but most blamed the growth of candidate participation in general, and the direct primary in particular. Intense candidate involvement degraded the nominee, the presidency, and the process. Presidential aspirants used to await the "action of the convention," and then made a few brief appeals. "That was a rational, a seemly procedure," the *Times* believed. Thanks to the primaries, Americans were no longer a people, but a mob." "Are party wreckers more desirable than party leaders—'bosses'?" the *Washington Post* asked. "Has not glorified populism as written into the election laws brought about conditions a hundredfold worse than what it was meant to correct?"[68]

Some observers, acknowledging the flaws, nevertheless hailed Roosevelt, "the national evangelist of direct primaries." This is a fight, the *Philadelphia American* announced, "to give the people the real power of electing their president by giving them the real power to select the party candidate. . . . The last barrier to popular government [is] being swept away."[69] In the struggle between democracy and republicanism democracy was gaining, but at the cost of the majesty and dignity of the presidency.

Eventually, Roosevelt won Republican hearts but Taft won the Republican nomination. The party "steamroller" of bosses and office-holders renominated the incumbent at Chicago. Roosevelt stormed out. But Taft's victory was hollow: He lost his best friend, and he lost his public. In July he complained to his wife: "Sometimes I might as well give up so far as being a candidate is concerned. There are so many people in the country who don't like me . . . [w]ithout knowing much about me."[70]

Satisfied with stopping Roosevelt's bid for the Republican nomination and determined to maintain some dignity, Taft resigned himself to a fall defeat. His brother, Charles Taft, believed that "The people are averse to the spectacle of a President going out on the hustings, and . . . Mr. Taft can get more votes by preserving the dignity of his great office." Taft eagerly agreed. "I have no part to play but that of the conservative," he declared. He would no longer try to run a "P. T. Barnum show." "I have been told that I ought to do this, ought to do that . . . that I do not keep myself in the headlines," Taft said. "I know it, but I can't do it. I couldn't if I would and I wouldn't if I could."[71]

Taft's appeals stressed this modesty, dignity, solidity, and safety. "For thirty years Mr. Taft has been active in public life," a broadside declared. "But with him *public life* and *publicity* have meant two entirely different things. . . . He hasn't any desire to see his name 'on the front page'. . . . Mr. Taft prefers to let the things he does stand on their own merits." He cherishes "some 'old-fashioned ideas' about the dignity of his office."[72] Taft was positioned as the authentic republican. The new art of "publicity" replaced oratory as the democratic seductress, wooing with idle boasts rather than real achievements.

The Democratic candidate, Governor Woodrow Wilson of New Jersey, also trusted these "old-fashioned" proprieties. He yearned to follow Taft's example. Wilson believed that "People do look for dignity in high office" and disliked "extended stumping tours." He would discuss "principles and not personalities" calmly and deliberately. "Why, every man concerned in this great contest is a pygmy as compared with the issues," he exclaimed. "What are men as compared with the standards of righteousness?"[73]

Candidates invoked "dignity" regularly yet inconsistently. The term was partly a cudgel, an ancient weapon from the republican arsenal to attack active candidates. To Taft, Roosevelt's disregard for dignity showed contempt for the masses; to Roosevelt, Taft's obsession with dignity showed a fear of them. But the concern also represented a desire for simpler times and clearer standards. Humanizing the candidate often humiliated him and destroyed illusions. "Th' less ye see iv a man . . . th' more ye think he's better or worse thin the rest iv us," Mr. Dooley explained.[74] As Roosevelt drew Wilson onto the stump, no one quite knew just what was dignified and what was not.

Wilson initially refused to mount a rear-platform campaign. "I don't mind talking," he explained to his friend Mary Allen Hulbert, "but I do mind being dragged over half a continent." His message could be telegraphed across the nation; he saw no need to play the celebrity in hamlet after hamlet, day after day. He even refused interview requests "because of . . . my desire to center all I have to say upon my speeches."[75]

But like Taft in 1908 and Parker in 1904, Wilson was compelled to stump. The college professor feared the Rough Rider, especially in this personality-obsessed polity. To the voters, Theodore Roosevelt "is a real, vivid person, whom they have seen and shouted themselves hoarse over and voted for, millions strong," Wilson fretted. "I am a vague conjectural personality, more made up of opinions and academic prepossession than of human traits and red corpuscles." No one would ever name a cuddly children's toy after Woodrow.[76]

The campaign overwhelmed Wilson. The expectations surrounding a modern president "terrified" him. One of his daughters, a social worker in Philadelphia, met a man who said that a Wilson victory would mean cheaper bread. "Think of the responsibility such expectation creates," Wilson sighed. "I can't reduce the price of bread."[77]

Wilson was also overwhelmed by the demands of the press. On his way to Denver, and yet another session with reporters, he asked "Do I have to go through that again?" The press, he learned, invaded a candidate's privacy and tried to impose its own agenda. Wilson was naive and stuffy in dealing with his "keepers." He resisted the notion that everything he and his family did and said was "news." Fed up, Wilson escaped occasionally to a private club in New York. "It's odd to have to run away from home for privacy," he told Mrs. Hulbert.[78]

The press, however, could cripple a campaign, Wilson learned. When asked about the volume of mail pouring into his home, Wilson said he felt like the frog that fell into the well: "Every time he jumped up one foot he fell back two." The next day one newspaper headlined: "WILSON FEELS LIKE A FROG." Wilson learned to mind his metaphors, stifle his protests, and rely on his charming aide, Joseph Tumulty, to compensate for his own frigidity.[79]

By succumbing to his advisers and agreeing to stump throughout the country, Wilson conceded that Americans wanted to see their candidates and that personalities mattered in the campaign. But he refused to pander. Even at brief stops he tried to instruct the public. He insisted on speaking extemporaneously, even though that hindered the distribution of his speeches by the Associated Press. "I cannot make speeches to a stenographer," he sniffed. He refused to pose plowing a field or milking a cow. When asked one morning to summarize a speech he would give later in the day because the baseball championship would monopolize all the afternoon wires, Wilson balked. "I have a feeling that the question of who is to be President is equally as important as who wins the world's series," he said.[80] Wilson viewed politics as education, not entertainment.

Wilson also refused to attack Taft. When their paths crossed in Boston, Wilson paid a courtesy call on the President, a rare moment when two competing nominees met during a campaign. Colonel George Harvey of *Harper's Weekly* thanked Wilson for his efforts "to elevate the tone of the campaign."[81]

Wilson exploited his discomfort on the stump—with more agility than Taft had in 1908. "It is a great pleasure for me to . . . greet . . . my fellow countrymen in this way," Wilson said in Union City, Indiana, "because I know they want to see what I look like, at least; not for the sake of my beauty, but for the sake of forming their own opinion as to what sort of chap I seem to be. But I would a great deal rather they would see the inside of my head than the outside of it."[82] These verbal acrobatics humanized Wilson to his audiences and proved that candidates could keep their dignity on the stump.

In searching for the proper tone when speaking to the public and the press, Wilson stumbled onto a conundrum. If campaigns were, as the *St. Louis Post-Dispatch* suggested, "summer school[s] of politics," were candidates the teachers or the pupils? In the nineteenth century, candidates were neither. Parties taught the voters while the candidates, to one degree or another, sat on the sides. Now candidates were considered the keynoters of the campaign and were condemned if their appeals were not sufficiently sublime. But they were also considered the peers, even the servants, of the voters. "Campaigns," the *New York Times* said, "are for the purpose of learning what voters think, and candidates rather spread their sails to the favoring breeze than impel themselves by their own individual bellows."[83] The contradictory demands of American democracy imposed unrealistic expectations on the candidates, who were supposed to lead enough so as to elevate the people, but not so much as to go beyond them.

Wilson also campaigned against campaigning even as he campaigned: "I have tried discussing the big questions of this campaign from the rear end of a train," Wilson declared in Indiana. "It can't be done. They are too big. . . . By the time you get started and begin to explain yourself the train moves off." Rather than highhandedly stopping there, he ended graciously: "I would a great deal rather make your acquaintance than leave a compound fracture of an idea behind me."[84]

Wilson's attacks on campaigning cheered those who despaired for the republic. Many agreed with him that "It is folly to try to speak to millions" and that the only purpose of these trips was "to let the people see the candidates." A campaign should not be an endurance test, one Democratic newspaper wrote. The tours were a "foolish . . . waste of energy." Better for well-rested candidates to think up new ideas and "in moderately short form entrust them to the newspapers to give to their readers."[85]

Gradually the people warmed to Wilson. "When an old fellow . . . slapped me on the back and shouted: 'Doc, you're all right; give it to 'em,'" Wilson recalled, he knew he had "'arrived' in politics." Noting that the professor was being called "Woody," "Kid," and "Doc," the *New York Times* declared: "The ice is broken."[86] This mounting enthusiasm illustrated what stumping could accomplish.

As Wilson became more comfortable on the stump, and more popular, the nominee of the fledgling Progressive party, Theodore Roosevelt, became more desperate. "Roosevelt has been outclassed," a newspaper claimed, "in his own specialty . . . of practical politics." The fall campaign had started magnificently for Roosevelt. The walkout from the

Republican party and the triumphant Progressive party convention exhilarated him. For the first time since 1900 he could carry the campaign publicly on his shoulders. And, unlike as in 1900, he would be at the helm. But Roosevelt's freedom from political constraints reflected his weakness, not his strength. Relying on a makeshift personal organization, shorn of his presidential and party powers, cut off from mainstream funds, Roosevelt had only his charisma. He understood what Bryan had learned repeatedly, that popularity was not necessarily popular support. At the voting booth, party loyalty remained more potent than star power. During a frenzied rally before the New Jersey primary in June, Roosevelt had knowingly said, "If you only vote as you shout, the thing is done."[87] Throughout the fall of 1912 it became clear that Roosevelt had the crowds but Wilson had the votes.

Roosevelt responded in the worst possible way. He became surly, dismissing "Professor Wilson" as a "schoolteacher" advocating "outworn academic doctrine[s]."[88] As the weeks dragged on and defeat loomed, Roosevelt also became weary and bored—fatal for a crusader. By October the bull moose had slowed. He was hoarse. He rambled.

Then, on October 14, Roosevelt's luck changed—for better *and* worse: He was shot in Milwaukee. His characteristic decision to deliver his speech with a bullet in his chest temporarily halted his campaign's slide. Roosevelt was amused that to "offset" the disproportionate denunciations of the previous nine months, "I have been praised in connection with the shooting with quite as extravagant a disregard of my deserts." Wilson suspended his stumping tour until Roosevelt recovered.[89]

By the time Roosevelt and Wilson held their final rallies, their fates were sealed. The crowds greeting Roosevelt were fanatic but fatalistic, while Wilson was able to ignite "a regular old-fashioned political meeting of 16,000 persons . . . into a wild, waving, cheering, yelling, roaring, stamping mob of enthusiasts," the *New York Times* reported. The cheers lasted for over an hour. The professor had learned how to stump. "We won in 1912," William G. McAdoo, vice-chairman of the Democratic National Committee and Wilson's son-in-law, recalled, "because the personality of Woodrow Wilson had captured the country."[90]

Woodrow Wilson's emergence as an active candidate exemplified the transformation of the presidential nominee. At first aloof and obsessed with dignity, he learned how to appeal to the people. Like his predecessors, he juggled modern demands with traditional sensibilities, democratic ideals with republican concerns. But, by Wilson's day, focusing on "men" spotlighted superficial personality tidbits rather than inherent character traits; and talking about popular "issues" was virtuous, not demagogic. Committed to discussing the issues but unwilling to commit political suicide, Wilson mastered the politics of personality.

V

For all his triumphs, Theodore Roosevelt's four national campaigns were exercises in frustration. In 1900 he discovered the joys of stumping, but he had to submit to McKinley's authority. As a result, he felt exploited. In 1904 he commanded but could not stump. He therefore worried about an outcome he never should have doubted. In 1908 his role was limited for he could act only through Taft. This frustration spawned the tragic break between the two friends. And in 1912 Roosevelt enjoyed unlimited authority and few constraints—but no chance of victory.

That Roosevelt's running mates and opponents shared this frustration offered little solace. Bryan suffered perennial defeat. The unsuccessful Parker was lost amid the changing campaign roles. When Taft won, his bold masquerade depressed him; when he lost, hewing to his anachronistic ways offered minimal comfort. The victorious Wilson, like Taft in 1908, found himself playing a game he loathed. All were caught between traditional sensibilities and modern demands.

"'Twud be inth'restin,' . . . if th' fathers iv th' counthry cud come back an' see what has happened while they've been away," Mr. Dooley thought. "In times past whin ye voted f'r prisidint ye didn't vote f'r a man. Ye voted f'r a kind iv a statue that ye'd put up in ye'er own mind on a marble pidistal. Ye nivir heerd iv George Wash'nton goin' around th' counthry distrributin' five cint see-gars." Twentieth-century Americans were conscious of the distance they had traveled from the teachings of the Founders. While they celebrated the democratization they also worried about a decline. Even as they brought the candidate closer to the people, they feared degrading him. Their commitment to liberal democracy was balanced by their concern for republicanism. The campaign was indeed a "A Test of the Nation"—and Americans continued to fear failure.[91]

SEVEN

Reluctant Runners,
1916–1928

The Man with the Best Story Wins
—*Headline in* The Independent, *May 1920*

"WE are unsettled to the very roots of our being. . . . All of us are immigrants spiritually" in the twentieth-century world, the journalist and philosopher Walter Lippmann observed in 1914. The emerging middle-class, consumption-oriented society was bureaucratic, technological, complex, and impersonal. "There are no precedents to guide us, no wisdom that wasn't made for a simpler age," Lippmann mourned. In all endeavors, from science to statecraft, Americans had to devise sophisticated new methods to "master" these novel conditions.[1]

This forbidding modern culture demanded a new kind of presidential campaign. The energetic campaigning of William Jennings Bryan and Theodore Roosevelt had subverted the traditional taboo and heralded these changes. Increasingly, bold innovations in campaigning were not only acceptable but necessary. Vying for attention with the various colorful diversions of the emerging leisure society, candidates had to work hard to showcase their personalities. To harness modern culture's new technologies and rational techniques, they turned to experts, for whom "mastery" entailed manipulating the voters systematically. Still, many candidates remained unwilling to pursue the presidency so intensively. The distaste for stumping lingered. Also, many of these attempts to rationalize the campaign, to influence the voters scientifically, would appear illegitimate, threats to individual autonomy. These concerns

133

helped keep alive traditional republican concerns—though in somewhat different forms.

I

Woodrow Wilson was well cast as America's usher into the modern world. Bespectacled, intense, yet eminently rational, the professorial President embodied the contemporary belief that reason could subdue anything, even American politics. Building on Theodore Roosevelt's legacy and his own academic theorizing, Wilson fashioned an activist presidency. As national networks in business grew, the federal government and its chief executive officer had to keep pace. Wilson forged a strong and modern presidency for a strong and modern nation. Like a good king, he dominated the nation's consciousness; like an effective prime minister, he shepherded through Congress a flock of Progressive reforms in banking, trade, and agriculture.

Rhetoric became a central tool in his approach. Believing that the President had the "only national voice" in the country, Wilson spoke to the people through the press, which ballooned to almost 2,500 newspapers averaging twenty-four pages per issue during his administration. The annual per capita consumption of newsprint exceeded twenty-five pounds, more than quadruple the rate in 1890. These increases swelled journalists' appetite for news: Wilson obliged them with formal speeches and informal press conferences.[2] Such direct lines of communication bypassed the party. In fact, the invigorated presidency, focusing on this singular representative who transcended politics, made parties appear to be parochial, crooked and somewhat marginal players in the presidential game.

The modern presidency had an international dimension, too. As Wilson contemplated his second-term prospects, the entire country looked anxiously overseas. Since the outbreak in 1914 of what would be known subsequently as World War I, most Americans had hoped to avoid Europe's mess; they cheered the President's immediate proclamation of neutrality. Although by 1916 Wilson had in fact inched toward "preparedness," he still hoped to run for reelection as the apostle of peace.

Preoccupied, Wilson postponed the ceremony notifying him of his nomination until Congress adjourned. He was willing to enact legislation to shore up Progressive support; he would continue to make speeches and hold press conferences; he would even make nonpartisan forays to such historic sites as Abraham Lincoln's birthplace. But he would not stump. "Bad taste is always bad judgment," Wilson insisted, claiming that "No candidate for President has ever been elected who went upon the stump."[3]

It was more than a matter of "dignity"; Wilson believed the President was too busy to campaign. "There's a lot of work going on that I have altogether too little time to attend to," he complained. Besides, he added, his record of four years should speak for itself—a President should "appoint counsel to address the jury."[4] Herein, Wilson offered a new rationale for presidential passivity: The President was too busy saving the world and reforming the nation to campaign actively.

Still, in the twelve years since Theodore Roosevelt had run from the White House, the traditional sensibilities had weakened. Wilson realized that some Democrats might mistake his humility for disinterest. When he refused to campaign while running a "nonpartisan errand," Wilson felt compelled to assure the state chairman that "My whole heart is in the campaign."[5]

Wilson recognized that attempting to remain presidential might cause "complications. . . . Inferences can be drawn, you know." Often, reporters missed his subtle distinctions. When he proclaimed that "Boasting of the record does not go very well with me," one reporter responded: "You did it very well in the acceptance speech." That was not boasting, Wilson insisted; "I think that was simply an exposition."[6]

Unwilling to sully himself with campaigning, Wilson relegated partisan tasks to lieutenants like Joseph Tumulty and Colonel Edward M. House. These aides mastered nineteenth-century techniques while experimenting with twentieth-century ones. The wise Colonel stressed the old-fashioned but still "essential element in success"—organization. "We must run . . . for Justice of the Peace and not for President," House explained; "We need not consider the disposition of 16 or 17 million voters, but the disposition of the voters in individual precincts."[7]

Approaching the voters as any modern businessman would—through mass advertising—House turned to an expert. Once, politicians like House were jacks-of-all-trades; now, they farmed out tasks to specialists in public relations and advertising. By 1916, advertising was well on its way to enveloping America in slogans and images. It had become professionalized, specialized, and even respectable—to a degree. The Democrats' director of publicity, Robert W. Woolley, and other admen recognized that the new leisure-oriented society required a different kind of campaign. Politics once commanded attention as the great American spectator sport; now, it had to compete with baseball, vaudeville, and other diversions.[8] Candidates would have to become entertaining, exposing their personalities and adorning their campaigns with the ephemera of modern popular culture.

In keeping with the latest commercial techniques, the Democratic campaign featured celebrity endorsements, moving-picture films, and colorful advertisements—though Wilson drew the line at "color" stories and photographs chronicling his family life. Woolley pictured Wilson as America's guardian angel of peace and prosperity. Thousands of billboards depicted, as Woolley described it, "the war demon held in leash, factories running in full blast, a contented workman with his dinner pail returning to a happy wife and two children who stand greeting him, the dome of the Capitol at Washington in the background, and above it, surrounded by golden clouds, an excellent picture of the President." Below the picture, in big white letters on a dark blue background, was the legend: "HE HAS PROTECTED ME AND MINE." Other posters simply announced: "HE KEPT US OUT OF WAR."[9]

Woolley's posters spoke directly and eloquently to a nation rapidly developing what poet Vachel Lindsay called a "hieroglyphic" civilization. To a people leery of oratory but still relatively innocent of pictorial deceit, the posters telegraphed Woodrow Wilson's personal commitment to avoiding war. The posters also cast the President as the nation's larger-than-life protector, beaming down upon Americans wherever they turned. It seemed to journalist Talcott Williams and others that "There was no fence or wall so high priced and no highway or railroad so sequestered" that it lacked Wilson's reassuring visage.[10]

As Wilson posed from his presidential perch, the divided Republicans nominated someone detached from their partisan squabbles, Justice Charles Evans Hughes. Formerly a Progressive Governor of New York, Hughes had repeatedly disavowed presidential aspirations since joining the Supreme Court in 1910. In 1912 the Justice, a stern figure with an Old Testament mien, had declared that "A man on the Supreme Bench who would run for public office is neither fit for the office he holds nor for the one to which he aspires." Many observers agreed, fearing the nomination of a sitting Justice would "prostitut[e] . . . our tribunal of last resort."[11] What could prevent ambitious justices from writing opinions appealing to the people and not the law? By 1916 the sanctity of the Court was clearly more precious than that of the White House. Gone were the days when the presidency was considered above politics; only the Supreme Court remained an apolitical preserve.

To compensate for this assault on the Court, Republicans praised Hughes in traditional terms as the people's reluctant but willing servant.

Colonel George Harvey of the *North American Review* rejoiced that "Never since this Republic demanded that George Washington become its first President has there appeared so striking an instance of the Office seeking the Man." Hughes respected the tradition that the presidency "should be neither sought nor refused by any American citizen." He feared that if he remained a Justice, people would accuse him of placing his own comfort and "preference to a particular position" above his "duty to the nation." With "deep regret" he resigned his life-long seat on the Court and accepted the nomination.[12]

As the leader of a divided party who had just spent six years insulated from American politics, Hughes faced many challenges. Every pronouncement, every meeting, every endorsement threatened his uneasy coalition of interventionists and isolationists, of Old Guard conservatives and Progressive reformers. Conscious of these risks, but anxious to reacquaint himself with the country and dispel the perception that he was—as Roosevelt sneered—a "bearded iceberg," Hughes decided to mount a vigorous campaign. "When I was a Judge I was 100 per cent Judge," he declared. "When I am a candidate for office I am 100 per cent a candidate." Republicans cheered, confident that Hughes could accomplish whatever it was they wished him to.

Hughes set out to prove that he was both "human enough to be President of the United States," and smart enough. He began his first tour, a 14,000 mile, thirty-nine day Western trek, in good spirits. In Detroit, Hughes "complied," *The Outlook* noted, "with the one unalterable tradition which has apparently become the foundation of every political candidacy"—attending a baseball game. Thousands cheered him at Tiger Stadium as he met baseball's great hitter, Ty Cobb. "How an American crowd enjoys paying homage to men who have fought their way to the top," a reporter accompanying Hughes exulted. "Truly this is a democracy. Two months before, Charles Evans Hughes was on the bench of the highest court in the world, with almost unlimited power. On August 7 he was simply one of the plain people, out among them . . . and ready to serve them."[13] This dispatch captures the contradictory impressions of celebrity and humility, of great achievement and democratic commonalty, essential to wooing the modern American voter.

Freed from the constraints of the Court, the "100 per cent candidate" marched triumphantly through the Midwest, showcasing his personality while addressing the issues. He was dignified but not aloof, indignant but not shrill, warmer than most people expected, and continually graced by the presence of the "sweet-faced" Mrs. Hughes.

Between extemporaneous attacks on Democratic corruption he embraced athletes, explored copper shafts with miners, and traded quips with cowboys. "By golly," said one surprised bystander, "there is nothing cold about him! He is a modest man, but he is all right." The *New York Evening Post* correspondent concluded that Hughes was "making one of the most remarkable records of successful campaigning of any presidential candidate in recent years."[14]

Some observers attributed the Republican victory in Maine's crucial September election to Hughes's brief swing through that state. In the nine cities Hughes visited, the Republican vote increased from the 1914 Congressional elections by 45 percent as compared to a gain of 24 percent elsewhere. Frederic H. Parkhurst of Bangor could find no reason for the disparity except the Hughes "presence."[15] Accounts like these tweaked the nose of Burchard's ghost and justified the stumping campaign.

Unfortunately for Hughes, the Maine victory marked the campaign's peak. By mid-September, cracks in the Republican façade were appearing. Indeed, the chasm between the Progressives and the Old Guard had undermined organizational efforts throughout the country. Hughes himself had suffered in California, when the Old Guard Republicans arranged a visit which at no time enabled Hughes to pay respects to the popular Progressive Republican Hiram Johnson, who was running for the Senate. At one point an unknowing Hughes was even in the same hotel as Johnson: An oversight became a snub. This incident was simply the most dramatic and best-known example of the quagmires Hughes stepped into repeatedly.

Furthermore, while these missteps received a great deal of attention, a combination of hostility from much of the press, and the campaign's own ineptitude, obscured many of Hughes's triumphs. While reporters wired objective accounts about Hughes on the stump, the editors back home pilloried him. Within the same week, for example, the *New York Times Magazine* could report that "Hughes Is Proving an Effective Campaigner," while *New York Times* editorials labeled him "The Frost-Bringer."[16] Hughes's insistence on speaking off the cuff, and his tendency to repeat the same speech at each stop, did not help matters. All too often, reporters had nothing new to report. When there was something newsworthy, without an advance text they missed their deadlines.

Republicans begged Hughes to indulge the press and to concentrate on "the whole hundred millions of the American people" rather than the small audience at hand. Hughes had to free himself from the orator's exclusive focus on his listeners. The all-important "average reader" was ignoring the speeches. In a telling slip equating the press with its audience, the protesters accused Hughes of slighting "the great American public."[17]

In addition to his now outmoded tactics, Hughes's persistent attacks on Wilson began to wear thin. Having been nominated, as William Allen White wrote, precisely "because he didn't stand for anything," Hughes found it difficult to be constructive. Wherever Hughes spoke, Robert Woolley had newspaper advertisements, billboards, and hecklers asking "What Would You Have Done?"[18] This question vexed Hughes. By avoiding specifics he remained vulnerable to attack as overly critical and irresponsible, a pallid contrast to the active President. Yet if he did speak out, he could be condemned for meddling and political pandering.

The carping, the disorganization, the division, and the grueling pace began to handicap Hughes and his campaign. Crowds became cooler. The nominee became increasingly shrill, labeling Wilson's foreign policy a "travesty," a "disgrace," and "traitorous." People wondered how this sober Dr. Jekyll had become a demagogic Mr. Hyde. "It is as if one of our most assured national assets had melted away under our eyes," *The Nation* mourned. "We feel intellectually poorer."[19]

Yet even as the Hughes campaign floundered, and traditionalists praised Wilson's restraint, Democrats brooded. Wilson refused to respond to Republican criticisms: Why should "a cannon" be used "to kill a fly," he asked arrogantly. But the President's disdain for politics, and his strict reliance on the record, were unduly lofty, Colonel House feared: "To hear him talk, you would think the man in the street understood the theory and philosophy of government as he does." As with Hughes, Wilson's extemporaneous speeches only exacerbated the problems. The President was being ignored. Missouri Senator William J. Stone wanted to sacrifice dignity to avoid defeat: "*A stump, my Kingdom for a stump,*" the Democrat begged.[20]

Wilson raised the rhetorical temperature of the campaign on September 29. Jeremiah A. O'Leary, president of an organization of Irish-Americans and German-Americans opposed to England and her allies, demanded that Wilson clarify his position on the European conflict. By then, hostility was growing against ethnic-American "hyphenates" like O'Leary. "I would feel deeply mortified to have you or anybody like you vote for me," Wilson wired O'Leary. "Since you have access to many disloyal Americans and I have not, I will ask you to convey this message to them."[21]

Wilson's telegram electrified the nation. The fact that Hughes had met with O'Leary further advanced the Democratic cause. Wilson seemed to have inspired himself with the telegram, too. His speech a few days later to the Young Men's League of Democratic Clubs addressed the "real issues of the campaign" for the first time. Thereafter, the President decided to deliver a few speeches throughout the country. Though it looked like a stumping campaign, and in fact was as effective as a stumping campaign, Democrats denied that the President was on the stump. "I am not making a speech-making campaign," Wilson insisted, as he greeted the thousands who swarmed to the stations simply to see the President.[22] Wilson and his supporters distinguished between formal speeches, which were acceptable, and short bursts of bombast from rear platforms, which apparently were not.

As he had done in 1912, Wilson campaigned against campaigning as he campaigned. He had always regarded a campaign as "a great interruption to the rational considerations of public questions." The scholarly politician told voters that he had hoped to find "an interesting, intellectual contest" but realized that "I should have known better."[23]

Even with Wilson's last-month surge and the effective Democratic campaign, the election was close. The Democratic grip on the White House was not secure. Also, for all his faults, Hughes still enjoyed a towering reputation; his campaign had stirred thousands. On Election Night, both Hughes *and* Wilson went to sleep convinced that the President had lost. Only after the West Coast votes were counted did Wilson's slim margin emerge: He had polled 9.1 million popular votes to Hughes's 8.5 million. Wilson thus won 277 electoral votes, only twenty-three more than Hughes, with California's thirteen electoral votes going to the President by merely 3,773 popular votes.

Hughes had overestimated the power of the stump. Operating on turn-of-the-century assumptions, he believed that by impressing individual voters who saw him he would, in effect, be deputizing them to spread his gospel. Like Roosevelt and Bryan, Hughes spoke to hundreds of thousands directly, and millions vicariously. However, by 1916 the American electorate was well on its way to becoming a mass audience which demanded that a candidate address it collectively. Wilson and the Democrats perceived this shift. While the party massaged the individual voter under Colonel House's watchful eye, Wilson addressed, and Woolley propagandized, the masses. Clearly, this method of campaigning suited both the taciturn Wilson and contemporary realities.

Increasingly, candidates would not only have to address the voters collectively but speak to them in the modern idiom of personal tidbits and popular culture icons. In this, Hughes was more successful than Wilson. While Wilson imperiously refused to open any windows onto his personal life, Hughes dragged his wife wherever he went; Mrs. Hughes was the first wife of a candidate to accompany her husband for the entire tour. Also, in meetings like those with Ty Cobb, Hughes revealed his fluency with the symbols of modern America. Though effective, and indicative of future trends, these touches were nevertheless insufficient to elect him.

The slim Democratic victory in California, combined with a 300,000-vote margin that chose Hiram Johnson as California's Republican Senator, refocused attention on Hughes's supposed snub of Johnson. Here was yet another cautionary tale for the itinerant candidate. But Hughes, who continued to insist that he did not know that Governor Johnson was at the hotel, dismissed such speculations. He attributed Wilson's victory to the effectiveness of the Democratic slogan "He kept us out of War."[24] This assessment hit the mark. In voting for Wilson, thousands of Republicans thought they were voting for peace—a misapprehension corrected only in 1917.

In blaming Hughes and the active stumping campaign for what was now considered a debacle, politicians were misled by both the dramatic quality of the Johnson snub and the high hopes that had imprisoned Hughes from the outset. But their errant conclusions also revealed a continuing distaste for rear-platform campaigns. Americans were more comfortable with Wilson's illusory passivity than with Hughes's aggressiveness. The president of the 1916 Republican Convention, Senator Warren G. Harding, embraced the conventional view that Hughes "would have fared much better had he gone to his summer residence . . . and remained there, and retained the halo about his head which came on his exceptional nomination."[25] Were Harding ever to be in Hughes's shoes, one could be sure, he would rest his feet—and his laurels—on his front porch in Marion, Ohio.

II

Yet even a candidate who stuck to the front porch had "to spend a lot of time standing upon his legs and talking about four or five things called issues," *The New Republic* would complain in 1920. Silence, it appeared, was no longer an option for the nominee. In a world where advertising reigned, only those who shouted were heard. The distinguished British philosopher Bertrand Russell lamented the change: "If I were to stand up once in a public place and state that I am the most modest man alive, I should be laughed at," he observed in 1922, "but if

I could raise enough money to make the same statement on all the busses and . . . along all the principal railway lines, people would presently become convinced that I had an abnormal shrinking from publicity."[26] The once great distinction between the front porch and the stump shrank, for the choice was no longer between silence and candor, but between a mellower or more aggressive campaign, a stationary or moving platform from which to speak.

Gone, too, was the fiction that the candidate could strike an authentic, albeit vicarious, relationship with the voter. Awareness increased that "There is interposed between the voter and his final judgment the whole mechanism of modern publicity," as *The New Republic* put it. "The final vote is not the result of direct acquaintance; it is the result of the news reports, the advertising, the oratory, the elusive rumors which are the modern substitute for direct acquaintance." In this "new age of publicity," Richard Boeckel of *The Independent* agreed, the publicity man had become the "president maker." Typically, the P.R. motto was: "The Man With the Best Story Wins."[27]

The new techniques of this new age inspired old-fashioned warnings. American virtue was again in danger, democracy again in decline. The modern cabals of "president makers" might be more sophisticated, but they were as dangerous as the conspirators whom the Founders feared. In doubting the morality of the leaders and the fortitude of the followers, contemporary Americans but echoed their politically paranoid ancestors.

As this sense of novelty mingled with traditional frustrations, Americans dreaded the 1920 campaign. Theodore Roosevelt was dead. Woodrow Wilson was ailing. And William Jennings Bryan was leading quixotic cultural crusades. The two major parties nominated Ohio politicians whose obscurity further emphasized the contrast with these "Titans." Republican Senator Warren G. Harding and Democratic Governor James M. Cox emerged as Ohio's fraternal but battling twins. Both were self-made newspaper publishers and prominent politicians. But Cox was an energetic urban powerhouse and Harding a laconic petit bourgeois of the small town. The two running mates heightened the contrast. Democrat Franklin D. Roosevelt was cosmopolitan, irrepressible, urbane, and eloquent; Republican Calvin Coolidge was provincial, dour, reactionary, and shy.

Republicans embraced the mediocre Harding as the antidote to the Wilsonian presidency. Tired of Wilson's "dictatorship," they argued that an average American was a more suitable president than would be an overachiever. "Warren Harding is the best of the second-raters," Senator

Frank Brandegee admitted. Harding was nominated in a traditional smoke-filled room by Old Guard Senators who wanted a deferential nominee. "My personality is of mere secondary importance," Harding said as he vowed party loyalty.[28] Republicans cheered, affirming that the party shaped the nominee's policies—that things were not the other way around. A Republican victory, then, would mark a return to the traditional, constitutional equilibrium between Congress and the President.

To peddle their old-fashioned, deferential candidate, Republicans put together a sleek advertising effort. All the icons of modern America—the flag, baseball, the movies—would be summoned to illustrate Harding's patriotism and dramatize his campaign promise to "Return to normalcy." Republican National Chairman Will Hays had been planning the campaign for two years. He was eager to "sell Harding and Coolidge to the country." Republicans recognized that the campaign was now "largely a matter of publicity." In advancing this "salesmanship campaign," the strategy was primary, the candidate secondary.[29]

Hays and other Republicans showered Harding with generic and rapid-fire praise, hailing "His poise of mind his soundness of judgment his hold on fundamentals . . . [and] his love of the people." These "vital qualities" would be trumpeted by such advertising men as Robert G. Tucker of Chicago, who simply wanted a candidate able to "dramatize whatever he does" for the newsreels. Projecting a candidate on thousands of movie screens across the country as a "'flesh and blood man,' a real human person," would make it "so much easier to put him through. . . . After all, the Americans . . . like to think of their leaders in a sentimental way."[30] The generic qualities, the emotional appeal, the analysis of "the candidate" as an interchangeable product and of "the Americans" as one massive market, characterized advertising's approach.

For the nominee, Hays scripted an "appealing story centered in the atmosphere of a charming small town." Harding would follow William McKinley's dignified path and campaign from his front porch. In case anyone missed the obvious parallel, McKinley's flagpole was moved from Canton, Ohio, to Harding's front porch on the aptly-named Mt. Vernon Avenue in neighboring Marion.[31]

Republicans rounded up the usual justifications for the front-porch campaign. Senator Henry Cabot Lodge recalled James G. Blaine's 1884 "Burchard Luncheon." Senator Boies Penrose feared that if asked difficult questions while traveling, "Warren's the kind of damned fool who would try to answer them." "This method of campaigning conforms to my own conception of the dignity of the office," Harding explained. He would make "deliberate statements" and not the easily "misquoted . . . extemporaneous utterances made from the tail end of a train." Dismissing the charge that he was hiding from voters, Harding rejected the symbolic fiction central to the rear-platform campaign: "Even through the most arduous travel that one could conceive, I could meet face to face only a very small proportion of the American people."[32]

Another Chicago advertising man, Albert D. Lasker, orchestrated many of the unprecedented publicity stunts dramatizing the Harding saga in Marion. He imported his major-league baseball team, the Chicago Cubs, to Marion to play a local team, the Kerrigan Tailors. He had Harding host seventy movie stars, led by Al Jolson, who sang "Harding, You're the Man for Us." Lasker even coined a slogan, "Let's Be Done with Wiggle and Wobble," for Harding to insert into a speech. The clever Lasker labored to keep his fingerprints off his handiwork: After dictating the slogan, he instructed Harding to make sure that it would be "spontaneously picked up" by reporters.[33]

Even without these Republican machinations, Governor Cox knew that the Democratic campaign would be difficult. The Great War, Wilson's failure to enlist the United States in the League of Nations, and his subsequent illness left the Democrats as enfeebled as their President. With finances limited, the party divided, the press hostile, and Cox naturally combative, the Democratic campaign centered on but one man—James Cox. From August on, Cox was perpetually in motion. He eventually visited every doubtful state, addressing over two million people while traveling 22,000 miles. Cox "is everything: manager, producer, director, leading man and caption writer," Roger Lewis noted in Collier's, invoking movie metaphors that revealed just how modern and story-oriented "everything" had become.[34]

On the stump, Cox was incisive and pugnacious. "That's right, Jimmie. Give them hell," a listener once yelled. "That man's a friend of mine," Cox shot back, recognizing a kindred spirit. Many Democrats were charmed. Even a hostile Hearst newspaper conceded that Cox was a "very winning personality" with a "most happy way of handling a crowd."[35]

But Cox's intensity and Harding's restraint created the effect, Roger Lewis noted, of a duelist whose opponent calmly plays solitaire. And all too often, especially when heckled, Cox's passion got the best of him. Friends had warned him that the "unforgivable sin in our politics is a lack of generosity." After Cox called Harding a "Happy Hooligan," the Chicago Tribune sniffed that "The barroom flavor of his campaign" indicated "a mind and character which do not belong in the White House."[36]

Cox tried to coax his opponent onto the stump. Failing that, he and the Democrats played to atavistic republican fears of the new advertising medium. Cox condemned his opponent's "salesmanship" campaign in tones that his successors, half a century later, would echo. "I do not subscribe to the idea of 'selling a candidate'. I believe in converting voters to the principles and policies enunciated by the platform and the candidates," the Ohioan declared. Franklin D. Roosevelt accused Harding of violating his "clear duty" as a candidate. "Photographs and carefully rehearsed moving picture films do not necessarily convey the truth," Roosevelt warned.[37]

The Democratic attacks and the torpor settling on Marion prompted Harding's advisers to reevaluate their strategy. As William Howard Taft had discovered in 1908, fewer people had the time, the money, or the desire to visit the nominee's home. After several weeks, those delegations that did come seemed remarkably similar to those that had just left. Reporters, who at first enjoyed serving their readers dollops of Hardingesque apple pie, grew tired of the unchanging menu. Only the Hardings themselves seemed not to have tired of the enterprise. Mrs. Harding often ushered surprised visitors into the now-famous home, where the Senator greeted them with a handshake, a pleasantry, and a smile.

But the Hardings' affability was not enough for many Republicans. The front porch symbolized passivity, even disinterest—the wrong message for a modern campaign. Republicans from all over the country demanded the candidate's presence. The campaign seemed headed for an anticlimax, but stumping would not help. Harding and his aides feared that a tour would produce slighted politicians whom Harding did not visit, an exhausted candidate, a loss of dignity, and "endless further difficulty with smooth running publicity" once the campaign left Marion.[38]

Harding eventually agreed to deliver a few speeches in selected cities. By September 25 he had concluded his front-porch campaign. Although he eventually made five speaking trips, he rarely indulged in rear-platform oratory. Like Wilson in 1916, Harding distinguished between giving dignified speeches to the people, and "whirlwind campaigning." Famed for his overblown speaking style prior to his nomination—his "bloviating," as it was known—Harding restrained himself in the campaign. "I could make better speeches than these, but I have to be so

careful," he confessed, as he, not the Democrats, "wiggled" and "wob-
bled" on such important issues as the League of Nations.[39]

Harding's landslide victory left few questions about the relative popularity of the two candidates. But the campaign did raise questions
about just what constituted authentic interaction between the candidate
and the people. Harding's statement that he could not meet all the
people implied that only direct contact between the candidate and the
people counted. The *New York Times*, however, appreciated the vicarious benefits of stumping: "Either directly or by descriptions given by
their friends [Americans] . . . get an idea of a candidate. He ceases to
be an abstraction and becomes a familiar figure in their mind."[40] Advertising executives like Robert G. Tucker trusted the newsreels to convey
the "flesh and blood man," the "real human person." Characteristically,
Tucker the adman trusted an artificial medium to convey truth.

It was also unclear just which truths were being conveyed. The
search for "color," for illuminating anecdotes and personality tidbits,
reflected the new premium on entertainment, on grabbing attention.
It also reflected the twentieth-century concern with "personality." As
Freudian psychology swept the nation, Americans began to view these
fragments as windows into a candidate's soul. But the increasingly nonpartisan, "respectable" press shied away from such speculation—as did
rival candidates. For now, personality traits functioned simply as lures.

III

Amid all the changes in the early decades of the twentieth century,
voters seemed to be choosing the nominee who appeared most traditional, most "presidential." In 1916 the incumbent who began campaigning earnestly only in October eked out a victory over his combative challenger. In 1920 a man who "looked like a president" and
luxuriated on his front porch for most of the campaign crushed his aggressive opponent. Yet the "traditional" behaviors were themselves modern: All candidates were telling a story. No candidate could be silent.
No candidate could avoid traveling to make some speeches by the end
of the campaign. Both Wilson and Harding had benefited from sophisticated advertising techniques. The twentieth-century ethos seemed to
demand a traditional mirage projected with modern devices.

In 1924 the incumbent Calvin Coolidge was determined to run a
quiet, dignified campaign. Coolidge had become President upon Harding's

sudden death in August 1923. An innocuous Vice President in a failing administration, Coolidge came to embody American pride and prosperity almost overnight. The coming campaign would test the Republican equation of peace and prosperity as well as the extent of Coolidge's transformation in the public mind.

As one of the most taciturn politicians in American history, Calvin Coolidge left much to the imagination of others. "Early in life" he discovered that "you don't have to explain something you hadn't said." His terse epigrams were read as assiduously as tea leaves. Among the well-circulated, and possibly apocryphal, stories was the one about a woman who told the President that she had bet a friend that "I could get more than two words out of you." "You lose," Coolidge responded.[41]

These bons mots and his perpetual Chesire Cat smile led some to believe that Calvin Coolidge was always playing a joke on the talkative world. Others were not so convinced. When Coolidge was nominated as Vice President, journalists who had covered him as the Massachusetts Governor gasped. "This is the worst man I ever knew in politics," a Boston Herald reporter said. William Allen White was one who believed that this "Puritan in Babylon" was a political genius. White considered Coolidge a "throwback to the more primitive days of the Republic"— perfect for an America anxious about modernity.[42]

Coolidge's philosophy of campaigning certainly was quaint. He could not "recall any candidate for President that ever injured himself very much by not talking." His natural reticence was intensified when tragedy struck barely a month after his triumphal nomination. Sixteen-year-old Calvin, Jr., stubbed a toe during a White House tennis match. The toe became infected and, on July 7, the boy died. The heartbroken father could not help but think that, somehow, "If I had not been President. . . . " Years later, Coolidge admitted that when Calvin, Jr., "went[,] the power and the glory of the Presidency went with him." To avoid even the appearance of a campaign "swing," the President limited his travels. "With the exception of the occasion of my notification, I did not attend any partisan meetings or make any purely political speeches during the campaign," he would later boast.[43]

Fortunately for the President and his party, the groundwork for victory had already been laid. Coolidge's triumph stemmed from the "amazing" revolution in public perception he and his advisers had engineered in the year before his nomination. Coolidge's apotheosis proved to the editors of The Nation that the "American people dearly love to be fooled, to worship politicians of whom they have created portraits which bear little or no resemblance to the originals." The "Coolidge myth," *The Nation* charged, "has been created by amazingly skillful propaganda."[44]

The Nation's cry of "Propaganda!" partially reflected the times, and partially the truth. Wilson's campaign promising to keep America out of war, and America's subsequent war to save democracy, introduced Americans to this science of systematically manipulating the "opinions of the masses."[45] As they did with so many other rationalizing innovations, Americans embraced propaganda wholeheartedly but nervously, at once celebrating its power and fearing its results. The cry of propaganda, therefore, was somewhat akin to older cries of "liar," of "demagogue"—our side spoke the truth, their side propagandized.

Coolidge's reputation had in fact been cultivated. In explaining why the President would not extend telephone greetings to various groups, an aide admitted that Coolidge's "reputation is built on his habit of keeping silent unless he has some definite idea to get across. . . . The country . . . likes his silence, and it would be a dangerous thing to tear down the picture which they have built." People would vote for Coolidge, not for his party or principles.[46]

This campaign of personality required a breezier speaking style. The formal oratory of a Bryan, even the bombast of a Roosevelt, belonged to an earlier era and a more issue-oriented campaign. A more leisurely, more democratic style was sweeping the nation. New textbooks on popular speech stressed "the conversational manner." This style relied on what advertising man Bruce Barton called the three "essentials of effective advertising copy: (1) Brevity. (2) Simple Words. (3) Sincerity." Calvin Coolidge mastered all three. The "President's own utterances will be the deciding factor" in the election, Barton exulted.[47]

In earlier times, relying on the "utterances" of a reticent President would have been difficult; but not in 1924. Reducing the supply of presidential statements increased both the demand and their ultimate value. Each presidential declaration packed more punch, for, with the advent of radio, one Calvin Coolidge speech could be broadcast throughout the entire country. Coolidge's clear voice and meticulous enunciation became familiar to radio listeners, especially after his campaign spent $120,000 for a series of "nonpartisan" radio addresses over 500 stations.

Radio had been used minimally in 1920—just one station had broadcast the election results to a handful of people. But by 1924, radio was an essential medium of communication. Over 530 stations broadcast to 1.25 million households. This "Aladdin's lamp" unleashed a flood of millennial expectations. Radio, many believed, would revolutionize campaigning. "It will knock the nonsense out of politics," George Baker, the head of the Republican National Publicity Bureau, predicted.[48]

Throughout the nineteenth century, Americans had greeted technological innovations with a mixture of hope and fear. The protective reflexes of the traditional republican society balanced what historian Daniel Czitrom calls the "ancient . . . dream of transcendence through machines."[49] Often, and especially given the behavior of the nominees, technology's impact was more limited than might have been expected. Innovations like the telegraph and the railroad created necessary yet insufficient conditions for change. But in the modern world, where technology was more influential and tradition correspondingly weaker, might not the technological cart leap ahead of the horse?

Many Americans believed that technology was destiny. Radio was not just an amplifier, not just an extension of a speech into the home, but the key to "an entirely new type of campaign," Bruce Barton exclaimed. A medium fostering an intimate style of communication, it would force politicians to talk directly and rationally to the American people. The repetition, the posing, the extravagance of the political hall sounded hollow in the living room. The radio, Barton explained, "enables the President to sit by every fireside and talk in terms of that home's interest and prosperity."[50]

Coolidge supplemented his limited but potent verbal campaign with an expansive visual campaign: He spoke to the nation in the modern language of photography. In their newspapers and movie theatres, Americans enjoyed seeing their President chopping trees, pitching hay, or greeting such visitors as Henry Ford and Thomas Edison at the White House. Of course, these apparently unguarded moments were carefully staged. In the spring, for example, White House secretary Edward Clark blocked distribution of a photograph of Coolidge at his family farm. Not only was it "undignified," Clark explained, but Coolidge's "costume," with its odd, clerical-type collar, "while true to life on the farm at Plymouth, is . . . so different from any other that I have ever seen depicting farm life that I doubt if the average farmer would believe it was real and not especially prepared for the occasion."[51] To convey the appropriate symbol in America's "hieroglyphic civilization," posed photographs were better than candid snapshots, illustrations more "real" than reality.

Meanwhile, the Democrats struggled with sobering realities. The party was torn between the more reactionary rural South and the more progressive urban North. On the hundred-and-third ballot in the longest and arguably most divisive of conventions in their long and contentious history, the Democrats nominated John W. Davis of West Virginia. Formerly Ambassador to the Court of St. James and Solicitor General of the United States, Davis was a most distinguished gentleman. But he had no power base and no distinct identity. Senator Robert M. La Follette's insurgent third-party candidacy appealed to Progressives, especially when they noted the most recent line in Davis's résumé—general counsel to financiers like J. P. Morgan. "Dr. Coolidge is for the Haves, and Dr. La Follette is for the Have Nots," H. L. Mencken wrote. "But whom is Dr. Davis for?"[52]

Davis had few illusions about his chances. He was, he admitted, "wholly without any machinery to handle . . . the details of running a presidential campaign." Among his early blunders, he vacationed at a "palatial" resort in Maine. Republicans gleefully described "the luxurious retreat where the Democratic candidate was to . . . rest from his lucrative labors in Wall Street" before beginning his campaign, Democrat Robert Woolley moaned. To sway the masses, Davis needed better symbols.[53]

Davis accepted the Democrats' central assumption that "Our chief asset in this campaign . . . is the personality of our candidates." He dutifully embarked on a 12,000-mile journey to showcase himself. Davis's speeches were eloquent, witty, generous, and statesmanlike. But they lacked passion. "Not once did he fire his audience," Robert Woolley reported. His speeches seemed better suited for the Supreme Court than the stump. In a twist that undoubtedly amused Hughes and Cox, Davis was condemned for being *too* dignified.[54]

Democrats were frustrated that the gallant Davis was, as Senator Key Pittman muttered, "flanked upon one side by a mummy and upon the other by a volcano." Ignoring La Follette, they futilely tried to embarrass "Silent Cal" into speaking, as the President confined himself to epigrams and nonpartisan appearances. Echoing Wilson, White House aides refused the many demands for speeches with talk of "official business." They feared that any hint of political publicity could destroy their carefully crafted illusion of nonpartisanship. At one point, a reporter asked the President: "Have you any statement on the campaign?" "No," Coolidge replied. "Can you tell us something about the world situation?" asked another, or "about Prohibition," asked a third. To which Coolidge again replied, "No." As the reporters filed out, Coolidge added solemnly, "Now remember—don't quote me."[55]

To further ensure their victory, Republicans tried to scare the nation into believing that the choice was between "Coolidge or Chaos." They encouraged the speculation that La Follette would get enough votes to throw the election into the House of Representatives. GOP strategists assumed that this would scare those who were undecided into voting for Coolidge.

For all the turmoil La Follette created, the campaign was in fact quite calm. The midnight oil did not burn in party headquarters; no one seemed passionate about any candidate. Many Americans refused even to think about the campaign until baseball's World Series ended.[56] Politics was rapidly becoming yet another spectator sport—and one of dubious popularity at that.

The campaign ambled to its predictable finish. Coolidge received almost 16 million popular votes and 382 electoral votes, totals just short of the Harding–Coolidge tallies in 1920. But the 1924 campaign did mark a turning point in presidential campaigning. Radio had begun to revolutionize politics. Advertising executives tightened their grips on campaigns, especially on Republican efforts. Pictures became more important as supporting material. Yet despite these popularizing touches, fewer voters came to the polls. The 1924 election marked the lowest percentage turnout in history. The search for what historian Arthur M. Schlesinger called the "Vanishing Voter" had begun.[57]

IV

In 1927, surveying the vast social changes since the turn of the century, Samuel G. Blythe of the *Saturday Evening Post* found "almost incalculable progress in production, in distribution, in transportation, in wealth, in science, the arts, in standards of living, in methods of amusement." Yet, politically, "we are right where we were seventy five years ago," Blythe complained. "Politics is a fixed, unmovable, archaic, invariable quantity in this country. It never changes." Politicians remained corrupt, and the voters remained passive.[58] While many bad political practices had persisted, Blythe's tantrum came at a time of remarkable transformation, especially for the presidential campaign. Amid the continuing obsessions with dignity and personality, with Burchardisms and swings around the circle, a new kind of presidential campaign—and a new role for the candidate—emerged. In the nineteenth century the republican inhibition insulated the campaign, and particularly the nominee, from change. Thus the nominee's role often appeared to be a quaint carryover from more innocent times. In the twentieth century, largely freed from this inhibition and with technology that centered upon him, the nominee often became a harbinger of change—though the paradoxical need to be a reassuring symbol of tradition remained.

The 1928 presidential campaign showcased this contradictory blend of the future and the past. The battle was principally fought via a modern contraption, the radio. The Republican candidate, Herbert Hoover, was a cool engineer who as Coolidge's Secretary of Commerce was the apostle of modernity. The Democratic candidate, Alfred E. Smith, was a street-wise New Yorker and Progressive Governor who symbolized the future America of diversity and tolerance. Yet Hoover was elected President to return America to the old-fashioned values of his Iowa boyhood, while Smith was defeated by the traditional hostility to Tammany pols and the more ancient animus against his Catholic faith.

From the moment in 1927 when President Coolidge pithily announced "I do not choose to run for President in 1928," Herbert Hoover had been the heir apparent. Secretary of Commerce and "Under-Secretary of all other departments," Hoover's presence was ubiquitous, his reputation towering. Hoover was the Great Humanitarian, the bureaucratic magician of postwar Europe and the flood-ravaged Mississippi Valley. He was also a political novice. The science of public relations, not the arts of demagoguery, forged his reputation. His was a world of achievements, procedures, and statistics. He had always relied on the kindness of journalists to publicize his good works. He disdained the world of glad-handing and backslapping, of speechmaking and ego-massaging. Keeping the level of discussion "decent," he would campaign as the ally of "General Prosperity." He would make speeches, he would consent to interviews, but he would not swing around the circle. Similarly, when meeting the public he would pose for pictures with babies, he would "shake their plump fists" if necessary, but he would not kiss them.[59]

While many Americans expected the no-nonsense Hoover to avoid such tomfoolery, many Republican politicians complained. They feared that Hoover's picturesque opponent would upstage him. They asked Hoover to turn in his "old-fashioned" double-breasted suits for more fashionable attire. Bruce Barton suggested that Hoover "do some fishing or tree-chopping, something that shows him a human being, not merely a candidate." Yet when Hoover went fishing he refused to be photographed, prompting lectures that "Candidates for office cannot escape the ubiquitous photographer." "We have rallied for five years around [Coolidge] the ice plant," politicians muttered, "and now the best we can hope for . . . is four passionate years in pious adoration of the adding machine.[60] Warren G. Harding looked better and better.

Unlike Hoover, Alfred E. Smith was a real politician. A proud alumnus of "F.F.M."—the Fulton Fish Market—Smith had risen from a Bowery tenement to the New York Governor's mansion. Smith played the city slicker, with his brown derby, "New Yawk" accent, fractured grammar, and familiarity with the ways of Tammany Hall. But Smith was also a Progressive reformer dedicated to modernizing government. "I suppose I could make a lot of speeches in the 'court-of-appeals language' of Charlie Hughes," he once admitted as he delivered, Bernard Baruch recalled, "a series of well-rounded sentences" in unaccented and flawless English. But, the Governor said, "That's not Al Smith."[61]

Al Smith had thrived as a politician by meeting the people; he looked forward to campaigning throughout the nation. Right after the northeastern wing of the still-divided Democratic party engineered his nomination, Smith retired to his Albany home to prepare his acceptance speech. "Many of the national issues were new to me," Smith would later admit, and he faced formidable opposition, especially among Southern Democrats. Evangelist Billy Sunday characterized Smith's male supporters as "damnable whiskey politicians, bootleggers, crooks, pimps and businessmen," and his female supporters as "streetwalkers." William Allen White thundered: "The whole Puritan civilization which has built a sturdy, orderly nation is threatened by Smith."[62] Smith would have trouble mollifying these self-righteous teetotalers, prejudiced Protestants and anxious farmers who, in many places, were the backbone of the Democratic party.

Unapologetic, Smith plunged into the fray. He campaigned throughout the country, championing the new emphasis on "the human side" of electioneering as if it were old-fashioned. He had no use for advertising executives. They might be "all right" to peddle commodities and invent such phrases as "It Fits Like a Glove," but the "only . . . sound theory of campaigning," he believed, was "to attempt to convince the public that you are better equipped to fulfill the duties" of office than your opponent. To do that, one had to be simple and sincere, and "amuse as well as instruct."[63]

A true democrat, Smith took his case to the people; a former amateur actor, he dramatized it. In major cities along his route he spoke extemporaneously, often tailoring his speeches to the particular locale. Milwaukee served as a backdrop for his Prohibition speech, Omaha for his farm relief address. These speeches hailed Democrats and blistered Republicans in "everyday language" punctuated with wild gesticulations. "Speechmaking alone," Smith sighed, "is an easy task"; the "travelling and handshaking," however, was exhausting. At hundreds of train stations throughout the West and the Midwest, locals would cry: "Come out here Al, and give us a look at you." Smith would stop, wave his derby, and charm the crowd. Believing that "short, hastily and poorly prepared speeches do more harm than good," he limited himself at these stops to pleasantries.[64]

Smith's colorful campaign amazed the nation. His Western tour demonstrated to one reporter that Smith's "personality is as radiant and compelling among the people of the wide-open, Republican spaces as among the cliff dwellers of his own Manhattan." He received the highest compliment a modern candidate could receive, short of winning: Executives said his tour had increased newspaper and radio audiences. While echoing the praise, the New York Times warned Smith not to be caught by "the fallacy of the crowd," wherein "ordinary curiosity which leads people to throng about" a candidate is mistaken for support.[65]

The Times was correct: Many voters remained fascinated, but doubtful. Too, Smith shot himself in the foot a few times, making the kind of arrogant remarks people expected from New Yorkers. When asked about the needs of "the states west of the Mississippi," Smith joshed: "What are the states west of the Mississippi?"[66]

Smith also discovered that, try as he might, he could not escape questions about his faith. He had settled the issue to his satisfaction even before the campaign began, in the Atlantic Monthly of May 1927. Therein, he avowed that there is no "conflict between religious loyalty to the Catholic faith and patriotic loyalty to the United States."[67] He then declared the issue closed.

But the issue persisted, fueled by ugly whispering campaigns. Smith reluctantly answered his critics on September 20 in Oklahoma City. Oklahoma's former Democratic Senator, Robert L. Owen, had branded Smith the "Tammany candidate." Smith blasted "Owen and his kind" for using "this Tammany cry" to raise the "red herring" of Catholicism. Smith denounced those "inject[ing] bigotry, hatred, intolerance, and un-American sectarian division into a campaign which should be an intelligent debate."[68]

Smith's outrage was justifiable—but impolitic. Equating worries about Tammany with religious bigotry did not still any fears about either his politics or his religion. And even tolerant Americans at the time wondered whether a Catholic could be independent of his Church. Smith was branded a "cry baby." Hoover, too, had been slandered, the Saturday Evening Post claimed, but was "too sensible, too sure of the common sense of the voter to rush to the stump to deny the silly stories . . . being circulated about him."[69]

Smith opponents who disliked attacking his faith picked up this cue, and expressed their dissatisfaction in more traditional terms. They condemned Smith for acting more like a wandering minstrel than a presidential candidate. Many particularly detested his last-minute offensive against Hoover. A "biff-bang, soak-him-on-the-snoot, kick-him-in-the-slats finish suitable to a Smith governorship fight in New York will spread out a bit thin when applied to a presidential fight in the United States," Samuel Blythe noted. Once again an aggressive Democrat appeared undignified and unpresidential.[70]

Smith was also defeated by a medium that had previously been kind to him—what he called the "raddio." By 1928 there were 8.5 million receiving sets in what the *New York Times* now called "radio-minded America." Americans continued to believe in radio's magic power, still viewing it as a talisman which would eliminate all the bad American political traditions; it inevitably would make campaigns shorter, more "national," more direct, more educational. "Radio has rendered the 'front-porch' campaign and the 'swing around the circle' obsolete," one authority quoted in *The Literary Digest* declared. Smith himself welcomed the new device as a vehicle for issues, not personalities, and for coupling the candidate with the voter.[71] But this direct contact did not transform the campaign so much as extend it. Even the optimists could not decide if radio would emphasize personality, as Barton predicted, or policies, as Smith hoped. The campaign and the candidates—warts and all—came into Americans' homes.

More than 40 million people listened to Smith's acceptance in August—after the speech was rescheduled to accommodate the networks. Broadcast over 100 stations linked with 57,000 miles of wire, the speech required an army of 1,500 engineers. This technical achievement was considered a fitting showcase for the Governor who had charmed New York radio audiences by being "an interesting talker." Major J. Andrew White of the Columbia Broadcasting System praised Smith's mastery of "the basic law of broadcasting, which is, 'Be Yourself'."[72]

But during the campaign, Smith's radio speeches were less effective than his personal appearances. His speaking style was too hot, too passionate, to be piped into the nation's living rooms. His voice, when amplified, became "tinny," he recalled. His voice also faded in and out because he wanted to see his audience from behind the "pie plate" radio microphone stuck in front of his face. Without the theatrical gestures and personal warmth, Smith's raspy, accented radio presence confirmed many Democrats' fears of the urban bogeyman. For better *and* for worse, Smith's voice became his calling card. Months after the campaign, a little girl met Smith and told her mother "He has the same voice that he had on the radio." Smith ruefully concluded: "Nothing makes such an impression on a person as the spoken word."[73]

Radio was kinder to Herbert Hoover. His subdued speech patterns, his clear voice, his flat, Midwestern accent, even his somewhat monotonous speeches, soothed Americans. His voice conjured up images of prairie tranquility rather than urban chaos. As the front-runner, Hoover had no incentive to stray from his original strategy. Smith could fulminate about his silence, but Hoover would not budge. Said Hoover: "Ours is not a campaign of opposition."[74] Not once did he mention Governor Smith by name. Not once did he plunge into controversy. In an implicit criticism of Coolidge, Hoover's conception of dignity did not even include accommodating photographers with colorful poses.

Hoover's routine during much of the campaign was that "of a business man rather than a candidate," reporter Ray Tucker noted. When he was not on one of his rare campaign trips, Hoover arrived early each morning at his Washington office. There, he answered correspondence and conferred with aides. Committed to an educational campaign and disdainful of ghost-writers, Hoover spent up to three weeks crafting each of his seven major speeches. More carefully prepared than most presidential addresses, these presentations were intelligent, "scientific," and boring.[75]

Hoover does not deliver speeches, the bombastic Smith scoffed, but "statistical essays." A presidential campaign should be "a debate," Smith believed. The people should hear directly from the candidate "about the issues." In short, the New York Evening World sighed, Hoover had waged "the dreariest, dullest and most inarticulate campaign ever."[76]

Making a virtue of his shortcomings, Republicans portrayed Hoover as a republican "man of action" in a sea of demagogic talkers. The Chicago Tribune conceded that Hoover was unusually quiet, "but when he has spoken it has been with . . . the weight of deliberate conclusion which should mark the utterance of the statesman." "What's The Matter With Hoover?" Katharine Dayton asked in The Saturday Evening Post. Echoing those who preferred McKinley to Bryan in 1900, she answered: Hoover is too busy "creating opportunities for livelihoods for literally hundreds of thousands of workers" to pose for pictures.[77]

Herbert Hoover's carefully drafted texts were a far cry from the spontaneous interactions between the politician and the people in Theodore Roosevelt's day. Politicians then took pride in their extemporizing. In 1916 both Wilson and Hughes rebuffed requests for advance texts. Indeed, until the day of a speech, Wilson confessed "I haven't finally determined what I am going to talk about."[78] Hughes and his successors eventually placated the press by releasing advance copies—which however they did not necessarily follow. This arrangement allowed the speaker to reach the national "market" while focusing on his immediate audience.

Nevertheless, what had once been a relatively informal and intimate interaction was now a national one. In "happier speaking times," Hoover sighed, nominees could "repeat the same speech with small variations. . . . Then paragraphs could be polished up, epigrams used again and again, and eloquence invented by repeated tryouts." Persistent press coverage shackled the nominee. "I want, if possible, to avoid making the same speech over and over," John W. Davis said in 1924, "and it requires no little ingenuity to find new words for the same tune."[79] Voters almost invariably did not want to hear a speech they had already read in the newspaper.

Speeches on radio had to be more controlled without being more formal. "The radio," Hughes observed, "demands precision, a decent restraint, and a more careful speech-structure. The repetitious utterances of a campaign orator, his excessive emotional outbursts, his strenuous efforts to reach his climaxes," may charm the immediate partisan audience "but go ill with the larger and more important" radio audience. At the same time, the "speaker does not like to have the audience walk out on him." Speakers with prodigious memories could memorize their speeches and serve both masters. But, increasingly, speakers had to choose between the immediate audience and the listeners at home. The real intimacy between the speaker and his audience was replaced by the artificial intimacy of the President speaking to what William Allen White in 1937 would call "John Q. Public."[80]

Speakers mourned their loss. When nominees hit the stump, they found that the shouting partisan crowds of the nineteenth century had been replaced by a more discerning audience: Listeners cheered or booed or snored, depending on whether the nominee was inspiring, controversial, or boring. Candidates like William Jennings Bryan prided themselves on their abilities to stir the audience, to win the voters' affections. But, as Al Smith complained, a microphone "never nods approval. It never stimulates [the speaker] by expressing dissatisfaction with his statements. . . . It is just a cold piece of metal suspended on a string." These limitations made Smith confident that broadcasting a speech in an empty studio without a live audience would never catch on. In fact, it would simply spur the experts to discover ways to gauge the response of the "privatized" audience now sitting at home.[81]

This shift, from a formal interaction among intimates to an artificial intimacy with a nationwide audience, was part of a broader transformation in the presidential campaign. Traditionally the campaign had been static, a lengthy discussion about two fixed entities—"The Republican" and "The Democrat." The rear-platform campaign allowed the nominee to be revealed to a particular locale, but the overall effect was that of a rotogravure, a still portrait, passed around the United States. Now the campaign was becoming a moving picture, a series of changing portraits with a beginning, a middle, and an end. This drama required changing sets in the forms of different places the candidate visited, a changing script in the form of new and different speeches, and—if possible—changing costumes and props. As the star of this show the candidate could not be passive, nor could he forget that every move he made was watched by an audience of a hundred million people. Increasingly, advertising executives replaced political bosses as producers and directors of this ever more elaborate show. Radio may have brought the candidate closer to the people, but the need for careful scripting had created a new distance.

Thus, despite Hoover's old-fashioned rhetoric, a modern campaign commenced. "One thing is obvious," Hoover strategists agreed, "this is purely and simply a Hoover campaign as distinct from a Republican campaign." For all the talk about party regularity and addressing issues, people counted for more, "policies for less."[82] Similarly, the Hoover campaign was not as high-minded as the nominee's lofty aspirations. Hoover affected a majestic indifference to the ugly whisperings flung against Smith. His calls for tolerance enabled him to appear righteous without jeopardizing the benefits he accrued from the anti–Smith campaign.

Hoover won, as predicted, with yet another Republican landslide. His victory seemingly marked the triumph of the Republican party, of general prosperity, and of the articulate yet passive candidate. In fact, all three were doomed.

V

The passive, dignified candidate was yet one more mirage in an age of illusions. By 1916, passivity—in its nineteenth-century sense—was out of the question. But, as Hughes discovered that year, and as Democratic challengers learned throughout the 1920s, distaste lingered for active, no-holds-barred campaigning from the rear platform of trains. Still, as Wilson and Harding realized late in their respective campaigns, the nominee could no longer avoid the people. By nineteenth-century standards Wilson, Harding, Coolidge, and Hoover were active and undignified, but to a twentieth-century polity they conveyed a sense of appropriate restraint. Bertrand Russell's observation was valid: Candidates had to proclaim their modesty—loudly. With the aid of the expanded Wilsonian presidency and increasingly sophisticated advertising techniques a candidate, especially an incumbent, could be active yet dignified. Passivity now meant campaigning within limits.

Republican concerns, however, had not died. Demagogues still lurked, democracy remained fragile. In fact, motion pictures and still photography, advertising and P.R., gave enemies of the republic a more potent and manipulative arsenal. Modern innovations kept alive ancient fears.

The advent of radio seemingly offered the perfect balance. By addressing the nation in a series of radio speeches, as Hoover did, a candidate could maintain his dignity while "facing" the people. Voters could judge both the issues and the candidate's character over the airwaves. But both Democrats and Republicans would discover in the 1930s that, while radio was an essential tool for the modern candidate, it was not quite sufficient. Stumping—and its dilemmas—would continue.

EIGHT

The President as
Campaigner

I don't know nothin' about politics.
—*President Franklin D. Roosevelt, 1940*

IN the 1930s, even as automobiles dotted the landscape and high-
ways crisscrossed the nation, the American romance with the railroad
continued. When Ben Hecht and Charles MacArthur wanted a setting
to convey both leisure and adventure, tradition and progress, the writing duo chose a transcontinental train ride. The result was *Twentieth
Century*, Hollywood's 1934 screwball comedy starring Carole Lombard
and John Barrymore. As in the movies, the special campaign train inspired and reassured Americans during the searing years after the stock
market's "Great Crash" in 1929. Such nostalgia also proved frustrating.
"We all remember what radio was to do to democracy in general and
political campaigning in particular," the *New York Times* sighed in 1936.
With a candidate broadcasting from the comfort of his library to millions in their parlors, "the old hot, dusty, sweaty business" of speaking
from rear platforms would end. But radio campaigning "has simply refused to live up to predictions," the *Times* complained. "The outcome
has been a campaign of personal appearances."[1]

Curiously, in the 1930s stumping was considered archaic when it
was still quite novel, proof of its persistent taint. Guardians of dignity
who could no longer brand it "unprecedented" deemed it anachronistic
in the radio age. Yet just as stumping became unnecessary, it became
entrenched. Before Franklin D. Roosevelt's four presidential campaigns,
the perennial question about the nominee was "Will he stump?" When

the candidate was an incumbent, the answer usually was "No." After Roosevelt the question, even for an incumbent, was "Just when will he begin?"

Stumping's resilience was not the only example of radio's unfulfilled promise. In the 1930s and 1940s radio emerged as a mixed blessing for democratic politics. On the one hand, radio brought the town meeting home; by 1940 it was the chief source of political information for 52 percent of Americans surveyed. Some even credited radio with doubling the number of voters from 1920 through 1936. But at the same time, the millenarians of the 1920s had been sobered. Dictators like Adolf Hitler and Benito Mussolini proved that demagoguery could flourish over the airwaves. Radio reawakened republican fears about a charismatic "superman" or a devious cabal seducing the nation. "Will Radio Kill Democracy?" Raymond Gram Swing of CBS wondered. The four Roosevelt campaigns from 1932 through 1944 provoked liberal-democratic cheers—and republican groans.[2]

I

As President, Herbert Hoover was doubly victimized—first by the unrealistic expectations that his election engendered, and then by the unexpected Depression. Hoover's hoped-for "chicken in every pot" became instead an unemployed man on every street corner. Thus the 1932 campaign required a new approach. Traits that endeared Hoover to the American public in 1928 now proved grating. He would have to act coy—and busy, hoping that Americans would appreciate his efforts. "Except for a few major addresses expounding policies of the administration I will not take part in the forthcoming campaign," he announced. The presidency demanded his "undivided attention." "The candidate is the President," Republican National Chairman Everett Sanders explained.[3] The defensive tone in justifying Hoover's passivity and the emphasis on duty, not dignity, hinted at the changing expectations.

Disdainful of Democratic nominee Franklin D. Roosevelt, most Republicans approved Hoover's plans. Though James Cox's running mate, and the two-term Governor of New York, Roosevelt was known as a lightweight. Bruce Barton sneered that Roosevelt, crippled by polio, "is essentially 'just a name and a crutch'."[4]

Roosevelt quickly confuted such cruel dismissals. He would make millions of Americans believe that "happy days" could come again. He began by displaying his virtuosity. The notification ceremony, with its demure interval between nomination and acceptance, was a quaint sham. Candidates no longer were unsuspecting draftees. They often pursued the nomination in primaries, and now knew instantly when they were nominated. Roosevelt decided to fly to the Democratic convention and accept the nomination in person. Delegates still unsure about these flying machines begged him not to come. His son John alighted after the long flight from Albany to Chicago a sickly shade of green, but the elder Roosevelt emerged refreshed. "You have nominated me and I know it," Roosevelt pronounced, dispatching with the century-old fiction, "and I am here to thank you for the honor." His precedent-shattering move marked his pledge to bring a "new deal for the American people" boldly and quickly.[5]

Roosevelt's trip to Chicago killed the notification tradition—the Republicans would stop after 1940—and changed the nature of the acceptance speech. Since the 1890s, acceptance speeches had explored the issues in depth. Although delivered orally at the notification ceremony, the addresses were meant to be read throughout the country. Even in the radio age, Al Smith delivered a 13,000-word laundry list on topics ranging from taxes and tariffs to reforestation and inland waterways. Roosevelt's 5,000-word speech was meant to be heard and not read, and showcased his personality as much as his policies. The irrepressible campaigner and the conversational medium invaded this sanctum of substance. To "My Friends," Roosevelt confessed that he would only "touch on a few" vital problems, approaching them as "you and I and the average man and woman" would.[6]

Few considered the move undignified, proof that the protocol had outlived its rationale. Many found the speech dramatic, even romantic, and happily interred "the notification farce." Some speculated that Roosevelt went to Chicago to "prove" that he was a normal man in spite of his polio. But others recognized the move as "typically Rooseveltian." The Governor "knew the value of drama in public office," his speechwriter Samuel Rosenman recalled, "and he understood the psychology of the American people of 1932."[7]

Shortly after charming millions with his acceptance, Roosevelt sailed up the New England coast with his family, ostensibly to vacation. Along the way he visited local Democrats, and was hailed wherever he went. When 50,000 people greeted him one Sunday in Hampton Beach, New Hampshire, Roosevelt recalled that his uncle Theodore once tried to inspect ships on a Sunday and was rebuffed. Thus, his aide Rexford Tugwell rejoiced, speaking "hardly a word of politics"—at least publicly—Roosevelt showed that he loved the outdoors; had "big sons who liked his company"; was the "paramount Democrat" embraced by local leaders; "was a Roosevelt"; and, for good measure, "was religious."[8] This candidate knew how to speak without words.

Clearly, Roosevelt intended to dominate the campaign. He dismissed warnings from his campaign manager, James Farley, against breaking the front porch "precedent." To Farley, the "weight of evidence" dictated a "traditional stay-at-home campaign"—stumping still was for losers. But Roosevelt could not resist. "You are you," another aide acknowledged, and "have the faculty of making friends on a campaign tour." Stumping also would quiet rumors about Roosevelt's health, and solidify his power base. He pooh-poohed fears of a verbal slip, vowing to "discuss every important issue of the campaign in a series of speeches." Rexford Tugwell wondered: Had Roosevelt "never heard of radio?"[9]

Roosevelt had not only heard of radio, he had mastered it. After speaking over it in 1924, he had embarrassed himself by asking "How did it sound?" while he was still on the air. But after over seventy-five talks during four years as a governor, Roosevelt delivered textbook examples of how to combine a genial tone and familiar language for maximum effect. Research showed that Americans projected various personalities onto radio voices.[10] Roosevelt's soothing tones, with just a hint of his patrician upbringing, had broad appeal. "All that man has to do is speak on the radio," one Republican would mutter when Roosevelt was President, "[and] the sound of his voice, his sincerity, and manner of delivery just melts me and I change my mind."[11]

Roosevelt's first campaign speeches demonstrated his mastery. He broadcast from his Hyde Park home rather than from a rally. Flattering his listeners, he sketched broad policies in "this quiet of common sense and friendliness," setting the stage for the campaign's "more detailed discussion."[12]

Though promising a campaign of education, Roosevelt in fact delivered one of subdued emotion, a cooler campaign tailored to a radio age. He and his successors would disappoint those who had predicted the triumph of reason, for appeals could be even more superficial over the radio. A mass-entertainment medium, radio demanded lowest-common-denominator approaches. "Radio broadcasting . . . must not be high hat," the "radio priest" Charles E. Coughlin would explain. "It must be human, intensely human." Recognizing that listeners could easily turn the dial to Charlie McCarthy or Amos and Andy, Roosevelt and other candidates had to seduce the voter with personalities, not with policies.[13]

In his first month as a nominee, Roosevelt had demonstrated his fluency in the visual and audio components of the modern campaign. His visit to Chicago showed he could captivate with grand gestures; his radio chat showed he could court with intimate touches. Yet for all his apparent spontaneity, the campaign was carefully planned. Louis Howe had mapped out Roosevelt's itinerary in February, and it was followed with but one minor adjustment. Just as Roosevelt learned to make his well-rehearsed radio "chats" seem ad-libbed, so did he make his calculated political moves appear spontaneous. This approach, stressing individual sincerity, would culminate in Roosevelt's attempt to "transcend" partisan politics and recast the presidency as a more personal and more powerful institution.[14]

The Governor billed his initial 8,000-mile journey through twenty-two states as a "look, listen and learn" tour. He insisted that his primary purpose was to study "at first hand the conditions . . . of every section" and "to talk with people." This statement, though pious, was somewhat true, for Roosevelt valued on-site visits. As President, he would teach his wife Eleanor how to read the nation's mood from the window of a railroad train. From town to town he repeated the same act: The six-car campaign special would pull into the station. Roosevelt, on the arms of his sons, would come out, wave, introduce his family, and leave. Engineers were scolded if they kept the train in a village longer than a minute.[15]

When Roosevelt made his few campaign addresses, his talk of a "new deal" for the "forgotten man," and his attacks on Hoover, sufficed. While some Democrats had to admit that their candidate was "disappointingly vague," even many Republicans welcomed Roosevelt's "bright, gay manner" after four years of Hoover's "sour" mien. According to the New York Sun, Roosevelt had the crucial—but quite modern—attribute for winning the American people, "picture personality." As for President Hoover, "Even when he is snapped out fishing he doesn't look happy."[16]

Hoover resented being the scapegoat for the Depression. The continuous sniping "depressed and hurt him," his secretary, Edward Clark, noted. These emotions bubbled to the surface amid the flat tones, forced gestures, and colorless language of Hoover's acceptance speech. "Today millions of our fellow countrymen are out of work," he mourned. "No man with a spark of humanity can sit in my place without suffering from the picture of their anxieties and hardships before him day and night." Amid this uncharacteristic display "of deep feeling," the New York Post detected "a new Hoover . . . trying to struggle out."[17]

Hoping for a new incarnation of their all-too-familiar candidate, Republicans begged Hoover to stump. Such Democrats as Senator Pat Harrison considered it a matter of responsibility, not strategy. Inverting the traditional order, he said "The President is a candidate; the people are entitled to hear from his own lips" what he believes. While praising Hoover's respect for "the solemn tradition which enjoins a President from engaging in the rough-and-tumble of political controversy," the *St. Louis Post-Dispatch* decided that the "unprecedented" Depression nullified "the traditions."[18]

Ultimately the Republicans' defeat in the mid-September Maine elections, rather than lectures about democratic responsibility, aroused Hoover. In early October, refusing to accept "Hideous misrepresentation . . . in silence" anymore, he launched his offensive with a ninety-minute speech in his native Iowa. The economic crisis had passed, he declared, implicitly justifying his shift from governing to campaigning. "We held the Gibraltar of world stability. The world today has a chance." The President's emergence as a fighter thrilled Republicans: "We heard you last night at Des Moines," a man yelled the next day. "Give us three more like that and it'll be all over."[19]

Hoover intensified his attacks. He stayed up late, night after night, perfecting each speech, cutting and pasting in a desperate attempt to satisfy the millions of radio listeners who demanded variety. These efforts culminated in Indianapolis, where Hoover excoriated Roosevelt for lying, evading, and offering a "shuffle" on questions instead of a "new deal." Hoover charged Roosevelt with profiteering from foreign bond sales as a businessman, then denouncing such sales now that he was a candidate.[20]

Though stung by these unprecedented insults from a President, Roosevelt was restrained. Mischievously, he noted that Hoover at first "sought to create the impression that there was no campaign just as he had sought to create the impression that all was well with the United States." Once Hoover realized he was a candidate, Roosevelt noted sadly, "dignity died." *That* the President campaigned was not a problem—it was now to be expected. *How* he campaigned was disturbing. Grandly paying "respect" to the President's "person and his office," Roosevelt illustrated how Hoover had forfeited his presidential dignity. In refusing to descend to Hoover's level and quibble about "private business affairs," commentators noted, Governor Roosevelt was the one acting presidential.[21]

The 1932 campaign concluded with a burst of activity on the stump and on the air. This bipartisan invasion of the airwaves was not always welcome. When a Hoover speech preempted the giggling Fire Chief, Ed

Wynn, millions of children went to bed disappointed. Six thousand out-raged parents called the stations to protest, reminding politicians that Americans turned on the radio for entertainment, not enlightenment. Radio's much-heralded extension of democracy into the homes annoyed many, especially when coverage was so extensive. Though the networks devoted barely 4 percent of their programing to news and politics, 46 percent of the listeners in one 1936 poll would want fewer political broadcasts, or none at all.[22] Whereas in the nineteenth century Americans had to seek out information about the candidates and contact with the campaign—and did, in the twentieth century, Americans had the candidates come to their homes—and rebelled.

All this hubbub provoked the ritual complaints that the campaign was "beneath the dignity of a great nation," as the *Saturday Evening Post* complained. "When the President and his opposing candidate take the stump, night after night, like an assemblyman or an alderman, the electorate learns to discount much that is said." But some relished the campaign's increasingly populist base. After Roosevelt and Hoover gave back-to-back speeches on October 31, the *Los Angeles Evening Herald and Express* commented that, rather than "being heard by comparatively few persons as was the case in past campaigns," the two candidates spoke to nearly 25 million Americans, making it "the greatest debate in American political history."[23]

Roosevelt's triumph repudiated the Republican party and vindicated his modern campaigning techniques. Walter Lippmann declared Roosevelt's campaign the most "wisely conceived . . . [in] recent history." Roosevelt broke traditions and helped redefine campaigning proprieties. His voice and presence set new standards in campaigning, solidifying "warmth" as a criterion for the presidency. Also, together with Hoover, Roosevelt buried the front-porch campaign yet again. "THE STAY-AT-HOME IDEA VANISHES," a surprised headline announced.[24] Finally, Hoover's campaign marked the increasing politicization of the presidency. "The candidate" was no longer "the President"—rather, "The President" was now "a candidate." But how could presidential dignity be preserved on the stump? In his subsequent campaigns, Roosevelt would master the difficult balancing act of president and candidate, between political and nonpolitical actions.

II

What makes "a successful candidate?" asked Democratic National Chairman James Farley, looking back on Franklin Roosevelt's reelection campaigns. As the architect of the Democratic juggernaut of the 1930s, Farley might have answered "organization." But Farley knew that a modern political sales force was only as good as its product. "The public has confidence," he mused, "in some men who aspire to office, in much the same way that the public has confidence in a good doctor without knowing much about the science of medicine. The quality is 'felt' rather than understood." Franklin Delano Roosevelt had that quality, Farley concluded, "to an exceptional degree."[25]

Roosevelt also knew how to display that quality to great effect. Taking full advantage of modern communications, he multiplied the contacts between the President and the people. He entered America's living rooms and dominated the front pages. He revived the White House press conference, meeting reporters 337 times in his first term alone. He invented the "fireside chat," an informal radio address whose debut inspired over half-a-million letters.[26] And he mastered the traditional weapons in the presidential arsenal—the on-site visit, the executive order, the formal policy speech.

This communication, however, was one-sided: The radio annihilated distance, yet increased it. Roosevelt spoke to "My friends" as if he were at their kitchen tables, except that he could not hear their response. The interaction was more intimate and more artificial. The burgeoning White House mail bags testified to the President's growth as a popular figure and to Americans' frustration with their silence. Eventually, public opinion polls would try to articulate the mass audience's response. Champions of democracy celebrated this popular dialogue; republicans feared its falsity.

This "dialogue" was central to Roosevelt's expanded presidency. The New Deal brought the federal government into the lives of the people as never before. As the government mushroomed, the presidency itself became "an institution," historians have noted. Yet Franklin Roosevelt, aided by radio's aggrandizing but human touch, made the relations between the people and their President appear more personal. "Millions of your children . . . appreciate more deeply than you will ever know your beautiful and unselfish administration," one former Republican would write.[27]

Similarly, Roosevelt revitalized the Democratic party, but recast it in his own image. Parties were increasingly passé in the modern world. Government encroached on the parties' traditional welfare services; professional and trade associations on their social and economic roles; and radio and movies on their entertainment functions. Even newspapers were becoming "objective." Roosevelt arrested party decline by mobilizing millions of new voters and strengthening the Democratic party as a national campaigning organization. It was, however, very much the "Roosevelt coalition." Party strength was no longer inversely proportional to candidate strength, but an extension of the candidate's organization, foreshadowing a time when the personal organization would render the party all but irrelevant. For now, Democrats did the political dirty work while the President stayed aloft as the leader of "all the people."[28]

As his uncle Theodore had in 1904, Roosevelt realized that his efforts reduced the 1936 campaign to one issue: "It's myself, and people must either be for me or against me." Using "simple illustrations that appeal to the average person back home," he would emphasize the New Deal's relief efforts. To exploit his "nonpolitical" status as "President of the whole people," he would delay declaring his candidacy. In mid-June, only days before the Democratic Convention in Philadelphia began, Roosevelt claimed that he had not even thought about the campaign. Asked why he was going to Philadelphia, he grinned: "Just for a good time. Just a nice little week-end party."[29]

Two weeks later, when the President accepted the nomination before over 100,000 Democrats at that "little" gathering, he asked Americans to "rendezvous with destiny" by rallying around his New Deal, not his party. He then retreated, opting for "a campaignless" summer. Recognizing, as Samuel Rosenman did, that nonpolitical trips were "the most effective political trips a President can make," Roosevelt deferred his few political speeches to October. Until then, he would "inspect" areas in the Midwest blighted by drought, and areas in the Northeast working on flood control. He would remain within a twelve-hour train ride from Washington, ready to rush back to the White House in an emergency. "And, of course," he confided to Farley with a wink and his trademark chuckle, "there won't be anything political about the inspection trips."[30]

These trips enabled Roosevelt to preserve presidential purity while attracting attention as an engaged chief executive. He refused "to link up human misery with partisan politics" during his "look-see" at various sites. As in 1932, he simply wanted to "see certain conditions at first hand." To prove that he was not on a political trip, he added "I am not going to any state fairs."[31]

"So far as the White House reporters can learn officially, there is no political campaign going on," columnist Raymond Clapper reported in August. Opponents muttered that this "role of dignified aloofness" was "far-sighted and shrewd." Many newspapers encased the word "nonpolitical" in quotation marks. How can you criticize a President who "speeds to the rescue of the drouth-stricken farmers in the West . . . instead of gallivanting around the country on campaign tours?" one critic whined.[32]

These fulminations delighted Roosevelt. But his "nonpolitical" phase could not last; the President could not long receive free air time for political fireside chats without making the debate about his speeches more than semantic. Republicans of course sought equal time for their candidate. And the director of two radio stations in Los Angeles deemed one "chat" a campaign speech and demanded payment. Simultaneously, Democrats began pressing Roosevelt to deliver more political speeches in October. Five, he insisted, would be sufficient, and those would remain on the "almost biblical plane." Unlike Hoover, he would not overdo it.[33]

Carefully, playfully, Roosevelt prepared for the shift. He announced that he would speak at the New York State Democratic Convention at the end of September. "That speech will be political, won't it?" a reporter asked. "Oh, no," he chuckled. Anticipating that the political and nonpolitical phases would blur, Republicans hoped to catch the President in his own lies. But Roosevelt avoided the trap. He continued to reassure radio listeners with his soothing voice and homey allusions. He never mentioned his opponent's name, and never attacked the Republican party, thereby preserving his nonpartisan posture. Still, Roosevelt made adjustments: He spoke more militantly, ridiculing Republican leaders, conservative "Liberty Leaguers," and the failed Hoover administration—though never the party rank and file. And he indulged in activities more befitting a candidate than a president. When serenaded in Syracuse, for example, rather than simply waving as he passed—as he had been doing for months—he stopped, joined the crooners, and sang "Pack Up Your Troubles in Your Old Kit Bag." His pleasure in the act was "genuine," a reporter wrote. "But he would not have yielded to the impulse prior to the beginning of his active campaign."[34]

Roosevelt thus improvised a protocol enabling presidents to campaign. With his perfect political pitch, he fashioned an approach allowing a president to exploit the powers of his office without being straitjacketed by its proprieties. When campaigning he injected a warmer, more personal touch to his comings and goings. Traditional notions of dignity, Roosevelt taught, could free a president, not just encumber him.

This loftiness, however, reinforced traditional republican notions of politics as demagogic and dirty. Roosevelt's hands-off approach taught his supporters that partisanship was illegitimate. At the same time, his

opponents saw this role of the dignified monarch as the work of a scheming politician. Whether they believed Roosevelt's presidency transcended it or was sullied by it, all could agree that politics was indeed
pernicious.

Roosevelt's panache whipped his enemies into a frenzy. He was the
republican nightmare, only interested in "self-glorification" and "personal government." His "escape" into what the *Chicago Tribune* called
"a jungle of glittering generalities" violated the democratic covenant as
well. Never before had a candidate refused to "make explicit pledges for
the future," the *Tribune* howled, forgetting the republican tradition of
silence. Cries of "Dictatorship!" filled the air.[35]

Republican beliefs that democracy was fragile and eloquence subversive were rejuvenated in the radio age. More and more middle-class
Americans were heeding European intellectuals' warnings about the
"unstable, credulous, irrational, and immoral" masses. Radio's ability to
stir millions unsettled those who no longer trusted the people and now
feared the crowds. "Democracy will be torn up by the roots if radio
broadcasting ever becomes the exclusive weapon of an Administration
seeking to perpetuate itself," William Randolph Hearst's *San Francisco
Examiner* warned. "A radio voice is only a phantom, as thin as the air
in which it rides and as ephemeral as a New Deal campaign pledge."
Voters had to decide: "DO WE WANT A SHOWMAN OR A
STATESMAN?"[36]

The Republican candidate, Alfred M. Landon, certainly was no
showman. The Kansas Governor was simple, direct, and sincere. This
country needs "less radio talks, less charm, less experiments, and a lot
more common sense," Republicans said. "Everything . . . about me is
the direct antithesis of the present executive," Landon declared.[37]

Ironically, an elaborate advertising campaign backed this "plain ordinary man." Businessmen long frustrated by the anachronistic ways of
the campaign welcomed the admen to politics; as with stumping, advertising had multiple debuts. The admen would sell Landon and "sell tax
phobia as they have automobiles, shaving soap, [and] cigarettes," a pundit noted. One proposed radio spot had a bridegroom reconsidering
marriage because the national debt came to $1,017.26 per person. Many
abhorred these commercial techniques. "Political appeals should be intellectual," Edward Klauber of CBS said as he rejected the "spot."[38]

Landon started strong. Dispensing with the traditional debate, he
decided to wage a vigorous campaign with a national speaking tour and
frequent press conferences. "It is not convenient for you to come out

and visit me on my front porch in Topeka," he would explain from his railroad car, "so I am glad to visit with you, as it were, from my back porch here." Before embarking on this crusade "for good government" he vacationed in Colorado. The visit at the Irene McGraw ranch was a publicist's dream, as photographs showed the candidate fishing, riding, hiking, and relaxing with his wife and children. Daily briefings helped complete the tableau of the All-American family at play.[39]

Landon's acceptance, however, was disappointing. During the nationally broadcast speech his voice was weak, his delivery awkward, and his timing poor—the crowd never had time to interrupt with applause. Of course, Republicans tried to put the best face on their nominee's limitations. Amos Pinchot urged Landon "not to try to improve" his delivery, because ineloquence sounded authentic. Landon is "a practical minded statesman" not "a glib promiser" or a "crooner," the *San Francisco Examiner* rejoiced. Still, most Republicans applauded when the party hired a voice trainer. But Landon had no time to practice. Anyway, he added, the White House is "an executive office[,] not a broadcasting station."[40]

Herein Landon revealed his naiveté. Campaigning in this "era of the news reel and the radio calls for a technique as deliberate as that of a Hollywood star," journalist Marquis Childs observed. "You could be homely and homespun, but if you didn't know how to put it across, you looked merely inept and foolish."[41] As Roosevelt continually demonstrated, illusions often were more important than realities. Under the lights of the camera and before batteries of microphones, Alfred Landon seemed to shrink, as did his reputation.

Landon continued to speechify, trying to match Roosevelt speech for speech, gesture for gesture. As the campaign wore on, pressure from the Republican right and Landon's own desperation pushed him to extremes, from which he then recoiled. In Maine, sounding like a Liberty Leaguer, he denounced a planned economy, whereas in Iowa, sounding like a New Dealer, he promised to increase farm subsidies. Landon "would have been a stronger candidate if he had sat on his front porch at Topeka throughout," Roosevelt's Secretary of the Interior, Harold Ickes, concluded.[42]

As Landon zigzagged toward the finish line, Roosevelt marched toward a landslide. The Republicans had hoped that by starting early they would force Roosevelt onto the stump. But, as Homer Cummings noted, the President "did not speak until he got good and ready." As people tired of Landon's oratory Roosevelt, apparently responding to their call, began to speak. Roosevelt's final push "generated . . . [w]hatever impetus and swing the campaign developed in its closing weeks," the Democratic expert in the fledgling science of polling, Emil Hurja, concluded.[43]

The President's swing around the "nonpolitical" circle, and Landon's unquestioning plunge into a stumping campaign, proved once again that candidates could not stay home anymore. Stumping was archaic, inefficient, and still dangerous—many believed that such efforts risked, and often lost, more votes than they ever gained. But since 1896 a generation had been raised knowing only the rear-platform campaign; Franklin Roosevelt had cast his first presidential ballot in 1904. With its red, white, and blue banners and colorful speeches, the stumping campaign had become "Typically American."[44] The undignified innovation was now an American tradition.

This tradition served both the candidate *and* the people. "There is something which a candidate gets from appearing in the flesh before an audience . . . which neither radio nor television can replace," Colonel Theodore Roosevelt, Governor General of the Philippines, had declared.[45] The candidate learned about the nation, receiving a firsthand look at conditions as well as direct reactions to his speeches and policies. Franklin Roosevelt was not merely being coy in labeling his stumping trips "look, listen and learn" tours.

As for the people, stumping seemed the best way to meet the candidate. Research showed that when Americans heard speeches in person rather than over the radio they were more satisfied, they listened more carefully, and they remembered more. Citizens appreciated the importance of "a flesh-and-blood presence," of seeing as well as hearing. Broadcast voices, pictures, or newsreels were simply not enough. They were "dead thing[s]," "phantom[s]."[46] To these first-generation users, disembodied voices and moving pictures were inauthentic, and the interactions between a candidate and the people through those media were suspect. Speeches could be ghostwritten, voices trained, pictures posed—only direct contact was real. In an increasingly mechanized world, Americans still wanted the personal touch.

Recognizing all of this, Roosevelt had settled on a formula which allowed a president to govern *and* campaign. Exploiting both the prerogatives of his office and the greater freedom of the candidate, he pulverized the opposition. He had given his campaign—and his avoidance of campaigning—an urgency that seemed linked to the national purpose. But few imagined that the two-term President would ever have an opportunity to ply these skills in another reelection campaign.

III

As the end of his second term approached, President Roosevelt dreamed of writing history at his Hyde Park estate. But he also wanted to complete the New Deal. The Supreme Court–packing controversy, the 1937 "Roosevelt Recession," and the revolt of conservative Democrats had weakened the President and made him anxious for vindication. Wary of becoming a lame duck if he decided to retire, Roosevelt equivocated. He ordered his aides not to acknowledge any of the letters begging him to run for a third term, lest his answers be misunderstood. When reporters pressed him, he replied "The weather is very hot."[47]

The third-term taboo could not be taken lightly. Initiated by George Washington and consecrated by Thomas Jefferson, it was a central republican tenet in a nation which continued to fear a strong federal government. In December 1938, 70 percent of those surveyed opposed a third term. In a world of Hitlers and Mussolinis, the no-third-term tradition became to many the "most potent" defense against "dictatorship."[48]

The pleas for a third term, however, were equally vehement, if initially less loud. Solicitor General Robert H. Jackson argued that in a democracy the people, and not some "extra-constitutional 'tradition'," should have the right to choose the next president. Germany's invasion of Poland in September 1939 turned the sporadic pleas into an incessant chorus. By April 1940, almost half of those surveyed wanted Roosevelt to remain as President, including many Republicans who detested the New Deal and Democrats who believed a third term "most undesirable."[49] In June, Germany conquered France. By July, when their convention began in Chicago, most Democrats were determined to draft the President. More and more, only those who opposed Roosevelt for other reasons spoke about the tradition: The "sacred" tenet had become a partisan brickbat.

Submitting, he claimed, only because of the crisis, Roosevelt forswore an ordinary campaign. He would eschew "purely political debate," he announced in his acceptance broadcast from the White House. The European war would chain him to his desk. Of course, he reserved the right to "call . . . attention" to "deliberate or unwilling falsifications of fact" which rivals might spread. The President would not campaign unless he had to.[50]

Throughout the summer, Roosevelt reminded prying journalists and anxious politicians of his no-campaigning vow, even while using his expanded presidential powers to advance his candidacy. Whenever he made a speech, he tried to insert "some late piece of news—war news or foreign news or news of production," Samuel Rosenman recalled. This technique of campaigning by governing culminated in September, when the United States offered Great Britain fifty aging destroyers for the rights to construct military bases on British possessions. This masterstroke, the beginning of what became known as "lend-lease," aided the Allies, evaded the congressional mandate of neutrality, helped nudge the public from isolationism toward interventionism, and illustrated Roosevelt's round-the-clock efforts to protect America, let alone his advantage as an incumbent. Opponents "could only talk," Arthur Krock of the *New York Times* noted. "The President acted."[51]

Roosevelt's 1936 inspection trips became military inspection tours. He visited major population centers near Washington, ostensibly to view military bases or defense-related factories. He was then pictured against "a background of guns, tanks, airplanes and fighting ships; not haranguing a political audience from the rear platform of a special train," the *New York Times* noted. Roosevelt claimed that his visits injected "pep" and quickened production. He toyed with his critics, asking them to define what was political and what was not. Was the Sermon on the Mount political? he would ask after the campaign.[52]

Roosevelt's loftiness frustrated many Democrats, who begged for more conventional politicking. He refused to visit many Democrats in need, but when he did, the presidential pose eclipsed party concerns. In Pennsylvania, for example, he followed the protocol of "nonpolitical" motorcades, riding in the front car with the Republican Governor and relegating the Democratic challenger to the rear.

"Annoyingly smart politics," these tours frustrated Roosevelt's opponents even more than his "nonpolitical" speeches had in 1936. The *Lynchburg News* declared all of Roosevelt's speeches and appearances "political."[53] Rejecting the distinction between the President's political and nonpolitical actions marked an important shift. An incumbent had run in all but three campaigns since 1900. In those four decades both Democrats and Republicans had urged the incumbent to adhere to the fiction and protect the presidency from politics—to a degree. But Roosevelt had so exploited the distinction that many now doubted that the presidency could be insulated from politics at all.

Despite this blurring, commercial considerations demanded a distinction. As in 1936, "nonpolitical" presidential pronouncements would be broadcast free. The newly enacted Hatch Act, limiting campaign expenditures to $3 million per party, made free publicity ever more important to the Democrats, and ever more resented by the Republicans. Preparing to address the Teamsters Union convention in mid-September, Roosevelt, as usual, professed not to know whether his speech would be political. The Teamsters offered to pay the $20,000 to broadcast the speech, but the Hatch Act limited contributions by organizations to $5,000. White House Press Secretary Stephen Early then announced that while he was "not saying it is going to be a political speech," the Democratic National Committee would purchase the time. Reporters wondered how Early and other White House aides could "keep a straight face." Well into October, whenever asked a "political" question, Roosevelt would shrug and say: "I don't know. I don't know nothin' about politics."[54]

As he had in 1936, Roosevelt also pretended to know nothing about his Republican rival. "Call him our opponent," he instructed. "Call him anything, but never call him bad names." Slandering him was ungentlemanly, while mentioning his name gave him publicity. But it was hard to ignore Wendell Willkie in 1940. In just a few months the obscure but respected utilities magnate had become the Republican nominee. Modern public relations techniques and an old-fashioned popular boom had helped draft the tousle-haired ex-Democrat. Willkie combined the small-town virtues of Indiana and the big-city smarts of Wall Street, the businessman's pragmatism and the politician's charisma. Half a million people had joined 4,000 Willkie Clubs. These devotees overwhelmed the Republican convention in Philadelphia. Willkie, the *New York Times* declared, was "the biggest smash since Mickey Mouse."[55]

Willkie's ascent indicated that Roosevelt was not the only politician who could live and die by the radio and the newsreels. Willkie was what later generations would call a media star, having become famous in an ever-dizzying spiral. Radio speeches fed press reports that led to a portrait on a *March of Time* newsreel and climaxed in April 1940, when he appeared on the radio quiz show "Information Please." At last the Republicans had a showman, too. Willkie knew that he could only beat Roosevelt by out-campaigning him, and relished the challenge. Americans vote for "men," not "policies," he said.[56]

Willkie luxuriated in the spontaneity of his effort. At Philadelphia he boasted: "I have no campaign manager, no campaign fund, no campaign headquarters. . . . I have no ghost writers. I've entered into no deals." He disdained all organizational details. Only years later did it emerge that Willkie was posturing, professing ignorance so as not to appear too calculating.[57]

Though he had been living in New York for years, Willkie decided to accept the nomination at Elwood, Indiana, his hometown. His acceptance speech eulogized the notification tradition and decried Roosevelt's compulsive innovating. "You all know that I accepted at Philadelphia the nomination of the Republican Party for President of the United States," Willkie said, dispensing with the quaint fiction. "But I take pride in the traditions."[58] Willkie did not know it, but this would be the last notification ceremony. Nevertheless, his appeal to Americans' sense of tradition was shrewd.

Willkie's speech, delivered in 102-degree heat, bored both the sweating masses in Elwood and the more comfortable radio audience at home. The speech also alienated party regulars. In promising, if elected, to preserve the New Deal and protect Europe, the Republican candidate bore a striking resemblance to the Democratic incumbent. One reporter suggested that to win the election Willkie should oppose the military draft. "I would rather not win the election than do that," Willkie replied.[59]

One area of disagreement with Roosevelt—and one effective thrust Willkie made at Elwood—concerned campaigning styles. Championing "the American political . . . tradition of face to face debate," Willkie challenged the President to "debate the fundamental issues" in joint appearances. Democrats said that no President ever debated his opponent directly, and doubted that such an activity would be "in keeping with the high office of the Presidency." "The President," Harold Ickes huffed, "cannot adjourn the Battle of Britain in order to ride the circuit with Mr. Willkie."[60]

While the country may not have been quite ready for direct presidential debates, Willkie appeared as the democratic David against an imperious Goliath. Roosevelt's refusal to debate focused attention on his posturing and his alleged megalomania. Willkie accused Roosevelt of believing, as did Hitler, Mussolini, and Stalin, that he was indispensable to his country. "He is the one whom the founders feared," the *Saturday Evening Post* thundered. Invoking the Lincoln–Douglas debate, and overlooking Lincoln's silence in 1860 and 1864, Republicans praised the all-American tradition of debate. Roosevelt could deliver speeches prepared by the literary staff "as well as any actor can read his lines," the *Chicago Tribune* acknowledged. "But can he give and take in a free debate?"[61]

The *Tribune*, along with most advocates of a debate, deplored Roosevelt's dependence on ghost-writers. Traditionally, Americans had been afraid of ghosts, assuming that such assistance corrupted the dialogue between president and people. It was common knowledge that Roosevelt did not draft his speeches. In fact, he collected governmental experts as enthusiastically as he did stamps. Raymond Moley, a Roosevelt ghost-writer, said Roosevelt would read almost anything as long as it sounded good. During the 1932 campaign, Moley claimed, when faced with two contradictory drafts for a tariff speech, Roosevelt had ordered: "Weave the two together."[62] Stories like this one proved to his foes that Roosevelt deceived himself as well as the nation.

Roosevelt loyalists, however, insisted that the President shaped every statement, denying that the uniformity of style found in Roosevelt's speeches was in fact a tribute to the staff's mimetic talents. For, despite their rising profile, ghosts had to remain invisible. After Stanley High pranced through Democratic headquarters in 1936 "proclaiming that he was off to write a speech for the President," a shocked Charles Michelson reprimanded him. Michelson explained that High had violated "the rules of the game, as a ghost is never supposed to admit that he is the author of a great man's utterance."[63]

Pleased to offer a popular contrast to the President, Willkie denounced Roosevelt's "duplicity" and contempt for democracy. "I can't fake things," Willkie boasted, as he refused to accept ghost-writers, pose for "phony" pictures, or even rehearse for newsreel speeches. These vows proved to a *Daily News* reporter that Willkie would not be "brain-trusted"—the new verb conveying the widespread awareness of Roosevelt's subterfuge.[64]

To heighten the contrast, and aware that his personal appearances excited voters, Willkie promised to speak "wherever and whenever two or more Americans are gathered in my honor." Willkie rejected the distinction between rear-platform and formal addresses. He would deliver a few "set" speeches on major issues, and over five hundred informal talks at settings as diverse as Jamaica High School in New York, the stockyards of Chicago, and the Hollywood Bowl. He admitted that his was "a political campaign. This is no military or educational inspection trip." In Buffalo he begged "Please, please, require this man, before you vote for him, to define what his program and policies will be."[65]

Yet for all of Willkie's piety, he was the Madison Avenue candidate. A galaxy of advertising luminaries, from Bruce Barton to Raymond Rubicam, advised the Republican campaign. Many other Willkieites worked for newspapers and magazines, including his manager, Russell Davenport, an editor at Time–Life. Championing the incumbent Roosevelt as the authentic candidate, CBS radio commentator Dorothy Thompson attacked these "glib copywriters who think you can slug this nation into an election."[66]

Inspired by the crowds—and, as one journalist noted, lacking in "self-discipline"—Willkie set a grueling pace. By the end of his campaign he would travel 18,759 miles by train, 8,884 by plane, and 2,000 by car. Within days his voice had been reduced to a rasp—which grated on his radio listeners. At first, experts had anticipated the clash of "two all-American voices." But Willkie whittled away his natural talent with his refusal to rehearse, his hoarse voice, his neglect of the radio audience when ad-libbing at campaign stops, and his disregard of time constraints, resulting in truncated speeches or, even worse for his strapped campaign fund, additional charges for radio overtime.[67] The excitement Willkie generated in person was lost over the airwaves. Campaign managers eventually hired a voice specialist for $250 a day, although many muttered that Willkie needed a policeman, not a doctor, simply to enforce silence.

Furthermore, the more Willkie spoke, the more he proved his running mate, Senator Charles McNary, right: "In politics you'll never be in trouble by not saying too much." In Pittsburgh, after promising to appoint a Secretary of Labor who (unlike the incumbent Frances Perkins) came from the unions, he added "and it will not be a woman either." In attacking the alliance between the New Deal and the bosses, Willkie accused "the third-term candidate" of perpetuating his power "through petty Hitlers right here at home." Willkie, Roosevelt roared, suffered from the occupational disease of the New York lawyer: "He talked too much."[68]

Yet, for all of Willkie's troubles, he was delivering some glancing blows. Crowds were enthusiastic. Democratic leaders begged the President to pick up the pace, for their sake and his. For a month after the Teamsters speech, Roosevelt continued to ignore politics in public. But by mid-October, some of Willkie's attacks made Roosevelt "fighting mad." After the election, Roosevelt told his opponent's manager that Willkie's campaign was "much more effective . . . than I expected. I had to abandon my policy of keeping quiet and go out and make a series of speeches. If I hadn't, you might have won."[69]

Roosevelt announced that the "systematic program of falsification of fact by the opposition" demanded a response. The President would make five speeches in the remaining three weeks, staying within a twelve-hour train ride of Washington. Although the trips would include "some inspection work," the Democratic National Committee would foot the bill. This about-face proved to Sam Rosenman, whose vacation had been cut short by the sudden decision to campaign, that "the American people just naturally refuse to be taken for granted." Roosevelt learned that Americans wanted to "hear the campaign issues debated by the candidates."[70]

Campaigning, then, was concerned not only with convincing Americans but with paying them respect. In *this* democratic era, the protocol of the stump illustrated the candidate's humility, his commitment to the democratic process, and his ties to the people. Rear-platform talks, handshaking, and speechmaking all served as symbolic exchanges, allowing the leader and the people to pay homage to each other. Also, in an era of increasing federal encroachment, the ritualized ceremony in which local pols "boarded the train" symbolically reasserted both the primacy of the individual states and the link between the candidate and the local organization. Just as a politician worried that the people no longer appreciated him when his events were poorly attended, so did the people worry about being unappreciated if the politician refused even to hold such events.

Roosevelt's three-week onslaught delighted the people and overwhelmed Willkie. At his first openly political speech, on October 24 in Philadelphia, the President exulted "I am an old campaigner, and I love a good fight." The crowd roared. In New York, Boston, Cleveland, and finally at home in Hyde Park on election eve, the old campaigner celebrated the New Deal while ridiculing his opponents. Ignoring Willkie, Roosevelt attacked Herbert Hoover and his successors in the conservative wing of the GOP, including (in a singsong gibe using only their last names) party chairman Joseph W. *Martin*, adman Bruce *Barton*, and isolationist Congressman Hamilton *Fish*. Roosevelt triumphed. As Raymond Clapper had observed in September, and Wendell Willkie discovered repeatedly, "A superman out of office is no match for a superman in office."[71]

Such "super" candidates burst onto the world scene during the 1930s, on the heels of the actual cartoon character. The Great Depression generated a worldwide call for strong men who could save the masses. However, traditional fears of strong centralized government, as well as a modern leisure culture that was already demonstrating its ability to trivialize, made the American "cult of personality" far less toxic than the European varieties.

Both Roosevelt and Willkie ran apparently modern campaigns promising a powerful personal presidency. Using the emerging mass media, each projected a pleasing personality to attract votes. Each struck a nonpartisan note, appropriate for the media age but portentous for party power. Roosevelt's campaign aroused more concern about one-man rule; Willkie's, more concern about seductive advertising. Though both appeared spontaneous and democratic, each operated from a strategy developed with experts. Roosevelt's ghost-writers and the Republicans' admen became scapegoats for campaigning ills, as observers assumed that such careful preparation and skillful manipulation were modern phenomena. Ironically, then, two candidates who inspired intense and seemingly authentic devotion during their campaigns, in the long run contributed to the growing distrust for the candidate and his campaign. These two new democratic heroes justified old republican fears.

IV

"Is there anyplace we could go, Mr. President, to find out about your fourth term intentions?" a reporter asked Franklin Roosevelt in June 1944. "My what?" the President chuckled. As long as America remained at war, Roosevelt knew he would have to remain as President. By mid-July, he was ready to announce that although "all that is within me cries out to go back to my home on the Hudson," if the Democrats nominated him yet again, he would accept. A good soldier, Roosevelt could not "leave his post."[72]

To oppose the President, the Republicans nominated the forty-two-year-old Governor of New York, Thomas E. Dewey. Trim, mustachioed, and energetic, Dewey enjoyed considerable fame from his days as a gang-busting prosecutor. Though somewhat stiff and self-righteous, he demonstrated impressive popular appeal in the presidential primaries. Having drafted him to lead a campaign of youth against the "tired old men" of the New Deal, Republicans fully expected Dewey to stump. Consequently, after conferring with Dewey, his running mate, Governor John W. Bricker of Ohio, announced: "We are going to cover the whole country." The campaign "will be complete, thorough and aggressive." This was, Dewey and his men assumed, the natural course.[73]

As President Roosevelt prepared to oppose Dewey with his well-practiced Commander in Chief routine, his situation was at the same time easier yet more difficult. After eleven years of the New Deal and three years of the Second World War, Roosevelt's stature, and that of his office, had grown. Roosevelt had expanded the presidency and so linked himself with his task that the two were inseparable and imposing as never before. The crisis made it easier to appear both engaged and presidential. But the greater expectations also fettered him. In wartime, presidential dignity became inflated but correspondingly easier to burst. In his acceptance, transmitted to the convention from San Diego, Roosevelt insisted that he would "not campaign, in the usual sense, for the office." In "these days of tragic sorrow," it would not be "fitting," nor could he "find the time." The wily veteran once again however reserved the right to "correct any misrepresentation."[74] This time, he would need an especially good excuse to campaign.

Roosevelt was also feeling too tired to campaign. He had aged, seemingly overnight. To refute the rumors that his emaciated appearance stirred, he engaged in well-publicized activities. His trip to the Pacific in August advertised his centrality to the war effort—as he conferred with commanders; and his courage—as he visited areas the Japanese had held. On his way home, he addressed civilian navy workers from a destroyer anchored in Seattle's Bremerton Navy Yard. The nationally broadcast speech was a disaster. The wind blew into Roosevelt's face, poorly adjusted braces cut into his legs, and angina pectoris gripped his chest. The President faltered, his poll ratings slumped, and the Democrats panicked.[75]

Meanwhile, the Republican campaign was building up steam. The first nominee born in the twentieth century, Dewey felt more comfortable than did his predecessors with modern tools like radio, advertising, and polling. Advertising's techniques, and its jargon, continued to invade the campaign. Public opinion polls were an essential tool in this "selling" job. Pioneered in the 1920s by marketing experts eager to quantify mass attitudes, polls gained political credibility in 1936, when Dr. George Gallup and others forecast "Alf" Landon's defeat. Scientific surveys "make the people more articulate," Gallup argued, praising polling as essential to the "democratic way of life." These democratic hosannas were accompanied by republican warnings that Gallup's polls would bring about the direct democracy the Founders feared. With constant surveys, popularity could eclipse virtue and leaders could become panderers.[76] Dewey and his men, for instance, relied on polls to identify popular issues, not just to chart personal appeal. The days of Samuel Tilden's door-to-door canvasses were long gone.

Even though he considered rear-platform talks "unseemly" in wartime, Dewey agreed with the admen that personal appearances in crucial states were essential. But, having learned from Landon and Willkie the dangers of speaking too soon and saying too much, Dewey would let the campaign build. He planned a restful August, a busier September, and an exhausting October. His stump appearances would be orchestrated, with reception committees at each stop receiving detailed instructions, including the height of the lectern for the diminutive candidate. Correspondents would marvel at this "Efficiency-Experted Tour for Votes." On the stump Dewey would remain calm, living up to his reputation, even among admirers, of being "cold as a February icicle."[77]

As much as he could, Dewey avoided unruly crowds. He counted on radio speeches which, in deference to his admen and their assessment of the nation's attention span, he would limit to twenty minutes. Dewey's smooth baritone would challenge Roosevelt's domination of the airwaves. The Dewey campaign's priorities were most apparent when 93,000 people, including dozens of movie stars, filled the Los Angeles Coliseum on September 15. Dewey delivered a dry exposition about Social Security. "My God, what was the matter with him?" a bored partisan gasped. Campaign manager Herbert Brownell, Jr., explained that Dewey did not want "a slam-bang rally type of speech," he needed "to get a constructive approach to the Social Security problem in the minds of the people all over the country who were listening in on the radio."[78] Dewey preferred broadcasting these radio speeches from an empty studio. Here at last was the kind of politician Al Smith never believed could have emerged.

Al Smith also would not have believed how central radio would become to both the Democratic and the Republican campaigns. Together, the two parties would purchase $2.5 million worth of airtime. The Democrats favored five-minute, vaudeville-style spots featuring politicians, celebrities, veterans, and war mothers. The Republicans preferred thirty-minute spots, supplementing Dewey's brief addresses with nonpartisan entertaining material.[79] Increasingly, production values counted—not the issues.

While the Democrats' traditional, warm, spontaneous approach seemingly contrasted with the Republicans' modern, cool, calculating one, the campaigns were more like different sides of a newly minted coin. Roosevelt's politics of personality was no more traditional than Dewey's opinion polls or flow charts. Roosevelt relied on modern expertise while Dewey played his own variation of the personality game. Still, for all the innovations, the candidates continued to do what many had been doing for decades: speaking and stumping.

Overall, Dewey's first tour received high marks. The *Detroit News* labeled him "the best campaigner the Republicans have had in the No. 1 position in a long, long time." Polls began to show Americans almost evenly split between the President and the underdog.[80] Back at the White House, Roosevelt and his aides noticed this surge in Dewey's popularity, and worried.

Roosevelt, who in retrospect had come to like Willkie and Landon, detested Dewey. He blamed Dewey for fanning the rumors about his health. In one Gallup poll, one-third of those surveyed predicted that poor health would prevent Roosevelt from completing his fourth term successfully. Roosevelt would have to face the people to prove otherwise, he told the cabinet. The President would "go" after Dewey and "make a real campaign."[81]

As he had in 1940, Roosevelt chose to begin at the Teamsters Convention. His entourage was nervous on the night of the Teamsters speech, September twenty-third. Haunted by memories of Seattle, they had begun to doubt him. But Roosevelt rose to the challenge. Ignoring his current opponent, Roosevelt recalled the "Hoovervilles" of 1933 and asked, "Can the Old Guard pass itself off as the New Deal?" Dismissing claims that the Democrats prolonged the Depression, he accused the Republicans of resorting to Adolf Hitler's "big lie" technique. Rising above the clapping and the laughter, the President's voice was clear and strong. "These Republican leaders have not been content with attacks—on me, my wife, or on my sons," he mock-seriously moped. "No, not content with that, they now include my little dog, Fala. Well, of course, I don't resent attacks, and my family doesn't resent attacks, but"—he paused—"Fala *does* resent them." Roosevelt explained that the Republicans had "concocted a story" that he had ordered the navy to retrieve Fala from an Aleutian island "at a cost to the taxpayers of two or three, or eight million dollars." When the feisty little canine heard of this canard, Fala's "Scotch soul was furious. He has not been the same dog since."[82]

Samuel Rosenman said he had never seen the President "in better form." As the union men shook the hotel ballroom with their cheers, Rosenman knew they shared the same thought: "The old maestro is back again." Even the anti-New Deal *Time* magazine conceded that Roosevelt still had "the old magic." The speech thrilled partisan Democrats across the nation. White House mail ran more than eight to one in favor of the speech.[83]

Out in the Midwest, Governor Dewey was outraged, especially by the implicit comparison to Hitler. Dewey hired additional radio stations to broadcast a reply to the President's "snide" remarks, signing personal notes to help pay the $27,496.46 required. That Monday night, September 25, in Oklahoma City, Dewey began on the high road. Recalling that Roosevelt had pledged not to campaign "in the usual sense," Dewey charged that a "speech of mud-slinging, ridicule and wise-cracks" was offensive in "these days of tragic sorrow." Claiming that he only wanted to keep the record straight, Dewey lambasted Roosevelt, accusing him of stumbling into war and prolonging the Depression. Dewey swore to save the nation from "the ill-assorted, power-hungry conglomeration of city bosses, Communists and career bureaucrats which now compose the New Deal."[84]

Throughout the country, Republican partisans cheered Dewey's rebuttal. Politicos from both parties rejoiced at the clash of two titans. "No Presidential campaign in the United States is ever a namby-pamby business," the *St. Louis Post–Dispatch* observed. "The people like a fighting campaign," the *Detroit News* added. "The truth, the brutal truth, will come out now."[85]

Yet this undignified exchange offended many citizens. Daily, more letters to the editor appeared in newspapers condemning *both* candidates. In thirteen big-city papers, three of every four letters about the speeches disapproved either of Roosevelt's attack or of Dewey's rebuttal. One North Carolinian complained that the campaign had been "reduced to the level of a street brawl."[86]

But it was Roosevelt's speech that provoked the greater response, by two-to-one. More than 80 percent of the letters about the speech assailed his bad taste. Even in newspapers that supported his reelection, almost three-quarters of the letters about the Fala speech were critical.[87] The correspondents complained most about the odious attempt to compare Dewey's tactics with Hitler's, and about the frivolous injection of a dog into political discourse. Such antics disgraced the President, some said. One Detroit resident wondered: When mothers are mourning and sons are dying, how can "this man" think it "fit to regale their ears with such insulting trash and triviality as the qualities and feelings of his dog!" To drive home the point, the author signed the letter "Nauseated."[88]

While the White House mail was overwhelmingly favorable, some of those who approved were defensive. "To hell with dignity when human lives are at stake," an innkeeper from Minnesota insisted. More soberly, Mrs. S. S. Watkins of Owensboro, Kentucky, begged the President not to make any more campaign speeches. "You are so far above such things, and I hope to keep my memory of you as this ideal President." Republicans speculated that the "asinine" speech would backfire. While Roosevelt's attack reassured worried partisans, no one wrote that the speech had converted them to Roosevelt's side.[89]

Two days after declaring Roosevelt's speech a "success," the columnist Arthur Krock reconsidered. Both campaign managers were discovering that "a great many people in this country" objected to this kind of electioneering, especially during wartime, Krock reported on September 28. "The tremendous popular reaction against Mr. Roosevelt" proved to a *Los Angeles Times* pundit that "The American people want serious discussions of serious matters in a manner befitting their intelligence."[90]

For once Roosevelt had been defeated by the medium he had befriended, the radio. Succumbing to the broadcasting imperative to entertain, he overlooked wartime sensibilities and traditional notions of presidential dignity. Without press accounts and published texts to filter the experience and mold their reactions, listeners took umbrage directly and immediately. As they sat in their living rooms, listening to candidates for the highest office in the land squabble like schoolboys, many Americans were appalled.

Chastened by the outrage, Dewey regretted his Oklahoma City speech, and called it the "worse damned speech I ever made." "It was all wrong" he admitted later. "I was attacking the dignity of the office I was seeking." In the future, he promised to avoid the gutter. Roosevelt, however, ignored the hostile undercurrent.[91] More concerned with activating his supporters than making new friends, Roosevelt could simply dismiss the criticism as the fulminations of an impotent opposition.

For the remainder of the campaign, Dewey continued his hard-hitting attacks against Franklin Roosevelt and his cronies. Dewey attacked the New Deal's incompetence, its ties to party bosses and labor leaders, its economic program, and its military strategy. When all else failed, Dewey waved the red flag, charging that "The Communists are seizing control of the New Deal."[92]

After the Fala speech, Roosevelt returned to his nonpartisan pose. He did, however, campaign by governing, wooing Italian and Polish voters by advocating aid for their respective homelands, and relaxing some wartime rationing. Asked in mid-October about his campaign plans, Roosevelt yawned: "I can't get frightfully interested in that sort of stuff now."[93]

But about ten days later, Roosevelt embarked on a brief stumping campaign. At his first stop, in New York City, he juggled his two roles. During the day he drove in his open-topped, bulletproof Packard through a thunderstorm, waving to the thousands massed along fifty miles of streets. This display demonstrated his stamina. That night he doffed his now-drenched candidate's hat and resumed his role as Commander in Chief, presenting a statesmanlike, if self-serving, address to the Foreign Policy Association. Roosevelt then visited Philadelphia, Chicago, and Boston. Disappointed that he could not visit more cities, he broadcast an exclusively political speech from the White House, a move he had avoided until this campaign.[94]

Dewey's aides crowed that Roosevelt's reemergence as "the Democratic candidate for President" justified their tactics. But Roosevelt's efforts truly reflected the joy he took in campaigning—he gained twelve pounds, and brightened in outlook. The efforts also revealed the President's growing contempt for Dewey. In his final full-length campaign address in Boston, Roosevelt's bitterness spilled over: "Never before in my lifetime has a campaign been filled with such misrepresentation, distortion and falsehood," he charged. These libels revealed "a shocking lack of faith in democracy." Less glib than the Fala speech and coming after a month of jousting, this statement raised few eyebrows. More and more voters came to expect the mudslinging—and yet another Roosevelt victory. When Governor Dewey finally conceded at 3 A.M. after losing on Election Day, Roosevelt turned to an aide and said, "I still think he is a son of a bitch."[95]

Even after the election, a bad taste remained in many mouths. Looking back, the *Charlotte Observer* speculated that if the millions of American soldiers who were fighting and dying to save the world for democracy had witnessed the contest, "They Would Be Disgusted." It had been, *The New Republic* agreed, "A Bad Campaign."[96]

———

The 1944 campaign in general, and the Fala speech in particular, became essential components of the Roosevelt legend. Historians later celebrated the speech as vintage Roosevelt, a moment of triumph.[97] That the popular antipathy about the speech and the campaign was buried in a heap of praise says much about Franklin Roosevelt the politician. From 1932 until his death in 1945, Roosevelt bewitched Americans with his political charms. The Fala speech showcased many of the qualities that made him a great politician—his ease, his sense of humor, his optimism. Furthermore, this reassuring evidence of his buoyancy came at a critical time, when the Democratic cause and the President himself seemed to be sagging. Especially for members of Roosevelt's inner circle, there was no reason to treat the speech as anything but a triumph. Why not believe that the magic that worked previously for him was potent that September night as well? Viewing the Fala speech as the turning point in the campaign made 1944 parallel both 1936 and 1940, when Roosevelt's last-minute efforts galvanized Democrats. Had Dewey upset Roosevelt, the Fala speech might have been viewed as a blunder. But in the wake of electoral victory in 1944, the legend of Roosevelt's virtuosity obscured the popular backlash against the speech.

Cheering the triumphant Fala speech not only fit the legend of Roosevelt's political prowess; it fit the new campaigning ethos that Roosevelt himself helped create. Just as the myth of Henry Clay's righteousness offered an idealized portrait of what a campaigner should do that reflected the values of America in 1844, the Roosevelt myth captured the ideal in its updated form a century later. In an era when campaigning was increasingly accepted and expected, it was only natural to inflate Roosevelt's image as a masterful campaigner. The fable of the Fala speech proved not only that stumping had become acceptable, but that campaigning skills now were qualities to be prized.

Still, concerns with presidential dignity persisted. Americans relished a partisan fight like good liberal democrats, but when they complained they sounded like their republican ancestors. More than simply a war-induced sensitivity, the discomfort with campaigning harked back to a nagging question throughout American political history: Just how should a candidate campaign? Criticism of the speech revealed that traditional concerns with presidential dignity lingered, that active and glib candidates still made many Americans uncomfortable.

V

"Modern campaigning will not be perfected," a Midwestern columnist joshed in 1944, "until it becomes possible not only to reason with a mother but to kiss her baby over the radio." This wisecrack, and other more serious analyses, pointed to the radio revolution in presidential campaigning that never was. Radio campaigning had its intricacies, but the "rules" of the presidential game stayed substantially the same.[98]

The continuities were clearest when it came to stumping, where changes in technology helped solidify its position in the campaign. The "swing around the circle" offered a structure wherein the candidate's story could unfold for newsreel, newspaper, and radio reporters. Candidates no longer had to fight obscurity from the back of a train, region by region. In fact, in an age of instant communication with one national market, candidates feared *overexposure*. To avoid a public overdose, candidates' appearances had to be rationed; tension had to be built, as in radio soap operas. Thus Roosevelt's excruciating mating ritual, generating mysteries about whether and when he would run—and Dewey's terraced strategy, culminating in an October blitz.

The limitations of radio also highlighted the advantages of stumping. Paradoxically, a medium that valued warmth could not fully convey it. Even as voters were seduced by the intimacy of the radio appeal, they missed the fullness and intensity of the personal exchange. In these radio days, stumping was essential—and expected.

Just as stumping's importance became more apparent, though, the live event became upstaged. The new technologies subordinated the needs of the immediate audience to those of the unseen millions in the theaters and living rooms of the great American continent. As 93,000 bored Deweyites discovered in Los Angeles in 1944, the radio audience of up to 65 million was that many more times important. In 1940, an adviser urged Wendell Willkie to appear at the Hollywood Bowl because the visit would trigger a "rain of publicity . . . which would be disseminated" throughout the country "via the many syndicated columns from Hollywood." A site was no longer important because of its electoral votes and political constellation, but its dramatic value and media constellation as well. The real people witnessing the scene were becoming props. The age of what historian Daniel Boorstin would call the "pseudo-event," whereby the event became less important than its coverage, had arrived.[99]

Fittingly, Franklin Roosevelt ushered in this era of liberal-democratic glories and republican terrors. When he took office, many considered the future of democracy to be "uncertain." Adapting to modern technologies and changing mores, he proved that democracy could produce vigorous leaders. He spurred an extraordinary liberal-democratic revolution. Ethnics, immigrants, and union workers plunged into the mainstream of American life. The government became the great champion of equity and equality. The presidency became at once more personal and more corporate, closer in appearance but more distant in fact, with the President functioning as "the American people's one authentic trumpet," in the words of Professor Clinton Rossiter.[100]

Roosevelt also helped propel the candidate toward the people. His three reelection bids capped the trend whereby Presidents campaigned. His four efforts, as well as those of his opponents, helped settle the century-long debate between active and passive candidacies. Henceforth all nominees, challengers and incumbents, would campaign energetically.

But rather than climaxing the movement toward a direct and democratic dialogue between the candidate and the people, this era also began the reign of the sleight of hand. Roosevelt's coquettish game of what was political or not gave politics and the presidency a bad name. With his pack of ghost-writers and his slick techniques in ethereal media, he epitomized the modern spectral candidate. To many, his very popularity confirmed their fears about his effectiveness and the masses' stupidity. His opponents, coached by advertising experts, were no more reassuring. "Photographs and carefully rehearsed moving picture films do not necessarily convey the truth," Roosevelt had chided Harding in 1920.

More than a decade later, he and his opponents seemingly proved the charge.

In truth, Roosevelt and his opponents were no more manipulative and no less independent than many of their predecessors. The scientific veneer and the brazenness of the new techniques, however, were novel. They came wrapped in a myth of invincibility which unsettled many Americans. From Adolf Hitler to Huey Long, from Orson Welles's "War of the Worlds" to Edward R. Murrow's coverage of World War II, Americans saw proof of radio's power. Even worse, pseudosciences like advertising and polling were in their infancy. As political scientist Pendleton Herring noted in 1940, politicians had not even begun to master "the more subtle ways of manipulating public opinion."[101]

In a century, the presidential candidate had come full circle. Originally hidden from the people by a fiction that he was above the partisan fray, when he finally entered the campaign the nominee remained obscured. Elaborate calculations rather than simple myths now camouflaged the candidate. Originally the projection of party experts, now he was the creation of his own technicians. No longer was the candidate pretending not to campaign; increasingly, he campaigned by pretending.

NINE

Televising the President, 1948–1964

Politics is show business.
—*Republican National Chairman Leonard Wood Hall, 1956*

IN Frank Capra's 1948 movie *State of the Union* Mary Matthews, played by Katharine Hepburn, reprimands her husband for allowing politicians to corrupt his grassroots, Wendell Willkie–like campaign. "That won't be Grant Matthews" giving a nationwide radio speech, Mary cries, "it will be a shadow, a ghost, a stooge, mouthing words that aren't you own, thoughts that aren't you own." Her husband, played by Spencer Tracy, throws out his bland, ghost-written text, and confesses to the American people: "I lost faith in you. I lost faith in myself." To the horror of the bosses and the experts, Matthews admits his speech is an "elaborately staged professional affair. . . . I thought I could hijack the Republican nomination. But I forgot . . . how quickly the Americans smell out the double-dealers."[1] In 1948, Americans believed they could "smell out" the occasional inauthentic candidate. Flush from victory in World War II, eager to embrace their self-proclaimed "American Century," Americans had little room for any doubts. By 1964, chastened by tepid campaigns and the continuing Cold War, Americans would question the authenticity of all candidates, as well as their own ability to detect such frauds.

In retrospect, the period from 1896 to 1944 would become a Golden Age of campaigning. As actors, the nominees were somewhat calculating and artificial, but on the whole appeared intimate and authentic. The "Campaign Special," rumbling through America morning, noon, and night, displayed the nominees in unguarded moments, be it Charles Hughes running to catch his own campaign train, or Al Smith greeting early risers in his P.J.'s. And while most of the rear-platform rituals highlighted the candidate's personality, the schedule was built around a series of policy addresses.

By 1964, advances in transportation and communication would make the candidate seem disembodied—airplanes would whiz him by; television would reduce him to an electronic mirage. The campaign would become paradoxical, with the nominee trying to camouflage himself, all the while participating in activities designed to expose him. This elaborate game would make Americans doubt both the candidates and themselves. The presidential candidate, many would fear, was simply another commodity being marketed.

I

In 1948 no one was sure just when the presidential sale was made. While many feared that admen could sell anything, including the presidency, to anyone anytime, others believed that most elections were decided even before the campaign began. Known as "Farley's Law" in honor of Franklin Roosevelt's campaign manager, James Farley, this perspective combined traditional fears of "Burchardization" with modern analyses of opinion formation. "Nine times in ten, the election results would be no different if the candidates stayed home," pollster George Gallup said.[2]

These doubts about campaigning dovetailed with the magnified sense of presidential dignity in the wake of World War II. The President was now "the leader of the free world," the term itself testifying to America's nuclear strength and anti-Communist fears. No president should play politics, for every word he uttered, every move he made, could determine the world's fate.

Unfortunately, Franklin Roosevelt's successor, Harry S. Truman, did not seem suited to be "the most powerful man on earth." Trim, amiable, and partial to blue-serge suits, "Harry" seemed more adept with a garden hose than a nuclear arsenal. It was hard to dislike the Missourian, but even harder to respect him. New Deal Democrats could not accept this failed haberdasher as the new Roosevelt. They hoped to retire the "interim President" in 1948. Truman, a World War I army Captain, snarled: "I was not brought up to run from a fight."[3]

Truman believed in aggressive campaigning. He and his aides recog-

nized that the parties had splintered into special-interest groups demanding government handouts, while the nation had coalesced into a
mass audience searching for an appealing "vote-getting picture" of the
President. Truman's aides instructed their boss to be more presidential,
systematizing for the rookie what had been instinctive for Roosevelt.
The "masses" watch "incidental gestures," not policies, the aides advised. Critics might scoff at "inspection tours," but the people would
respond. In "selling" himself as a candidate, a President "must resort to
subterfuge—for he cannot sit silent," one memorandum acknowledged.[4]
In the 1940s these sentiments remained hidden from the public—though
not for much longer.

Aping his predecessor, Truman took a "nonpolitical" trip to California in June 1948, to accept an honorary degree from Berkeley. "I
thought I had better come out and let you look at me to see whether I
am the kind of fellow they say I am," he told thousands at railroad
stations along the way. In fifteen days Truman gave seventy-six
speeches, seventy-one of them "off the cuff." He greeted crowds at any
hour, dressed on occasion in his bathrobe. Again and again poor staff
work, public apathy, and Truman's verbal slips muffled the occasional
cheers. Barely 2,000 people showed up in Omaha's 10,000-seat coliseum.
Lacking Roosevelt's light touch, when Truman joked about his nonpolitical trip he destroyed the illusion. And, dedicating an airport in
Idaho, he praised the "brave boy" who died "for our country." The
grieving mother whispered that her *daughter* "was killed right here."[5]

While rehashing Roosevelt-era complaints that the trip did not fool
anyone, critics especially condemned Truman's "off the cuff" speeches.
Roosevelt "never uttered a sentence in a public address that was not
fully considered and written down in advance," the Kansas City Times
lectured. The Washington Post reminded Truman that now, the whole
world was listening to him. One verbal slip could trigger an international crisis.[6] In sacrificing the authenticity of extemporaneous speeches
for the dignity and safety of prepared texts, Americans revealed their
growing Cold War anxiety.

The President's behavior appalled "Mr. Republican," Robert A.
Taft, who accused Truman of "blackguarding Congress at every whistle
stop in the West." The Ohio Senator erred. He used railroad shorthand
for a "hick" town so trivial that it did not merit a regular stop, forcing
conductors to toot their whistles in order to signal engineers when a
stop *was* necessary. By 1948, to avoid offending townspeople, railroad
men spoke of "flag stops" or "flag stations." Taft's faux pas helped sal-
vage Truman's journey, contrasting the Democratic everyman with the

Republican plutocrats. Harry Truman had found his political voice on what he now called his "Whistle Stop Tour."[7]

Nevertheless, Republicans felt cocky; they had many candidates who seemed more "presidential" than Truman. Thomas E. Dewey, still Governor of New York, considered the campaign an inconvenience. Invoking the claim of executive dignity, aides insisted that Dewey "is fully engaged with the work of the legislative session and cannot actively seek the nomination." But Minnesota Governor Harold Stassen's victories in the Wisconsin and Nebraska primaries upset Dewey. Suddenly finding time to campaign in Oregon, Dewey set out to prove that he was not the human icebox. Shaking hands from Sweet Home to Brownsville, he indulged in local rituals, even eating raw beef at Grant Pass with a fur-clad group who fancied themselves the "Cave Men." He also debated Stassen over the radio. Dewey won the Oregon primary, rousing his campaign and leaping to the nomination.[8]

Dewey savored his nomination as a harbinger of victory. Farley's Law, the power of advertising, and the fear of lapsing into undignified behavior, as he had in 1944, convinced Dewey that full stumping campaigns were passé. The future leader of the free world would campaign sparingly. In deference to local Republican candidates and to tradition, Dewey would traverse the nation, but the prospective president would offer nothing more controversial than the promise to "build in this country a sense of fair play and of unity and give and take." On September 9, pollster Elmo Roper stopped taking polls. Dewey, he declared, was "almost as good as elected."[9]

Harry Truman's rip-roaring campaign made Dewey's seem even more elevated and platitudinous than it was. In his acceptance, after itemizing the Democrats' benefits to each constituency, Truman called a special congressional session, on what was known in Missouri as Turnip Day. Now, Truman said, the nation could judge the Republicans' commitment to fair housing and lower prices. As expected, the Republican Congress refused to enact Truman's "Fair Deal." Truman would continue to peddle this mix of calculated folksiness, playing Santa to Dewey's Scrooge; the Midwestern farm boy to the Eastern city slicker.

After the special session, Truman marked the long summer days. Come September, he would start "a campaign tour that is going to be a record for a President of the United States." He dismissed the concerns with dignity, opting instead to champion democracy in a "people's crusade" which would "give 'em hell."[10]

Truman began with a rousing Labor Day speech to auto workers in Detroit's Cadillac Square, in what would become the Democrats' traditional opening. Over the next two months, Truman delivered twenty-six odes to Democratic largess, and 244 "whistle stop" talks. "Homespun Harry" adhered to the campaign train ritual: The high-school band played "Hail to the Chief." The local beauty queen (or union man, or Kiwanis chief) presented a bushel of apples (or head of lettuce, or city hall key). Better briefed than in June, Truman saluted the Democratic Pooh Bahs, dazzled folks with some local trivia, and commented on a relevant national issue. "And now," he would smile, "howja like to meet ma family," basking in the applause as he introduced "the Boss"—his wife—and "the Boss's boss"—his daughter. In under ten minutes he would be on his way.[11]

Beneath the trifles and the jokes that "Dewey" rhymes with "Hooey," Truman made his campaign a referendum on democracy. He also exploited republican fears. His "whistle stop" rituals honored small-town America, the last bastion against modern decline. An old-fashioned democrat who rejected technology and its manipulations, Truman denounced the "expensive Republican propaganda" and its "sleeping polls." Having defended both democracy and republicanism, Truman posed as the man of courage and candor. "I have been going all over the United States . . . telling the people what the issues in this campaign are," he boasted to his audiences, while Dewey refused to "talk to you man to man, face to face, about what he would do if he were elected."[12] In Harry Truman's capable hands the stumping campaign became traditional and appropriate; the passive campaign, modern and illegitimate.

While clever, many of Truman's antics were undignified—and unprecedented. Bess Truman told her husband to run the way he did when he was "campaigning for county judge," thereby treating the President as just another mortal politician. Never before had a President campaigned so bluntly or so intensively. Even Roosevelt had avoided such brazen confusion of his political and official roles. "He's stopped trying to be President," one observer lamented. "He's being Truman now." Still, Truman's partisans praised the tour's democratic nature, celebrating the "curious American flavor" of his appeals. Most citizens writing to Truman encouraged him and suggested even more rhetorical flourishes—quite a contrast to the lectures on propriety most nineteenth-century candidates received.[13]

Each day the crowds ratified Truman's tactics, growing larger, louder, and wilder. Most pundits were too committed to Farley's Law, too blinded by the polls, and too appalled by Truman's tactics to take the crowds seriously. The crowds simply were honoring the office, not the man, they insisted. Still, as Dewey continued distributing clichés—"The next thing we know he'll be endorsing matrimony, the metal zipper and the dial telephone," Tallulah Bankhead teased—he sensed his campaign drifting. His campaign manager, Herbert Brownell, Jr., canvassed over 125 Republican leaders. All but one said "Don't rock the boat."[14] Dewey respected the consensus, lost, and inevitably had to shoulder the blame alone.

Truman's victory overturned both Farley's Law and Burchard's legacy. Even with modern polling, no one could verify whether farmers, unions, the entire Roosevelt coalition, or Truman himself proved decisive.[15] Just as uncertainty did not stop earlier generations from blaming Clay, Blaine, or Hughes, this generation credited Truman. Passivity was now considered more dangerous than campaigning; dignity could no longer keep the candidate from the people. The candidate's interaction with the millions he could reach really did matter, Americans decided. Main Street defeated Madison Avenue, rejecting Roosevelt's legacy of the pseudo-event. Campaigning—the "old-fashioned" way—apparently counted.

With the certainty of hindsight, Dewey and his campaign were repudiated. Americans welcomed the defeat of the slick, manipulative, efficiency-experted "Young & Rubicam and Hollywood" campaign. In good republican fashion, new technologies like polling were deemed subversive. "We are proud of America for clouding up the crystal ball, for telling one thing to a poll-taker, another thing to a voting machine," essayist E. B. White exulted. Unpredictability is an "essential part of freedom," the *St. Louis Star-Times* explained.[16]

Truman and his men encouraged these obituaries for Madison Avenue. Falsely contrasting authenticity and calculation, Democrats celebrated Truman's triumph, overlooking his years of preparations. Truman and his aides claimed there were "no devious plans," there was no "high strategy."[17] Boasts like these ensured that plans would *always* appear devious. Once Americans discovered how much calculation modern campaigning entailed, their disappointment—and cynicism—would be all the greater.

Even considering Truman's weakness and Farley's Law, Dewey's passivity seemed foolish. Had he not learned from Roosevelt's example, and from the Oregon primary, that the people demanded an active campaign? Dewey was "passive" only by mid-twentieth-century standards, but he had campaigned more energetically before. His behavior can only be understood by recalling that in 1948 Communism was spreading, Berlin was blockaded, war raged in the Middle East and China. Since the last election, the President had acquired the ability to destroy the world. Dewey decided to campaign cautiously, as if the world's fate was in his hands. Truman's campaign was anachronistic and reckless, even though the world it recalled reassured Americans. A Dewey victory might have injected more dignity into the campaign. Instead, the messy personal campaign emerged as America's "traditional" salvation. Nuclear proliferation and fears of Communism would continue to cast a shadow over the campaign, but they would fail to revolutionize this now-enduring American institution.

II

Harry Truman had redeemed the rear-platform campaign, confirming its legitimacy. The human touch prevailed. But neither ancestral notions of dignity nor modern campaigning techniques had quite died with Dewey's campaign. Candidates could no longer be passive, but they still had to be dignified. Advertisers and pollsters, though cowed, were not defeated. Modern contraptions would not be rejected; they would be more artfully employed. Trumanesque intimacy would have to be mass-produced.

The 1952 campaign was inevitably confusing. Truman's earlier campaign seemingly offered the model for all, and aspirants like Senator Robert Taft whistle-stopped during the first half of 1952. But airplanes promised faster travel, and television tempted politicians to forego the tour entirely. By 1952, 17 million TV sets were in service, exciting hopes, similar to the ones that greeted radio, of bringing government closer to the people.

Before choosing a marketing strategy, though, politicians had to find a product. The World War II hero Dwight D. Eisenhower was the leading Republican candidate, except that he was not running, was not a Republican, and was not even in the United States. General Eisenhower said that he would run only if the people insisted. Millions were ready to draft him—but party leaders preferred Taft. Eisenhower would have to earn his nomination. The republican dream, that he could stand for election and await the people's call, had vanished. In June, Eisenhower returned home, resigned his commission, and began to campaign.

Distasteful as stumping was to him, Eisenhower could not afford to campaign like Dewey. Now, the no-nonsense general had to smile when politicians boomed "Hi, podner!" and smothered him with bear hugs. And the master of terse commands also had to make lengthy speeches. After mumbling through his first televised speech, Eisenhower threw his prepared talks "out the window." This declaration of independence from ghost-writers demonstrated Eisenhower's sincerity and let the people "determine what manner of man" he was, the *New York Times* applauded.[18] At a convention watched by 51 million viewers, Eisenhower was nominated.

To oppose the national hero unfamiliar with politics, the Democrats drafted Adlai E. Stevenson, a politician unfamiliar to the nation. In April, barely one-third of those surveyed identified the balding, cerebral Princeton alumnus as the Governor of Illinois. Stevenson did not want to run. Asked what he would do if nominated, he replied "I'll shoot myself." Stevenson tired of "the nauseous nonsense" and the "all-things-to-all-men demagoguery that are too much a part of our political campaigns." He considered personalities irrelevant; candidates should address issues "sensibly and truthfully." In relenting and accepting the nomination, Stevenson welcomed the campaign as "a great opportunity to educate and elevate. . . . Let's talk sense to the American people," he cried.[19]

Stevenson planned a campaign that was old-fashioned yet modern. He refused to "insult" the people by mouthing clichés from a train, and had no interest in chatting with local pols. With an ethic more suited to earlier times, Stevenson launched a campaign of speeches. Television beamed his urbane policy pronouncements into millions of living rooms, while the airplane offered a sedate atmosphere for perfecting the texts.

"Prop-stopping"—with occasional whistle stops—allowed Stevenson to roam the continent. But it also insulated him. There were no midnight or 6 A.M. calls for a bathrobed candidate. Local politicians could not hop aboard for a quick conference with the nominee. Stevenson could land only in cities with airports large enough to accommodate his chartered jet. And, while the uncommitted might walk to the downtown railroad station to see a candidate, only partisans would trek to the suburban airfields. The plane is "sure speedy," one politician noted, "but how many votes are up there?"[20]

When he landed, Stevenson motorcaded into town. Candidates had used such cavalcades of cars for decades, though never so extensively. A motorcade through downtown could expose the candidate to thousands. But it was grueling. You smile "until your mouth is dehydrated by the wind," and wave "until the blood runs out of your arm," Stevenson would remember. Sometimes the fancy cars provoked more cheers than the candidate. In 1952, operatives were still accustomed to the comforts of the campaign train. During a day-long motorcade through Connecticut, nature began making its demands on the participants. But a motorcade "cannot pull up to a service station," Professor John Kenneth Galbraith recalled. "No car can break away, however desperate the occupants." There are "few more exacting ordeals than a Presidential campaign," Stevenson often muttered.[21]

Television also both helped and hurt. TV made Stevenson a "star" overnight. His eighteen half-hour talks, on topics ranging from atomic energy to the one-party press, averaged 3.6 million viewers, more than twice the size of his radio audience. Surveys found that Stevenson gained more support among TV viewers than among the general public. But he had his video problems. His constant revising, and his refusal to rehearse, often forced him to rush as he neared the end of his half-hour, bobbing his head and swallowing his words. And by refusing to wear makeup, and preferring texts to teleprompters, he ended up showing the viewers too much of his freckled forehead.[22]

More generally, staffers feared that Stevenson's wit amused the masses without converting them. Bons mots promising that if the Republicans "will stop telling lies about the Democrats, we will stop telling the truth about them" were not harsh enough. Stevenson had to send his opponents reeling, not chuckling. He had to get his audiences cheering, not nodding assent. Accusations of elitism irked Stevenson: "You'll just have to forgive me if I go on trusting your intelligence," he pouted. Voters often left his speeches more impressed with themselves for appreciating his cerebral style than with Stevenson himself.[23]

Eisenhower, on the other hand, had mastered the touches but avoided the issues. He could lend dignity to even the most carnival-like settings. The campaign centered on a whistle stop tour, while television, airplanes, and motorcades extended his reach. Such whirlwind campaigning exorcised Dewey's ghost. Eisenhower stuck to generalities because he could. People were thrilled to see the war hero, but many often left before he started "talking politics." Still, his halting delivery helped contrast the honest, if fumbling, soldier with the glib "egghead." Making a virtue of necessity, partisans praised Eisenhower's "character" as enough of a policy. "What Ike has to sell," an aide confessed, "is his rugged, incorruptible honesty. . . . There's no use trying to dress him up as an expert in all phases of civil and political affairs."[24]

This "hack politician approach" disappointed many. *The New Republic*'s columnist TRB said that comparing Stevenson's speeches with

Eisenhower's was like comparing "one of Emerson's essays and an advertisement for bubble-gum." Even Eisenhower would later admit that the Republican strategy gave "too much weight to nationwide familiarity with my name" and not enough to "principle."[25]

Many knew that one of Eisenhower's few policy pronouncements, a pledge to go to Korea to handle the conflict there, originated with a ghost-writer. Surprisingly, few objected to the source. Both Eisenhower and Stevenson had begun to believe in ghosts, albeit reluctantly. "Organizing a presidential campaign is about as intricate as planning a large-scale invasion," the General realized; he could not do it all. Stevenson, too, had "confronted . . . the ugly reality" that he would have to use "researchers"—he refused to call them "speechwriters." Still, Eisenhower insisted that he could never deliver someone else's draft "intact as my own." When Stevenson came across phrases he disliked while delivering a speech, he often stopped and winced. He blamed these lapses for contributing to his bad "TV image."[26]

Ghosting had become more legitimate since the New Deal, but the resistance remained. "Ghost-writing has debased [our] intellectual currency . . . and is a type of counterfeiting which invites no defense," Supreme Court Justice Robert H. Jackson bellowed in a 1949 case.[27] Candidates and the public preferred that the ghosts disappear, but the campaign remained haunted.

In mid-September, Democrats tried to avenge Republican charges of corruption. Eisenhower's running mate, Richard M. Nixon, had a secret $18,000 fund to cover his expenses as a California Senator. Many urged Eisenhower to drop Nixon from the ticket. On September 23, right after the top-rated "Milton Berle Show," Nixon delivered what came to be known as the "Checkers Speech" to almost 60 million people. Nixon's maudlin defense, during which he invoked his wife and his dog, inspired a flood of telegrams which saved his political life.[28]

Critics blamed television for Nixon's "corny" defense. Jack Gould of the *New York Times* warned against "television turning politics into a coast-to-coast vaudeville show." This criticism revealed more about the anxiety surrounding the new technology than about any changes in politics. Checkers was as relevant to the Nixon affair in 1952 as Fala had been to the New Deal in 1944—politicians did not have to learn about cheap sentiment from television. TV did, however, make Nixon an instant celebrity. In late August, less than half of the people surveyed could identify Nixon.[29] Three weeks later, reporters flocked to cover his campaign; crowds, to hear him speak. Alert observers, including Nixon, recognized television's power.

Television could also derail a campaign. Some experts believed that most half-hour speeches wasted $75,000 or so. Television was supposed to "capture" nonpartisans, but uncommitted viewers often changed the channel or griped. After one speech preempted TV's most popular show, a flood of telegrams proved that Americans "liked" Ike, but they "loved" Lucy. Also, Rosser Reeves of the Ted Bates ad agency discovered that few viewers remembered much of what Eisenhower or Stevenson said; their messages did not "penetrate."[30]

Reeves generated scripts for over fifty commercials featuring Eisenhower, his wife Mamie, and "Mr. and Mrs. America." Eisenhower at first feared that "a spot campaign would not be dignified." It smacked too much of toothpaste, he said. Once settled, Eisenhower proved most accommodating. He "cut" 40 television spots one day, 25 radio spots the next. Aided by cue cards with eight-inch-high letters so that he could dispense with his glasses, his "natural" look preserved in the klieg lights by makeup, Eisenhower genially "Answer[ed] America." A typical exchange had a woman holding a shopping bag and complaining, "I paid $24 for these groceries! Look—for this little!" Eisenhower responded: "A few years ago, those *same* groceries cost you $10. Now—twenty-four! Next year, thirty! That's what will happen, unless we have a change!" Never before had a nominee participated in such an artificial and "scientifically" planned endeavor. Between takes, Eisenhower muttered: "To think that an old soldier should come to this."[31]

Before they were broadcast, word of the spots leaked. Condemning the Madison Avenue hucksters, Stevenson said "This isn't Ivory Soap vs. Palmolive. . . . This is a choice for the most important office on earth." Republicans, including Reeves, denied the ads existed, yet within three weeks the broadcasts began.[32]

Although the Democrats had their own agency and envied the Republicans' resources, their attack was sincere. Advertising, and its attendant fears, had been creeping into the campaign for decades. The "merchandising" style of campaigning originated with Mark Hanna in the 1890s. Ever since Albert Lasker helped Warren Harding in 1920, advertisers had been injecting "business" principles into campaigns—especially Republican ones. But in 1952 the blatancy of the Republican appeals, the prominence of admen like Reeves throughout the campaign, Eisenhower's complicity, and the apparent effectiveness of the spots, intensified these concerns. With three agencies on their payroll, the Republicans appeared to have been hijacked by the admen, who respected no boundaries. Advertisers like Lloyd G. Whitebrock believed that admen should limit themselves to "time buying" and "technical advice." CBS policy, an executive recalled, "held that television commercials may be used to sell merchandise but not to sell ideas."[33] Reeves and his cohorts made the candidates and the people objects, one to be sold, the other to be swayed. The men in gray flannel suits replaced the power brokers and foreign agents of republican demonology. With their power and expertise, they would subvert the nation. TV advertising became the bogeyman of the modern campaign.

The nominees had become both more important and less autonomous. Truman's victory thrust them onto center stage, but advertisers and other experts now controlled their destiny. Even though both Eisenhower and Stevenson began as reluctant campaigners, their supporters—and Dewey's spectre—disallowed such quaint sensibilities. Use of the airplane further enslaved the nominees to the whims of politicians across America, and to an accelerated campaign. Truman's 20,000-mile jaunt paled before Stevenson's 32,000 miles and Eisenhower's 50,000. The sore throats and stomach ills that afflicted each entourage testified to the grueling pace. In the future it would only get worse.

Also, even though their campaigns were carefully planned, both candidates played the innocent. Republican Senator Henry Cabot Lodge, Jr., claimed that Eisenhower had no tactics: "We've never had any tactics in this campaign." After Eisenhower's landslide victory, Republican officials stopped Rosser Reeves from analyzing the spots' impact. Republicans did not want to show that their "mandate for a change" varied "according to the intensity of the spot campaign," an insider reported. Whenever someone tried to coach Stevenson, he bristled: "If they don't like me as I am, *tant pis!* I won't pretend to be anything else." All this posturing implied that politics was demeaning and generated unrealistic expectations about the virtues of American candidates. "Stevenson's attitude to politics has always seemed that of a man who believes love is the most ennobling of human emotions while the mechanics of sex are dirty and squalid," Theodore White observed in 1960. Adlai Stevenson—and the American people—continually forgot that "public affairs and politics are linked as are love and sex."[34]

Nearly eighty thousand letters poured into Springfield after Stevenson's defeat. Many who had voted Republican explained that they loved his campaign but hated his party. Over the years, memories of Stevenson's eloquence and elegance would blot out the amateurishness and elitism. Stevenson's campaign would be remembered for its oratory, Eisenhower's for its commercials. Stevenson's effort would become the paradigmatic campaign of substance, Eisenhower's the campaign of show business and fluff. Indeed, Stevenson's campaign was a remarkable

achievement, a monument to the democratic dialogue at its best. After
150 years, the presidential campaign had evolved to a point where a
candidate could address the people seriously and substantively. But Stevenson lost. And therein lay the true lesson for many. Losing ennobled
Stevenson and sullied American politics. Stevenson's may have been a
remarkable campaign—but it was not a successful one. Talking about
issues was nice, but celebrities with jazzy campaigns won elections. The
gap between expedience and virtue seemed greater than ever.

III

As the 1950s progressed, people wondered what TV was doing to America. Radio simply extended reality, but television transformed it, un-
leashing, many feared, a struggle for America's soul. Americans valued
television as their "most important source of ideas, apart from interper-
sonal contact," while fearing it as "a monster uprooting established patterns of activity." By 1955, television had entered 35 million homes,
commanding attention five hours per day in the average household.
Politicians like Governor Dewey and broadcasters like Walter Cronkite
appreciated TV's "X-Ray" ability to detect "insincerity"; its potential to
be a "medium for the truth," as Senator Taft termed it. Yet some worried
that TV's apparent integrity would spur politicians to greater artifice.
Acting sincere on TV was not the same as being honest. Once again,
Americans glorified the good old days of campaigning that their ancestors so disliked. Cronkite feared that, with television, the superficial
charmer would always defeat a brilliant but "ugly little man with a bald
head." Are we destined for "government by Hooper Rating?" he wondered.[35]

The Democrats exploited this nostalgia and fear by championing
their "old-fashioned"—and cheaper—approach. Stevenson's 1952 campaign provided the vocabulary for the attack. In 1956, the battle lines
formed quickly. "There is no substitute for personal campaigning—the
old handshake and the pat on the shoulder," Democratic National
Chairman Paul M. Butler said. His Republican rival, Hugh Scott, disagreed, reasoning that even if millions see a candidate on the stump,
"Most will not hear what he says. What's that compared to getting into
every voter's living room?" Scott's successor, Leonard Wood Hall, added
that only elaborate productions would attract viewers. "Politics," he declared, "is show business."[36] Torn between technology and the status
quo, politicians reflected the public's mixed signals about the modern

campaign. This confusion characterized the hybrid campaigns that Stevenson and Eisenhower mounted.

Eisenhower expected to run, and win, on his own terms. Peace and prosperity boosted his approval ratings to 75 percent. Then, on September 23, 1955, the sixty-five-year-old President suffered a heart attack. It appeared he would retire, but in February Eisenhower decided to run again. He would "wage no political campaign in the customary pattern." He would "inform the American people" about his administration's deeds "through means of mass communication." "Doctor's orders or no, I would not have conducted the same sort of campaign in 1956 as I had in 1952," Eisenhower later explained. Traditional concerns and modern realities ruled out whistle-stopping; the "first duty of a President" remained discharging "the responsibilities of his office." Five or six TV appearances would suffice. "We are in a new age—an electronics age," his press secretary, James C. Hagerty, explained.[37]

For his part, Adlai Stevenson expected an easy renomination, followed by another grand campaign. But then Yale-trained, coonskin-capped Tennessee Senator Estes Kefauver challenged him. Kefauver championed nationwide primaries that would enable the people of each party to choose the nominee. The primaries had long languished as formalities, mocking "our democratic processes," Kefauver believed. Eight of the twenty-six states that held primaries in 1916 had abandoned them. Recently, primary victories for Dewey in 1944 and 1948, and for Eisenhower in 1952, had advanced their respective nominations, while losses by Willkie in 1944 and Truman eight years later hastened their respective retirements. Still, primaries remained sideshows—party bosses ruled: Most convention delegates were chosen by fellow politicians. In 1956, New Hampshire held the earliest primary. The nonbinding preference poll took place on the second Tuesday in March, during "mud season"—the time for New England politicking, after the snow and before the plowing.[38] Although only eight delegates were at stake, Kefauver gambled that a victory would catapult him into the public eye. It did. Later that month he won the Minnesota primary, too. Primaries would never be ignored again.

"I'm tired of losing elections," Stevenson fumed. Choosing personalities over policies, expedience over virtue, Stevenson agreed to match Kefauver handshake for handshake. He plunged into the Florida campaign, in his way. Muttering "I'm no five dollar whore," Stevenson pursued voters in barber shops and department stores, at factories and supermarkets. But campaigning like a "candidate for deputy sheriff" did not suit the Princeton patrician. When a girl offered him a stuffed alliga-

tor, Stevenson snarled, "For Christ's sake, what's this?" An aide explained that he should have thanked her and said "I've always wanted
one of these for the mantelpiece at Libertyville." Amused but not fully
enlightened, Stevenson retold that story, guaranteeing, his aide winced,
more votes for Kefauver, "who was born knowing what to do with an
out-thrust alligator."[39]

This "retail" campaigning contrasted with the "wholesale" campaigning of 1952 and injected a new element into presidential politics.
Never before had presidential candidates sought out the voters so ag-
gressively. Although campaigning rituals had the nominee appear as a
mendicant in search of a voter's favor, the people always approached
the candidate at rallies, train stations, prop-stops, and motorcades. Now
the candidate was a beggar, stalking voters between lingerie counters in
department stores. Privately, Stevenson agonized. "No one worthy of
being President should act like a panhandler," he snapped. One day,
after wriggling into a cowboy outfit to lead a parade, Stevenson sighed:
"*God*, what a man won't do to get public office."[40]

The rise of the primary and the emergence of the candidate as mendicant signified a victory for democracy. Contact between the voters
and their leaders expanded, and for the first time a popular nomination
was possible. Yet while many advocated direct primaries in theory, few
were impressed by them in practice. Proving that the republican distaste
for democracy lingered, primaries were criticized for being unseemly and
destabilizing. Even though Stevenson clinched the nomination with victories in Florida and California, he agreed. The primaries were undignified, "banal," and exhausting. By the time he was nominated, he was
"squeezed and wasted," he confessed.[41]

The primary fight demonstrated that, this time, Stevenson was running to win. He admitted that in 1952 he had "spent far too much time
on texts, at the expense of politics." He proposed "the greatest grassroots campaign in all political history." The campaign was managed by
a Philadelphia ward boss, James Finnegan, who would mobilize precinct
workers. Advertising techniques supplemented the old-fashioned organization. "Our whole operation is an exercise in PR," the Democrats'
director of publicity, Samuel Brightman, exclaimed. After being turned
down by over a dozen advertising agencies who feared offending Republican clients, the Democrats hired a smaller firm, Norman, Craig and
Kummel, who shot "The Man from Libertyville," a series of "folksy"
spots about the candidate at home. Stevenson was filmed answering
mail, picnicking on his lawn with Philadelphia's mayor, and talking
about the high cost of living with his pregnant daughter-in-law—with

the all-important shopping-bag prop. When a twenty-man film crew with a 3,000-pound dolly invaded his home, Stevenson complained "How do you expect me to act folksy in front of so many people?"[42]

The "folksy" imperative, central to the Truman, Eisenhower, and now Stevenson campaigns, illustrated the politicians' attempts to peddle nostalgia, and their realization that TV worked best as a vehicle for personalities, not issues. Also, as the first divorced nominee, Stevenson had to improve his family "image." In 1956, Americans knew more about Stevenson, including his marital status. "If a man can't run his family, he has no business trying to run the country," a Midwesterner muttered.[43]

Stevenson also had to compete with the legend of 1952. He alternated between grand calls for a "new America"—detailed in lengthy position papers—and jabs at Eisenhower, "the part-time President." Stevenson "says many of the same things he said in '52 but he says them in plainer language," El Paso's Democratic chairman rejoiced. Still, devotees mourned that "We've lost much of the tone and quality of 1952 utterances." Stevenson's paeans to "hard-hitting factual debate" began to sound phony.[44] His intensive whistle-stopping and prop-stopping undermined his live TV appearances. All too often he appeared harried and unprepared while speaking. In trying to serve all masters, Stevenson was failing television, the most important one. Increasingly, in contrast to the 1952 crusade, 1956 seemed like just another campaign, and Stevenson just another politician.

Meanwhile, Republicans fretted more about medical charts than opinion polls. On June 8, Eisenhower underwent surgery for ileitis. He now had even less interest in campaigning. Americans worried, as pollsters asked whether they believed another heart attack or another stomach operation was the more likely. Eisenhower looked especially bad on TV: his face was drawn, his voice sounded husky. "That's why Ike will have to go out on the road," professionals noted. To spur the President, his aides overstated Stevenson's strength. "You don't win campaigns with a diet of dishwater and milk toast," Vice President Richard Nixon warned.[45]

In yielding, Eisenhower hid behind semantics. He was "probably doing a little bit more than . . . originally planned," but he was "not going to go barnstorming" or "whistle-stopping." His 50,000 miles in 1952 was "what I call barnstorming." Cartoonist Herblock sketched the President motorcading through a crowd and asking "Who's Whistle-Stopping?" "I like to go out and see people," Eisenhower grinned.[46]

Both Eisenhower and his critics assumed it was proper for presidents to campaign, testament to Franklin Roosevelt's legacy. Democrats viewed Eisenhower's descent from his "pedestal" as an admission of weakness. As usual, history was recast to justify contemporary practice. The border between the powers of the presidency and the pressures of politics was so "broad and vague" that during the past half century each President had struck his own balance, columnist Raymond P. Brandt explained. Eisenhower's shift, only after his doctor "gave the green light," dramatized his swift recovery, and justified the charade.[47] Stevenson's gain had been his loss: Luring Eisenhower onto the stump energized the Republican campaign.

Stevenson's attempt to inject issues into the campaign also boomeranged. He advocated banning hydrogen-bomb testing and ending the draft—positions which were noble and farsighted but risky. At best the reasoning was too abstract; at worst it made the Democrats appear weak on defense. Stevenson's choice of issues became especially unfortunate when, in late October, in two terrifying weeks, Great Britain, France, and Israel captured the Sinai Peninsula from Egypt, while the Soviet Union crushed Hungary's anti-Communist uprising. Americans wondered if World War III had begun. Eisenhower reassured the nation, speaking "not as a candidate for office, but as President of the United States." His already commanding lead thereafter increased by an estimated five percentage points in the popular vote. Stevenson, who chuckled that millions took "refuge *with* Eisenhower *from* Eisenhower's disastrous" foreign policy, would never be President.[48]

Predictions that 1956 would "be the year in which people saw their last campaign train" proved groundless. Stumping was still considered "real campaigning." Just as stumping showed the man behind the radio voice, it confirmed the TV image, verifying that the candidate was not some mirage projected into this "magic lantern." And, by whistle-stopping into the heart of downtown, a candidate announced that he was not some Ali Baba whisked around on a magic carpet.[49] Prop-stopping would gradually replace whistle-stopping, but stumping would persist, a comforting antidote to modern pyrotechnics. Advertising and TV rendered the stumping campaign obsolete—except that candidates continued to stump.

The televised stumping campaign, however, was no panacea. Ideally, stumping allowed nominees to maintain close contact with voters, whereas television extended the campaign's reach. But television also trafficked in artificial images, and frequently upstaged the live event. With the perfect campaign as unattainable as the Holy Grail, the over-extended candidates watched the demands on them proliferate. They had to continue as actors on the stump, while carefully honing their images in the TV studio.

After nearly a decade, Americans remained awed by television's potential and disappointed by its mediocrity. The *Saturday Review* could rejoice that "The America of 150,000,000 souls" was returning "to the era when politicians and people met face to face," while pioneers like Sig Mickelson of CBS would recall how TV's artificiality and superficiality "shattered" their "optimism." By 1960, polls would show that two out of three Americans believed that commercials used untruthful arguments; they were beginning to doubt the "medium of truth." Yet, by a ratio of five to four, they preferred a campaign of televised speeches to stumping tours. The *Washington Post* television critic advocated a bill "requiring absolute honesty in TV political campaigning."[50] The springs of their naiveté still running deep, Americans turned to Congress for help.

IV

The congressional committees overseeing communications policy searched for ways to channel the televised campaign. Under Section 315(a) of the Communications Act of 1934, if networks granted free time to any "legally qualified" candidates, they had to grant it equally to all, be they Democrats or Vegetarians. The networks feared losing lucrative programing hours to a parade of candidates. If Congress would suspend this "Equal Time Rule" during the 1960 campaign, the networks offered to donate up to eight hours for what Robert W. Sarnoff of NBC called "Great Debates" between the Republican and Democratic nominees.[51]

Support for debates had ballooned since 1940, when Franklin Roosevelt waved off Wendell Willkie's challenge. Some candidates had debated during primaries, including Dewey and Stassen in Oregon in 1948 and Kefauver and Stevenson in Florida eight years later. As the patron saint of the campaign, Stevenson embraced the cause. Testifying before Congress, Stevenson declared that "face to face" substantive discussions would redeem the "democratic dialogue." Stevenson and his allies designated the Lincoln–Douglas debates as their model, forgetting Lincoln's passivity and Douglas's charade when they ran for President. "To hear the candidates discuss the great issues of an earlier America, people rode all day by buggy or wagon; they waited for hours for the candidate's train; they stood in the sun and rain and listened," Stevenson gushed.

"They wanted to know about the issues and where the candidates stood."[52]

This red, white, and blue version of history inflated faith in the ability of television, the "most powerful medium of communication," to "serve the public good," as Stevenson said. The debates became the latest political panacea. A great debate would bypass the ghost-writers and admen who interposed themselves between the candidates and the people. Everyone could judge the candidates fairly and directly. Candidates would speak to millions with "sanity, and on the basis of factual presentation," Senator Mike Monroney of Oklahoma predicted. Debates "would end the tendency to reduce everything to assertions and to slogans," Stevenson concluded. "It might even help to restore what we seem to have lost—our sense of great national purpose."[53] Many embraced debating as an alternative to whistle-stopping, let their expectations soar, and—as usual—were disappointed.

The debates enhanced the sense that the 1960 campaign marked "a quantum jump in American history," as *Harper's* said.[54] As the age of Roosevelt and Eisenhower ended, the G.I. Joes succeeded the generals. Born in the twentieth century, these new leaders were less rooted than their elders. Freer of party commitments, comfortable on TV, they would embrace the modern campaign.

———

Senator John F. Kennedy of Massachusetts epitomized this new American. He was blessed with a wealthy family, good looks, and a beautiful wife. A typical celebrity, he was famous, it seemed, simply for being famous. His campaign literature illustrated the circularity of this approach, stressing his "Unique Voter Appeal," his "Nation-wide Prestige and Fame," his status as a "Top Television and Platform Personality." Who was more desirable than a "tireless sparkling campaigner," the pamphlet implied; what better guarantee of future popularity than present renown?[55]

After Kefauver's 1956 efforts, primaries became natural springboards for young politicians like Kennedy. In the primaries, Kennedy's mystique partly defused the still powerful taboo against a Catholic president.[56] Jack Kennedy was no Al Smith. His faith was a non sequitur, a mere speck in his all-American tableau. The tired ethnic joke for once seemed appropriate: This good-looking son of Harvard didn't *look* Catholic. In primary campaigns that infuriated Protestant opponents like Senator Hubert Humphrey, Kennedy implied that a vote for him was a vote against bigotry. Come convention time, such aspirants as Stevenson and Senator Lyndon B. Johnson, both of whom waited, trusting the old system, lost. And come the general election, the primary victory emerged as Kennedy's freshest credential, proof that he was both popular and electable.

The reputation of the Republican nominee, Richard Nixon, had also been forged on the campaign trail—for better *and* worse. Nixon's initial runs for Congress in 1946 and for the Senate in 1950 became legendary for their Red-baiting. In his 1952 vice-presidential campaign, Nixon slammed Adlai Stevenson and his "Ph.D." from the "College of Cowardly Communist Containment." Nixon's resurrection after the Checkers speech marked his more positive contribution to the campaign. By 1956, he was following Eisenhower's advice to "Give 'em heaven" and became "the best campaigner we've got, bar none," one Republican official said.[57] The Vice President also exhibited his eloquence on his diplomatic missions, especially during his July 1959 "Kitchen Debate" with the Soviet Premier, Nikita Khrushchev. Victories like this on the world stage anticipated Nixon's plan to run as a statesman, the anti-Communist hatchet man gone mellow but not soft.

Nixon was self-conscious about his campaigning. He despised the "Tricky Dick" label. He claimed he had "never engaged in personalities in campaigns," distancing himself from the tactic that made him famous. To prove his virtue, Nixon exiled his TV people to an office one block *east* of Madison Avenue. At the same time, he was haunted by Dewey's failure and Eisenhower's lethargic second term. Truman's victory taught Nixon that most votes are decided in the last two weeks of the campaign. Nixon wanted, therefore, to begin slowly, peaking at the end. To prove that a Republican campaign could be "exciting and even inspiring," Nixon promised to campaign in all fifty states.[58] This pledge was a tribute to modern America, to the new states of Alaska and Hawaii, and to advances in jet travel. Not since Franklin Roosevelt's acceptance in 1932 had a candidate offered a campaign tactic as an indicator of policy. Nixon's promise harked back to the nineteenth century, when a campaign was offered as a candidate's bond, a guarantee of his conduct once elected. Of course, traditionally, passivity reflected virtue; but by 1960 the opposite was true.

Nixon was a one-man band. He begged Americans to ignore party affiliation and decide on the basis of what the candidates "say" and "believe." By championing "the man" rather than his "party"—though not his personality—Nixon acknowledged the Republicans' minority status as well as the decline of party power. Nixon "reduced us all to clerks," a Republican official fumed.[59]

Kennedy and his aides considered Nixon a vulnerable candidate lacking in "humor, spontaneity and warmth." Kennedy would ignore Stevenson's noble example and simply project a pleasing persona. Truman's victory had addicted journalists to the ebbs and flows of the "race" for the presidency, John Kenneth Galbraith noted. Each candidate had to maintain the appearance of being "a hot campaigner" without burning out.[60] Like Nixon, Kennedy would try to pace himself. Like Nixon, once plunged into the whirlwind, he would campaign like mad.

Nixon's campaign stumbled when he bumped his knee on a car door in North Carolina: He was hospitalized for twelve days with a knee infection. This setback freed him from his fifty-state pledge, advisers suggested. But Nixon refused to quit, even as his fever returned.

Nixon had barely recovered when it was time for the first debate. Initially, as the front-runner, he opposed such a risky venture. But since August 22, when the House of Representatives shouted approval for the Senate's suspension of the Equal Time Rule, Americans had been applauding their return to the spirit of Lincoln and Douglas. Public pressure for a debate became "irresistible," Nixon would recall. Besides, he fancied himself an ace debater and trusted his TV instincts. His aides began quibbling with Kennedy's men about the timing, lighting, and staging. The networks wanted a head-on clash, but the politicians demanded a safer format, with panels of journalists participating in the quartet of hour-long meetings. This format, many grumbled, guaranteed that the "Great Debates" would be neither.[61]

On the night of September 26, 1960, seventy million Americans watched their leaders joust. The television studio, Charles Kuralt of CBS observed, became 1960's "front porch." Fearful of slipping on one of the "invisible banana peels" strewn across the sound stage, both candidates were cautious, if not a bit too deferential. "I subscribe completely to the spirit that Senator Kennedy has expressed tonight," Nixon proclaimed. The "goals are the same for all Americans. The means are at question," Kennedy acknowledged. Dazed viewers tried to follow the abstractions, statistics, and technicalities, but, many confessed, "The more we listened the more confused we got." Nixon's restraint especially disappointed his fans, who sent hundreds of telegrams pleading for the old Nixon's "brass knuckles" approach. "Dignity and responsibility" are fine, Fulton Lewis, Jr., complained in his radio commentary. But this "mutual admiration society" was sickening.[62]

More important than what the candidates said was how they appeared on the small screen. Political folklore tells how the tanned, athletic Kennedy surmounted the stature gap and won the election. As

Theodore White wrote, Nixon was "half slouched, his 'Lazy Shave' pow-
der faintly streaked with sweat, his eyes exaggerated hollows of black-
ness, his jaws, jowls, and face drooping with strain." After the debate
thousands of viewers, including Nixon's mother, called to ask if he was
ill. In the future, Nixon and his supporters would quote surveys that
had Nixon triumphing on radio, and Kennedy on television.[63]

In videotapes of the first debate viewed three decades later, the contrast between Kennedy and Nixon shrinks. Nixon shifts and smiles
wanly, but he is nothing like White's sallow-cheeked, three-day-bearded
apparition. Sweat forms at the base of Nixon's chin, but spittle dances
between Kennedy's teeth. The exaggerated response reveals the great
expectations that burdened Nixon—he failed in not delivering a knock-
out blow. It also illustrates a phenomenon that would become increasingly common, whereby the press would "spin" events into ever greater
spirals, until minor affairs became major. Most important, the distorted
impressions reveal the shock of the television close-up. On the stump,
candidates panted and wheezed and "bloviated." William Jennings
Bryan reeked of sweat and alcohol from his gin rubdowns; Theodore
Roosevelt gave choppy, bombastic speeches. TV's X-ray vision demanded a "perfect" image.[64] Watching the debates, Americans stared at
their candidates for an hour not through their eyes but, in a sense,
through the all-seeing, critical eye of CBS. Faced with their candidates'
spittle and sweat they overreacted, perceiving one as smoother and
better-looking than he was, and the other as more ghastly than he was.
Thus was an American myth forged whose lessons no candidate would
forget.

Nixon's pallor focused unprecedented attention on the production
details of the debate, revealing the effort behind every television appearance and stripping one more layer of illusion from the American public.
"Fire the makeup man," Republicans cried. In fact, *both* candidates had
spurned CBS's top makeup artist, although Kennedy took some makeup
around the eyes and Nixon used "Lazy Shave" to cover his stubble.[65]
Nixon's experience underscored the value of makeup and the importance of lighting. In a medium where rain looked real only when faked,
the illusion created was the defining political reality. For the next debate, Nixon hired a makeup artist and drank four milkshakes a day to
restore his weight and "color."

Still, makeup artists were even more suspect than ghost-writers.
Makeup was for actors, not politicians; it was artificial, even effeminate.
Before the debates, Democrats had charged that Nixon thinned his eye-
brows to appear less fiendish, while Republicans said Kennedy changed

his hairstyle to appear less boyish. Both candidates denied the make-
overs. After the debate the nominees used makeup more often, but the
idea of it still remained tainted. When Nixon accused him of a "bare-
faced lie," Kennedy said he knew Nixon did nothing bare-faced because
"I've seen him in a television studio, with his makeup on."[66]

After all the fanfare about a democratic dialogue, this concern with
images upstaged the policy discussions. Before the second debate, the
candidates' aides engaged in their own version of the Cold War, with
Nixon's men lowering the thermostat and Kennedy's men surreptitiously raising it. For the third debate a week later, ten degrees Fahren-
heit and three thousand miles separated the candidates, as Nixon spoke
from a frosty television studio in Los Angeles, and Kennedy from New
York.

While broadcasters like NBC's Sarnoff celebrated this "powerful
new instrument of democracy," most Americans were more sober. At
best, the debates supplemented but did not supplant conventional campaigning. The awaited transformation had not come about. Walter
Lippmann praised television as a "truth machine," while Nixon would
complain that "what is in a man's head" should be more important
"than the type of beard he may have on his face." Dr. Frank Stanton
of CBS argued that Americans were fulfilling the original function of
the Electoral College—choosing "from among men known to them" by
catching the candidates "in the act of being alive." On the other hand,
historian Henry Steele Commager argued that Washington, Jefferson,
Lincoln, and Wilson all would have lost debates like these that prized
"the glib, the evasive, the dogmatic, the melodramatic," over "the sincere, the judicious, the sober, the honest in political discussion."[67] In
short, Americans reacted to the debates as they reacted to the campaign. Once again, disappointment followed great expectations. Once
again, "personalities" seemed to upstage "issues." As usual, Americans
appeared two-faced. In the quiet of their homes they professed devotion
to rational discussions, not emotional outbursts—but on the campaign
trail they were often passionate, occasionally ribald, and far more genuine.

Still, the debates roused millions and energized the campaign. Over
600,000 people mobbed Kennedy's motorcade in Ohio the day after the
first debate. People shouted "You look as good in person as you do on
TV," making the link explicit. As Kennedy passed teenagers shrieked,
and the mob undulated as fans jumped up and down. Nixon's crowds
escalated in size and intensity, too, In Pennsylvania, one woman
knocked the Vice President down while trying to kiss him on the lips.

With the "rear-platform" campaign, candidates finally caught up with the transportation and communication revolutions that had transformed nineteenth-century America. Theodore Roosevelt emerged as the paradigmatic twentieth-century president, charming the people with his energy and his personality. Still, it was considered undignified to campaign from the White House. Aware that silence would be expected during his 1904 effort, President Roosevelt made lengthy speaking tours in 1902 and 1903. (*Smithsonian Institution*)

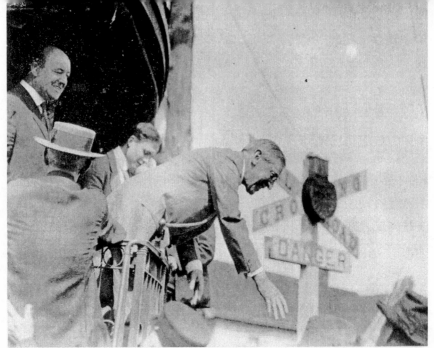

Candidates found it increasingly difficult to avoid the stump. In 1912, Woodrow Wilson agreed to reach out to the people (*above*) only after his advisers insisted. When running for reelection four years later, he became the first presidential incumbent to stump during the general election campaign. In 1924, the dour Calvin Coolidge avoided the stump—marking the last time a major-party nominee would remain passive. Yet even Coolidge felt compelled to engage in some publicity stunts, as evidenced by his willingness to pose in an Indian headdress for photographers (*below*). (*Library of Congress*)

Herbert Hoover never learned how to use pictures and gestures effectively. During the Great Depression, when President Hoover was photographed fishing in his high starched collar, the people were not quite reassured that prosperity was "just around the corner." (*Library of Congress*)

Hoover's Democratic rival in 1932, Franklin D. Roosevelt, knew how to thrill the people in the press and in person, as he did during his July 1932 yachting "vacation" to Hampton Beach, New Hampshire. Such appearances were carefully staged. By gripping his son James for support, this vigorous, upbeat man could hide the fact that polio had rendered his legs all but useless. (*Franklin D. Roosevelt Library*)

WILLKIE RETURNS TO ELWOOD, INDIANA, WHERE HE MADE HIS OFFICIAL ACCEPTANCE SPEECH ENDORSING MOST OF ROOSEVELT'S NEW DEAL POLICIES

Media-savvy candidates chose dramatic settings as they whistle-stopped, prop-stopped, and motorcaded throughout America. In 1940, Wendell Willkie began his unsuccessful challenge to Franklin D. Roosevelt in his hometown of Elwood, Indiana (*above*). (*Smithsonian Institution*) For his part, President Roosevelt embraced the traditional pose of presidential passivity—while campaigning actively. But during his final, 1944 campaign, his hardhitting "Fala" speech provoked a heated reaction. Many Americans felt that Roosevelt had unduly politicized the presidency and demeaned the war effort. (*Library of Congress*)

Traditional tactics retained their appeal long after they became anachronistic, as Democrat Harry S. Truman demonstrated in his 1948 "whistle-stop" campaign. The "all-American" tradition remained popular because it thrust the candidate among the people. In the future, security concerns would discourage such intimate scenes. (*Library of Congress*)

"Who's Whistle-Stopping?"

The television age furthered the technological revolution while perpetuating traditional tensions. When campaigning for reelection in 1956, President Dwight Eisenhower pretended that he was not campaigning. Here, a cartoon shows Eisenhower innocently asking "Who's Whistle-Stopping?" while campaigning vigorously by motorcade. (*Herblock, copyright © 1956 in the* Washington Post)

The televised Nixon–Kennedy debates of 1960 were supposed to purify the campaign and bring the candidates home to 60 million Americans. Yet the subsequent controversy about the candidates' makeup and images upstaged the more substantive discussion about issues. Still, as these two photographs from their first debate reveal, Richard Nixon was not quite the sallow-cheeked, three-day-bearded apparition of subsequent mythology. (*Library of Congress*)

by Garry Trudeau

Wary candidates avoided another debate until 1976, when neither Democratic challenger Jimmy Carter nor Republican incumbent Gerald Ford felt confident enough to veto such a meeting. That year, nominees seemed far too concerned with the production details of the debate, as Garry Trudeau's *Doonesbury* cartoon complained (*above*). (Doonesbury, *copyright © 1976 G.B. Trudeau, reprinted with permission of Universal Press Syndicate*) When a technical glitch imposed 27 minutes of silence during the first debate, both Carter and Ford acted so cool as to be frozen in place (*below*). (*Gerald R. Ford Library*).

REAGAN
BUSH'84

*President Reagan and
Ethnic Americans*

"America is too
great for
small dreams"

Ronald Reagan's two presidential campaigns showcased
the candidate as icon, actor, and image. Carefully tailored
campaign pamphlets like this one from the 1984 campaign
showed that democracy had triumphed: The candidate
now had to pursue the people. But the age-old tension
between dignity and candor, between the president as king
and the president as prime minister, between liberal
democracy and traditional republicanism, persisted. Many
wondered whether the ever-more-sophisticated campaign
tactics imperiled the candidate's virtue. (*Max and Elaine
Mandis Collection of Political Memorabilia; photo by B. D.
Troy*)

Broadcasting these receptions triggered similar reactions elsewhere. Until the debates, both candidates had been somewhat reserved. It was television that provoked frenzies usually associated with Elvis Presley, or even, as Pennsylvania's Governor David Lawrence muttered, "the Messiah."[68] Television appearances made politicians famous in this new age.

Kennedy and Nixon received unprecedented TV exposure beyond the debates as the networks enjoyed their respite from the Equal Time Rule. For the first time, nominees appeared more on news shows and public interest programs than on paid political broadcasts. No longer simply preaching to the converted, candidates now had to convert the uncommitted. To achieve that, the candidates offered the mass electorate full self-portraits. On shows ranging from Jack Paar's late-night talk show to Walter Cronkite's news specials, TV invaded the candidates' homes, and their privacy. Previously, the most intimate glimpse of a candidate had come during the staged spots from Stevenson's farm; the most informal interactions had been the ritualized yet extemporaneous rear-platform talks. Now, with fifteen or thirty minutes to fill, these new interview shows were intimate and informal but trivial. Interviewers feared arid expositions on the issues, and candidates feared controversy. Nixon was asked why people did not like him, and if his daughters "have been working as hard on their schoolwork as you have on the campaign." "When you run for the Presidency your wife's hair or your hair or something else always becomes of major significance," Kennedy sighed. "I don't think it's a great issue, though, in 1960."[69]

By appearing as full-blown personalities and by moderating their message to reach more people, the candidates eventually became more palatable. But the greater exposure brought greater risks too. The cameras' intense gaze and the interviewers' prying questions forced candidates to be self-protective and calculating while trying to appear natural. Jacqueline Kennedy's response to a question about entertaining in the White House—"It's so hahd (hard) to get help nowadays"—alienated all those who could not afford help at all, one voter wrote. And after Kennedy appeared on the "Tonight" show, viewers complained that Jack Paar's "usual brassiere jokes," while at least "above the belt," demeaned the presidency. With news shows struggling to amuse, and with newsmakers appearing on entertaining shows, the lines between politics and entertainment, between propriety and exploitation, blurred. "I should say the most important thing about the business of government and politics is not to bore the people," Nixon confessed during his appearance on "Tonight."[70]

In the last weeks of the campaign, with the result still in doubt, the nominees staggered around America like punch-drunk boxers in their fifteenth round. Their hands were swollen and bruised after being tugged and grasped thousands of times. So many people generated such a confetti "blizzard" in Los Angeles that Kennedy gagged on gobs of the little papers and had to clean out his ears. As Kennedy found it harder to wake up each morning, he would stir only when his aide Dave Powers whispered: "What do you suppose Nixon's doing while you're lying there?"[71]

Ever mindful of Dewey's legacy, Nixon also refused to quit. He launched a Herculean ten-day finale. Every night, for the last week, from 7 to 7:15 P.M., he spoke to the nation via television. On Sunday, November 6, he jetted to Alaska, fulfilling his "historic" pledge. A "candidate for the Presidency should go to every state so that he knows what America is all about," he declared, arguing that the campaign educated the candidate as well as the voters.[72] After a four-hour Election Eve telethon featuring show girls, Hollywood celebrities like Ginger Rogers, and his wife Pat along with their daughters Julie and Tricia, Nixon ended his crusade.

The election was as close as predicted. Had as few as 14,000 voters out of a record sixty-nine million switched (or, as some speculated, had fewer corpses voted in Chicago and Dallas), Nixon would have won. In that case, his fifty-state pledge might have established a new standard for candidates, becoming the necessary human complement to the mechanized campaign. Instead, it became the symbol of Nixon's stubborn and unfocused drive. Dewey's campaign now had its opposite pole—a warning that activity for its own sake was equally unsafe.

As a good candidate should, Kennedy affirmed the traditional naiveté by making a statement that "the message" counted, not the "technique": "A political candidate who does not utterly believe in the ability of the people to sense the truth, and in the desire of the people to know the truth, had better start looking for a job elsewhere." Less grandly, after the election he admitted: "It was TV more than anything else that turned the tide."[73] The charade of immaculate conception continued. This gap between fact and fiction, between what people saw and what politicians wanted them to believe, would only grow.

In looking back on the campaign, Nixon listed the three lessons that most observers learned in 1960. First, the campaign was simply too long. The huge television and radio audiences made it unnecessary for candidates to endure "the physical, mental, and emotional wear-and-tear that both Kennedy and I experienced." Second, the candidate must "save himself" for the major events. A candidate's time and energy had to be rationed, not dissipated. Finally, but "regretfully," Nixon concluded that he paid "too much attention to what I was going to say and too little to how I would look. . . . One bad camera angle on television can have far more effect on the election outcome than a major mistake in writing a speech," he noted ruefully.[74] As Stevenson had done, Nixon learned to discount substance. If Nixon ever ran again, he vowed, he would be shrewder, more careful, more scientific. He would not dismiss Madison Avenue tactics, he would master them. But for now, Nixon retired to private life—and the nation turned to its new hero and his young wife.

V

President Kennedy's assassination as he motorcaded through Dallas while preparing his reelection effort overshadowed the 1964 campaign. Although the sniper's bullets could not quite shatter the campaign of personal appearances, they did prompt serious second thoughts. Yet despite the skittishness of Secret Service agents and editorialists alike, neither President Lyndon B. Johnson nor his Republican challenger, Barry M. Goldwater, would be deterred from an active stumping campaign.

An Arizona Senator, Goldwater had survived a bruising Republican primary campaign and convention. He offered conservative answers to the unnerving questions about racism, the Vietnam War, and urban decay that had emerged. "We must and we shall return to proven ways—not because they are old, but because they are true," he declared in his acceptance speech. His campaign slogan, coined by the Leo Burnett advertising agency, affirmed "In your heart you know he's right." "Yes," wags responded, "far right."[75]

After Johnson's enthusiastic nomination at the Democratic convention, a straightforward clash seemed likely. Johnson and Goldwater disagreed about fundamental issues like Social Security and nuclear proliferation. "I'm not one of those baby-kissing, hand-shaking, blintz-eating candidates," Goldwater said. He envisioned a "lofty, rational presentation of contending political beliefs"—a crusade, not a campaign.[76]

With only sixty days to convey to 182 million people an "image of what you are really like and what you really believe," Goldwater realized that "you can't do it personally." Campaigning today "depends upon good television and radio plus press coverage," he figured. "Actually, it's getting back to the older days where the candidate didn't too actively campaign." He would not duplicate the "extreme activity" of "Dick

Nixon," who hit "every State" and wore himself out. Goldwater said he
wanted to sleep in his own bed "at least once a week."[77]

Goldwater's calculations revealed that the half-life of political memory was shrinking: It had taken sixty years for Burchard's example to
be forgotten, and twenty years for Farley's Law to be disproved; but
Dewey's spectre haunted politicians for only twelve years—until Nixon
offered a counter example. By 1968, Nixon would be the only politician
still wary of "extreme activity." More and more, candidates, like short-
sighted generals, would be fighting only the most recent of battles.

For his part, Lyndon Johnson found an intense campaign as irresistible as a Texas barbecue. This larger-than-life character with the face of
a hound dog and the mind of a fox never did anything in moderation.
He pooh-poohed advisers—especially Kennedy men like John Kenneth
Galbraith—who warned that "People do not want the President to get
too much in the fray." Johnson wanted a "new mandate from the people
[to] further the cause of social reform." Lacking Eisenhower's excuse of
failing health, and Roosevelt's ability to play-act convincingly, Johnson's
professions of disinterest were most transparent. When he characterized
the traditional Labor Day campaign kickoff as a trip to Detroit "to speak
to a group of workingmen who invited me," reporters like Dan Rather
mocked the "little charade."[78]

Johnson blurred the roles of President and campaigner even more
than Truman had. His first consideration remained "carrying out the
duties of the Presidency." Still, Johnson used America as his stage—and
his charity case. He alternated between playing the amiable county sheriff and acting as the most powerful man in the world. "Get in your cars
and come to the speakin'," he yelled as he motorcaded, grasping every
hand in reach. As "President of all the people," Johnson praised leading
Republicans so often that some wondered whether Eisenhower was on
Johnson's ticket. The flow of farm aid, disaster relief, food stamps, and
pay raises he released overwhelmed the opposition. To demonstrate his
commitment to defense, Johnson jetted to Omaha and inspected the
Strategic Air Command; to demonstrate his compassion, he flew into
flood-stricken Montana with a $4.5 million check.[79]

This combination of imperial power and government grants, of presidential perks and local "pork," awed Americans. "Santa Claus" Johnson traveled in grand style, using Air Force One as reindeer and sleigh.
He was constantly accompanied by security men, military aides, political
advisers, reporters—and one aide with a nondescript briefcase, the
holder of the codes that could trigger nuclear Armageddon. Here was

the most dramatic proof of the President's power and the stakes of the election.

Johnson justified his travels, his trappings, and his largess with democratic rhetoric. At his July 24 news conference, he explained that the "purpose of elections" was "to discuss the issues" and allow "the people, in their wisdom," to "make a good decision." "Personalities" were irrelevant; the personal touch, however, was not. "The people want to see their President in person," he explained after traveling 10,000 miles in one week in October. "They want to hear first hand what he believes." No longer a separate function, campaigning now was an essential part of the President's job. As historian James MacGregor Burns would lament, the White House had become a "round-the-clock, round-the-year campaign headquarters."[80]

Johnson's political mastery frustrated Goldwater. To get closer to the people, the Arizonan whistle-stopped through the Midwest. Even though the tour was self-consciously labeled a "rendezvous with nostalgia" and a "throwback," politicians still sensed the need for this kind of campaigning. An amateur pilot, Goldwater preferred prop-stopping. But, whether by train or by plane, he was stymied: He did not know how to attack the man while respecting the office, how to mobilize extremists without sounding like one. Before the campaign, Goldwater met Johnson more or less secretly and agreed not to exploit the delicate issues of civil rights and the Vietnam War. Yet as the campaign progressed, he began asking "Would you buy a used car from Lyndon?" and chanted that all Johnson did was "lie and lie and lie." Still, when crowds cursed Johnson's name, Goldwater chided: "Don't boo the office of the Presidency."[81] His more vociferous supporters did not quite understand the subtleties of gentlemanly engagement.

Goldwater's debility gave Johnson little incentive to debate. After 1960, the Great Debates bathed in a nostalgic glow. Many assumed that joint appearances would become institutionalized. But Nixon's example had taught well the lesson that the challenger should not be granted a podium: The Democratic-controlled Senate tabled a resolution to suspend the Equal Time Rule for 1964. Johnson and his supporters masked their political calculations by arguing that an incumbent should not debate. "There is too much security involved and there could be a question of life and death involved in each reply," reporter Cedric Foster explained.[82] In the shadow of the Cold War, presidential dignity—and democracy—appeared ever more fragile.

Johnson had no qualms, however, about hiring an outside advertising agency, Doyle Dane Bernbach, to depict Goldwater as a trigger-happy, Social Security–slashing extremist. The Democrats' most controversial ad, conceived by a consultant, Tony Schwartz, dissolved from a scene of a little girl picking flowers into the expanding mushroom cloud of a nuclear explosion. Although Goldwater was never mentioned, the "Daisy" commercial enraged Republicans: "Instead of meeting Senator Goldwater face to face, in a series of TV debates, like the great debates of 1960, Mr. Johnson is hiding behind a series of shocking television commercials," party chairman Dean Burch complained.[83] The Democrats pulled the ad. Still, Republicans could now censure the "Madison Avenue" Democrats.

Six weeks later, the roles reversed. A pro-Goldwater group produced a thirty-minute film called *Choice* that painted the Democrats as the party of pornographers, black rioters, and corrupt politicians. Democratic Chairman John Bailey could now mount his high horse and condemn "the sickest political program to be conceived since television became a factor in American politics." Goldwater stepped in, previewed *Choice*, and canceled it. "This," he snapped, "is a racist film."[84]

The candidates themselves had been peripheral to both these efforts. The new divorce between the candidate and his message harked back to the days before stumping, when parties spoke for candidates. To most voters, candidates were no longer flesh-and-blood actors, traveling America, but disembodied "images," hollowed out, falsified. Words and their medium, speeches, had been replaced by images and their medium, staged commercials.

In his zeal to win, Johnson had sullied the Democrats and ushered them into the modern world. Both parties had achieved strategic and moral parity. The Democrats might place their commercials during "The Addams Family," and the Republicans during "The Lawrence Welk Hour"; the Democrats might highlight the President's distinctive voice, and the Republicans Goldwater's handsome face; but all of these were technicalities. The campaign that year was not "between President Johnson and Senator Goldwater," but between their respective advertising firms, Charles Kuralt of CBS half-joked.[85]

Most Americans were now inured to the appeals. Campaign advertising had become so commonplace that DDB's large role in the Democratic campaign escaped notice. How else could the candidate reach the electorate? No matter how many eighteen-hour days a candidate puts in, "the potential number of voters who get his message in person is still dismayingly small," *Newsweek* observed. Publicity was what counted. Advertising budgets tripled, to $8.5 million for the Democrats and $16 million for the Republicans; and the length of political broadcasts plummeted, from thirty-minute speeches to thirty- and sixty-second spots.[86] In 1952 the simple fact that spots were contemplated provoked outrage; in 1964 only tasteless commercials merited notice. Americans had accepted the ubiquity of advertising in television, and of television in politics.

Admen at once viewed themselves as omnipotent while denying they could, as critics alleged, subvert democracy. There is a lot of guesswork involved even in selling soap or toothpaste, George Gallup insisted. If advertising men were as powerful as critics feared, "they would be so fabulously rich that they couldn't be bothered by making a few dollars managing the advertising and promotion of political campaigns."[87]

Just when it appeared that there was no more mud to splatter, and that the Democrats could chill their champagne, one of Johnson's closest aides, Walter Jenkins, was arrested in a men's room for indecent conduct. To the Republicans, Jenkins's arrest epitomized the cloud of corruption enveloping Johnson's cronies and, they feared, America itself. As Republicans pondered how best to exploit the issue, a Soviet coup ousted Nikita Khrushchev, upstaging the Jenkins scandal and rallying Americans around the President. By mid-October, then, the only suspense remaining concerned the magnitude of Johnson's landslide.

Once again an American campaign began with great promise and ended in the gutter, and as usual the mourners treated the phenomenon as unprecedented and viewed earlier campaigns too benignly. *Time* found the 1964 campaign "one of the most disappointing ever" and longed for 1960, which now became a "vigorous, meaningful campaign." In this television age, the underhanded "image" from the Daisy commercial, rather than a particularly nasty phrase, made the biggest impression. Television and advertising unfairly became the scapegoats. The millennial hopes that had greeted television had vanished, making the disappointment more acute. Six of ten Americans polled advocated "changes . . . in the way political campaigns are conducted," especially "less mudslinging and distortion of issues." Americans also wanted shorter and cheaper campaigns, clearer issue discussions, and television debates as a standard feature.[88]

Most jeremiads ignored television's contributions to democracy and, more broadly, overlooked the progress of Franklin Roosevelt's democratic revolution as demonstrated by the growth of primaries, the decline of bosses, and the continuing march of the disenfranchised into American politics. Each election from 1948 on had provided examples illustrating the vitality of American democracy: Truman's upset, Eisenhower's crowds, Stevenson's speeches, Kennedy's debate with Nixon, Goldwater's ideological appeal, Johnson's mandate. The televised stumping campaign exposed nominees as never before to more people than ever before. Later generations would consider John Kennedy's campaign indicative of the secrecy surrounding the private lives of public figures, but at the time, the 1960 contest was a model of openness. Thanks to television, political knowledge in the latter twentieth century transcended the issues, the cardboard representations of individuals, and their formal appearances. Americans returned, as CBS's Frank Stanton argued, to the days of the early Republic when the electors took the full measure of the man.

Yet these stirring portraits were repeatedly soiled; the great expectations for each campaign were never met. In 1948, Dewey's dignified approach derailed his candidacy rather than exalting the presidency. In 1952 and 1956, Stevenson and Eisenhower tried to transcend politics and ended mired in it. The Kennedy–Nixon debates degenerated from policy discussions into makeup contests; and the Johnson–Goldwater clash went from ideological exposition to mud-wrestling. To worried observers in each campaign, personality loomed larger and larger as a determining factor. Most presidential campaigns had experienced such falls from grace—they were part of the pattern of republican degeneration and redemption throughout American history. But these descents had evoked unprecedented concern. The rise of television and the proliferation of advertisers made many fear that something fundamental had changed, that the new tactics made politicians too potent and the voters too weak to resist. Republican National Chairman Dean Burch proclaimed that, thanks to TV, "Presidential campaigns are a sham."[89]

VI

During the 1952 Republican convention, cameramen followed Dwight Eisenhower into his apartment. As he entered, the television set in the corner caught his eye. "On it, startled, "I saw myself moving through my own front door," he recalled.[90] A decade later, politicians were accustomed to seeing themselves on TV. In fact, with each campaign they became more and more self-conscious, assuming that millions were scrutinizing every move they made, every word they uttered. Eating from the apple of knowledge changed politicians and their constituents alike. In 1960, John Kennedy and his brother Robert reacted to Martin Luther King's arrest in Atlanta spontaneously. The candidate called

Mrs. King, while his brother called the Georgia judge who was holding the civil rights leader. "The best strategies are always accidental," Kennedy later observed.[91] In future campaigns, few politicians would act so quickly without trying to predict the potential impact; even if a politician acted decisively, few Americans would believe the gesture genuine.

As calculated cynicism replaced Eisenhower's sense of wonder, the people began to doubt themselves. The new campaign took voters for idiots, not idiot savants. Political scientists delicately suggested that "The people lack the conceptual tools that aid in making order out of chaos."[92] Many Americans fought this suspicion that their minds could be controlled. The belief that Farley's Law still held, that campaigns did not matter much, flourished alongside the contradictory sense that campaigns mattered all too much, that anything could be sold to the American public.

This charade inhibited serious analysis of campaigns. In yet another example of technology's attenuated impact on American politics, the revolution in assessing political attitudes occurred long before politicians would embrace it. Politicians employed the latest techniques, but as Rosser Reeves discovered in 1952, they were unwilling to assess their effectiveness. They wanted virtue, not tactics, to seem authoritative. Instead, politicians relied on the changing folk wisdom. Dewey's campaign traumatized Nixon's campaign, which then traumatized Goldwater's efforts. Dismayed by their 1952 loss, Stevenson and his intellectuals in 1956 acted like ward heelers; four years later, Kennedy's men distanced themselves from the tactics of both Stevenson campaigns. Eisenhower learned how to be presidential from Roosevelt, while Johnson mimicked both Roosevelt and Truman. The oral law flourished; science was feared.

Many were afraid that America's political soul was at stake. The techniques were becoming more sophisticated, and more ubiquitous. The confusion—and the doubts—could only intensify.

TEN

A Cross-Country
Marathon

The reach of the individual campaigner doesn't add up to diddly-squat
in votes.
—*Nixon aide H. R. Haldeman, 1968*

THROUGHOUT the 1960s and 1970s the civil rights movement
and the antiwar movement, women's liberation and gay liberation, Hip-
pies and Yippies convulsed American society. Among other things,
these radicals demanded a "new politics," a new approach to American
democracy. As the search for a purer process mounted on the left, new
political forms emerged in the mainstream as well. "The new politics is
the art of communicating a candidate's message directly to the voter
without filtering it through a party organization," political consultant
Joseph Napolitan would write in 1972.[1] The candidate now stood at the
center of the campaign, simultaneously serving as the chief icon in the
literature, the leading actor on the stump, and the dominant image on
television. A master of the "new politics," establishment-style, Napolitan put the most democratic "spin" on this phenomenon. Many were
more skeptical. The campaigns were expensive, exhausting, and dangerous in a society more like Dodge City than Shangri-la. For all the efforts,
voter turnout was dwindling, dissatisfaction was soaring, and experts
had yet to prove just what a campaign accomplished.

Two spectres haunting the 1968 campaign—the memory of Robert F.
Kennedy and the message of Marshall McLuhan—offered contradictory
guidance. By some counts, both Kennedy brothers had been martyred
to the American compulsion to "press the flesh." Why not simply rely

on television to broadcast the candidate's message, many wondered. But by 1968, television itself was in disrepute. The "X-ray machine" had become the "idiot box," a medium for distortion, not truth. In claiming that "the medium is the message," McLuhan, a Canadian professor turned media guru, taught that campaigning on television was fundamentally different from campaigning in person. TV speeches could not substitute for personal contact, despite the risk of assassination. Furthermore, "Anyone who looks as if he *wants* to be elected had best stay off TV," McLuhan warned. Like anchormen, politicians had to appear "cool," not hot. The republican ethos now had a modern rationale—and the hybrid campaign, combining broadcasting and stumping, accessibility and humility, persisted.[2] A new class of experts—called "consultants," not "pols"—would guide the candidates. These technocrats, along with the burly Secret Service agents, spun an elaborate cocoon that insulated the candidates from the people even as the candidates pursued the people.

I

Amid all the novelties of 1968, one familiar figure hoped to triumph. Richard Nixon turned to the experts to capture the presidency and atone for his debating sins. The aspiring President's men had to erase the "loser" image that had stuck to their boss during his political exile in California and Manhattan, and somehow adapt his style to television. In a classic circular strategy, they trusted primary victories to make him seem like a winner. The second hurdle, media visibility, was more daunting.

Quoting McLuhan right and left, Nixon's men produced a series of TV programs in which Nixon answered questions from "average" citizens. The panelists could ask any question, and did, quizzing Nixon about the Vietnam War, civil rights, and farm policy. These televised town meetings offered a model for the electronic democracy of the future. Here he was, Nixon recalled, the "man in the arena," standing alone and facing the people.[3]

In fact, these apparently spontaneous dialogues were stage-managed by Roger Ailes, who had produced Mike Douglas's talk show before entering politics. Bud Wilkinson, the genial former college football coach, hosted the shows to project sincerity. The studio audience consisted of Republican partisans primed to cheer. Demographic experts cast the panelists as cynically as they cast Coca-Cola commercials, charting each questioner's sex, age, social class, and ethnicity. Made-up and relaxed, Nixon could sling the same canned answers he had been honing for years. When asked about "the accusation . . . that your views have shifted and are based on expediences," he admitted "There is a new Nixon, if you are talking in terms of new ideas. . . . In terms of what I believe in the American view and the American dream, I think I am just what I was eight years ago."[4] Answers like these appeared personal, sounded authentic, and committed the candidate to nothing—just what Dr. McLuhan had ordered.

Following his advisers and acting presidential, Nixon snatched the Republican nomination. His platitudes offered a soothing alternative to the mounting Vietnam protests. Richard Nixon, the man of a thousand resentments, the pit bull of American politics, would again pose as an apostle of unity and peace.

"I am not going to barricade myself into a television studio and make this an antiseptic campaign," Nixon claimed. This posture proved that candidates still felt compelled to appear accessible. But Nixon would pace himself. There would be "no baby-kissing, no back-slapping, no factory gates." He visited Key Biscayne frequently to maintain his tan. He eschewed nighttime rallies because they usually were too late for TV coverage. Nixon was subordinating the stumping campaign to his multimillion-dollar advertising effort. He agreed with his advance man from 1960, H. R. Haldeman, that "The reach of the individual campaigner doesn't add up to diddly-squat in votes."[5]

Through it all, Nixon portrayed himself as the traditional campaigner adrift in the modern world. His campaign published position papers on 167 different issues—although the *New York Post* suggested that he make it an even 170 "by adding Vietnam, the cities, and civil rights." He pretended that he was above suggestions such as the one Roger Ailes made that he try "slightly whiter makeup on upper eyelids." Dismissing "images" as unimportant, Nixon rejected "the advice of the public relations experts who say that I've got to sit by the hour and watch myself. The American people," he declared, "may not like my face but they're going to listen to what I have to say."[6]

Nevertheless, Nixon's effort was curiously lethargic. He was so anxious to avoid replicating his 1960 self that he began to resemble Thomas Dewey. On the stump, Nixon was stiff. *Both* he and his listeners seemed bored. Even the much-vaunted advertisements were not that effective: Nixon rarely appeared in his own commercials, contributing to the impression of an insulated candidate who feared the people would reject him as he was. By October, Nixon's estimated fifteen-point lead of the previous month had vanished. Nixon and his men assembled in Key Biscayne to jumpstart their flagging effort.

Fortunately for Nixon, and his admen's reputations, the Happy Warrior, Hubert H. Humphrey, was fighting an unhappy campaign. Humphrey's presidential hopes had been dashed by John F. Kennedy in 1960, only to be resurrected four years later when Lyndon Johnson chose the Minnesota pharmacist-turned-liberal-crusader as a running mate. By the time Vice President Humphrey became the Democrats' standard-bearer at their 1968 convention in Chicago, though, the long-sought trophy was tarnished. The clashes between protesters and policemen that erupted outside the Chicago Hilton dramatized the party's divided state.

Humphrey could not even find a Vietnam policy. Lyndon Johnson demanded total loyalty. "The President has not made me his slave," the Vice President feebly insisted. Only later would Humphrey admit "I had become like the oldest son—and I couldn't make the break" thereby capturing the Oedipal pathos of his position.[7]

Humphrey's impotence only exacerbated the problems of the disorganized and underfunded party. Democratic consultants such as Joseph Napolitan and Tony Schwartz were eager to show their own mastery of McLuhan's "cool medium." In September, Napolitan played some radio spots for Theodore White, lamenting, "They're wonderful . . . [but] we'll never get enough money to put them on air."[8]

Trying to transcend the divisions, Humphrey stumped from dawn till midnight, day after day. He was determined, "even if I had to hire a station wagon . . . [to] go out across the country and . . . carry the message." On the stump, Humphrey was exuberant. He loved "armpit politics." But such a campaign seemed frivolous when hecklers shouted "Dump the Hump" and threw tomatoes.[9]

Humphrey appeared on many local television programs, offering a low-budget but authentic contrast to "The Richard Nixon Show." But Humphrey could not tailor his long-winded style to the telegraphic demands of TV; he was too "hot." In Pittsburgh one night, he fielded only four questions during a thirty-minute program. Professor Henry Kissinger of Harvard groaned, "If Humphrey is elected, we will hear announced on an afternoon, 'The President will address the nation tonight from 8 until 11'."[10]

To heighten the contrast with the "Madison Avenue slick" Nixon, Humphrey called for a debate before the American people. The Vice President mocked his opponent as "Sir Richard the Chicken Hearted" and "Brand X." Nixon bristled but did not budge. He remembered that

Senator Humphrey in 1964 had voted at Johnson's behest against suspending Equal Time rules that included every minor party candidate in network debates. Nixon claimed he would "take on anybody," except the American Independent party candidate, Alabama Governor George C. Wallace. Had Humphrey excluded Wallace, Nixon probably would have tried to include him, for Nixon had no intentions of debating. Republican congressmen blocked the Democrats' newfound desire to waive the Equal Time requirements with the longest filibuster since 1854.[11]

Slowly, Humphrey's campaign began to woo Democrats back. On September 30, in a nationally televised speech, Humphrey took the vice-presidential seal off his podium—literally—and called for a bombing halt in Vietnam. Although this declaration of independence was belated, alienated Democrats terrified of a Nixon presidency warmed up to Humphrey. By the time Nixon's men gathered in Florida, the public was fed up with both nominees. Fully 43 percent of those surveyed would have preferred someone other than Nixon *or* Humphrey.[12]

In the last few weeks of the campaign, Nixon added some radio addresses to his schedule and appeared on TV interview programs like "Meet the Press." The Nixon camp had learned that voters disapproved of a candidate floating into the White House on a cloud of silence. Nixon is "so cocksure of winning he acts as if he doesn't have to tell us what he will do when he becomes President," a North Carolina woman complained.[13] By Election Day, the race turned out to be as close as 1960, with only half-a-million votes separating Nixon and Humphrey. But with 302 electoral votes, thirty-two more than required, Nixon emerged as the winner and, in retrospect, the genius.

While Americans were still marveling at Nixon's "comeback," a young journalist named Joe McGinniss showed how McLuhan's spirit had corrupted the Nixon effort. *The Selling of the President 1968* captured all of the President's admen in the process of remaking the campaign and subverting democracy. "Voters are basically lazy, basically uninterested in making an *effort* to understand what we're talking about," one memorandum lectured. "The next guys up will have to be performers," Roger Ailes said. The book voiced the contemporary assumptions that voters were fools, candidates empty vessels, and consultants omnipotent. "If Ruth Jones of New York had been buying [commercial] time for Hubert Humphrey instead of [for] Richard Nixon," Joseph Napolitan would write in his own book, "Humphrey would have been elected President."[14] McLuhanites not only repealed Farley's Law and insisted that campaigning mattered; they preached that the most trivial tactic, the most obscure technician, could determine the outcome. *The Selling of the President* was a milestone in Americans' drift toward political cynicism. The 1970s became the Age of Aquarius for the flower children, but it was the age of self-consciousness for politicians, and of wariness for voters.

II

As President, Richard Nixon continued to apply the lessons of 1968. He limited such spontaneous appearances as press conferences, averaging only seven per year—down from Franklin Roosevelt's average of two per week. He also maximized coverage of staged events, be they "prime time" televised presidential addresses or a phone call to the men on the moon in July 1969.

Characteristically, Nixon would take the pose of presidential passivity to its extreme. He would be reelected simply by "doing my job." "He doesn't have to campaign . . . to establish his identity," said H. R. Haldeman, now the White House Chief of Staff. "He's been exposed for twenty-five years." Even after his renomination, reporters would find that around the White House, "It bordered on treason to call Nixon a candidate."[15]

Nixon's most effective campaigning did, in fact, occur as President. His 1972 foreign-policy successes illustrated how the campaign could motivate a President. Trips to the People's Republic of China in February, and to the Soviet Union in May, made the President an historic personage, no longer a mere politician. Images of Nixon in front of the Kremlin's onion domes and on top of China's Great Wall were beamed home in living color and helped boost his approval ratings by 13 percent in one year.[16]

This, then, was the public Nixon—dignified and accomplished. He towered over the pygmies who opposed him at home, just as he overwhelmed the dour Communists he met abroad. But the private Nixon was as insecure as ever: He considered the election "a fight to the death." With most journalists "out to get us," Nixon and his men had to be "as tough, ruthless and unfeeling as they are."[17]

The press presented a natural target for Nixon. Reporters were no longer the deferential scribblers of Theodore Roosevelt's day. In the 1960s reporters became more critical, recoiling from the government's aggressive "news management" during the Vietnam War, and reflecting the growing radical critique of American society, especially the doubts that impartial truths existed at all. No longer compelled to be "objective," reporters became more skeptical, more interpretive.[18] In becoming gadflies rather than mouthpieces, journalists went from an essentially cooperative relationship with politicians to an adversarial one. It became increasingly apparent that journalists did not merely mirror what happened, they shaped the news.

Journalists also became more conspicuous, for television gave its reporters star quality. At the same time, the power of the press became more concentrated as, like so many other American industries, it became nationalized, bureaucratized, and homogenized. National chains gobbled up and consolidated independent papers. By the end of the 1970s, 97 percent of American cities would have only one daily, and 71 percent of American newspapers would be chain-owned. The chains also acquired as many radio and TV stations as the antitrust laws allowed. Recognizing their common interests, "prestige papers" like the *New York Times* worked with the television networks to expand press prerogatives, most notably in the Pentagon Papers case. People began to fear the power of the "media"—a word invented by advertising agencies to encompass the networks, newspapers, and magazines. In 1972, old "newsmen" like Theodore White loathed this "outsider's term," but for Nixon's men the term characterized the arrogant institution dominated by the "liberal elite."[19] Convinced that these Northeastern parochials were out of touch with America's "silent majority," Nixon's men set out to master the media's conventions. They could reach the public via TV and radio, and did not need reporters as conduits. By controlling access to the White House and staging events that the press had no choice but to cover, Nixon's men hogtied their enemies.

This same bunker mentality led Nixon's men to fancy themselves above the law. They justified any action, no matter how irregular, by pointing to the hostile forces around them. Wary even of their own party's establishment, they established an independent effort, called the Committee to Reelect the President, aptly known as CREEP. This combination of paranoia and zeal began a series of petty crimes, evasions, and abuses of power that snowballed into the Watergate scandal.

Throughout the 1972 campaign, even after evidence linked CREEP with the June break-in at Democratic headquarters, Watergate failed to stir the American people. While some dismissed it as typical election-year hijinks, others could not believe that anyone would bother eavesdropping on the Democratic National Committee. There was no need to sabotage Democratic efforts; the Democrats were doing a perfectly good job of it on their own.

In the wake of the 1968 debacle, Democratic insurgents had pushed through a series of reforms to "open" the party's nominating process. A commission chaired first by South Dakota's Senator George S. McGovern, and then by Minnesota Congressman Donald M. Fraser, sought to bring the people into the selection process and increase the representation of blacks, women, and young people at the national convention. The most tangible result of this democratizing push was more primaries, twenty-three in all, sprinkled throughout the first half of 1972.

McGovern noted the changing political rules, and announced his candidacy on January 18, 1971, earlier than any other major modern presidential candidate. The former history professor then began a lonely trek through Iowa and New Hampshire, armed with a band of young supporters and faith in his anti–Vietnam War views. His surprising strength in both the Iowa caucuses and the New Hampshire primaries gave him a momentum which eventually catapulted him ahead of his sixteen competitors. McGovern had realized that, under the new system, enthusiastic volunteers and dramatic victories that grabbed media attention mattered more than traditional party organization.

Popularizing the nominating process and parceling it into a series of local elections made stumping all the more important. Candidates saw that campaign swings in primary states could bring them victories. Local politicians and reporters confirmed this belief. When George Wallace was shot while shaking hands in a suburban shopping center before the Maryland primary, 60 percent of a nation traumatized by too many assassinations called for limited campaigning. But stumping was "a vital phase of our democratic process," the Milwaukee Journal insisted. As the candidates vowed to continue "pressing the flesh," Americans applauded this courage on the stump and at the polls.[20]

While most Americans appreciated that the primaries were more democratic than the boss-centered alternatives, they also found the Democratic primaries confusing. This "weird system," as historian Arthur Schlesinger, Jr., called it, generated excitement, educated many, toughened the candidates, and involved "a not too unreasonable cross-section of the country." But the primaries were also lengthy, chaotic, undignified, unpredictable, and excessively concerned with trivial differences among the contenders.[21] Yes, the people wanted democracy—but too much of it seemed to leave them alienated and bored.

George McGovern soon learned that success in state primaries did not guarantee success overall. Once nominated, this insurgent had to welcome traditional Democrats without alienating his "army" of primary supporters. At the convention, any attempts McGovern's forces

made to control the delegates or ally with party stalwarts were denounced as the "old politics" of boss rule. To many of the fifty million
TV viewers, the convention seemed overrun by long-haired kids in tie-
dyed T-shirts. McGovern was "a threat to the nation," a South Carolina
newspaper exclaimed. For the first time since polling began, "The nominee of the party lost ground" at his own convention, Democratic party
activist Ben Wattenberg would note. "We should have had a coat and
tie rule," a McGovernite later admitted.[22]

To help unite the new Democrats and the old, McGovern chose
Senator Thomas Eagleton of Missouri as his running mate. Eagleton was
young, Catholic, and popular with blue-collar ethnics. Unfortunately,
during the convention he neglected to mention that he had been hospitalized three times for nervous exhaustion. When word leaked shortly
thereafter, McGovern first declared himself "1,000 percent for Tom Eagleton." But the story would not die. McGovern was stuck. If he kept
Eagleton, thousands would abandon the ticket. If he scuttled Eagleton,
he would appear to be just another politician, eager to win at all costs.
Two days after his endorsement, McGovern began hinting that Eagleton should resign. Within the week, Eagleton was out.

With Eagleton's withdrawal, and the thickening ethical clouds
around Nixon's White House, the Freudian Revolution finally reached
the presidential campaign. Since the turn of the century, politicians and
journalists had shied away from publicly discussing candidates' private
lives. "Personality" had come to mean colorful tidbits that humanized
the candidate. The alleged infelicities of Wendell Willkie, Franklin Roosevelt, Dwight Eisenhower, John Kennedy, and Lyndon Johnson,
among others, were not considered "news." The rumor mill often
worked overtime, but public discourse remained more or less genteel.

The "liberation" of the 1960s and the "narcissism" of the 1970s
helped make the private public. What historian Christopher Lasch calls
the "therapeutic sensibility" invaded politics. Americans began to scruti-
nize each candidate as intensely as they scrutinized themselves. The
eighteenth-century concern with reputation was too limited; the nineteenth-century concern with the soul too lofty. The search for character
in the late twentieth century became a hunt for behavioral clues illuminating an individual's psyche. At the same time, the critical press became anxious to expose politicians. By 1987, the executive editor of the
New York Times, Max Frankel, would instruct his staff that American
presidents "have no 'right' of privacy. Their lives, their personalities,
their finances, their families, friends and values are all fair game for fair

reporting."[23] How else could Americans protect themselves from crazy or crooked Presidents?

By the end of July, the demons that would torment McGovern's efforts had already emerged. The Eagleton affair impugned McGovern's candor and competence. "Leadership?" one New Yorker asked. "Why the man can't even lead himself." Voters viewed the campaign as a dry run of the presidency. If McGovern could not even organize his campaign, the *Philadelphia Inquirer* sneered, he would never manage "the most powerful nation in the world."[24]

McGovern had trouble adjusting to the scale of the general campaign. An entourage of over one hundred reporters prevented the intimate contact he enjoyed during the primaries. One invasion of a Texas supermarket "destroy[ed] canned fruit displays, terrif[ied] early-morning shoppers in their hair curlers, and infuriate[d] store managers," his manager, Gary Hart, recalled. Similarly, McGovern's Boeing 727s could land only at major airports. The demands of the media and of jet travel thus forced McGovern into formalized activities in bigger cities. He and his new running mate, Sargent Shriver, each visited three media markets a day. The candidate would swoop down, motorcade to a downtown rally or a television station, speak to a crowd or to an interviewer for a few minutes, and be on his way. "They're only going to show one event a day on TV in Los Angeles," one aide noted, "so why should we do two?" Ignoring their culpability in the matter, reporters sniffed that the campaign had turned into "an airborne media device" wholly "lacking in substance."[25]

McGovern himself was frustrated by what one aide called "this panicky running around in search of another television camera somewhere." He wanted to debate the President about "the issues." If Congress would not cooperate and suspend the Equal Time Rule, the two candidates should buy time together to debate. With the public so suspicious of both politicians and the media, McGovern argued, "confidence" could only be "restored by voters seeing and judging the candidates as they meet face to face."[26]

Nixon dismissed McGovern's "dishonest" debate challenge. He schemed with Haldeman to plant a question asking McGovern how he voted in 1964 when Johnson upheld the Equal Time Rule. Nixon admitted that he had "changed" his position, that he realized that "It would be injurious to the national interests for the President to debate his opponent." McGovern responded that Nixon was "afraid of the people" and reminded Nixon of his earlier contention that debates "give voters the opportunity to see the real man, not the synthetic product of public relations experts." In the twelve years since their debut, the debates had gained a talismanic quality. "A Kennedy–Nixon debate belongs to the golden era of television," a *New York Times* editorial sighed.[27]

Nixon's silence frustrated McGovern. Often, the networks reported the President's activities, and then paired McGovern's actions with those of a cabinet member traveling as part of the Republicans' "surrogate" campaign. Thus, McGovern was the "candidate," and the President was the President. In September, McGovern visited forty cities, while Nixon left Washington only five times. The desperate Democrat tried to bully the President onto the stump, calling Nixon barbaric, genocidal, and Hitlerian. Nixon's administration went from being the "most corrupt in recent history" to the "most corrupt since the days of Warren Harding" to the "most corrupt in the two centuries of American government." These attacks undermined McGovern's image of positive idealism and made him appear reckless.[28]

Privately, Nixon seethed. He considered this the "dirtiest campaign in history against a President." At one of his rare press conferences, he took note of the attacks. The "President who went to China and to Moscow, and who has brought 500,000 home from Vietnam, has been called the Number One war-maker in the world," Nixon said, speaking about himself in the third person. He of course refused to "respond in kind."[29] To Nixon, his landslide victory endorsed both his campaign tactics and his policies.

In 1968 and 1972, Nixon continued his twenty-year swing between playing the ambitious democrat and the virtuous republican. The "new Nixon" established a reputation for calculation and media mastery while professing nonpartisanship. Only in 1990, in his fifth volume of memoirs, would he admit, as he had in the 1950s, that all candidates "must learn to use television."[30] Nixon's ambivalence mirrored the nation's: Americans wanted both an innocent and a Machiavellian. Characteristically, Nixon tried to oblige.

This campaign, more than most, left many Americans bitter, disagreeable, and bored. McGovern's hostility and Nixon's passivity obscured the substantive issues dividing the candidates. Most voters do not perceive "all that much difference" between the two candidates, Haynes Johnson reported. In fact, that year, the candidates and the parties had divergent world views—social scientists found voters more concerned with issues in 1972 than they had been two decades before.[31] If this campaign could be perceived as lacking in substance, perhaps the problem was in the political system itself, and not with the candidates.

The Watergate cover-up scandal helped convince many that the problem indeed lay within the system. Watergate and Nixon's eventual downfall, coming on the heels of the turbulent 1960s, made Americans' traditional skepticism about politicians and the political system appear inadequate. One poll estimated that in 1976 only 35 percent of Americans trusted the government in Washington "to do what is right," down from 54 percent in 1972 and 75 percent in 1958.[32] At the same time, the scandal triggered an orgy of campaign reform. Now, optimists hoped, the presidential campaign would finally be "fixed."

III

As Americans approached their nation's bicentennial, they yearned for an electoral overhaul. The media's growth, the sixties' upheaval, Eagleton's shock treatments, Vice President Spiro Agnew's indictment, and Nixon's crucible all helped rip the ties that traditionally bound the press and the politicians. With a politician's character flaws able to undermine a candidacy, let alone a presidency, the press would be ever more vigilant. Inspired by the New Journalism and the success of Theodore White's *Making of the President* series, a cottage industry of books exposing the campaigns and the candidates grew. It was a new game in which disclosure counted and nothing was too trivial, for the personal was now political.

In December 1974 the Governor of Georgia, Jimmy Carter, announced his candidacy for the Democratic nomination. Carter's greatest national achievement so far had been stumping the panel on the game show "What's My Line?" But he and his young advisers sensed an opportunity. To a nation feeling "betrayed," Carter promised: "I'll never lie to you." To a people troubled by a "lack of competence," he asked: "Why not the best?"[33]

As a one-term governor forced by law to retire, Carter did not have much of a record. He asked to be judged by his campaign. Inverting traditional sensibilities, Carter boasted that his upcoming unemployment would free him to "devote all my time to the race, while other governors and senators will have to sacrifice their campaign efforts to duties of office. Or vice versa." Carter promised to "talk with" the American people—"not to" them—"at the factory, the supermarket, the service station." In the next twenty-two months, he would cover half a million miles and over a thousand cities, delivering 1,495 speeches.[34]

This approach accentuating personal campaigning fit the changing institutional environment. Independent candidates and the mass media had been sapping party strength for years. Fewer citizens were identifying with parties, and more voters were willing to vote for "the best man" rather than their party's leader. Increasingly, candidates had to court reporters instead of party bosses.[35] Imitating McGovern, Carter and his aides theorized that if they could do "Better Than Expected" in early primaries, they would establish credibility and snare the nomination. This strategy pleased Democrats in Iowa and New Hampshire, who timed their contests to receive maximum attention from candidates and reporters.

In 1972 a broken-down offset printing press forced Iowa Democrats to hold their precinct caucuses in January, so they would have enough time to duplicate and distribute the results. This arrangement made their vote the first in the nation. Four years later, Iowans promoted their early caucuses to candidates and journalists. "I knew each wanted to be where the other was," the Democratic state chairman, Tom Whitney, would recall, identifying the symbiotic relationship between candidates and the media. In January, Whitney's—and Carter's—strategy succeeded. Carter's slate of delegates received more than twice the votes of any other candidate's. Even though this procedure was merely the first step of many in choosing forty-seven of 3,008 delegates for the convention, reporters were looking for a winner—and found Jimmy Carter.[36]

Although his candidacy was the product of cynical calculation from Georgia to Iowa, Carter emerged as a political messiah. To prove that he would "address the issues with truth, openness, and common sense," Carter released hundreds of position papers. Still, he peddled the myth of his campaign as his greatest credential. "I started campaigning for President last January," he said in South Dakota in May 1976. "Nobody knew who I was. . . . But we started working one living room at a time."[37] Anxious for honest men who did not hide behind Madison Avenue–produced façades, Americans melted at Jimmy Carter's oft-flashed smile.

Implicitly, much of Carter's message was "I am not Richard Nixon." Republicans were worried. Having originally replaced Spiro Agnew as Vice President in 1973, Nixon's successor, Gerald R. Ford, was the first President never to have faced the national electorate. With his self-deprecating comments that he was "a Ford, not a Lincoln," and after a few stumbles in public, this former college football star and Yale Law School graduate became the national klutz. Ford did not even have the luxury of an easy nomination. Former California Governor Ronald Reagan launched a bruising primary campaign that was only decided at the Republican convention. Early polls placed Ford thirty points behind Carter.

To top it off, Ford was ineffectual on the stump. With more candor than class, his consultant Stuart Spencer said: "Mr. President, as a campaigner you're no fucking good!" Personal appearances could not "reach enough people," seemed "unpresidential," and highlighted what a more diplomatic adviser called the President's "poor" communication skills. Ford had to become "television oriented." He had to hide behind the trappings of the presidency and avoid the stump. Reporters would be "skeptical," aides acknowledged, but "They would nevertheless have to report the President's actions as being Presidential." The campaign plan directed the President to exploit Americans' soft spot for sacrifice, and say he was using "this Bicentennial year" to improve the electoral process by "campaigning on the issues."[38]

With both candidates angling for more exposure, neither could refuse to debate. For two years, citizens had been lobbying the Federal Communications Commission to broaden its interpretation of the Equal Time Rule. In September 1975, the FCC reversed its 1962 opinion and allowed networks to broadcast debates without providing equal time to minor party candidates—*if* the debates were "bona fide news events" not sponsored by the networks. Partisan needs and ideological demands converged. A nonpartisan voter education group, the League of Women Voters, would sponsor the debates.[39]

Optimism abounded. "The '76 Presidential Debates, more than any other event during our Bicentennial year, could reaffirm our democratic institutions and revitalize voter interest," the League telegraphed both candidates. The Kennedy–Nixon debates had taken their place in the American pantheon of democratic discourse, in line with the Declaration of Independence, the Bill of Rights, and Lincoln–Douglas. Gallup polls estimated that seven out of ten Americans echoed these views.[40]

Applying the lessons of Nixon's makeup, Americans watched the debate preparations. Since 1960, TV had lost its innocence. People were more aware of the scheming behind politics, especially televised politics. A nominee "would no more travel without his makeup man than he would without his press secretary," Joseph Napolitan explained, testifying to the proliferation of experts who crafted the candidates' "image." As in 1960, however, the candidates' representatives vetoed a direct exchange. In each of the three ninety-minute debates, a panel of reporters would pose questions. "Doonesbury" cartoonist Garry Trudeau pictured the debate moderator explaining that both candidates had been "made up and lit in exactly the same way," were "sitting behind matching lecterns," and were "wearing identical blue suits. Now then," the moderator falters, "which of you is Governor Carter?"[41]

Meanwhile, the fall campaign's desultory beginning made the "Great Debates" seem all the more important. Suddenly, in September, official business kept Ford in Washington. Every day, Ford arranged to be photographed doing something presidential, be it signing bills, hosting celebrities, or checking Carter's latest move—raising government support payments, for instance, when Carter complained about farm prices. Although they knew the President was toying with them, network producers could not resist the backdrops that the President's Rose Garden provided. "The White House is the greatest set television ever had," TV critic Sander Vanocur marveled.[42]

Carter denounced Ford for "hiding" from the people, and yet again trumpeted his hyperactive campaign of openness. But while Ford perhaps was too guarded, Carter was too glib. In an interview with *Playboy* magazine, Carter contemplated the relationship between his religious and political views. To illustrate Jesus's "impossible standards for us," Carter admitted, "I've looked on a lot of women with lust. I've committed adultery in my heart many times." He continued, "Christ says, Don't consider yourself better than someone else because one guy screws a whole bunch of women while the other guy is loyal to his wife." Having proved, he hoped, that he was not a prig, Carter added that his "religious beliefs" would help "prevent" him from doing what "Nixon or Johnson did—lying, cheating and distorting the truth."[43]

A slip like Carter's was almost inevitable during a twenty-two-month talkathon which served as an extended exercise in self-revelation. In an atmosphere of moral transition, when one President had lost office because his character flaws were exposed, and wherein an obscure one-term Governor was offering his character as his primary credential, the line between public and private blurred. If the President was the paragon of American morality, how could he navigate these waters when they turned choppy?

The *Playboy* affair climaxed just before the first debate, increasing the yearning for a more elevated discourse. "[Now,] perhaps we can get down to a campaign of issues rather than images," the *Atlanta Constitution* hoped. Because by 1976 the people had become so cynical, and politicians so self-conscious, the debates *had* to seem spontaneous. "The candidate must appear as if he hasn't spent all his time preparing for the first debate—but, in fact, he should have spent most of his time in preparation," one congressman advised. Both candidates tried to act casual. "He's been reading for half an hour here and an hour there," Ford's press secretary Ron Nessen said, neglecting to mention Ford's four fat briefing books and a pile of suggestions, including one to limit the President's "liquid intake" prior to the hour-and-a-half contest. "I am not going to go off and practice against a dummy opponent or memorize any cute speeches or things like that," Carter insisted.[44] The debates were the last preserve of the "old-fashioned," authentic candidate, the best opportunity for voters to see the individual up close. The candidates' posturing only widened the credibility gap.

No debate could have fulfilled the expectations built up over the previous sixteen years, the first Carter–Ford debate especially so. For over an hour the candidates nervously exchanged statistics and jargon, just as Kennedy and Nixon had done. Washington columnist Joseph Kraft, among others, found himself "bored to the point of yawning, and often confused." Toward the end, Carter seemed about to soar to the oratorical heights both had avoided so far. He began speaking about the "breakdown of the trust among our people in the. . . ." when a 25-cent capacitator shortcircuited, silencing both TV and radio relays. For twenty-seven minutes, while engineers tried to restore the sound, the two men vying for the presidency of the United States stood silent and motionless, except for a moment when the cameras panned away and the two wiped their brows.[45]

The audio gap proved that this debate was not a bona fide news event but a television show. When the broadcast signal stopped, so did the debate, even though the candidates could be heard in the theatre. Moreover, the gap illustrated the consequences of overprograming the candidates. The fear of making an improper move paralyzed them. Standing in their matching blue suits on the symmetrical sound stage, they served as twin monuments to the tyranny of television. Hyperconscious of their every move in front of 85 million viewers, Carter and Ford acted so cool as to be frozen in place.

In the second debate, held two weeks later in San Francisco, three separate sound systems guarded against technical errors. But then the thing the candidates *most* feared occurred. Ford declared "There is no Soviet domination of Eastern Europe." "That is the dumbest thing I ever heard!" Carter's aide Stuart Eizenstat rejoiced offstage. Yet, at first, few viewers noted Ford's gaffe. His pollster Robert Teeter calculated, immediately after the debate, that Ford had "won" by an eleven-point margin. Smelling a good story, reporters pounced. With each news show, with every headline, Ford's initial victory would slip away until

Teeter's polls estimated Ford losing by forty-five percentage points.[46] By the time he retracted five days later, Ford had aggravated his own Achilles heel: Millions were questioning their President's intelligence.[47]

The slip *was* revealing. Ford responded to the gaffe the way he had responded to the news earlier that week that Secretary of Agriculture Earl Butz had told a racist joke to the Watergate whistle-blower, John Dean, and the popular singers Sonny Bono and Pat Boone. Ford reprimanded Butz, who then equivocated for three days before resigning. In accepting the resignation, Ford called Butz "good and decent."[48] For three days, stories about Butz, about the Republicans' troubles with blacks, and about Ford's mental sluggishness dominated the headlines. Ford's rhetorical liberation of Eastern Europe, coming just days after the Butz stonewall, had again exposed a stubborn yet indecisive man.

To Ford's good fortune, Carter was unable to capitalize on these mistakes. As in 1972, the Democratic nominee faltered in going from a series of local primaries to a national campaign. The *Playboy* brouhaha made Carter more restrained in public. Under the scrutiny of the national press, Carter's nuanced answers to direct questions about tax reform and abortion appeared evasive. "I used to like Carter's honesty and sincerity, but I'm just turned off now," a retired grocer told reporters. Carter's thirty-point lead had all but disappeared.[49]

Ford's final two-week blitz illustrated just how empty a campaign could be. All those weeks of tending the Rose Garden had not improved Ford's speaking abilities. To compensate, his media men produced six half-hour TV programs, costarring the President and the baseball-catcher-turned-game-show-host Joe Garagiola. Balding and cherubic, Garagiola looked like Ford's distant cousin. He made Ford feel more comfortable while appearing more presidential. Garagiola as everyman lobbed easy rhetorical pitches to the President: "How many world leaders have you dealt with?" Garagiola would ask. "One hundred twenty-four leaders of countries around the world, Joe," Ford would intone. "How many do you get at a shopping center rally, maybe 32,000 people?" Stuart Spencer boasted. "*This* is a way to reach 2 million."[50]

Celebrity endorsements were a staple of twentieth-century campaigning. As early as 1916, Charles Evans Hughes had posed with Ty Cobb. In planning the 1948 campaign, Truman's aides had recognized the value of being photographed with great men like Albert Einstein. More recently, in 1972, Nixon had counted Billy Graham and Jackie Gleason in his corner, while McGovern relied on "hipper" celebrities like Shirley MacLaine and Warren Beatty. But these celebrity endorsements were brief spatters of glitter on an otherwise serious canvas. The

more important endorsements came from the city boss, the state senator. In the post–party era, celebrities had eclipsed party pols. Celebrities
attracted publicity which in the modern calculus attracted votes. They
were also powerful guides in the still-daunting waters of commercial television. Yet never before had a candidate, let alone a President, relied on
one celebrity so heavily. Ford hoped to benefit from Garagiola's popularity and his common touch, implicitly saying, "See, I'm no politician. I'm
famous but a regular guy, just like Joe."

Ford's comeback gave Carter the narrowest victory in the Electoral
College since 1916: 297 votes to 241. Less than two million popular
votes, 2 percent of the total, separated the winner from the loser. The
margin was close enough so that Ford's Eastern European gaffe—or any
of half-a-dozen other incidents—could be considered the key to the defeat. Ford's gaffe joined Nixon's makeup in political folklore and solidified the debates as trivial yet crucial, proof that minor incidents could
have major consequences.

Carter's emergence marked a triumph for American democracy. An
obscure peanut farmer had become President of the United States by
speaking to the people wherever he could find them. For good measure,
he and his opponent had debated before the entire country. And yet,
leading figures from both parties attacked both the candidates and their
campaigns. "I don't think I've seen an emptier, pettier campaign,"
George McGovern said. Neither Carter's talkathon nor the debates triggered the substantive issue exchange good democrats craved. In fact, all
these democratic techniques served simply to expose the individual. "Issues are only a means to establish personal qualities with voters," Robert
Teeter had lectured at one White House staff meeting. "Personalities
[are] far more important."[51] The republican concern with character, in
its modern gossipy form, was subverting the seeming triumph of liberal-
democratic campaign techniques, as well as faith in democracy itself.
Still, Americans were getting what they responded to—what they
wanted.

IV

By the time Jimmy Carter and Ronald Reagan snared their respective
nominations in 1980, most Americans were already fed up with the presidential campaign. The Iowa caucus and the New Hampshire primary
forced the public campaign to begin in January, not September. With
nationally televised debates, carefully produced commercials, and end-

less controversies, the primary campaigns had become so elaborate that the fall campaign seemed only the final episode of a long and tawdry TV miniseries.

As President, Jimmy Carter suffered the most dramatic fall from public grace since that other dour engineer, Herbert Hoover. At home, Carter struggled with an energy crisis and with "stagflation," the combination of inflation and unemployment. Overseas, Iran kidnapped American embassy personnel in November 1979, and the Soviet Union invaded Afghanistan a month and a half later. The impossible standards Carter the candidate set haunted Carter the President. Ninety-five campaign promises gave him less room to maneuver than did vague calls for a "New Frontier." The man who had promised never to lie turned out to be as political as anyone else. When, for example, Carter hesitated to fire his budget director and scandal-tainted crony, Bert Lance, his twenty-two-month campaign for purity looked like a sham. The great expectations Carter initially provoked only fueled greater frustration with democracy itself.

Senator Edward Kennedy, the link to the Democratic martyrs of the 1960s, would only have opposed a Democratic incumbent whose popularity had sunk to Carter's low of 25 percent in September 1979, and who had alienated so many insiders. Still confident in his campaigning abilities, Carter planned an all-out primary effort. The foreign-policy crises, however, changed the political equation. With Americans rallying around their President, and Carter confident that the hostages would be freed quickly, he no longer needed to campaign. As he holed up in the Rose Garden, he explained: "I, as President, have got to maintain the accurate image that we do have a crisis, which I will not ignore until those hostages are released." This commitment to the "image" of crisis reflected the modern parlance and priorities in presidential leadership. Still, Carter acknowledged that a President should campaign. "I'm a campaigner, I'm a candidate," he admitted. "And I look forward to the time when the hostages are released and I can go out and campaign actively."[52]

Although Carter's admission appeared to set new standards for presidential candor it deepened public cynicism. Carter was simply playing Franklin D. Roosevelt's game. As the crisis dragged on, Carter pushed the charade to new heights—or depths. At 7:13 A.M. on April 1, just in time for the morning news shows on the day of the Wisconsin primary, Carter announced that the Iranians had made a "positive step." When this hope proved false, the President "no longer seemed decent and honorable, but manipulative," an aide admitted.[53]

Carter's advisers reevaluated the Rose Garden strategy. The link to Democratic regulars, Robert Strauss, believed that Carter would have "absolutely locked up Connecticut big" if he had visited even once. Whether true or not, this claim reflected the belief that being passive hurt doubly, by depriving the campaign of the candidate, and by angering those who wanted the candidate to campaign. "The people like him when they see him, but they don't like him now," a Carter strategist admitted. Carter's poll ratings began to slump. On April 30, a week after a hostage rescue attempt failed, Carter decided he was no longer needed in Washington every day. Democratic Senator Robert C. Byrd applauded the release of the fifty-fourth hostage. The President of the United States had been dragged onto the stump.[54]

Although, as he had promised, Carter "whipped Senator Kennedy's ass," the victory was hollow: He wrecked his choirboy image. A Herblock cartoon pictured Carter and his press secretary Jody Powell walking past men in lab coats charting the "1980 Presidential Political Polls." "Well," Carter says, "let's see what our domestic and foreign policies will be today."[55] Such a cartoon was a far cry from the 1852 caricature of "Managing the Candidate." Now, the President was independent of his party. He was the boss, helped by "specialists" like Powell and the all-important pollsters, whose political calculations were based on scientific research samples rather than "instinct." The candidate had gone from being a pawn to being just as devious as the rest. Nominees had lost both their insulation and their innocence.

Ronald Reagan found the primaries a happier, though no less exhausting, experience. The conservative war-horse and retired Hollywood cowboy began by trotting, not running. He immediately took full advantage of the Secret Service protection offered to candidates after Robert F. Kennedy's assassination. Wherever he went, Reagan was surrounded by a nest of agents and handlers who made him appear "presidential." "It wouldn't do any good to have him in, going to coffees and shaking hands like the others," his campaign manager, John Sears, sniffed. "People will get the idea he's an ordinary man, like the rest of us." Reagan's aides limited his contacts with the press, shielding their boss from making controversial attacks on liberals and from embarrassing moments that revealed his ignorance as to just who was the President of France and what kind of federal aid New York City had received. "I guess he doesn't want any tough interviews," his press assistant shrugged.[56] Traditionally, the primaries required more informal "retail" campaigning, as Adlaï Stevenson had learned in Florida in 1956. This cocoon that the Secret Service and the consultants spun around

Reagan blurred the line between primary campaigning and the general election campaign.

Like Carter, Reagan learned that he had to be accessible. "If you're going to use a Rose Garden strategy, you better have a Rose Garden," Reagan's aide Lyn Nofziger sighed. After losing in Iowa, the Reagan men settled on just the right balance between privacy and access, passivity and activity. Reporters noted that even though Reagan was a private man wary of the press, he loved pressing the flesh. "I don't think the two don't go together," Reagan said. "I happen to like people."[57]

This formula helped Reagan win the New Hampshire primary and, eventually, the nomination. As that nomination loomed, one Republican emerged who rejected the preparation and the crowdsmanship of the Reagan campaign. While others pandered to the National Rifle Association in New Hampshire, John B. Anderson, a little-known congressman from Illinois, declared for gun control. While his rivals flipped pancakes, drove tractor–trailers, and kissed babies, Anderson addressed issues. By championing the democratic exchange, he became the modern incarnation of republican virtue. "Somehow we accept the idea that if you press enough flesh, by some strange alchemy it turns you into an adequate President. I don't," he proclaimed.[58] In April, Anderson abandoned his party, establishing the "National Unity Campaign," with a 350-page platform. Anderson gambled that enough people were fed up with the two nominees to join his efforts. Polls showed that many Americans blamed the poor choice of candidates on the flawed electoral system. While Anderson may not have been the solution, he had accurately diagnosed the problem.

With a crippled incumbent and an unproven challenger, a debate seemed unavoidable. The League of Women Voters, acting as "surrogates of the people," again offered to sponsor.[59] The League decided to include Anderson, whose poll ratings were as high as 15 percent. White House aides worried that Anderson would gain credibility and steal more votes from Carter than from Reagan. Anderson would provide the excuse for avoiding the debate, as George Wallace had done for Richard Nixon in 1968.

Carter's refusal overshadowed the typical debate about the debates, which usually centered around lighting and timing and other theatrical details. It reopened the controversy about his refusal to debate Kennedy during the primaries. Most Americans disapproved of Carter's decision. Once again he had politicized his image. The press insisted that debates mattered, and that Carter's refusal mattered too.

That participation in debates became a mark of respect for one's rivals and for the democratic process revealed how entrenched debating had become. The "bona fide news event" fiction freed the events from the tyranny of the Equal Time Rule and the grip of the Congress. And now that President Ford had debated in 1976 without endangering the republic, even that fig leaf was gone. Just as it took stumping decades to be accepted, long after all the technological hurdles had been jumped, only now would debates become standard. As always, the candidates had cloaked their political considerations in pieties. But candidates did not debate, or stump, until it was in their best interest, meaning that they either could benefit from the activity or could not afford to boycott it. In institutionalizing debates, politicians recognized the importance of television and the fact that both major candidates were needed to draw a big audience—individual speeches would no longer draw the masses.

When Reagan and Anderson met on September 21, 1980, the debate itself proved less interesting than the debate that had preceded it. Carter's absence detracted from the aura—and the audience. ABC broadcast the movie *Midnight Express* instead. The postmortems ignored the two debaters and focused on the missing President. "It was a disaster for Carter," Michael G. Gartner, the editor of the *Des Moines Register and Tribune* decided. "People here like to know where candidates stand. There's a strong moral sense about it."[60]

For all its limitations, the debate had allowed millions of Americans to spend an hour with Ronald Reagan and John Anderson. This opportunity was especially welcome in light of the increased awareness of the consultants who kept Reagan under wraps. In August, Reagan had proposed resuming "official relations" with Taiwan, and questioned Darwinian evolution. These statements reflected the candidate's right-wing sensibilities but upset the Republican strategy of moderating his image. Reagan therefore spent much of September insulated from the press and the people. He stuck to his basic stump speech, boring himself and his audiences. His aides interposed themselves between Reagan and reporters, muttering "No interviews" and letting their elbows fly. "There is too great a chance that somebody will throw something at you from left field that you're not aware of, that you haven't heard of," a Reagan aide explained. "Our job is to elect the guy President."[61] "Electing the guy" and engaging the people seemed contradictory goals. As Nixon had done, Reagan's men viewed the press as the enemy. The candidate, it seemed, had to be protected from the press, the people, and himself.

Carter's men also wanted to keep their candidate in check. They feared that the President's contempt for Reagan would bubble over and reignite talk of Carter's "mean streak." But Carter would have to face the people, having overplayed the Rose Garden strategy during the primaries. Carter began with town meetings and bill-signing ceremonies in September, followed by a fuller stumping schedule in October.

By early October neither Reagan nor Carter had mastered their respective demons. In Ohio, Reagan declared that trees created more air pollution than did automobiles. Signs on trees sprouted, pleading "Chop me down before I kill again." That same week, Carter claimed that a Reagan victory would divide Americans, "blacks from whites, Jews from Christians, North from South, rural from urban."[62] With doubts about both candidates persisting, neither could avoid a debate.

The match was set for October 28. "I think appearance is more important than a whole bunch of facts—how you look, how you act, and how you present yourself," William E. Timmons, Reagan's deputy campaign manager, predicted. "Reagan will be calm, cool and collected and the President will be tense."[63] Twenty years after Kennedy and Nixon clashed, the debates had been shorn of grand expectations. They were now simply the wildest of cards in a high-stakes poker game.

The Carter–Reagan debate marked a clash between two styles, between a linear, formalistic print culture and McLuhan's blurry visual culture, between a politics of issues and a politics of images. Carter played Nixon to Reagan's Kennedy, contrasting the democratic man of substance with the republican personification of virtue. Carter, tight-lipped, flashing forced smiles at inappropriate moments and, looking like a parson, preached that there are "no simple answers to complicated questions." On the other hand, Reagan was friendly and paternal, blocking Carter's jabs with a smile and a nod. "There you go again," the sunny Californian chided the uptight Georgian, when Carter alleged that Reagan would cut Social Security payments. In closing, Carter slipped and thanked "the people of Cleveland and Ohio for being such hospitable hosts during these last few hours in my life."[64] Ronald Reagan the ex–movie actor and sportscaster who had costarred with Bonzo the chimp beat Jimmy Carter the nuclear engineer who had apprenticed with Admiral Hyman J. Rickover.

As drama, the debate fared well at the box office but was panned by the critics. One hundred and twenty million Americans watched the last-minute show; most were disappointed. Both candidates had been coached, and dished out carefully prepared morsels. "Only those with shallow minds would attempt to dispose of great problems of global importance with off-the-cuff answers," historian Henry Steele Commager lamented. "The American presidency is too exalted an office to be subjected to the indignity of this technique." Douglas Cater, who helped resurrect the debates in 1976, declared the present ones a failure. These debates "confounded" the "democratic process." Have "we . . . grown acculturated to synthetic political pap in the same way we fancy the processed fast foods as substitute for a more nutritious diet?"[65]

Still, the debates appeared decisive. Throughout the fall, polls had placed the two front-runners within percentage points of each other, with Anderson's candidacy fading each week. On Election Day, Reagan won 51 percent of the popular vote, 10 percentage points more than Carter, and 489 electoral votes to Carter's 49. Anderson received 7 percent of the vote, just enough to qualify for federal financing and stave off bankruptcy. Estimating that Carter dropped 10 percentage points during the campaign's final forty-eight hours, the Gallup organization declared the shift one of the most dramatic ever observed. The last-minute Iranian announcement of terms for the hostages' release benefited Reagan, but the debate also hurt Carter.[66] Few doubted that as powerful an instrument as the debates could be ignored in future campaigns; even fewer were happy with the way the debates were being used.

On Election Eve, as the nation's secular high priest, Walter Cronkite, recited the president-elect's résumé, many despaired that a former Las Vegas pitchman and "B" movie star would fill Washington's chair. Yet Reagan had campaigned longer and harder than had most modern candidates. He was no Jimmy Carter rising from the ashes of Watergate, or even a George McGovern emerging from senatorial obscurity. Reagan the politician had been in the public eye for almost twenty years. He left a substantial paper trail of speeches and policy decisions. As the most ideological major party nominee since Barry Goldwater, he had clear positions on every major issue facing the American people—defense, abortion, the economy. He could be accused of being simplistic; he could not be accused of being vague or uncontroversial.

At the same time, Reagan was aided by a corps of professional campaigners, some of whom had been helping Republicans since Nixon. Along with Reagan's homegrown aides like Michael Deaver, they insulated the candidate. Marshall McLuhan's theories were discredited among academics, but these men continued to believe in them, and run campaigns by them. The previous decade had proved the media omnipotent, no longer "The Responsive Chord" but "The Second God," in the words of one Democratic McLuhanite, Tony Schwartz. With the "medium" the "message," personalities were more important than issues, feelings more important than thoughts, impressions more important than facts. These cowboys hurled epigrams as enthusiastically as McLuhan had: "Truth is a print ethic," Schwartz preached; "Television elects Presidents," Deaver taught.[67] They were not so much immoral as amoral, thrilled with their power and their high-tech toys.

These men considered Ronald Reagan the "perfect" candidate. "He does whatever you want him to do," his manager, Edward J. Rollins, rejoiced.[68] Reagan was "telegenic" and used to taking direction. The result was an image that belied the conservative war-horse he was. Reagan was the most ideological and the most evanescent candidate of the modern era. Without the conservative grounding, he would have floated away. Without the image-making, he would have sunk under the weight of his rhetoric. Reagan and his men would exploit this paradox to the fullest over the next eight years.

V

As President, Reagan played Franklin Roosevelt to Carter's Hoover, arguing that there was no cause for malaise but malaise itself. Reagan "brought pride back" to an America buoyed by an economic upturn. After the unhappy tenures of Johnson, Nixon, Ford, and Carter, he proved that a President could still be popular and powerful.

Reagan also capped the institutional transformation of the presidency begun during the New Deal. Franklin Roosevelt smuggled experts, including ghost-writers, into the White House; Ronald Reagan openly embraced such assistants. Reagan acknowledged the fifty-year-old fact that the modern President was more chairman of the board than Lone Ranger. Ghost-writers like Peggy Noonan took off their sheets and achieved celebrity as "speech-writers." "You're getting his sound," White House Special Assistant Richard Darman told Noonan. "Actually, you may be recreating his sound, and it sounds very natural to him."[69] Darman recognized that the modern corporate presidency blurred the individual and the institutional; that assistants and the president were often one and the same.

Reagan's White House was preoccupied with securing favorable news coverage. Increasingly, the "news" meant TV. Since the networks lengthened their news shows to thirty minutes in 1963, TV news had blossomed. Daily, 100 million Americans watched news shows. Anchormen like Walter Cronkite and David Brinkley became as famous as—and more trusted than—the Presidents they covered. From dawn to midnight, from "Good Morning America" to Ted Koppel's "Nightline," it seemed that news dominated the medium. At the same time, the medium's entertainment values began to infect the news. Scholars no longer spoke about an "electric mirror" reflecting reality but a "flashlight in the attic," spotlighting particular items of interest. Television's economic, technological, and temporal demands biased the news in favor of black-and-white stories that grabbed attention and elicited emotion, all in two minutes or less.[70]

Like drug pushers catering to an addict's needs, Reagan's aides met every morning at 8:15 A.M. to plan the day's news coverage, to choose the "line of the day." Exploiting TV's "structural" biases, they offered one major story a day, dramatically illustrated. The "visual is as critical as what we're saying," Deputy Chief of Staff Michael Deaver preached.[71]

In this scenario, reporters were props at best and pests at worst. Reporters could upstage the day's theme with alternative, or even critical, stories. Reagan held even fewer press conferences than Richard Nixon had. Reporters would joke: "Covering the President means never having to say you saw him."[72] In an inversion from the nineteenth century, the Presidents' private life was publicized and his public concerns were obscured.

Like dupes at once delighted and dismayed by a hoax, Americans succumbed to and condemned this government-by-polls. Reagan enjoyed approval ratings of 60 and 70 percent, but cynicism about American politics became endemic. The presidential campaign season—prolonged by the primaries—became the forum for a year-long wail. Hundreds of journalists scrutinized the candidates in search of the telling flaw. The media hordes had become so pivotal that they too merited coverage. Typically, journalists exposed their own crimes while continuing to commit them. In February 1984 the *Los Angeles Times* ran a story about the illegitimate origins of the Iowa caucuses. But while showing how Iowa officials puffed up this exercise, the *Times* further inflated the event, echoing one candidate's assessment that "On February 20, the Democrats of Iowa will be the most powerful citizens on earth."[73] This approach, which built on the traditional American dichotomy between lofty sentiments at home and crass emotions in the field, only deepened the cycle of cynicism. The media acted cynically, treated cynical candidates cynically, and reported everything even more cynically.

"There's got to be a better way," many sighed, as the primaries became a focal point of dissatisfaction. As early as 1976 a Louis Harris survey estimated that four voters in five wanted the primary system changed. Since that time the system had only grown longer, more expensive, and more chaotic, and the public had become more resigned. Yet the present system had many benefits as well. The primary system

opened the process, allowing underdogs like Jimmy Carter to emerge
and inviting tens of millions of Americans to participate. Primaries functioned as basic training for presidents, allowing them to "fine-tune" essential political skills.[74] The system was unwieldy, inefficient, and cum-
bersome—as was democracy.

This open system was naturally biased toward active candidates and
suspenseful campaigns. Devoting hundreds of reporters and millions of
dollars to covering the nomination fight, the media was loathe to have
a winner declared immediately. As a result, reporters often sought to
knock the front-runner and promote his closest challenger. Similarly,
the voters often wanted the candidate to "earn" the nomination, and
did not respond well to talk about "inevitable" candidates.

Walter Mondale suffered through these biases. Carter's Vice President came into the campaign well-organized and well-known. But talk
of the "inevitability" of his nomination hurt him and helped account
for Senator Gary Hart's strong showing in the New Hampshire primary.
Mondale's counterattack finally extinguished the doubts that had
haunted him since 1974, when he had confessed: "I do not have the
overwhelming desire to be president which is essential for the kind of
campaign that is required."[75] Mondale did not want to spend the rest
of his life in Holiday Inns. This confession of humility should have been
an asset, and would have been in the nineteenth century. But by the
1970s, the ideals had been inverted. The 1984 primaries let Mondale
prove that he had "what it takes" for the modern campaign—a cast-
iron stomach for eating ethnic foods; bionic limbs for round-the-clock
handshaking and stumping; and a motor mouth.

By the time Mondale was nominated he was a better campaigner
but a weakened candidate. He was exhausted, and his faults had been
exposed. He stumbled, bruised and bleeding, into the ring with the well-
rested and undisputed campaigning champion, Ronald Reagan.

As with Carter and Reagan in 1980, and McGovern and Nixon in
1972, Mondale and Reagan offered the American people a stark choice.
Mondale was a New Deal Democrat, trusting the federal government as
an instrument of justice. He favored arms control, abortion, and higher
taxes to reduce the federal deficit. Reagan, on the other hand, was a
Goldwater Republican, committed to a smaller government, a defense
buildup, curbs on abortion, and spending cuts, not tax increases. The
two candidates' political strategies reflected their differing philosophies.
Mondale took his campaign of issues to the New Deal coalition in the
Northeastern "Rust Belt," while Reagan relied on television and care-

fully crafted appearances to bolster his new coalition anchored in the California to Florida "Sun Belt."

Mondale officially opened his general election campaign by marching in New York City's Labor Day parade at 9 A.M. Unfortunately, the streets were empty. The picture of the candidate wandering down the desolate streets symbolized the old-fashioned assumptions burdening the Democratic campaign, and the shoddiness of Mondale's advance work. Later that day, the President appeared at a twenty-minute pep rally in Northern California with sky-divers, hot-air balloons, and 40,000 people shouting "U.S.A.! U.S.A.!" Therein the pattern was set. In one week, Mondale would make twelve appearances in nine cities, trying to hit three media markets each day and answering questions wherever he went. That same week, Reagan spoke six times in four stops, concentrating mostly on posing for the nightly news. He took no questions. A week later, to disprove Mondale's charge that he was "the most isolated President in American history," Reagan would consent to a ten-minute news conference, his first since July 24—and the longest exchange with reporters during the entire campaign.[76]

Ronald Reagan believed in stumping. "It's a good idea—and it's the American way," he declared in Iowa.[77] With their Hollywood flair, their understanding of media needs, and their attention to detail, Reagan's aides mounted a great show. They made appearances on the stump one more installment in the daily soap opera they produced and directed. In so doing, they undermined stumping's role as the necessary human complement to the mechanized campaign. Reagan's appearances became one more media event, one more stage-setting for one more sound bite.

Though aware they were being manipulated, print reporters dutifully wrote about the Reagan juggernaut, while TV producers broadcast the red-white-and-blue extravaganzas. After all, the President of the United States was "news." Reporters often noted that the events were "well-orchestrated," but the image overwhelmed the disclaimer. Conversely, while reporters appreciated Mondale's openness, they exploited it. Mondale generated too many stories each day. These stories raged out of control as versions abounded, conflicted, and occasionally prompted denials, further muddying Mondale's message.[78]

Mondale and his advisers peddled his awkwardness as a sign of authenticity. They naively trusted the people or the press to "assert" themselves and demand more substance from Reagan, the campaign manager Jim Johnson would recall. "I'm not comfortable in front of television and I'm afraid I never will be," Mondale confessed. Echoing Adlai Stevenson, Mondale rejected the notion of "somebody . . . manufacturing me . . . coloring my hair and whatever."[79]

As with his doubts about spending his life in Holiday Inns, Mondale's refusal to adapt to TV violated the contemporary code for candidates. To many, the contrast in appearances had less to do with authenticity and more with efficiency. In their self-appointed role as the people's surrogates, reporters judged a campaign by the quality of its "retail" campaigning. "When a candidate can't get his own campaign organized, I begin to ask whether he can run the country," the editor of *Adweek* said.[80]

Mondale's posture was disingenuous, for he did consent to some coaching. In fact, Democrats had as many political consultants and advance men and advertising strategists as Republicans did. Mondale and the Democrats were moaning more about the Republicans' effectiveness than about their tactics. True, Republicans took the strategy a step or two further, but Reagan and Mondale were more similar to each other than either one was to Adlai Stevenson. In losing all presidential elections but three in the four decades of the television age, Democrats had made the "image" campaign their issue. But it was not so much a Democratic issue as a loser's lament.

Nevertheless, Mondale's critique went to the heart of the Reagan paradox and uncovered a division in the White House. All wanted an "aggressive campaign," not a "Rose Garden strategy," entailing at least forty days on the stump. Reagan's men realized that even the incumbent had to approach the people. They disagreed, however, about whether the campaign should be ideological or patriotic. The "hawks" wanted a "bold campaign" that would revitalize the right-wing agenda on social issues, economic reform, and defense. This stance would allow Reagan to continue playing Ronald Reagan, conservative. The "patriots" preferred that the campaign remain sugary, or, as Richard Darman put it, "relatively nonspecific programmatically." This approach stressed patriotism, not conservatism, and themes, not policies. Reagan endorsed this approach by recalling that he "never mentioned" his plans for welfare reform "in the campaign for reelection" as California Governor. He "didn't want to politicize it." Reagan would ignore "what's-his-name," avoid the press, and wrap himself in the American flag. Phrases like "the opportunity society," "a positive vision of our citizens and our country," and "freedom's next step" abounded.[81]

Reagan saw politics as sordid. The President, the premier American politician of the 1980s, was therefore characterized by his campaign director, Ed Rollins, as someone who was "not a political man but has superb people instincts that probably turn out to be better political instincts" than most professionals have.[82] This paradoxical position of the apolitical politician played into traditional republican conceptions. Yet at heart it betrayed a cynicism about what the public might believe, and only deepened public disaffection.

Still, even Reagan would have to debate. "It's become an expected part of the campaign," Dorothy Ridings of the League of Women Voters observed. As in 1980, the expectations were considerably scaled down. Observers grumbled that these were merely "carefully programmed joint appearances" and not debates; that "TV personality was the determining factor"; and that "makeup and lighting" counted over all else. Although academics and pollsters remained skeptical, most believed that the debates would be decisive.[83] The metaphors surrounding the debates (the "Super Bowl," "sudden-death," "Do-or-die") and the mythology that had grown (Nixon's makeup, Ford's blooper, Reagan's "There you go again") reflected the consensus. For that reason, no candidate could afford to skip the debates—or treat them casually.

In fact, by 1984, to go into the debates without intense preparation would have appeared suicidal or arrogant rather than courageous or authentic. Experts, from makeup artists to ghost-writers, were now an accepted part of politics. Candidates boasted about their elaborate preparations, rather than downplaying them as Carter and Ford had done eight years before. During debates, details counted. Every camera angle had to be considered, every color coordinated, every stage set. The two camps would quibble about production details, produce voluminous briefing books, and then run the candidates through mock debates. One of the issues that Democrats never successfully mined during the 1984 campaign was "Debate-gate." Somehow, one of Carter's 1980 briefing books had ended up in the Reagan camp. All of Reagan's aides had been struck by bouts of amnesia concerning the details, although clearly some chicanery was involved. But few Americans seemed perturbed by such hijinks, and no one questioned the need and value of the briefing books themselves.

In the first debate, on October 7 in Louisville, Kentucky, Mondale's intensive preparations paid off. As usual, the candidates filled their brief responses with jargon and statistics—the tools of substance—while reporters and viewers focused on each candidate's presence. Mondale, looking confident, kept on asking about the deficit. Reagan, looking wan and a little disoriented, repeated one automatic response. Reagan's closing statement was feeble. After standing on his feet doling out prepackaged dollops of wisdom for ninety minutes, the seventy-three-year-

52 SEE HOW THEY RAN

old was tired. The Mondale campaign had hit a "home run," Reagan's manager, Ed Rollins, would later admit.[84]

Mondale rose from "Loser to Underdog," once again proving the significance of debates. For the first time, even publications like the conservative *Wall Street Journal* worried about Reagan's age. The flagging Mondale effort revived. Crowds grew. Fundraising picked up. The press fed the phenomenon by headlining "DEBATE MOMENTUM PUTS ZIP BACK INTO MONDALE CAMPAIGN."[85]

Putting his own "spin" on his candidate's off-day, Senator Paul Laxalt charged that Reagan "was brutalized by a briefing process" that included six dress rehearsals. In 1960, the excuse would have been more devastating than the failure. Reagan sulked that "If I had as much makeup on as he [Mondale] did, I'd look younger too." Even Ronald Reagan, the "Great Communicator," would have a hard time convincing people that Mondale had mastered television theatrics better than he had. Reagan's response did betray his belief that image was more important than substance; that, as the *Washington Post* huffed, "The amount of rose in the cheek—is what voters are swayed by."[86] But this was precisely Reagan's lesson to American politics. He—and the political system—were too foregone to play the innocents. Makeup did not become the issue it had been in 1960, for when in 1984 people said that Reagan looked old, they meant he looked old even with the camouflage of Michael Deaver and company.

The second debate, held on October 21 in Kansas City, was ostensibly about foreign policy. The candidates stuck to the script, clashing about "Star Wars," Lebanon, and arms control. But the debate really was a stylized confrontation, with Mondale's supporters looking for more signs of weakness in the President, and Reagan's supporters waiting for a gesture showing that the Gipper was still at the top of his game. True to form, Reagan joked "I'm not going to make an issue about Mr. Mondale's age and experience." In one deft move, the old performer had wooed back his audience. The low expectations that Reagan had to fulfill were reflected in a *Baltimore Sun* headline the next day: "PRESIDENT DIDN'T STUMBLE."[87] That's all he had to *not* do. Reagan had survived the debate—and the election.

As expected, Reagan wiped out Mondale, winning 525 electoral votes to Mondale's thirteen. Mondale blamed his loss on television. He feared that "American politics is losing its substance. . . . It's losing the depth that tough problems require to be discussed, and more and more it is that 20-second [TV network news] snippet." Mondale's chief speechwriter, Martin Kaplan, was asked whether *anyone* could have defeated

Ronald Reagan. Echoing his boss, Kaplan suggested "Robert Redford or Walter Cronkite."[88]

Mondale's critique assumed that the people were helpless in the face of a stirring image. "If voters are really swayable by a smile and a commercial, what are we saying about our democracy?" Ben Wattenberg asked. "That the voters are jerks. I don't believe it." "Whether it is a candidate with a bullhorn on the caboose of a train, broadcasting on radio, or using most every television station in the land, the American people know integrity, courage, leadership, vision," another columnist, Carl Rowan, claimed. "They have [done so] in every time, age and stage of communications technology."[89] Rowan's perspective, however, was decidedly not that of the majority: In 1984, politicians no longer had faith in the people—and the people no longer had faith in themselves.

VI

Ronald Reagan "fundamentally understands that politics is communication with leadership, and he probably puts communication above substance," one of his former press aides, Leslie Janka, observed during Reagan's second term. "Carter was just the flip side of that. He put substance ahead of politics."[90] In both 1980 and 1984, voters had been offered stark choices in campaigning styles. Balancing the demands of his office with his commitment to substance, Jimmy Carter had run a somewhat passive but issue-oriented campaign. With his aides pressing him to avoid controversy, Ronald Reagan had run an active but relatively silent one. Four years later, Regan continued to avoid substance and was even more passive than Carter had been, while Carter's Vice President, Walter Mondale, ran an active and substantive campaign. These four stances paralleled the positions staked out in the 1840 and 1844 campaigns by Martin Van Buren, William Henry Harrison, James Knox Polk, and Henry Clay. The differences between the two sets of campaigns revealed the great distance that the presidential campaign had traveled. Henry Clay's activity paled by comparison with that of the most passive of the modern candidates, while Reagan's relative silence outshouted the pronouncements of all but the loudest of his nineteenth-century predecessors. Still, the parallels were striking, as was the fact that in the 1980s, as in the 1840s, no position appeared completely legitimate. Both Carter and Mondale were repudiated as losers, while Reagan's two victories carried with them a taint—a sense that, as with Polk's 1844 campaign, the tactics were unsporting even though they worked.

The democratic vision of the early twentieth century had soured. The rise of liberal democracy had activated the candidate, involved the people, and injected issues into the campaign. At the same time, the triumph of technology had promised a saner and more substantive politics. But the republican heritage had never been fully erased—the doubts about democracy and about campaigning lingered. And America's technological capacities outstripped contemporary proprieties. Like prematurely developed adolescents, American politicians found themselves capable of actions they could neither fully understand nor control. For all its progress over a century and a half, the problem of the presidential campaign persisted.

E L E V E N

The Search for Virtue in the Presidential Campaign

Why am I doing this?
—*Michael Dukakis, 1988*

"CAN WE focus on the issues and not the personalities and the mud?" an uncommitted voter asked during the second presidential debate of 1992. As the other 208 panelists applauded, the three leading presidential candidates responded. "I think it depends on how you define it," President George Bush equivocated. Still, he agreed: "I mean, I think in general, let's talk about these issues. Let's talk about the programs." Ross Perot boasted: "I don't have any spin doctors. I don't have any speechwriters. Probably shows." Bill Clinton fumed: "I'm just as sick as you are by having to wake up and figure out how to defend myself every day. I never thought I'd ever be involved in anything like this."[1]

Once again, a seemingly trivial campaign exchange was in fact a profound attempt to solve the enduring conundrum of American politics. All three candidates accepted the essential distinction in American political rhetoric between issues and personality. "Issues," meaning a detailed discussion of particular policies, connoted substance, rationality, and respect for the people; "personalities," meaning a focus on character traits and past actions, betrayed superficiality, emotionalism, and contempt for the voters. According to each campaign, "our" candidate addressed the issues; "their" candidate indulged in personalities.

Surveys conducted in 1988 showed that by margins of three and four to one, Americans deemed "issues" more important than "personality" in choosing a president.[2] This demand for "issues" conveyed voters' frustration with the empty, meaningless presidential campaign. At the same time, candidates could not ignore the public's search for a president of good character. "I believe that character is a part of being president," George Bush insisted early in the second debate. Back in 1987, Michael Dukakis, the sacrificial lamb of 1988, had agreed, declaring: "The next President of the United States will face challenges that no campaign position paper can possibly anticipate. But what can be measured in advance is the character of the person who will confront those challenges."[3]

By 1992, Americans had evolved an elaborate campaign ritual, with the candidate at the center. A nominee won the presidency through a grueling cross-country blitz of preening, parading, gladhanding, back-slapping, baby-kissing, and debating. In 1992 candidates and pundits repeatedly congratulated themselves for being more serious, more substantive, more virtuous than in the past. Nevertheless, by Election Day the candidates were exhausted and the nation was demoralized. Barely half of those eligible had bothered to vote. Two-thirds of those surveyed criticized one or both of the candidates for being "too personally negative"; 43 percent said that the campaign had not made them "feel proud to be an American." "Cynicism pervades. Nothing seems genuine," the *New York Times* reported. "For the truth be told, much of America just doesn't like its three candidates for President."[4]

I

"Why am I doing this?" Governor Dukakis asked as he rushed around the nation in 1988. Stripped of the armor that the republican taboo had provided to the passive nineteenth-century nominees, modern candidates bore the brunt of the people's frustration with the "joyless," "churlish," "nasty" campaigns. Although he won, George Bush was called a wimp, a racist, and a demagogue. For his efforts, Dukakis was branded "humorless, whining, ungenerous, murky in program, dreary in rhetoric"—and this by a supporter.[5]

Despite traveling more than half a million miles and shaking thousands of hands, the candidates remained aloof. One layer of insulation, provided by the Secret Service, testified to the violence blighting modern America. The second layer, provided by the political consultants, testified to the caution and pseudo-science gripping modern politics. Thus, America's paradoxical political campaign thrust the candidate toward the people while trying to shield him from them.

Clearly, stumping during the primary helped a winner emerge. But after the conventions, its impact was less clear. In the television era, there were far more effective ways to reach the people than whistle-stops and prop-stops. In seeking to explain why candidates still stumped, political scientists retreated into double negatives. "No one is absolutely certain that whistle-stop methods produce no useful result," Nelson W. Polsby and Aaron Wildavsky concluded in their popular textbook on elections.[6]

Still, the candidates hit the campaign trail, fourteen-hour day after fourteen-hour day. Again and again, contradictory expectations clouded their efforts. By 1988, Americans' appetite for personal information about their candidates seemed endless. Even before any primary votes were cast, the character question sank two Democratic candidacies. In May 1987, former Senator Gary Hart withdrew when word leaked of his involvement with a Miami model. That fall, Senator Joseph Biden quit amid reports that he had plagiarized in law school and had lifted rhetoric from other politicians. At dinner tables throughout the land, Americans debated whether they preferred a morally flawed nominee with whom they agreed, or a Mister Clean whose views they disliked. Strict democrats deemed character irrelevant. They wanted to know where their candidate stood on the issues. But individual peccadilloes often illuminated more serious flaws. Thus, Hart's extracurricular adventures confirmed doubts about "his judgment and credibility," *Newsweek* wrote, while Biden's rhetorical larceny substantiated fears that he was shallow.[7]

Unsure which course to chart, both Bush and Dukakis wavered. In accepting the nomination, Dukakis emphasized character, not issues. "This election is not about ideology; it's about competence," the diminutive Bostonian declared at the Democratic convention, presenting himself as trustworthy. Yet as his campaign progressed—or, as some would say, degenerated—he became known as a "policy nerd," interested in technicalities, not personalities. Frustrated, Dukakis insisted during the debates, "I'm a reasonably likable guy." He also began campaigning with his wife. By introducing her husband as "my passionate partner for twenty-five years," Kitty Dukakis hoped to prove, one reporter noted, "that the man was not just a brain in a jar."[8]

Dukakis's romantic republican view of campaigning crippled his efforts. He assumed that Bush's rhetorical crimes would not pay. "Friends, this is garbage," Dukakis said of the slurs directed against him. "This isn't worthy of a presidential campaign." "The Packaging of George Bush," a series of Democratic ads, attacked Republicans for doing "anything" to win. "They'd like to sell you a package," the narrator intoned, "Wouldn't you rather choose a president?" These ads, however, fed the general disgust with campaigns without refuting Bush's charges or illustrating Dukakis's virtue. Many viewers thought the commercials were pro-Bush.[9]

Like so many of his predecessors, Governor Dukakis stepped up his stumping campaign to demonstrate his virtue and his accessibility. "As a candidate who's viewed as emotionally distant, he needed that contact with the press and the voters," his communications director, Kirk O'Donnell, explained. Although O'Donnell claimed that his boss excelled at "retail politics" and "became a much better candidate," Dukakis remained stiff on the stump until the final few weeks.[10] His discomfort with modern populist politics often undermined his efforts to broaden his appeal. In one "photo opportunity" intended to illustrate his commitment to national defense, Dukakis donned a helmet and climbed into an M-1 tank. He ended up looking more like Snoopy fighting the Red Baron than General Patton defending freedom. This ridiculous image epitomized Dukakis's ineffectual campaign, his inability to choose between emphasizing character or issues, between pandering and educating.

In 1988, George Bush was less ambivalent than his opponent, and correspondingly more successful. The Vice President began with the issues and retreated into personalities. In his "final" instructions to Peggy Noonan, the speechwriter working on his acceptance speech, Bush insisted: "No personal attack on Dukakis.... Just the issues."[11] Yet Bush's campaign featured a visit to an American flag factory and a refusal to say the "L-word," thereby treating his rival's liberal beliefs as a schoolboy would treat a girl with cooties. Despite his stated preference, Bush became known as the campaign's mudslinger.

Bush decided to "go negative" in the spring, when he trailed by seventeen points in the polls and had a "negative rating" of 40 percent, twice that of his opponent. After eight years as Reagan's vice president, the *Washington Post* reported, Bush was still known as a "wimp, wasp, weenie. Every woman's first husband." In a move that would become legendary among consultants, Bush's campaign director, Lee Atwater, told his aide James Pinkerton, "We're gonna have to use research to win this campaign. You get me the stuff to beat this little bastard and put it on this three-by-five card." Pinkerton listed the Governor's positions on taxes, defense, and the polluted Boston Harbor, his opposition to the death penalty, mandatory drug sentences, and a bill mandating recitation of the pledge of allegiance at school, and—lifting a move from the Democratic primary contender Al Gore—his support for a prison furlough program that enabled a convicted murderer, Willie Horton, to rape a woman and terrorize her fiancé.[12] "It's a wonderful mix of liberalism and a big black rapist," one Republican would confess. A "focus group" assembled in Paramus, New Jersey, soured on Dukakis when presented with Pinkerton's "negative cluster." At a meeting on Memorial Day weekend at the Bush estate in Kennebunkport, Maine, Bush's advisers urged a negative campaign. "Two things voters have to know about you," Roger Ailes told Bush. "You can take a punch and you can throw a punch." Instinctively distancing himself from the decision, Bush said, "Well, you guys are the experts."[13]

In June, Bush began mentioning Willie Horton in his speeches. In September, the National Security Political Action Committee broadcast an ad juxtaposing photos of a swarthy Dukakis with Willie Horton's mug shot, claiming, "Dukakis not only opposes the death penalty, he allowed first-degree murderers to have weekend passes from prison." Barbara Bush later complained that even though it was "a pro-George independent committee—not our campaign" that used "the image of a sinister looking Willie Horton, who was black.... We got blamed for dirty politics and racism." Still, when the Republicans broadcast an ad attacking Dukakis's "revolving door" approach to crime, they did not need to mention Willie Horton's name.[14]

Bush convinced himself that he was attacking Dukakis's record, rather than indulging in personalities. Secure in his identity as a gentleman and a champion of "the quiet man," Bush cut loose. Dogged by what he dismissed as "the vision thing," the demand for the bold rhetoric that Ronald Reagan loved—and that so many Reagan critics hated—Bush found his "vision" by demonizing Dukakis. "I will not be deterred by the age-old ploy of calling it negative campaigning," he vowed, claiming that he had "an obligation" to say, "Here's where I stand and here's where he stands." As George Bush embraced what he called "the Norman Rockwell vision of America—the vision of kids and dogs and apple pie and flags on parade," he declared Dukakis and the liberals "out of the mainstream." "Ideology matters," the Vice President proclaimed as he elevated slurs into symbols.[15]

Both candidates' contradictory and changing strategies obscured fundamental policy differences. The tumult of the 1960s and 1970s had made many voters more passionate about certain issues, and most candidates had responded accordingly. Michael Dukakis and George Bush disagreed about social issues, defense, and the best way to reduce the budget deficit. They released reams of position papers detailing their views on issues ranging from abortion and air pollution to Zimbabwe and Zaire. With the explosion of news coverage, reporters generated more stories about issues, even if the overall percentage of substantive coverage decreased. Nevertheless, few voters were satisfied that the candidates addressed these differences. By the end of October, even George Bush yearned for substance. "I want to get back on the issues, and quit talking about him," Bush told his consultant Roger Ailes. "We plan to do that Nov. 9," the day after the election, Ailes replied.[16]

———

Although the 1988 campaign was not the dirtiest campaign ever, it did leave one of the longest hangovers. Bush's negative campaign, particularly his Willie Horton coup, came to represent the worst in American politics, and in American society. Democrats shocked by their defeat blamed Willie Horton, rather than the many tactical errors they and their candidate made. Analysts looking for proof of America's superficiality, narrow-mindedness, gullibility, nihilism, cynicism, conservatism, and racism pointed to Willie Horton. Books entitled *Why Americans Hate Politics* and bemoaning *The Betrayal of American Democracy* used Willie Horton as Exhibit A in arguing "that American democracy is in much deeper trouble than most people wish to acknowledge," that "the substantive meaning of self-government has been hollowed out." The media scholar Kathleen Hall Jamieson used the Willie Horton commercial as a launching pad for her book *Dirty Politics*, proclaiming in 1992 that "William Horton and Michael Dukakis are now twinned in our memory."[17] Four years of retrospectives attributing Bush's victory to Horton had indeed coupled the Democratic loser and the convict.

George Bush recognized such talk as an attack on his mandate. He defended his legitimacy by casting the discussions as attacks on the American people and the democratic process. The President said that the "ability of the American people to judge candidates on the issues and not, as many cynics claim, on the basis of imagery," was "consistently underrated." Eager to emphasize that he, not his handlers, had won the election, he insisted that campaigns "are ultimately about ideas and leadership.... No consultant can make up for a candidate who is deficient in these vital areas."[18]

II

The backlash against the 1988 campaign shaped the 1992 contest. Anxious to repudiate the sins of 1988, all three major candidates claimed to address the issues and avoid the mud. At the same time, each candidate staked out a position on one side or another of the great divide between republicanism and liberal democracy. Bill Clinton confronted the issues, pitching his campaign as the cure for twelve years of Republican evasions. George Bush and Ross Perot began by positioning themselves as men of character, qualified to face whatever issues arose. Inevitably, all three candidates confused the two positions.

Ross Perot appeared as an unconventional candidate especially suited to the antipolitics of the moment. In fact, the Texas billionaire was simply the latest in a parade of saviors who had vowed to free American politics from politicians. Hoping to parlay humility into popularity as George Washington had, Perot announced on *Larry King Live* that he would run only if drafted. This lofty eighteenth-century pose with a twentieth-century media twist was done in classic nineteenth-century style: just as by Andrew Jackson's time the claim of disinterest was often belied by behind-the-scenes politicking, Perot hired legions of "volunteers." Even after he "withdrew" from the campaign in July, Perot spent $500,000 a month maintaining sixty-four campaign offices.[19]

A typical nonpolitical candidate, Perot promised to purify politics by remaining dignified. "I hate the mud wrestling in politics," Perot said. "I think it's obscene."[20] Clearly, he was appealing to the ancient and unattainable goal of a high-level campaign, while cashing in on the public's frustration with George Bush.

In July, with his campaign growing, and the press probes into his life intensifying, Perot abandoned the race he had not yet entered. When he returned ten weeks later, he shifted his position, though he still attacked politics. "Not only is Government a mess, politics is also a mess," he said when "accepting" his volunteers' "request" to run. But forgetting his earlier claim that "the American people don't care about issues," Perot vowed not to "spend one minute answering questions that are not directly relevant to the issues that concern the American people." He would campaign to save America from its four-trillion-dollar debt.[21]

In shifting from character to issues, Perot began to sound more like Andrew Jackson than George Washington. But even more than Perot redux, Bill Clinton's presidential quest marked the culmination of more than a century of speechmaking and policy proposing by candidates. Clinton pinned his presidential hopes on the people's desire to focus on the issues, in particular, as the famous sign in Little Rock declared, on "THE ECONOMY, STUPID."[22]

Clinton ran as the quintessential democrat who enjoyed politics and loved talking about the issues wherever he could find an audience. He wanted to be prime minister, not king. From the start of his campaign he renounced the public's traditional desire for an "ideal man." In early

September of 1991, he and his wife, Hillary, acknowledged that their marriage had weathered rocky moments. "If the standard is perfection, I can't meet it," Clinton confessed.[23] Echoing the relativism of the 1960s' counterculture, Clinton repudiated the ancient demand for virtuous leaders.

Clinton the democrat rooted his modern vision of a rational, concerned citizenry in the past. "This country was set up over 200 years ago by people who believed they had a moral obligation to vote, and who knew if they were well acquainted with the issues, well acquainted with the politicians... that this country would last forever as a democracy," he said in his standard stump speech. In the age of mass media, more and more Americans questioned their own competence and rationality. By 1992, the political scientist Samuel Popkin's ardent defense of the "Reasoning Voter" characterized voting as a "gut" decision of "low-information rationality," akin to the kinds of decisions Americans made as consumers. Scholars now restated republican doubts about the masses in scientific terms.[24]

A Clinton victory would prove that the masses could act rationally, Democrats argued. Just as Republicans would try to cast Clinton's emphasis on issues rather than character as fraudulent and dangerously modern, Democrats tried to cast Bush's emphasis on character as irrelevant and contemptuous of the voter. "Too many people have voted on base instincts and diversion and division," Clinton said. "This will be a test in this election not just of my character but of the larger character of the American people."[25]

To George Bush, the best man was far more important than the best policies. Diluting Hamiltonian virtue with a recipe for niceness, Bush compared voting for president to deciding who "you'd like to have sitting across from you at the dinner table." Bush saw himself as a man of character, a worthy successor to Washington. As an incumbent, he would stand wrapped in what Max Weber calls the "charisma of office." He would preserve his dignity by minimizing campaigning and avoiding forums like MTV. Russ Hodge, a Bush adviser, complained that the desire to be "presidential" sank several "ideas that might have...helped him get his message out."[26]

Bush repeatedly talked about "trust," "character," "honor," "leadership," and the need to "live a good example." In accepting his renomination as vice president, Dan Quayle praised Bush as a man "whose public and personal life are the embodiment of character.... Every day in that Oval Office, I see the dedication of a husband, father and grandfather; the self-reliance of an entrepreneur; the courage of a Navy pilot; the dependability of a loyal friend; the compassion of a man of faith; and the wisdom of the man who married Barbara Bush."[27]

Quayle's litany portrayed George Bush as the exemplar of traditional values against the Democratic relativists. The Democrats did not shower Bill Clinton with a similar cascade of adjectives. The Republicans' definition of character reached back to the nineteenth-century realization that individual morality cultivated public virtue. Bush embraced the expanded republican notion of the president as "an ideal man" at home and in the office.[28]

The Republican National Convention drew the line clearly, condemning Clinton and the Democrats as immoral. By declaring a "cultural war" on them, Pat Buchanan and others also rejected the progressive, rational, and bureaucratic values underlying Clinton's issue-oriented campaign. As in Washington's day, the republic was imperilled. Warnings that Clinton lacked "moral authority" and would ruin "a nation we still call God's country" made this clear.[29] Only a virtuous nominee could save America.

Even once the general campaign began, Bush preferred playing the dignified republican to the hell-raising democrat. He tried to avoid directly attacking his rival. The National Guard conference in mid-September gave Bush a natural forum for condemning Clinton as a draft evader. Instead, Bush acted presidential. "I want to tell you that I do feel strongly about certain aspects of the controversy swirling around Governor Clinton," he said elliptically, "but I didn't come here to attack him."[30]

George Bush was far more verbose and active than any nineteenth-century candidate had been. Still, he stressed the role of the president as virtuous caretaker whereas Clinton emphasized activism in campaigning and governing. A president is more than the sum of his policies, Bush explained. "[A] lot [more than issues] goes into it. Caring goes into it.... Strength goes into it.... Standing up against aggression. That's not specific in terms of a program. This is what a president has to do."[31]

The fall campaign, then, should have been a showdown between the two warring traditions of American politics, between the liberal-democratic yin and the republican yang, between the idea of the presidency as a bully pulpit for a prime minister and as a throne for an ideal king, between a campaign of issues and a campaign built on character. The campaign could have updated the late-nineteenth-century debate between the "Man" and the "Platform": one hundred years later, voters were more independent of parties, but the dilemma persisted.[32]

In fact, each candidate discovered that he could not follow his instincts and gravitate toward a particular pole. The competing traditions of republicanism and liberal democracy could not be distilled so easily nor resolved so neatly. Each candidate had to try to satisfy the American people's conflicting demands.

III

Although Ross Perot enjoyed remarkable success in addressing the issues, his campaign foundered on doubts about his character. Initially, people had rallied around Perot himself, but by October more Americans embraced the message than the messenger.[33] Perot tried to have it both ways. He pronounced character questions irrelevant, yet he offered his résumé as his greatest credential—echoing the nineteenth-century candidate William Henry Harrison, who offered his reputation "as a pledge of my future course."[34] With the degeneration of Perot's infomercials into thirty-minute puff pieces praising his happy blonde family, it seemed that character was "relevant" when Perot praised himself and "irrelevant" when the press pursued the truth.

Bill Clinton also learned that campaigns do not survive on policies alone. Voters' eyes often glazed over as the Governor rattled off statistics about AFDC and EITCs (Aid to Families with Dependent Children and Earned Income Tax Credits). Americans did not want a walking encyclopedia for president.

The problem was more than the modern voters' television-reduced attention spans. The issue-oriented campaign was not an obvious antidote to republican elitism. Like Thomas Jefferson, Americans trusted the "ploughman" over the "professor"; folk wisdom over intellectual acumen. The populist sensibility demanded politicians who could address issues intelligently while keeping the common touch. Even in the modern age of the expert, Americans preferred politicians who could master policies without Master's degrees. Polls conducted in 1992 proved that anti-intellectualism threatened to derail a campaign of policy wonks. Many voters, overlooking Clinton's rise from poverty and his twelve-year-old daughter, inferred from the Clintons' Ivy League pedigrees and his focus on issues that the Clintons were a childless power couple born with silver spoons in their mouths.[35]

In a political culture that considered politicians—and government—necessary evils, Clinton's great assets became liabilities. His political ability, his very love of the process, his desire to accommodate everybody, appeared devious to reporters and voters alike. Throughout the primary campaign, his standard speech claimed: "We can be pro-growth and pro-environment, we can be pro-business and pro-labor, we can make government work again by making it more aggressive and leaner and more effective at the same time, and we can be pro-family and pro-choice." In the fall, Dan Quayle called such waffling "pulling a Clinton."[36]

At the same time, accusations of womanizing, draft dodging, and drug use taught Clinton that if he did not define his character, his opponents would do it for him. Questions about his virtue threatened his democratic appeal. As summer approached, his campaign languished. "So far as I'm concerned, we're at zero," Clinton told his staff. "We might as well have been like any member of Congress and kissed every ass in the Democratic party. I don't think you can minimize how horrible I feel, having worked all my life to stand for things, having busted my butt for seven months and the American people don't know crap about it after I poured $10 million worth of information into their heads."[37] Even after clinching the nomination and surviving many smears, Clinton the rationalist still viewed campaigning as pouring information rather than providing inspiration or engendering trust.

Clinton's advisers drafted a top-secret "Manhattan Project" to repackage the candidate. The project acknowledged that character and image counted. Having been weaned on TV, Clinton's "post-Beatles" advisers treated politics as a cross between education and entertainment. "We had to go to nontraditional news sources because we were not trying to convey news," Mandy Grunwald, Clinton's "thirty-something" media consultant explained. "We were trying to convey biography and personality." Perot would be perceived as the "Larry King candidate," whereas Clinton first exploited MTV, the Nashville Network, and other popular formats. The "merchandising" style of modern politics decreed that candidates had to be packaged and peddled on popular media.[38] If John Kennedy could joke with Jack Paar on the *Tonight Show* in 1960, and Richard Nixon could say "Sock It to Me" on *Laugh-In* in 1968, Bill Clinton could play the saxophone for Arsenio Hall.

Not surprisingly, Clinton's "pop culture" campaign unsettled some observers. "I wouldn't have dreamt of going on MTV," the 1984 Democratic nominee Walter Mondale said. "It just wasn't done. There was a dignity to running for the Presidency." Nearly every innovation in campaigning, from stumping to debating to advertising, has raised similar hackles. Like William Jennings Bryan, Clinton's people valued democracy—and accessibility—over proprieties. "Willie Sutton said he robbed banks because that's where the money was," Clinton campaign consultants James Carville and Paul Begala explained. "The Clinton campaign used nontraditional media to spread its message because we had to."[39]

The new Bill Clinton was unveiled at the Democratic National Convention in July. Clinton went from being a draft-dodging, noninhaling policy wonk to the "Man from Hope," born in the twentieth-century version of a log cabin. Reporters eager for a new angle cooperated, changing the brands they stamped on the candidate almost overnight. Hillbilly origins certified the candidate as a moral exemplar and one of the people.[40]

"I believe the best way for me to demonstrate my character is to make sure people know the whole story of my life and my work and my family and what I'm fighting for in this election," Clinton said, clinging to his precious policy appeals. But in the capable hands of Clinton's campaign workers, "the whole story" emphasized traditional values and overlooked some of the novelties that Clinton had first relished. His daughter, Chelsea, suddenly emerged. His wife, Hillary, traded in her powersuit for an apron, forgot earlier boasts that voters would be getting "two" leaders "for the price of one," and challenged Barbara Bush to a chocolate chip cookie baking contest. Emphasizing New Age, process-oriented qualities, Clinton and his running mate, Al Gore, created intimacy with the people rather than establishing distance. In his vice presidential acceptance speech, Gore shared the pain of his young son's car accident. He praised Clinton's "values" and his "plan" rather than more traditional and seemingly objective character traits. Not to be outdone, Clinton recalled his father's death and his mother's breast cancer.[41] In America's twelve-step culture, confessions of family trauma expiated all kinds of sins. This was a far cry from the focus on issues Clinton had promised—or expected.

Meanwhile, President Bush charted an opposite path, trying to stand on character while inching toward a more populist campaign. Bush refused to expose his inner self. He talked about values to give the character issue salience. "Sure we must change, but some values are timeless," Bush said in his acceptance speech, responding to Clinton.[42] As they had done so effectively with Reagan, Republicans obscured debates about particular issues in a cloud of rhetoric about virtuous values. Bush implied that he could not solve every problem, but that his heart was in the right place. The Democrats shared intimate experiences to humanize themselves and transcend mere policy positions; the Republicans used their policy positions to express core beliefs.

An aloof and dignified pose emphasizing Bush's virtue was risky, especially during a recession. Bush could not pretend that, like Franklin D. Roosevelt, he was so busy solving problems he did not have time to campaign. Furthermore, the eighteenth-century protocols no longer held. Even an incumbent had to be one of the people. In February, at a conference of the National Grocers' Association in Orlando, Florida, Bush seemed unfamiliar with a supermarket scanner. Ensconced in the Secret Service's security bubble for twelve years as both vice president and president, Bush was "amazed by some of the technology"—and ridiculed for being so dignified that he was out of touch.[43]

Bush appeared disengaged on the issues as well. Asked in April to name a single domestic policy goal for his second term, he faltered. "Single goal?" Bush asked. "Oh, there are several goals, and I've been spelling them all out. I think education reform certainly would be right up at the top.... It's awfully hard to single out one area, however."[44]

Finally, to show that he was engaged, to inject passion into his campaign, Bush went into "attack mode." Resigned to the fact that campaigns were brutal, Bush plunged in, with no intentions of educating the people. Hewing to his themes of "trust" and "character," he ended up attacking his opponents' integrity rather than their policies. He dismissed Clinton and Gore as "Bozos"—until Mrs. Bush objected. At Bush campaign rallies the Democratic nominee was condemned as "disloyal to his country" and "a sissy."[45] Such rhetoric was particularly striking for an incumbent who had been busy posturing as the more suitable and dignified king.

The 1992 campaign was ultimately fought on multiple fronts with sometimes conflicting strategies. Clinton's nationwide democratic policy seminar added a touch of the *Beverly Hillbillies,* just as Bush's republican country club recruitment project occasionally approximated a fraternity hazing. Ross Perot criticized both campaigns for indulging in "politics as usual," while he overstated and sidestepped like a master politician.

Bush's insistence on acting presidential (when convenient) and his sporadic attacks on "all this mud wrestling" (when he was not mudslinging himself) confirmed Clinton's distinction between personal and political integrity. Good men did not always make good leaders. In polls, twice as many voters deemed Bush and not Clinton personally moral. However, two or even three times as many voters considered Clinton and not Bush a strong and caring leader. Presidential aides begged Bush to emphasize the question of "truth"—where Clinton was vulnerable—rather than "trust"—where the President was vulnerable.[46]

For all his rhetoric about the issues and for all the concerns about his "character," Ross Perot in the end based his campaign on personality. In a celebrity-obsessed culture that confused success with virtue, the most famous billionaire in the land was a natural leader. His candidacy underscored the link between popular and political culture in a nation where more people watched the Super Bowl than voted for president.[47] Perot's supporters first experienced him through the tabloids and on TV. News reports about Perot's Bahamas retreat or his art-filled office seemed straight out of *Lifestyles of the Rich and Famous*.

The debates highlighted Perot's emphasis on personality. He appeared to "win" the first debate by being the most entertaining, joking that he was "all ears" in searching for "a fair way" to "clean this mess up." But his running mate James Stockdale's performance in the vice-presidential debate proved that Perot's "grassroots movement" was a one-man show. In later debates, this candidate of supposedly fresh ideas sounded stale with his constant promises to have congressmen quit "throwing rocks" and work together. Perot was offering personal skills as a policy.[48]

Unlike his opponents, Clinton harnessed his discomfort. He made his commitment to addressing issues the mark of character. From the start, Clinton and his aides stigmatized all criticism as echoes of the "Republican attack machine's" 1988 slanders. On ABC's *Prime Time Live*, Hillary Clinton called rumors about her husband's sex life the "daughter of Willie Horton," a diversion that "keeps real issues out."[49] This response illustrated the Clinton strategy: first focus on the economy, then attack the Republicans' tactics without rebutting any charges.

Clinton's people characterized the "character" question as the province of gossips, not the ancestral preserve of the Framers. On *Donahue*, Clinton refused to talk about his marriage, the draft issue, or drug use. "I don't believe I or any other decent human being should have to put up with the kind of questioning you're putting me through," the candidate snapped. This approach struck a chord among alienated voters. "Given the pathetic state of the United States at this point—medicare, education, everything else—I can't believe you spent half an hour of air-time attacking this man's character," one woman yelled at Phil Donahue.[50] Chastened, Donahue turned to "the issues."

This backlash freed Clinton from trying to be something he clearly was not. Before the second debate, he acknowledged his success in lowering expectations. "People know I'm not perfect," he said. They wanted to know if he could lead. When asked if Americans trusted Clinton, George Stephanopoulos sidestepped: "I think trust is not the right word.... They understand he's a human being. He's always said he's not perfect, but he's committed and tenacious and caring."[51] Such apologias were a far cry from the Bush campaign's traditional paeans to character.

Still, the strategy worked, making Clinton look dignified and substantial. In endorsing Clinton, the editors of *The New Republic* echoed his relativistic redefinition of character: "He has shown the character to emerge from a difficult childhood to take advantage of some of the best education the world has to offer; he has shown the ability not merely to package his politics, but to think through the intricacies of policy that support it."[52]

Clinton's strategy made those who addressed issues appear substantial, authentic, and virtuous. Being a good democrat became the path to republican virtue. Words and not images starred in most Democratic commercials. By Election Day, no question went unasked, no issue was unaddressed. Many observers speculated that 1992's subdued campaign redeemed American politics. "Lectures loaded with facts, figures and issues have replaced the slick image and propaganda productions of past U.S. elections," *Time* rejoiced.[53]

In reality, the restrained look of the 1992 campaign was as artificial as its predecessors. The Democratic campaign aped the techniques of the designer Ralph Lauren—the candidates had that casual air achieved only at great effort. As campaigns oscillated between republicanism and liberal democracy, they also wavered between substance and style. Neither a campaign of issues nor a campaign of personalities guaranteed a decorous discussion. The pettiness was due less to popular culture and television than to the calculations of ambitious men prospecting for popularity.

Campaigning history was littered with examples of supposedly high-minded debates that were simply charades. For all the pretensions to uplift, most campaigns remained common; most candidates preferred to posture. Considering a candidate's personal qualities generated a fusillade of superficial symbols—even when politicians were not mudslinging. Nineteenth-century talk of Andrew Jackson's heroism or of William Henry Harrison's log cabin was no more meaningful than contemporary discussions of George Bush's World War II bombing-runs or Bill Clinton's hometown. Similarly, talk about particular policy proposals easily degenerated into empty sloganeering. "Waving the bloody shirt" was as frivolous as conjuring up the specter of Willie Horton—although Republicans in the 1880s had insisted that there was no more important issue than loyalty to the Union, just as their successors branded law and order essential.

In 1992 the jogs, the sartorial changes, and the issue-oriented appeals were simply more sophisticated forms of popular pandering. Campaign handlers were better than their predecessors at covering their tracks and crediting the candidate. "Bill Clinton ran a perfect 1988-style Republican presidential campaign," Russ Hodge of the Bush/Quayle camp conceded. "It was smooth, it was efficient, it was aggressive and ahead of the curve, it was skillful in its mastery of symbols and the press, and it was not married to any orthodoxy." Dan Quayle paid Clinton the highest of compliments. "If he runs the country as well as he ran the campaign, we'll be all right."[54]

———

By the twentieth century, and certainly by 1992, the distinction between campaigns devoted to issues and those built on personalities had blurred. Candidates generated a haze of contradictory attitudes and strategies. Modern candidates were particularly promiscuous, addressing the issues while exhibiting good character, preserving republicanism while expanding liberal democracy, appearing substantial while campaigning with style. In fact, the two categories were often mutually reinforcing—Clinton's successful campaign for "change" muted doubts about his character, just as Ronald Reagan's pleasing personality seemingly diluted his extremist views.

Yet despite the often artificial nature of these distinctions, the leading candidates represented two conflicting and enduring strains within American politics. Psychobiographers can boil the basic difference between Clinton and Bush down to their respective backgrounds, contrasting the son of a patrician senator with the product of a drunken stepfather. But whatever their personal experiences, the two candidates were riding central streams in American political thought. Bush appealed to traditionalists who prized charisma over bureaucracy, emotions over intellect, the past over the future. If these latter-day republicans doubted the intellect of American voters, they compensated by trusting the people's virtue and their ancestors' virtue. Clinton, by contrast, believed in rational, orderly procedures, idealizing America's political arena as an expanded policy seminar. His appeals had little romance, little trace of Reagan's "shining city on the hill" or Lincoln's "last best hope on earth." He looked to the future, trusting progress, rationality, democracy.[55]

Exit polls showed that on Election Day most voters chose between these conflicting visions. Those eager for experienced leadership voted for Bush. Clinton and Perot supporters were most interested in change (50 percent of Clinton voters; 44 percent of Perot voters) and having the best plan (30 percent of Clinton voters; 28 percent of Perot voters). Even as they elected him, less than half the voters polled considered Clinton "trustworthy enough to be President," but more than half trusted him to "get the economy moving." Clearly, the nominees had succeeded in linking their candidacies to particular stances, and the voters had chosen what they wanted from the man and the message.[56]

IV

Bill Clinton won the presidency, but he did not win the war between issues and personalities, between America's past and America's future, or between his personal past and his political future. The character questions of 1992 caught up with him. The struggle for America's political soul and within Americans' political soul would continue.

Clinton interpreted his victory as a mandate for change and for his issue-based politics. Many hoped, along with Tom Rosenstiel of the *Los Angeles Times*, that a successful Clinton presidency would help the country "step back from the faulty syllogism that a candidate's private behavior reveals something deeper about his public character and deserves greater attention than his public record." Yet in 1992 Clinton had not received many more votes than Michael Dukakis had in 1988. The new president entered the White House without the reservoir of faith in his character that had kept so many of his predecessors afloat. When the inevitable political troubles began, his pollster Stan Greenberg feared, the Clinton presidency would sink, partly as a result of the unresolved character questions.[57]

Through much of 1993, President Clinton staved off the character crisis with a flurry of policy initiatives promoting the change he had promised the American people. The passage of his economic program, NAFTA, national service, and aid to Russia, along with an economic upturn, buoyed his presidency. Even his ambitious health care program seemed destined for passage. By the end of the year, such policy successes had been upstaged by talk of Whitewater investments, White House counsel Vince Foster's suicide, and sexual escapades in Arkansas. "I have fought more damn battles here for more things than any President has in 20 years...and not gotten one damn bit of credit from the knee-jerk liberal press, and I am sick and tired of it," Clinton fumed.[58]

Rather than divorcing questions of character from issues of governance, Bill Clinton's presidency recoupled them. A nation full of armchair psychologists attributed Clinton's political failings to his personal shortcomings. The *Newsweek* columnist Joe Klein chided the President for being "indiscriminate, casual and irregular" in foreign policy, domestic policy, and his personal affairs. "The character flaw Bill Clinton's enemies have fixed upon—promiscuity—is a defining characteristic of his *public* life as well."[59] In 1994, Republican attacks on this unvirtuous President helped end the Democrats' forty-year reign in Congress.

Viewing the elections—and Bill Clinton's presidency—in historical perspective reveals that many of the dilemmas that faced the Founding Fathers persist; lines linking the traditional republican ideology with more contemporary concerns emerge. Chief among these is the continuing obsession with virtue. In a world of marathon campaigns and spin-doctors, politics still seems distasteful. In 1988, George Bush's campaign chairman, James A. Baker III, graced the cover of *Time* with his Democratic rival. When Baker saw himself pictured under the headline, "BATTLE OF THE HANDLERS," he considered it "the worst day of his life," the *New York Times* reported.[60]

Many politicians tried to transcend their demeaning profession. Whenever presidents stood for office, they acted as if campaigning somehow diminished both the office and the man. In 1984, Ronald Reagan's campaign chairman called the incumbent president, two-time governor, and four-time presidential aspirant "nonpolitical." The "Rose Garden" strategy of both Gerald Ford and Jimmy Carter reflected this republican sense that governing was worthy of a president, campaigning was not. Such charades undermined the legitimacy of campaigning and fostered cynicism. "I find it appalling that a lot of well-established people don't understand how important political skills are to governing," James Carville complained. "If you don't... [get reelected] you are never going to get anything done."[61]

While sanctioning these masquerades, Americans celebrated those strategists who secured success at any price. Candidates like Dukakis and Mondale were despised for losing. Political consultants like Roger Ailes, Lee Atwater, and David Garth became celebrities, emulated and envied as American success stories. The "Romeo and Juliet" romance in 1992 between the Republican strategist Mary Matalin and her rival James Carville inspired a movie and a best-selling memoir written by the two, who married in 1993. Virtue, while valued, had its limits.

This ambivalence about ambition and success goes beyond politics. At the beginning of the 1990s, many Americans felt that after a decade of rampant ambition, they now had to pay the piper. Authors celebrated the end of the "Predators' Ball," as judges sent financiers like Michael Milken to jail. Milken and his pals became the latest characters in the American morality play warning against ambition that stretched from Henry Clay through Jay Gould to Richard Nixon in history, and from Captain Ahab through Jay Gatsby to Sherman McCoy in literature. While still valuing Horatio Alger, Americans feared that ambition debauched otherwise good men. Ambitious but virtuous politicians were hard to find. Thus, even though Americans in the 1980s and 1990s were less moralistic than their ancestors, they scrutinized candidates more carefully, assuming that everything counted, that the smallest of incidents could reveal the man. This emphasis on personality was considered to be the least dignified aspect of the modern campaign. "Character" traditionally connoted socially sanctioned behaviors that revealed whether or not an individual was good. Nevertheless, this new focus on idiosyncratic behaviors and personal image marked a return to the Founders' republican notion that good character was the most important requirement for a good president.

In the eighteenth century, Americans had believed that only gentlemen who knew a candidate intimately could assess his character. Two centuries later, television was supposed to have allowed the American public to "x-ray" a candidate's personality. Instead, many feared, TV had become the most potent weapon in the modern demagogue's arsenal of artifice. Those who attacked the "electronic election" complained that nominees were no longer authentic, that they were created by handlers. Ghostwriters and consultants were routinely acknowledged, as observers matter-of-factly referred to "Peggy Noonan's acceptance speech, which Bush recited at the 1988 Republican convention." Still, each candidate claimed that his rival was held hostage by handlers. "The Vice President seems willing to do anything they say," the Democratic campaign manager Susan Estrich charged in 1988. I want a "real person," one voter grumbled.[62]

Handlers were the modern-day "adversaries of republican government," seducing the people with images and sound-bites instead of intrigues and rhetoric. A direct line could be drawn from Alexander Hamilton's warning in *Federalist* 68 against demagoguery and cabals, through William Henry Harrison's attack on ambitious politicians acting like "auctioneers," through William Randolph Hearst's characterization of Franklin D. Roosevelt as "a chanter or a crooner," to the *Boston Globe's* speculation in 1988 about the "mischief" a "devious" candidate could "make with a quiver of finely honed commercials and 15-second sound bites." The "body of the people" remained in danger of "corruption" from unscrupulous candidates or manipulative cabals.[63]

Television had become the republican bogeyman, realizing traditional fears of a debased polity through modern means. "Politics is a more simplistic, less subtle, less thoughtful pursuit today" than it was a generation ago, Richard Nixon lamented in 1990. "The reason for the change is television." *Time's* essayist Lance Morrow blamed TV for making the "issues...as weightless as clouds of electrons, and the candidates mere actors in commercials." "The media's dietary habits are not particularly healthful," Carville complained. "They kind of like their high-fat foods, like cheese fries and patty melts: Gennifer Flowers, Hillary's hairdo. They're not too big on the garden vegetables of the campaign, like job creation and health care costs." Walter Cronkite's 1952 warning against handsome charmers became cliché; most assumed that in the age of television, a homely but Lincolnesque candidate would lose to a good-looking rival.[64]

These jeremiads overlooked television's democratic benefits, its ability to introduce the candidates to millions of people. TV was neither as influential nor as revolutionary as its critics assumed.[65] Yet again, a new technology, after failing to save the campaign, bore the blame for its decline. And once again, the traditional dilemmas underlying the voters' continuing frustrations were ignored. Soundbites about "No New Taxes" were, in fact, more substantive than Harrisonesque slogans about "Log Cabins and Hard Cider." These tirades against television betrayed contempt for a democratic medium that brought politics to the masses, and revealed a continuing nostalgia for "good old days" that never really existed.

The republican distrust of the people lingered in what was supposed to be the world's greatest democracy. Most voters, Nelson Polsby and Aaron Wildavsky wrote, "are not interested in most public issues most of the time." Bush's 1988 victory showed that "if something is correctly packaged, virtually anything can be sold," one reporter sneered. Increasingly, scholars, reporters, consultants, and candidates treated the people like idiots. The people even condemned themselves—or their neighbors. In one 1988 poll, 35 percent of those surveyed felt that "voters" did not make a strong enough "effort . . . to find out about the candidates."[66] Modern American politics not only kept alive the Founders' initial doubts that democracy could work, but seemingly proved them. The people remained unworthy of the great responsibility democracy bestows on each citizen.

Throughout two centuries of changes in the press, the party, and the presidency itself, despite the expansion of liberal democracy and the contraction of republicanism, Americans returned to fundamental questions about power. In 1992, when Bill Clinton deemed not using the power of the presidency a "character issue," he thrust the campaign back to the Framers' constitutional debate.[67] With his liberal-democratic orientation, Clinton saw politics as an opportunity to exercise power for the public good. From that came his faith in government and politics. For all the changes over the years and all its conflicting conceptions, liberal democracy advocated using the people's power to advance their own interests. As a result, issues were central to campaigns. Candidates debated not *whether* they would use government, but *how* they would use it to serve their constituents.

At the same time, Bush reverted to the fear of power that had motivated the American revolutionaries. Most leaders intend to be "humble, modest, and just.... But the possession of power soon alters and vitiates their Hearts," *Cato's Letters* warned. Eighteenth-century republicans had mistrusted power, government, politicians—as do their modern successors.[68] Then and now, virtuous leaders serve as the only line between democracy and dictatorship. They promise dignity, a sense of proportion. The pressures of a democratized popular culture add the demand that personality be entertaining, but ultimately, Americans want an "ideal man" to keep government in check while embodying their greatest hopes and beliefs. Thus, fighter pilots like George Bush guarantee stability and virtue, philanderers like Bill Clinton don't.

The fear of power fluctuates from election to election, from crisis to crisis. In the past, Americans had turned to democratic activists during times of national emergency. As a Franklin Roosevelt or a Bill Clinton promised to use government to fix things, the fear of power took a back seat to the fear of economic ruin. But both Roosevelt and Clinton were preceded by people like Warren G. Harding and Ronald Reagan, who offered their pleasing personalities and apparent good characters as proof of governmental restraint. In 1920, Harding's call for "normalcy" offered a respite from Woodrow Wilson's activism, as well as the disruptions of world war.[69] Sixty years later, Reagan's combination of patriotism and lassitude subordinated discussion of particular issues to a general promise that smaller government would revitalize America. But passivity needed prosperity—Herbert Hoover was no more successful with Harding's appeal in 1932 than George Bush was with Reagan's in 1992.

V

"It was a pretty empty campaign," James K. Glassman wrote in *The New Republic* in 1988, "but face it, we're a pretty empty country these days." The tendency in these attacks to sugar-coat the past, be it the Lincoln-Douglas debates or the Kennedy-Nixon debates, also reflected the republican fear of national decline. "1988, you're no 1960," *Time* magazine pronounced, with no hint of irony, and little memory of the frustrations of 1960. Americans continually looked back to a mythic golden era. "We used to have marvelous presidential elections," John Chancellor of

NBC sighed.[70] As they longed for those "good old days," Americans forgot that Arcadia could always be found twenty years earlier—that Americans had always believed previous elections to be better than the present ones.

Simultaneously, the public continued to search for a new tactic to save American politics. "Thanks to you, Larry, and to the other programs that I've been invited on, I've been able to relate to people in a way that I can't if I'm just dependent on eight-second sound bites on the evening news," Clinton told the talk-show host Larry King. King and others believed this flattery and welcomed 1992's new "talk-show democracy." King immodestly placed his show "at the center of this talk-show phenomenon" that promised to "break down that mystique" leaders cultivated, and would replace "America's low-calorie sound-bite diet."[71]

Ironically, these republican fears and fantasies sustained the essentially democratic practice of stumping, which was no longer a novelty but a tradition. The comparisons used to justify stumping revealed its importance—and the distance traveled in 150 years. John F. Kennedy compared campaigning to a "lawyer" addressing a "jury"; others compared it to a job applicant interviewing with his "employer."[72] These comparisons testified to the businesslike rhetoric of modern Americans; few contemporaries would compare candidates to Coriolanus or Caesar, as their ancestors had done. Such comparisons also acknowledged the democratic nature of this exchange: the people determined whether a candidacy would live or die.

Candidates came to believe that stumping was the only way to campaign. "If we put him in front of cameras all day, he wouldn't think he had campaigned," Hubert Humphrey's director of scheduling noted during the 1972 primaries. "The best way for a political candidate to be able to communicate is to go directly" to the public, said Bush's chief of staff, John Sununu, endorsing what he called a "see-me-feel-me-touch-me" campaign. "Get out there and go into the malls. Let people look the candidate in the eye while he's...talking about issues."[73]

Even if candidates did not want to campaign, they often felt they had no choice. Until the voters finally spoke on that first Tuesday after the first Monday in November, the campaign mostly took place on America's front pages and television screens. To a great extent, campaigns became prolonged fights for positive media exposure. Candidates had to vie for attention daily, not only with each other, but with the myriad distractions of an entertainment-drenched society. "How are you going to get people to not click on a Goldie Hawn movie and click on an hour of President Clinton?" Bush's aide Margaret Tutweiler asked, posing the fundamental challenge of modern politics.[74] To help, politicians became fluent in the language and mores of media—slogans became "sound bites"; visits to politically important locales became "exposure" in "regional media markets."

Recent political history fed the belief that stumping counted. On the campaign planes, every underdog was a "Harry Truman"; every front-runner, a "Tom Dewey" or "Richard Nixon in 1960." In 1992, all three candidates vied for the honor of being viewed as Harry Truman's successor. Candidates aspired to be John F. Kennedy and, after 1988, Ronald Reagan. When the Democratic vice presidential candidate, Lloyd Bentsen, chided his Republican rival, Dan Quayle, saying, "You're no Jack Kennedy," the smooth-talking elderly senator appeared Reaganesque. Even in the scientific age, political myths about past successes were more potent than political scientists' skeptical empirical studies.

Many candidates admitted that, to a large extent, they were playing a confidence game. By greeting crowds of screaming partisans they "reinforc[ed] previous convictions"—the one outcome academics since the 1940s were sure campaigning accomplished. And, even if staged, these rallies helped make the candidate appear more presidential, and the campaign more winnable. Ironically, most losing efforts ended with a burst of such campaigning, one final attempt to captivate the nation. Both Dukakis's 1988 campaign and Bush's 1992 campaign ended with what Dukakis called a last-minute "surge." Crowds increased in size and intensity. Dukakis displayed a vigor he had previously lacked. "It's doable," John Sasso of the Dukakis campaign exclaimed, making the eventual loss all the more devastating.[75]

Stumping expressed confidence in oneself, as well as in the outcome. Modest men did not win a major party nomination. After months of stumping for votes in the primaries, and often years of stumping in local elections, candidates came to believe in their own powers of persuasion.

There were other, more tangible, outcomes to stumping as well. As candidates moved from one media market to another, they fortified their coalitions and acknowledged that, under the Electoral College system, the presidential campaign was really fifty-one separate elections. The decline of political parties and the proliferation of interest groups made these activities especially important. Even in an era of mobile phones and Fax machines, the personal touch and local pride remained important.

While candidates wooed particular regions and interest groups, they also kept their eyes on the national audience. To the extent that governing had become a "Permanent Campaign," with a constant need to rally the people, stumping tested an essential presidential skill.[76] Campaigns functioned as elaborate auditions for the rhetorical themes and central policies that would shape the coming presidency. George Bush's clunky but straightforward cry—"Read my lips, no new taxes"—resonated throughout his presidency, complicating the budget process and creating a backlash when he broke his promise.

Still, had American politics evolved in an orderly fashion, by the mid-twentieth century stumping would have gone the way of the human tail, webbed feet, and other outmoded adaptations. But the modern campaign grew haphazardly, shaped by the changing institutional and technological environment, a divided political ideology, and the constant calculation of candidates and their advisers. Vast changes over two centuries in communications, transportation, the party system, and the presidency itself created the necessary conditions for change. These developments made it possible, even desirable, to stump, to debate, but they were not enough. The surprising persistence of the republican remnant distorted the otherwise "natural," democratic evolution of the presidential campaign. Throughout the nineteenth century, this atavistic obsession with virtue had kept candidates off the stump long after technological developments, party needs, and the growth of the presidency demanded such participation. Once candidates entered the campaign, republicanism left a lingering taint, a sense that most campaigning was unseemly and undignified.

Initially, stumping had demonstrated the candidate's commitment to party ideals, his willingness to peddle the party's policies. It also demonstrated respect for the people. By the 1990s, it was a declaration of the candidate's authenticity and independence, proof that the voters would be electing a "real person." As skepticism about the campaign grew, stumping became more important, calming many republican fears. The same ideological impulse that initially inhibited stumping now perpetuated it. On the stump, the candidate faced the people, emerging from behind the blue smoke and mirrors of the modern campaign.

Countering the republican fears of artificiality and demagoguery, candidates, "in the flesh" and "pressing the flesh," broke down television's mythical "fourth wall." Even with elaborately staged "pseudo-events," by meeting citizens at factory gates and beauty shops, at baseball stadiums and barbecues, candidates emerged from behind their makeup and their studios, their consultants and their advertising budgets, and revealed themselves to the people. The impromptu and intimate nature of many of the exchanges humanized the campaign and the candidates. When candidates plunged into crowds, their Secret Service agents tensed, their handlers worried, but many citizens cheered. By taking to the stump, whether it won votes or not, candidates forged a direct and human link with the voters.

In keeping with the growing demands of American democracy, the presidential nominee had moved from the periphery to the center of the campaign. Stumping focused attention on the individual, his personality and his character. While speaking about the issues, a candidate confronted a series of obstacles that assessed his moral fiber and psychological makeup. Trading in the accepted democratic currency—issues—candidates could be judged by the traditional republican standard—character. They could showcase their policy positions and their personalities at the same time. Thus could the dueling gods of liberal democracy and republicanism be pleased, to a degree.[77]

VI

Such is the modern American presidential campaign. It is, on the one hand, a remarkably sophisticated endeavor, dependent on the latest technology to transmit sights and sounds to almost 250 million citizens. On the other hand, the ritual is strikingly primitive, as Americans continue to struggle with the question that vexed their ancestors: Who shall lead us? Americans are still looking for a leader to advance political positions, to embody the hopes of the nation, to be greater than themselves, and to make them feel good.

The modern presidential campaign reflects its mixed ancestry and haphazard growth. The campaign is a monument to democracy, the most inclusive leadership selection process in the world. From Eastern Europe to South America, aspiring democrats look to the United States for inspiration in establishing free elections. Never before have so many American voters participated in so many stages of the process. Women and blacks now have the franchise. Discriminatory poll taxes and literacy tests have been outlawed. Primaries involve millions in what had been the nominating prerogatives of a handful of party bosses. Voters enjoy greater access to the nominees than ever before, and are exposed to an unprecedented amount of information about each nominee's personal life and policy views. By the end of the presidential campaign, few biographical facts remain unearthed, few political issues remain unaddressed.

At the same time, the presidential campaign has disillusioned millions with its nonsense and its manipulation. More Americans choose not to exercise their right to vote than anywhere else in the world. Primaries seem endless, pointless, and unnecessarily weighted in favor of showmen not statesmen. The cynicism is so deep that even when candidates act nobly, their motives are questioned, and even when candidates have substantive differences, the disagreements are ignored. Increasingly, policy positions themselves have verged on becoming mere poses, simply the currency used to showcase personalities. And the stumping pentathlon, forcing candidates to drudge through snow, flip flapjacks, munch kielbasas, and drive tanks, deters many qualified people from even considering a run for the presidency. "Broder's Law," named for the Washington columnist David Broder, suggests that anyone willing to subject himself to the indignities of the current campaign thereby reveals "that he is too loony to be trusted with the office."[78]

In some ways, modern American politics is afflicted by the worst of both the democratic and the republican legacies. In the nineteenth century, the rise of liberal democracy had countered the elitist and overly dignified republican campaign. Stumping made the candidates more accessible and forced them to address the issues. But the late-twentieth-century amalgam in which hyperactive candidates expose themselves from coast-to-coast lacks substance *and* dignity. If George Washington's stiff silence was the republican thesis, and William Jennings Bryan's bombastic crusades were the liberal-democratic antithesis, Jimmy Carter's *Playboy* interview makes for a most unappealing synthesis. Trying to be all things to all people, too many modern candidates end up being of little use to anyone.

These conflicting traditions created a political schizophrenia of sorts. Today, each candidate claims that he addresses issues, his rivals plot strategies; he is virtuous, "they" are corrupt. As a result, American politics enjoys a renewable virginity, a sense each time that this campaign will be different, more honorable, more substantive. Yet, inevitably, the campaign soon becomes the "worst ever," as partisanship intensifies and the disappointments of previous years are forgotten. Finally, on Election Day, Americans celebrate the greatest democracy on earth and the "sacred ballot box" that solves America's conflicts peacefully. This republican morality play undermines Americans' faith in themselves, then renews it.

The simultaneous triumphs and humiliations of the presidential contest illustrate why the campaign will not be fixed so easily. Welcome advances often spawned unfortunate consequences. Primaries democratized the process and disillusioned millions. Television brought the candidates to the people, while creating a new artificial distance. Polling articulated—then subverted—the opinions of the masses. The interest in character has come at the cost of a commitment to policy. The greater demands on active candidates, as well as the increasing scrutiny of their entire lives, have produced more openness at the cost of the individual's dignity and the institution's majesty.

The problem of the presidential campaign is not a matter of mechanics. If engineers tried to invent the ideal democratic process, many would design a system as inclusive and comprehensive as the one that evolved. Over the years, the American drift toward liberal democracy has short-circuited the least democratic aspects of electoral politics, including the Electoral College, the republican taboo, and the boss-centered party nominating system. Rather than tinkering with the primaries or with federal funding or with anything else, reformers need to inject civility, substance, openness, and dignity into the present system—commodities that cannot be produced on demand. America needs a campaign that can accommodate the Walter Mondales who do not relish a two-year merry-go-round of Holiday Inns; a George Bush has to be able to stick to "the facts" as he had hoped. At this point, any candidate who took it easy, or took the high road, would be dismissed as a poseur or a loser. Before changing the electoral system, Americans have to determine just how their ideal candidate can be dignified yet accessible, issue-oriented yet intimate, acceptable to lofty editorialists yet electric on the streets, as "sensible" as Adlai Stevenson and as charming as Ronald Reagan.

These dilemmas bring us back to the fundamental conflicts the Founding Fathers failed to resolve. Shall the president be a king or a prime minister, the most virtuous man or the most representative one? Should the people—or their betters—decide? Should the decision be based on careful calculation or tempered emotion? Typically, the Founders tried to finesse the problems, and created a contradictory system that operates today in ways very different from those they imagined. It is no wonder that two hundred years later, Americans remain miffed.

"Democracy begins in conversation," the Progressive philosopher John Dewey declared on his ninetieth birthday.[79] Until presidential candidates broke the republican code of silence and began conversing with the people, American elections could not be considered "democratic." Candidates had to face the people, reveal themselves, and commit themselves publicly. The dialogue with the people was a mark of respect, and a sign of a dynamic democracy. It also was an essential tool of leadership, solidifying the president's role at the center of the American political universe.

Only a few decades after the candidates entered the conversation, the opposite problem looms. Candidates say so much that they appear to be saying nothing. Much of what they do say is dismissed as calculating. Candidates need occasionally to trust to silence, to think, but there is no time for that on the three-media-market-a-day campaign trail. They end up speaking at the people, not to the people. While this verbosity appears to be a gain for liberal democracy at the expense of republicanism, it merely follows the form and not the essence of democracy. The solution, however, is not to stop the conversation, or to impose artificial limits on it by restraining campaigns or candidates. Rather, Americans have to acknowledge their contradictory expectations for the candidates and the campaign, and continue to seek a balance, between inspiration and education, between openness and dignity, between the man and the message, between liberal democracy and republican virtue.

APPENDIX A

Electoral and Popular Votes for Major Presidential Contenders, 1789–1988

Year	Candidates	Parties	Electoral Vote
1789	*George Washington*	No party designations	69
	John Adams (VP)		34
	John Jay		9
	Miscellaneous		38
1792	*George Washington**	No party designations	132
	John Adams (VP)		77
	George Clinton		50
	Thomas Jefferson		4
	Aaron Burr		1
1796	*John Adams*	Fed	71
	Thomas Jefferson (VP)	Dem-Rep	68

NOTE: Minor parties are not included; only major-party vice-presidential nominees are mentioned.

Italics = winner   * = incumbent

ABBREVIATIONS: Fed, Federal; Dem-Rep, Democrat-Republican; Dem, Democratic; Rep, Republican; Anti-Fed, Anti-Federalist; Ind-Rep, Independent-Republican; Nat Rep, National Republican; Anti-Mas, Anti-Masonic Nullifiers; Lib, Liberal; Nat Dem, National Democratic; Con Un, Constitutional Union; Lib Rep, Liberal Republican; Prog, Progressive; States, States Rights; Amer Ind, American Independent.

Year	Candidates	Parties	Popular Vote	% Pop. Vote	Electoral Vote
	Thomas Pinckney	Fed			59
	Aaron Burr	Anti-Fed			30
	Samuel Adams	Dem-Rep			15
	Miscellaneous				33
1800	*Thomas Jefferson*	Dem-Rep			73
	Aaron Burr (VP)	Dem-Rep			73
	John Adams*	Fed			65
	C. C. Pinckney	Fed			64
	John Jay	Fed			1
1804	*Thomas Jefferson* * (George Clinton)	Dem-Rep			162
	C. C. Pinckney (Rufus King)	Fed			14
1808	*James Madison*	Dem-Rep			122
	C. C. Pinckney (Rufus King)	Fed			47
	George Clinton (VP)	Ind-Rep			6
	Votes Not Cast				1
1812	*James Madison* * (Elbridge Gerry)	Dem-Rep			128
	De Witt Clinton (Charles Jared Ingersoll)	Fusion			89
	Votes Not Cast				1
1816	*James Monroe* (Daniel D. Tompkins)	Rep			183
	Rufus King	Fed			34
	Votes Not Cast				4
1820	*James Monroe* * (Daniel D. Tompkins)	Dem-Rep			231
	John Quincy Adams	Ind-Rep			1
	Votes Not Cast				3
1824	*John Quincy Adams* (John C. Calhoun)	Dem-Rep	115,696	31.9	84
	Andrew Jackson (John C. Calhoun)	Dem-Rep	152,933	42.2	99
	Henry Clay	Dem-Rep	47,136	13.0	37
	William Crawford	Dem	46,979	12.9	41

Year	Candidates	Parties	Popular Vote	% Pop. Vote	Electoral Vote
1828	*Andrew Jackson*	Dem	647,292	56.0	178
	(John C. Calhoun)				
	John Quincy Adams*	Nat Rep	507,730	44.0	83
	(Richard Rush)				
1832	*Andrew Jackson**	Dem	688,242	54.5	219
	(Martin Van Buren)				
	Henry Clay	Nat Rep	473,462	37.5	49
	(John Sergeant)				
	William Wirt	Anti-Mas	101,051	8.0	7
	(Amos Ellmaker)				
	Miscellaneous and Not Cast				13
1836	*Martin Van Buren*	Dem	764,198	50.9	170
	(Richard M. Johnson)				
	William H. Harrison	Whig	549,508	36.6	73
	(Francis Granger)				
	Hugh L. White	Whig	145,352	9.7	26
	Daniel Webster	Whig	41,287	2.7	14
	Other				11
1840	*William H. Harrison*	Whig	1,275,612	52.9	234
	(John Tyler)				
	Martin Van Buren*	Dem	1,130,033	46.8	60
	James G. Birney	Lib	7,053	.3	
1844	*James Knox Polk*	Dem	1,339,368	49.6	170
	(George M. Dallas)				
	Henry Clay	Whig	1,300,687	48.1	105
	(Theodore Frelinghuysen)				
	James G. Birney	Lib	62,197	2.3	
	(Thomas Morris)				
1848	*Zachary Taylor*	Whig	1,362,101	47.3	163
	(Millard Fillmore)				
	Lewis Cass	Dem	1,222,674	42.4	127
	(William O. Butler)				
	Martin Van Buren	Free-Soil	291,616	10.1	
1852	*Franklin Pierce*	Dem	1,609,038	50.8	254
	(William R. King)				
	Winfield Scott	Whig	1,386,629	43.8	42
	(William A. Graham)				
	John P. Hale	Free-Soil	156,297	4.9	

Year	Candidates	Parties	Popular Vote	% Pop. Vote	Electoral Vote
1856	James Buchanan (John C. Breckinridge)	Dem	1,839,237	45.6	174
	John C. Frémont (William L. Dayton)	Rep	1,341,028	33.3	114
	Millard Fillmore	American	849,872	21.1	8
1860	Abraham Lincoln (Hannibal Hamlin)	Rep	1,867,198	39.8	180
	Stephen A. Douglas (Herschel V. Johnson)	Dem	1,379,434	29.4	12
	John C. Breckinridge (Joseph Lane)	Nat Dem	854,248	18.2	72
	John Bell (Edward Everett)	Con Un	591,658	12.6	39
1864	Abraham Lincoln* (Andrew Johnson)	Rep	2,219,362	55.1	212
	George B. McClellan (George H. Pendleton)	Dem	1,805,063	44.9	21
	Votes Not Cast				81
1868	Ulysses S. Grant (Schuyler Colfax)	Rep	3,013,313	52.7	214
	Horatio Seymour (Francis P. Blair)	Dem	2,703,933	47.3	80
	Votes Not Cast				23
1872	Ulysses S. Grant* (Henry Wilson)	Rep	3,597,375	55.6	286
	Horace Greeley	Dem/ Lib Rep	2,833,711	43.8	
	(B. Gratz Brown) Thomas A. Hendricks				42
	B. Gratz Brown				18
	Other and Not Cast				20
1876	Rutherford B. Hayes (William A. Wheeler)	Rep	4,033,950	48.0	185
	Samuel J. Tilden (Thomas A. Hendricks)	Dem	4,284,885	50.9	184
1880	James A. Garfield (Chester A. Arthur)	Rep	4,449,053	48.3	214
	Winfield Scott Hancock (William H. English)	Dem	4,442,035	48.2	155

Year	Candidates	Parties	Popular Vote	% Pop. Vote	Electoral Vote
1884	*Grover Cleveland* (Thomas A. Hendricks)	Dem	4,911,017	48.9	219
	James G. Blaine (John A. Logan)	Rep	4,848,334	48.2	182
1888	*Benjamin Harrison* (Levi P. Morton)	Rep	5,444,337	47.8	233
	Grover Cleveland* (Allen G. Thurman)	Dem	5,540,050	48.7	168
1892	*Grover Cleveland* (Adlai E. Stevenson)	Dem	5,554,414	46.0	277
	Benjamin Harrison* (Whitelaw Reid)	Rep	5,519,802	43.0	145
	James B. Weaver (James G. Field)	People's	1,027,329	8.5	22
1896	*William McKinley* (Garret A. Hobart)	Rep	7,035,638	50.9	271
	William J. Bryan (Arthur Sewall)	Dem	6,467,946	46.8	176
1900	*William McKinley** (Theodore Roosevelt)	Rep	7,219,530	51.7	292
	William J. Bryan (Adlai E. Stevenson)	Dem	6,358,071	45.5	155
1904	*Theodore Roosevelt** (Charles W. Fairbanks)	Rep	7,628,834	56.4	336
	Alton B. Parker (Henry G. Davis)	Dem	5,084,401	37.6	140
1908	*William Howard Taft* (James S. Sherman)	Rep	7,679,006	51.6	321
	William J. Bryan (John W. Kern)	Dem	6,409,106	43.1	162
1912	*Woodrow Wilson* (Thomas R. Marshall)	Dem	6,286,214	41.8	435
	Theodore Roosevelt (Hiram W. Johnson)	Prog	4,126,020	27.5	88
	William Howard Taft* (James S. Sherman)	Rep	3,483,922	23.2	8
1916	*Woodrow Wilson** (Thomas R. Marshall)	Dem	9,129,606	49.3	277

Year	Candidates	Parties	Popular Vote	% Pop. Vote	Electoral Vote
	Charles E. Hughes (Charles W. Fairbanks)	Rep	8,538,221	46.1	254
1920	Warren G. Harding (Calvin Coolidge)	Rep	16,152,200	61.0	404
	James M. Cox (Franklin D. Roosevelt)	Dem	9,147,353	34.6	127
1924	Calvin Coolidge* (Charles G. Dawes)	Rep	15,725,016	54.1	382
	John W. Davis (Charles W. Bryan)	Dem	8,385,586	28.8	136
	Robert M. La Follette (Burton K. Wheeler)	Prog	4,822,856	16.6	13
1928	Herbert C. Hoover (Charles Curtis)	Rep	21,392,190	58.2	444
	Alfred E. Smith (Joseph T. Robinson)	Dem	15,016,443	40.8	87
1932	Franklin D. Roosevelt (John N. Garner)	Dem	22,821,857	57.3	472
	Herbert C. Hoover* (Charles Curtis)	Rep	15,761,841	39.6	59
1936	Franklin D. Roosevelt* (John N. Garner)	Dem	27,751,612	60.7	523
	Alfred M. Landon (Frank Knox)	Rep	16,681,913	36.4	8
1940	Franklin D. Roosevelt* (Henry A. Wallace)	Dem	27,243,466	54.7	449
	Wendell L. Willkie (Charles L. McNary)	Rep	22,305,755	44.8	82
1944	Franklin D. Roosevelt* (Harry S. Truman)	Dem	25,602,505	52.8	432
	Thomas E. Dewey (John W. Bricker)	Rep	22,006,278	44.5	99
1948	Harry S. Truman* (Alben W. Barkley)	Dem	24,179,345	49.6	303
	Thomas E. Dewey (Earl Warren)	Rep	21,991,291	45.1	189
	J. Strom Thurmond	States	1,176,125	2.4	39
	Henry A. Wallace	Prog	1,157,326	2.4	

Year	Candidates	Parties	Popular Vote	% Pop. Vote	Electoral Vote
1952	*Dwight D. Eisenhower* *(Richard M. Nixon)*	Rep	33,936,234	55.2	442
	Adlai E. Stevenson (John J. Sparkman)	Dem	27,314,992	44.5	89
1956	*Dwight D. Eisenhower** *(Richard M. Nixon)*	Rep	35,590,472	57.4	457
	Adlai E. Stevenson (Estes Kefauver)	Dem	26,022,752	42.0	73
1960	*John F. Kennedy* *(Lyndon B. Johnson)*	Dem	34,226,731	49.7	303
	Richard M. Nixon (Henry Cabot Lodge)	Rep	34,108,157	49.5	219
	Harry F. Byrd				15
1964	*Lyndon B. Johnson* *(Hubert H. Humphrey)*	Dem	43,129,484	61.1	486
	Barry M. Goldwater (William E. Miller)	Rep	27,178,188	38.5	52
1968	*Richard M. Nixon* *(Spiro T. Agnew)*	Rep	31,770,237	43.4	301
	Hubert H. Humphrey (Edmund S. Muskie)	Dem	31,270,533	42.7	191
	George Wallace	Amer–Ind	9,906,141	13.5	46
1972	*Richard M. Nixon** *(Spiro T. Agnew)*	Rep	47,169,911	60.8	520
	George S. McGovern (Sargent Shriver)	Dem	29,170,383	37.5	17
	Other				1
1976	*Jimmy Carter* *(Walter F. Mondale)*	Dem	40,830,763	50.1	297
	Gerald R. Ford* (Robert Dole)	Rep	39,147,793	48.0	241
1980	*Ronald W. Reagan* *(George Bush)*	Rep	43,267,462	50.7	489
	Jimmy Carter* (Walter Mondale)	Dem	34,968,548	41.0	49
	John Anderson	Ind	5,588,014	6.6	
1984	*Ronald W. Reagan** *(George Bush)*	Rep	54,455,074	58.8	525

Year	Candidates	Parties	Popular Vote	% Pop. Vote	Electoral Vote
	Walter Mondale (Geraldine Ferraro)	Dem	37,577,137	40.6	13
1988	*George Bush (J. Danforth Quayle)*	Rep	48,886,097	53.4	426
	Michael S. Dukakis (Lloyd Bentsen)	Dem	41,809,074	45.6	112
1992	*William Jefferson Clinton (Albert Gore, Jr.)*	Dem	43,728,375	43.0	370
	George Bush* (J. Danforth Quayle)	Rep	38,167,416	37.5	168
	Ross Perot (James B. Stockdale)	Ind	19,237,247	18.8	0

1789–1800 Prior to the election of 1804, each elector voted for two candidates, with the runner-up becoming Vice President. The Twelfth Amendment to the Constitution changed this procedure.

1816 Four different Federalists received vice-presidential votes.

1824 The election was decided in the House of Representatives because no candidate received a majority of the electoral vote. There were no distinct party designations that year.

1840 The Democratic National Convention failed to choose a vice-presidential nominee. John Tyler succeeded William Henry Harrison, who died in office on 4 April 1841.

1848 Millard Fillmore succeeded Zachary Taylor, who died in office on 9 July 1850.

1864 Andrew Johnson completed Lincoln's second term, after Lincoln's assassination on 14 April 1865.

1872 Horace Greeley died before the electoral votes were counted. His votes were split among three men who had not received any popular votes.

1880 Chester A. Arthur succeeded James A. Garfield, after Garfield's assassination on 2 July 1881.

1900 Theodore Roosevelt completed McKinley's second term, after McKinley's assassination on 6 September 1901.

1920 Calvin Coolidge succeeded Warren G. Harding, after Harding's death on 2 August 1923.

1944 Harry S. Truman succeeded Franklin D. Roosevelt, after Roosevelt's death on 12 April 1945.

1956 One Democratic elector from Alabama voted for Walter B. Jones instead of Stevenson.

1960 Fifteen electors refused to vote for Nixon and cast their votes for Byrd. Lyndon B. Johnson succeeded Kennedy, after Kennedy's assassination on 22 November 1963.

1972 Gerald R. Ford, who became Vice President after Spiro T. Agnew resigned, completed Nixon's second term, after Nixon resigned on 9 August 1974.

APPENDIX B

Newspapers, Radio, and Television in the United States, 1790–1990

Year	Population	Number of Daily Newspapers	Average Daily Circulation	Households with Radio	Households with TV
1790	3,929,214	8	n.a.		
1800	5,308,483	24	n.a.		
1810	7,239,881	26	n.a.		
1820	9,638,453	42	n.a.		
1830	12,866,020	65	n.a.		
1840	17,069,543	138	n.a.		
1850	23,191,876	254	758,454		
1860	31,443,321	387	1,478,435		
1870	39,818,449	574	2,601,547		
1880	50,155,783	971	3,556,395		
1890	62,947,714	1,610	8,387,188		
1900	75,994,575	2,226	15,102,156		
1910	91,972,266	2,600	24,211,977		
1920	105,710,620	2,441	33,028,630	1,250,000 (1924)	
1930	122,755,046	2,086	42,947,824	12,049,000	
1940	131,669,275	1,878	41,132,000	28,048,000	975,000 (1948)
1950	150,697,361	1,426	53,829,000	40,700,000	3,875,000
1960	179,323,175	1,763	58,882,000	48,504,000	46,312,000
1970	203,235,298	1,748	62,108,000	46,108,000	60,594,000

Year	Population	Number of Daily Newspapers	Average Daily Circulation	Households with	
				Radio	TV
1980	226,542,518	1,745	62,201,840	79,968,240	76,300,000
1990	250,410,000 (estimate)	1,655	62,649,218	91,100,000	92,100,000

n.a.: not available

NOTE: In the early nineteenth century there were many more weekly newspapers than dailies. There were 70 weeklies in 1790; 422 in 1820; 1,141 in 1840; and 1,902 in 1850.

SOURCES: *Historical Statistics of the United States, Colonial Times to 1970, Bicentennial Edition* (Washington, D.C., 1975), A 1–8, R 93–105, 232–257; 809; Alfred M. Lee, *Daily Newspaper in America* (New York, 1947), pp. 717–718, 725–726; Michael Emery and Edwin Emery, *The Press and America*, 6th ed. (Englewood Cliffs, NJ, 1988), p. 623; *Statistical Abstract of the United States, 1990* (Washington, D.C., 1990), p. 48.

Manuscript Collections Cited

Adam Badeau Papers, Library of Congress, Washington D.C.

Bruce Barton Papers, State Historical Society of Wisconsin, Madison, WI

John Bell Papers, Library of Congress

John Bigelow Papers, Rare Books and Manuscripts Division, New York Public Library, New York, NY

James G. Blaine Papers, Library of Congress

Blair Family Papers, Library of Congress

William Jennings Bryan Papers, Library of Congress

James Buchanan Papers, Microfilms of the Historical Society of Pennsylvania, Philadelphia, PA

"Campaign Speeches and News Coverage, 1964," Lyndon B. Johnson Library, Austin, TX

William E. Chandler Papers, Library of Congress

Edward T. Clark Papers, Library of Congress

James S. Clarkson Papers, Library of Congress

Henry Clay Papers, Library of Congress

John M. Clayton Papers, Library of Congress

Grover Cleveland Papers, Library of Congress

Clark Clifford Papers, Harry S. Truman Library, Independence, MO

Roscoe Conkling Papers, Library of Congress

George B. Cortelyou Papers, Library of Congress

James M. Cox Papers, Wright State University Archives, Dayton, OH

John Jordan Crittenden Papers, Library of Congress

Homer S. Cummings Diaries, Microfilm Edition, Special Collections Department, University of Virginia Library, Charlottesville, VA

David Davis Family Papers, Illinois State Historical Society Library, Springfield, IL

John W. Davis Papers, Sterling Library, Yale University, New Haven, CT

Thomas E. Dewey Papers, Rush Rhees Library, University of Rochester, Rochester, NY

Stephen A. Douglas Papers, Department of Special Collections, the University of Chicago Library, Chicago, IL

Stephen Early Papers, Franklin D. Roosevelt Library, New Hyde Park, NY

Millard Fillmore Papers, Microfilm Edition, Buffalo and Erie County Historical Society, Buffalo NY

Hamilton Fish Papers, Library of Congress

Gerald R. Ford Papers, Gerald R. Ford Library, Ann Arbor, MI

Papers of Gerald R. Ford Staff Secretary, Gerald R. Ford Library

James A. Garfield Papers, Library of Congress

Richard Goodwin Files, Pre-Presidential Papers, John F. Kennedy Library, Boston, MA

Ulysses S. Grant Papers, Library of Congress
Horace Greeley Papers, Library of Congress
Hanna–McCormick Family Papers, Library of Congress
Benjamin Harrison Papers, Library of Congress
William Henry Harrison Papers, Library of Congress
Rutherford B. Hayes Papers, Rutherford B. Hayes Presidential Center, Fremont, OH
Will Hays Papers, Indiana Division, Indiana State Library, Indianapolis, IN
Ken Hechler Papers, Harry S. Truman Library
Charles Dewey Hilles Papers, Sterling Library, Yale University
Frank Hitchcock Papers, Library of Congress
Louis M. Howe Papers, Franklin D. Roosevelt Library
Charles Evans Hughes Papers, Library of Congress
Lyndon B. Johnson Papers, Lyndon B. Johnson Library
John F. Kennedy Pre-Presidential Papers, John F. Kennedy Library
Robert F. Kennedy Pre-Administration Political Files, John F. Kennedy Library
Abraham Lincoln Papers, Library of Congress
George B. McClellan Papers, Library of Congress
William McKinley Papers, Library of Congress
Manton Marble Papers, Library of Congress
Louis T. Michener Papers, Library of Congress
George Fort Milton Papers, Library of Congress
Miscellaneous Manuscript Collection, Library of Congress
Edwin D. Morgan Papers, New York State Library, Albany, NY
Office of the Press Secretary, Papers, Gerald R. Ford Library
Alton B. Parker Papers, Library of Congress
Franklin Pierce Papers, New Hampshire Historical Society, Concord, NH
James Knox Polk Papers, Library of Congress
Michael Raoul–Duval Papers, Gerald R. Ford Library
Rosser Reeves Papers, State Historical Society of Wisconsin
Whitelaw Reid Family Papers, Library of Congress
Franklin D. Roosevelt, Papers as Governor of New York, Franklin D. Roosevelt Library
Franklin D. Roosevelt, Official File, Franklin D. Roosevelt Library
Franklin D. Roosevelt, President's Personal File, Franklin D. Roosevelt Library
Theodore Roosevelt Papers, Library of Congress
James H. Rowe, Jr., Papers, Franklin D. Roosevelt Library
Carl Schurz Papers, Library of Congress
William H. Seward Papers, Microfilm Edition, Rush Rhees Library, University of Rochester
Horatio Seymour Papers, New York State Library
Alfred E. Smith Papers, New York State Library
Adlai E. Stevenson Papers, Illinois State Historical Society
William Howard Taft Papers, Library of Congress
Zachary Taylor Papers, Library of Congress
Robert Teeter Papers, Gerald R. Ford Library
Harry S. Truman Papers, Harry S. Truman Library
Harry S. Truman Papers, President's Secretary's Files, Harry S. Truman Library
Lyman Trumbull Family Papers, Illinois State Historical Society
Martin Van Buren Papers, Library of Congress

Robert Walker Papers, Library of Congress
Elihu B. Washburne Papers, Library of Congress
Henry Watterson Papers, Library of Congress
William C. Whitney Papers, Library of Congress
Wendell L. Willkie Papers, Lilly Library, Indiana University, Bloomington, IN
Wendell L. Willkie Presidential Campaign Papers, Sterling Library, Yale University
Woodrow Wilson Papers, Library of Congress
Robert W. Woolley Papers, Library of Congress

A Guide to Abbreviations in Notes

NEWSPAPERS AND PERIODICALS CITED

AlAr	Albany Argus
AlEJ	Albany Evening Journal
AtlC	Atlanta Constitution; Atlanta Journal and Constitution
AtMo	Atlantic Monthly
BalS	Baltimore Sun
BosG	Boston Globe; Boston Daily Globe
CharM	Charleston Mercury
CharO	Charlotte Observer
ChiST	Chicago Sun–Times
ChiT	Chicago Tribune
CSM	Christian Science Monitor
CinE	Cincinnati Daily Enquirer
ClPD	Cleveland Plain Dealer; Cleveland Daily Plain Dealer
Col	Collier's
DMN	Dallas Morning News
DenP	Denver Post
DesMR	Des Moines Register
DetFP	Detroit Free Press; Detroit Daily Free Press
DetN	Detroit News
HarpW	Harper's Weekly
HarC	Hartford Daily Courant
IlSR	Illinois State Register
Ind	Independent
JAH	Journal of American History
JoWh	Jonesborough Whig and Independent Journal; Jonesborough Whig
LitD	Literary Digest
LAT	Los Angeles Times
LouCJ	Louisville Courier–Journal; Louisville Daily Courier–Journal
LouD	Louisville Democrat
MilJ	Milwaukee Journal
MinST	Minneapolis Star and Tribune
NAR	North American Review
NasU	Nashville Union
Nat	The Nation
NatI	National Intelligencer; Daily National Intelligencer

Niles	Niles' National Register; Niles' Register
NOP	New Orleans Times–Picayune; New Orleans Daily Picayune
Nwswk	Newsweek
NYH	New York Herald
NYHTr	New York Herald Tribune
NYM	New York Mirror; New York Evening Mirror
NYS	New York Sun
NYT	New York Times
NYTM	New York Times Magazine; New York Times Book Review and Magazine
NYTr	New York Tribune; New York Daily Tribune
NYW	New York World; New York Evening World
NYer	New Yorker
OSJ	Ohio State Journal; Ohio Daily State Journal
Out	The Outlook
PhB	Philadelphia Evening Bulletin
PhI	Philadelphia Inquirer; Philadelphia Daily Inquirer
PSQ	Political Science Quarterly
POQ	Public Opinion Quarterly
RoR	American Monthly Review of Reviews
SatEP	Saturday Evening Post
SatR	Saturday Review
SFChr	San Francisco Chronicle
SFX	San Francisco Examiner
SLPD	St. Louis Post–Dispatch
TNR	The New Republic
USNWR	U.S. News & World Report
WasU	(Washington, D.C.) Daily Union
WasG	Washington Globe
WasP	Washington Post

ADDITIONAL ABBREVIATIONS

ABP	Alton Brooks Parker
AES	Adlai E. Stevenson
AL	Abraham Lincoln
BB	Bruce Barton
BH	Benjamin Harrison
CEH	Charles Evans Hughes
DNC	*Proceedings of the Democratic National Convention*
FDR	Franklin D. Roosevelt
FDR-Gov	Franklin D. Roosevelt, Papers as Governor of New York, Franklin D. Roosevelt Library
FDR-OF	Official File, Franklin D. Roosevelt Library
FDR-PPF	President's Personal File, Franklin D. Roosevelt Library
FDR-press	Presidential Press Conferences of Franklin D. Roosevelt, Microfilm Edition
FP	Franklin Pierce

GC	Grover Cleveland
GF	Gerald Ford
GMc	George B. McClellan
HG	Horace Greeley
HS	Horatio Seymour
HST	Harry S. Truman
HST-PSF	President's Secretary's Files, Harry S. Truman Library
JAG	James A. Garfield
JB	James Buchanan
JFK-pre	John F. Kennedy Pre-Presidential Papers, John F. Kennedy Library
JGB	James G. Blaine
JKP	James Knox Polk
LBJ	Lyndon B. Johnson
LBJ-64	"Campaign Speeches and News Coverage, 1964," AC 70–29, Lyndon B. Johnson Library
MVB	Martin Van Buren
PConf	Press Conference; Press and Radio Conference
RBH	Rutherford B. Hayes
RFK-pre	Robert F. Kennedy Pre-Administration Political Files
RNC	*Proceedings of the Republican National Convention*
SAD	Stephen A. Douglas
TR	Theodore Roosevelt
TR-Lett	Elting E. Morison, ed., *The Letters of Theodore Roosevelt*, 8 vols. (Cambridge, 1951–1954)
USG	Ulysses S. Grant
WHH	William Henry Harrison
WLW-IN	Wendell L. Willkie Papers, Lilly Library
WLW-Yale	Wendell L. Willkie Presidential Campaign Papers, Sterling Library
WW	Woodrow Wilson
WW-Link	Arthur S. Link et al., eds., *The Papers of Woodrow Wilson*, 53 + vols. (Princeton, 1966–)
ZT	Zachary Taylor

Notes

PROLOGUE. *"What Has America Done to Deserve This?"*

1. Donald Morrison, ed., *The Winning of the White House 1988* (New York, 1988), p. 230; Kitty Dukakis with Jane Scovell, *Now You Know* (New York, 1990), p. 220.
2. *Time*, 14 Nov. 1988, p. 19.
3. Throughout this work, either "the people" or "Americans" is used as a shorthand phrase to summarize the emerging or prevailing opinion. *Nwswk*, 1 Feb. 1988, cover.
4. Elizabeth Drew, *Election Journal: Political Events of 1987-1988* (New York, 1989), p. 262.
5. Sidney Blumenthal, *Pledging Allegiance: The Last Campaign of the Cold War* (New York, 1990), p. 5.
6. Robert Westbrook, "Politics as Consumption," in *The Culture of Consumption*, ed. Richard Wightman Fox and T. J. Jackson Lears (New York, 1983), pp. 145, 171, 151; Robert Spero, *The Duping of the American Voter* (New York, 1980); *NYT*, 30 Oct. 1988, 1:30.
7. David S. Broder, *The Party's Over* (New York, 1972); Michael E. McGerr, *The Decline of Popular Politics* (New York, 1986), pp. 171-179.
8. Jeffrey K. Tulis, *Rhetorical Presidency* (Princeton, 1987); *BosG*, 9 Nov. 1988, p. 18.
9. *Time*, 3 Oct. 1988, p. 18; Peter Goldman, Tom Mathews, et al., *The Quest for the Presidency* (New York, 1990), p. 418; Peggy Noonan, *What I Saw at the Revolution* (New York, 1990), p. 108.
10. *Time*, 14 Nov. 1988, p. 66; *NYT*, 30 Oct. 1988, p. 1; Goldman, Mathews et al., *Quest for the Presidency*, p. 192.
11. Jimmy Carter on NBC, "Evening News with Tom Brokaw," 13 Oct. 1988; *NYM*, 23 Oct. 1852, p. 1.

CHAPTER ONE. *Standing for Office in an Age of Virtue*

1. This work does not attempt to redefine republicanism. While republicanism has become an explanatory catchall for too many historians, the term is a useful shorthand for traditional attitudes toward campaigning. Nineteenth-century Americans often spoke of nominees diverging from republican paths.
2. Carter Diary Entry, 1 Apr. 1776, *The Defence of Injur'd Merit Unmasked* (n.p., 1771), p. 10, both in Charles S. Sydnor, *American Revolutionaries in the Making* (New York, 1965), pp. 48-49, 143.
3. Forrest McDonald, *Novus Ordo Seclorum: The Intellectual Origins of the Constitution* (Lawrence, 1985), p. 73.
4. Edmund S. Morgan, *Inventing the People* (New York, 1988), pp. 203, 199; Sydnor, *American Revolutionaries*, pp. 48, 53.
5. John Adams quoted in Bernard Bailyn, *The Ideological Origins of the American Revolution* (Cambridge, 1967), p. 135.

6. Alexander Hamilton [Publius], "No. 71," Edward Mead Earle, ed., *The Federalist* (New York, n.d.), pp. 464–465. See Michael Kammen, *People of Paradox* (New York, 1973), pp. 97–116, 242–244.
7. Hamilton, "Nos. 70–71," *Federalist*, pp. 454, xli, 455.
8. On the Electoral College as "democratic" see Shlomo Slonim, "The Electoral College at Philadelphia," *JAH* 73 (June, 1986):35–58.
9. The *Constitution* and *The Federalist* do not directly address the question of the candidate's role. Hamilton, "No. 68," *Federalist*, pp. 441, 444; James W. Ceaser, "Political Parties and Presidential Ambition," *Journal of Politics* 40 (Aug. 1978):718, 720.
10. *Massachusetts Centinel*, 26 Mar. 1788, in John P. Kaminski and Jill Adair McCaughan, *A Great and Good Man: George Washington* (Madison, 1989), p. 97; George Washington to Marquis de Lafayette, 28 Apr. 1788, Washington to Alexander Hamilton, 28 Aug. 1788, Washington to Hamilton, 3 Oct. 1788, all in W. B. Allen, ed., *George Washington* (Indianapolis, 1988), pp. 392, 417, 422.
11. James Thomas Flexner, *Washington: The Indispensable Man* (Boston, 1969), p. 214.
12. Washington to Catherine Macaulay Graham, 9 Jan. 1790, in Allen, *Washington*, p. 537; John Frederick Schroeder, ed., *Maxims of Washington* (New York, 1854), pp. 317–318.
13. Jeffrey K. Tulis, *Rhetorical Presidency* (Princeton, 1987), p. 69. See Leo Braudy, *Frenzy of Renown* (New York, 1986), p. 462.
14. Flexner, *Washington*, p. 270.
15. James Madison, "No. 10," *Federalist*, pp. 53, 60.
16. Campaigning practices evolved haphazardly. Candidates remained passive longer in the more conservative South and when running for governor. Madison to Washington, 2 Dec. 1788, in Sydnor, *American Revolutionaries*, pp. 48, 143, n. 13.
17. Perry M. Goldman, "Political Virtue in the Age of Jackson," *PSQ* 87 (Mar. 1972): 58.
18. Frank Luther Mott, *American Journalism*, 3rd ed. (New York, 1962), p. 169; Paul F. Boller, Jr., *Presidential Campaigns* (New York, 1984), pp. 11, 13.
19. (Harrisburg, PA) *Magician*, 4 July 1840, p. 1.
20. Merrill D. Peterson, *Adams and Jefferson* (New York, 1976), p. 88.
21. M. J. Heale, *The Presidential Quest* (New York, 1982), pp. 2–4, 14–22.
22. Ibid., p. 3.
23. By 1836, every state but one had adopted the General Ticket System. In South Carolina, state legislators chose presidential electors until 1868. See Richard McCormick, *The Presidential Game* (New York, 1982), p. 160.
24. Thomas Jefferson to Edward Carrington, 16 Jan. 1787, in Merrill D. Peterson, ed., *The Portable Thomas Jefferson* (New York, 1975), p. 414; Robert H. Wiebe, *The Opening of American Society* (New York, 1984), p. 295.
25. Andrew Jackson to L. H. Coleman, 26 Apr. 1824, in John Spencer Bassett, ed., *Correspondence of Andrew Jackson*, 7 vols. (Washington, D.C., 1926–1935), 3:249.
26. Just how "Jacksonian" and how "democratic" the revolution was remains debatable, but most historians recognize that Jackson symbolically dominated his era. Carl N. Degler, *Out of Our Past*, rev. ed. (New York, 1970), p. 140; *Niles*, 16 Apr. 1831, p. 126; Alexis de Tocqueville, *Democracy in America*, J. P. Mayer, ed. (Garden City, NY, 1969), p. 60.
27. Bancroft in Degler, *Out of Our Past*, p. 137; Tulis, *Rhetorical Presidency*, p. 27; Andrew Jackson to MVB, 18 Sept. 1831, Jackson to David Burford, 28 July 1831, both in Bassett, 4:350, 321.

28. Letter of Sherrod Williams, 7 Apr. 1836, in William Ogden Niles, *The Tippecanoe Textbook* (Baltimore, 1840), pp. 76–77.
29. C[harles] Hammond to Henry Clay, 21 Jan. [1840], Clay MSS.
30. Kammen, *People of Paradox*, pp. 243, 223.
31. J. G. A. Pocock, *Machiavellian Moment* (Princeton, 1975), p. viii.
32. "Gen. Harrison's Speech at Columbus," *Niles*, 27 June 1840, p. 265.

CHAPTER TWO. *To Stand or to Stump?*

1. Ronald P. Formisano notes that the new party forms depended on a "flow of information that had simply not existed in 1800," in *The Transformation of Political Culture* (New York, 1983), pp. 247, 262. On the people as a "crowd" see Jean H. Baker, *Affairs of Party* (Ithaca, 1983), p. 285. Entry, 2 Nov. 1840, in Allan Nevins, ed., *The Diary of Philip Hone*, 2 vols. (New York, 1927), 1:506.
2. Some of these techniques had been around for decades, but the scale of activity in 1840 was unprecedented. Nathan Sargent, *Public Men and Events*, 2 vols. (Philadelphia, 1875), 2:107; Baker, *Affairs of Party*, p. 269.
3. Differing interpretations include that of Richard P. McCormick, who buries the republican demand for passivity too quickly, arguing that, by 1844, calculation and not tradition "inhibited" nominees. This chapter argues that the ideological prohibition and the caution were mutually reinforcing. M. J. Heale considers all subsequent Whig nominees active candidates who "prepared the way for the whistle-stop campaigns." This claim exaggerates Whig activity and disregards half a century of resistance prior to William Jennings Bryan's whistle-stop tour in 1896. Richard P. McCormick, *The Presidential Game* (New York, 1982), pp. 203, 226; M. J. Heale, *The Presidential Quest* (New York, 1982), p. 107.
4. In this work, a candidate is called "active" if he campaigned for election by making speeches and public appearances. A candidate is deemed "passive" if he did not make public appearances, even if he worked in the background, writing private letters and planning strategy. Similarly, a candidate's public statements determine his "forthrightness."
5. Nicholas Biddle to Herman Cope, 11 Aug. 1835, in Reginald C. McGrane, ed., *The Correspondence of Nicholas Biddle* (Boston, 1919), p. 254; Richard S. Elliott, *Notes Taken in Sixty Years* (Boston, 1884), pp. 120–121.
6. WHH to John Owen et al., 19 Dec. 1839, in William Ogden Niles, *The Tippecanoe Textbook* (Baltimore, 1840), pp. 85–86.
7. WHH to Sherrod Williams, 1 May 1836, in Charles S. Todd and Benjamin Drake, *Sketches of the Civil and Military Service of William Henry Harrison* (Cincinnati, 1840), p. 154; OSJ, 27 Dec. 1839, p. 3.
8. *Gen. Harrison's Speech at the Dayton Convention, September 10, 1840* (Boston, [1840]), p. 2, Letter of WHH, 13 May 1840, both in WHH MSS; "Speech of General Harrison Delivered at the Old Hamilton Convention," 1 Oct. 1840, p. 6, MVB MSS.
9. WHH quoted in *Niles*, 27 June 1840, p. 265; *WHH at Dayton*, p. 2.
10. *WHH at Dayton*, p. 6; WHH to Harmer Denny, 2 Dec. 1838, *Tippecanoe Almanac for 1841* (n.p., [1841]), pp. 58–59.
11. Such silence was typical. The 1840 Democratic platform addressing issues was unprecedented for a national party. Letter of David Gwynne, J. C. Wright, and O. M. Spencer, 23 Feb. 1840, reprinted in *AlAr*, 31 Mar. 1840, p. 2.
12. Thomas Cooper to Nicholas Biddle, 29 Apr. 1837, in McGrane, ed., *Correspondence*

of Biddle, p. 272; [Thomas Hart Benton], *Thirty Years' View. By a Senator of Thirty Years*, 2 vols. (New York, 1856), 2:204.

13. Letter of Gwynne, Wright, and Spencer, p. 2.

14. *Boston Morning Post*, 10 June 1840, p. 2; *WasG*, 10 July 1840, p. 1; *Extra Globe*, 16 June 1840, p. 31, MVB MSS; *AlAr*, 27 Mar. 1840, p. 4.

15. *AlAr*, 8 Apr. 1840, p. 4; Major L. Wilson, *Presidency of Van Buren* (Lawrence, 1984), p. 204; *Lafayette* (IN) *Free Press*, 27 Oct. 1840, p. 1; Robert Gray Gunderson, *Log-Cabin Campaign* ([Lexington], 1957), p. 74; *AlAr*, 29 May 1840, p. 4.

16. "WHH at Hamilton Convention," p. 6; WHH, 6 June 1840, quoted in *Niles*, 20 June 1840, p. 246; *AlEJ*, 5 June 1840, p. 2.

17. Letter of WHH, 13 May 1840, p. 5; Francis P. Blair, Sr., to Andrew Jackson, [17] June 1840, Blair MSS.

18. WHH quoted in *Lafayette* (IN) *Free Press*, 27 Oct. 1840, p. 1.

19. Ibid.

20. "WHH at Hamilton Convention," pp. 6–7; *WHH at Dayton*, pp. 5–6.

21. "WHH at Hamilton Convention," p. 8.

22. *AlEJ*, 11 June 1840, p. 2; *AlEJ*, 20 June 1840, p. 2.

23. *CharM* and *DetFP* quoted in *AlAr*, 21 July 1840, p. 4; (Harrisburg, PA) *Magician*, 4 July 1840, p. 1.

24. The Democrats, however, won the historical victory. Most historians portray Harrison as a fool and a tool of the Whig managers. The Harrison papers reveal a more impressive man. See Arthur M. Schlesinger, Jr., *Age of Jackson* (Boston, 1945), p. 292.

25. *OSJ*, 30 Jan. 1840, p. 4; *WasG*, 29 June 1840, p. 1; *Songster* (n.p, n.d), p. 55, WHH MSS.

26. *AlEJ*, 2 July 1840, p. 2; Wilson, *Presidency of Van Buren*, p. 197.

27. MVB to Sherrod Williams, 20 Apr. 1836, MVB MSS; Andrew E. Norman, ed., *The Autobiography of Martin Van Buren* (New York, 1983), p. 226, n. 1; [MVB] to [Andrew Stevenson et al.], [29] May 1835, frag., p. 4, MVB MSS.

28. MVB to Stevenson, [29] May 1835, p. 4; MVB to John B. Cary et. al., 31 July 1840, in *Niles*, 22 Aug. 1840, p. 393.

29. Proceedings of the Baltimore Convention, 16 May 1840, *Extra Globe*, 16 June 1840, p. 1, MVB MSS.

30. *AlEJ*, 23 Sept. 1840, p. 2; *AlEJ*, 29 Sept. 1840, p. 2.

31. *AlEJ*, 5 Sept. 1839, p. 2.

32. The Whigs mischievously lifted the phrase "climax of affectation and dandyism" from a Democratic attack on President John Quincy Adams's 1828 tour. *AlAr*, 15 Aug. 1828, quoted in *AlEJ*, 20 July 1839, p. 2. *AlEJ*, 8 July 1839, p. 2; *Daily Advertiser*, quoted in *AlEJ*, 23 July 1839, p. 2; *Boston Atlas*, reprinted in *AlEJ*, 23 Jan. 1840, p. 2; *AlEJ*, 31 July 1839, p. 2; *AlEJ*, 10 July 1839, p. 2; *AlEJ*, 24 July 1839, p. 2.

33. MVB to John M. McCalla et al., 4 July 1840, in *Niles*, 8 Aug. 1840, p. 364.

34. Dillon Jordan to MVB, 18 Nov. 1840, Th[omas] L. Hamer to MVB, 18 Nov. 1840, both in MVB MSS.

35. "O.K.," short for "Old Kinderhook," was Van Buren's nickname; the "Old Hero" was Harrison. Clement Eaton, *Henry Clay and the Art of American Politics* (Boston, 1957), p. 142; Richard L. Rubin, *Press, Party, and Presidency* (New York, 1981), p. 43; 3 Nov. 1840, in Allan Nevins and Milton Halsey Thomas, eds., *The Diary of George Templeton Strong*, 4 vols. (New York, 1952), 1:151.

36. Candidates remain central throughout this narrative, but only as they approached the twentieth century did they begin to shape their own campaigns.
37. *Democratic Review* quoted in Wilson, *Presidency of Van Buren*, p. 192; Edmond C. Watmough to Robert J. Walker, 7 Sept. 1844, Walker MSS.
38. Cave Johnson to JKP, 10 June 1844, in Charles G. Sellers, Jr., *James K. Polk*, 2 vols. (Princeton, 1966), 1:109; Letter of JKP, 15 May 1843, in *Niles*, 26 Oct. 1844, p. 125.
39. JKP, 12 June 1844, in *Niles*, 6 July 1844, pp. 294-295.
40. Walker helped procure Polk's nomination, and also ran the embryonic national committee in Washington, serving, in effect, as the first Democratic National Chairman. R[obert] J. Walker to JKP, 30 May 1844, pp. 1-2, JKP MSS.
41. JKP to J[ohn] K. Kane, 19 June 1844, J[ohn] K. Kane to JKP, 29 June 1844, both in JKP MSS.
42. For debate on Polk's "fraud" see Merrill D. Peterson, *The Great Triumvirate* (New York, 1987), p. 363 and Sellers, *Polk*, 2:120. JKP to John K. Kane, 19 June 1844, in *Niles*, 6 July 1844, pp. 294-295.
43. JKP to Committee of Charlotte, NC, 2 July 1844, JKP MSS; Harrisburg (PA) *Democratic Union—Extra*, 31 Aug. 1844, p. 3.
44. *NasU*, 5 Oct. 1844, p. 2; *NasU*, 3 Oct. 1844, p. 2; *NasU*, 11 Oct. 1844, p. 2.
45. *AlEJ*, 26 Oct. 1844, p. 2; *NYTr*, 11 Oct. 1844, p. 2; Jones in *AlEJ*, 18 Oct. 1844, p. 2; Jackson in *NYTr*, 19 Oct. 1844, p. 2.
46. J. W. Goode et al. to JKP, 21 Sept. 1844, JKP MSS.
47. J. George Harris to JKP, 24 Sept. 1844, J[ohn] Catron to JKP, 26 Sept. 1844, p. 3, G[eorge] M. Dallas to JKP, 9 Oct. 1844, all in JKP MSS. See Polk drafts 25 Sept. 1844, JKP MSS.
48. *Charleston (SC) Courier*, reprinted in *JoWh*, 24 Apr. 1844, p. 1; *JoWh*, 17 July 1844, p. 1.
49. *NasU*, 23 Apr. 1844, p. 2.
50. H[enry] Clay to Joseph Gales, Jr., and William W. Seaton, 3 May 1844, in *Niles*, 11 May 1844, p. 161.
51. Robert Letcher to J. J. Crittenden, 21 June 1842, in Peterson, *Great Triumvirate*, p. 353; [Henry] Clay to [J. J.] Crittenden, 19 Apr. 1844, in Crittenden MSS; Clay to [Joseph Gales, Jr., and William W. Seaton], 17 Apr. 1844, in *Niles*, 4 May 1844, pp. 152-153.
52. At first, Clay's letter did not appear to be a political blunder, as Van Buren also opposed annexation. But when the Democratic Convention repudiated Van Buren and nominated Polk, Texas became an issue, spelling trouble for Clay in the South and West. Peterson, *Great Triumvirate*, pp. 360-361.
53. H[enry] Clay to Stephen F. Miller, 1 July 1844, in *Niles*, 3 Aug. 1844, p. 372; H[enry] Clay to Thomas M. Peters and John M. Jackson, 27 July 1844, in *Niles*, 31 Aug. 1844, p. 439.
54. *NasU*, 3 Oct. 1844, p. 2; *Rochester Advertiser* in *AlAr*, 11 Sept. 1844, p. 2; J. George Harris to JKP, 24 Sept. 1844, JKP MSS.
55. H[enry] Clay to [Joseph] Gales, Jr., and [William W.] Seaton, 23 Sept. 1844, in *Niles*, 5 Oct. 1844, p. 74.
56. See *AlAr*, 13 Aug. 1844, p. 2.
57. *NasU*, 30 Aug. 1844, p. 2.
58. Henry Clay to John M. Clayton, 22 Aug. 1844, p. 3, Clayton MSS.
59. 2 July 1844, *AlAr*, p. 2. On Whig appreciation for "the personal character of a ruler"

see *Louisville* (KY) *Jour[nal]*, reprinted in *Niles*, 10 Aug. 1844, p. 392. See also Warren I. Susman, *Culture as History* (New York, 1984), pp. 273–274.

60. The often incorrect conclusions that contemporaries drew are more relevant to this
    study of perceptions than are historians' more accurate analyses. What matters here
    is that many Democrats and Whigs *believed* that the letters cost Clay the election.
    For conflicting views see Daniel Walker Howe, *The Political Culture of the American
    Whigs* (Chicago, 1979), p. 144; Lee Benson, *The Concept of Jacksonian Democracy*
    (Princeton, 1961), pp. 135–136. Millard Fillmore to Henry Clay, 11 Nov. 1844, Clay
    MSS.

61. Clay's image among contemporaries was that of a compromiser, even a gamester,
    and a dictator. He became a statesman and a saint after he died. On Clay's image
    and on the origins of the phrase see Peterson, *Great Triumvirate*, pp. 380–385, 286–
    289. "Eulogy of Mr. [James] Brooks," A. H. Carrier, *Monument to the Memory of
    Henry Clay* (Philadelphia, 1858), p. 395; William H. Barnum quoted in *AtlC*, 21
    Aug. 1892, Whitney MSS.

62. Comparing the letters of the four candidates written during the campaign and pub-
    lished in *Niles' National Register* reveals that Clay wrote many brief letters. With
    his letters so accessible, and some of his positions so slippery, he made himself
    vulnerable. Van Buren wrote ten letters, averaging approximately 2940 words. Har-
    rison wrote six letters, averaging approximately 723 words. Polk wrote two letters,
    averaging 351 words. Clay wrote seventeen letters, averaging 684 words.

63. Charles Augustus Davis to John Jordan Crittenden, 2 Oct. 1844, pp. 1–3, Critten-
    den MSS.

CHAPTER THREE. *An Age of Parties, 1848–1856*

1. "Managing the Candidate" (New York, 1852), Print Division, Library of Congress.

2. William Safire traces the term "stumping" to 1716 when Ann Maury's *Memoirs of
   a Huguenot Family* recorded that one of the "head men" in a Saponey Indian town
   would speak while standing on "a great stump of a tree. . . . so that being raised,
   he might the better be heard." By 1838, Safire writes, the term "was part of the
   American political vocabulary." William Safire, *Safire's Political Dictionary*, rev. ed.
   (New York, 1978), pp. 701–702. NYM, 8 Nov. 1852, p. 2.

3. George Spring Merriam, *The Life and Times of Samuel Bowles*, 2 vols. (New York,
   1885; reprint ed., Ann Arbor, 1976), 1:29.

4. This approach recognizes the ideological differences between the Whig and Democratic parties, but minimizes the differences between Democratic and Whig politicians. Politicians embraced similar strategies and attitudes on the campaign trail.
   The contrasts that do emerge reflect different party realities, not attitudes: The
   Democrats came closer to the common party ideal than the Whigs. M. J. Heale
   emphasizes the differences between the parties, and views the candidates' actions
   as illustrative of the Whig party position. An analysis of Whig party newspapers
   reveals that the candidates' actions often deviated from Whig norms. Their rivalry
   linked the Whigs and Democrats symbiotically. See M. J. Heale, *The Presidential
   Quest* (New York, 1982), pp. 83–132 passim; Ronald P. Formisano, *The Transformation of Political Culture: Massachusetts Parties, 1790s–1840s* (New York, 1983), p. 309.
   See also Charles G. Sellers, Jr., "The Equilibrium Cycle in Two-Party Politics,"
   POQ 29 (Spring 1965):16. *Democratic Review* 15 (Dec. 1844):531–532, in William R.
   Brock, *Parties and Political Conscience* (Millwood, NY, 1979), p. 19.

5. Many Democrats and Whigs remained uncomfortable with the idea of party, Whigs probably a little more so. Still, this discomfort did not blind most Whigs to the new realities. See Daniel Walker Howe, *Political Culture of the American Whigs* (Chicago, 1979), pp. 52-53. WHH to John Owen et al., 19 Dec. 1839, in William Ogden Niles, *Tippecanoe Textbook* (Baltimore, 1840), pp. 85-86; Kirk H. Porter and Donald Bruce Johnson, eds., *National Party Platforms*, 4th ed. (Urbana, 1970), pp. 3, 10, 16, 23.

6. Considering partisan identity fixed, contemporaries concentrated on mobilizing adherents rather than gaining converts. Richard Jensen, "Armies, Admen and Crusaders, Types of Presidential Campaigns," *History Teacher* 2 (Jan. 1969):36.

7. Thurlow Weed Barnes, *Life of Thurlow Weed*, 2 vols. (Boston, 1883-1884), 2:76.

8. Weed's counterparts included his Democratic rival in New York, Edwin Croswell and the Kentucky Whig operator John J. Crittenden. By 1840, both parties held periodic national conventions but lacked permanent structures. Legislation in 1845 established a uniform date for the selection of presidential electors in each state, forcing simultaneous campaigns. As a result, in 1848 the Democratic National Committee (DNC) was formed. Still, it was active only in congressional and presidential years. Whigs relied on ad hoc campaign committees. A permanent rival to the DNC emerged in 1856 with the Republican National Committee. See Cornelius P. Cotter and Bernard C. Hennessy, *Politics Without Power* (New York, 1964), pp. 15-21. Roy F. Nichols, *Disruption of American Democracy* (New York, 1948), p. viii; Barnes, *Life of Weed*, 1:105, 137.

9. James MacGregor Burns, *Vineyard of Liberty* (New York, 1983), p. 516.

10. 30 Aug. 1843, in Allan Nevins, ed., *The Diary of Philip Hone, 1828-1851* 2 vols. (New York, 1927), 2:667. See Michael Schudson, *Discovering the News* (New York, 1978), pp. 12-60 passim.

11. Horace Greeley, *Recollections of a Busy Life* (New York, 1869), p. 137; Alfred McClung Lee, *The Daily Newspaper in America* (New York, 1937), p. 384; Darrow quoted in Bernard A. Weisberger, *The American Newspaperman* (Chicago, 1961), p. 104.

12. The Democrats in 1848 pioneered the use of campaign textbooks. In 1856 Republicans published a textbook as well. In 1876 the Democratic campaign manager Abram S. Hewitt transformed the textbook from an assortment of campaign documents into an essential campaign tool.

13. Greeley's peers included Weed's political and journalistic rival, Edwin Croswell of the *Albany Argus*, as well as Samuel Bowles of the whiggish but independent *Springfield* (MA) *Republican*. Although the relations between a particular editor and the party varied, all promoted local and national candidates enthusiastically.

14. Glyndon G. Van Deusen, *Horace Greeley* (Philadelphia, 1853), p. 95.

15. This account emphasizes their particular archetypal skills, but the three were versatile. Weed edited newspapers and served in his state assembly; Greeley served in Congress briefly and ran for president in 1872; and Seward bargained with associates as adeptly as he communicated with the public. Among Seward's peers were the eloquent but uncompromising Massachusetts Senator Charles Sumner and Senator Stephen A. Douglas of Illinois.

16. Originally, governors also stood for election and did not run. During this period, however, gubernatorial passivity waned; presidential passivity did not. Glyndon G. Van Deusen, *William Henry Seward* (New York, 1967), p. 109.

17. For example, Seward began a speech at a Whig mass meeting in Boston on October 15, 1848, this way:

    In the hour of darkness which hung over the Roman republic when Julius Caesar, with his legions, flushed with the conquest of Germany, was on his way to march to subjugate the liberties of Rome, and when Pompey, upon whom all hopes were cent[e]red to take command of the army, had withdrawn and taken position in Africa—at that moment, when the people of Rome were divided and distracted, and while some were persuading to submit to Caesar, and others offered other leaders under whom the republic might find safety—Cicero expressed himself in these words: "I can easily know whom I ought to avoid, but not whom I ought to follow."
        Such is the nature of the question which the whigs of the United States are now called upon to decide.
        (George E. Baker, ed., *The Works of William Henry Seward*, 5 vols. [New York, 1853–1884; reprint ed., New York, 1972], 3:286.)

18. This sketch has focused on the Whig party, which was less organized and more antiparty than the Democrats. These characterizations are even more applicable to the Democrats.

19. Lewis Cass to Zadoc McKnew, 8 Dec. 1851, "Zadoc McKnew," Miscellaneous Manuscripts, Library of Congress.

20. Lewis Cass, 30 May 1848, in William T. Young, *Sketch of the Life and Public Services of General Lewis Cass* (Philadelphia, 1853), pp. 360–362.

21. The *New York Tribune*, *Albany Evening Journal*, Jonesborough (TN) *Whig*, *New Orleans Weekly Delta*, (Washington, D.C.) *Daily Union*, and *Detroit Daily Free Press*, from the Democratic Convention in May 1848 through Election Day, paid less attention to Cass than to any other nominee during the 1840s and 1850s. There were only four serious discussions of Cass's behavior. See *AlEJ*, 29 May 1848, p. 2; *NYTr*, 3 Sept. 1848, p. 2; *Cincinnati Gazette* reprinted in *JoWh*, 12 July 1848, p. 2; and *WasU*, 20 Sept. 1848, pp. 2–3. Roy F. Nichols, *Invention of the American Political Parties* (New York, 1967), p. 374.

22. Democrats would not object to military heroes—that was part of Cass's appeal. But they were not desperate for a hero, and demanded party loyalty from their candidates.

23. Taylor, a slaveholder, was especially popular among Southern Democrats, even though Democrats were more wary of Taylor than were Whigs. Once he declared himself a "decided Whig," Taylor's Democratic support faded. Still, thousands of Southern Democrats deserted their party and voted for Taylor. Joseph G. Rayback, *Free Soil: The Election of 1848* (Lexington, 1970), pp. 34, 41–42, 45–46, 53, 306.

24. ZT to Colonel [Joseph] Taylor, [Summer, 1846], in Barnes, *Life of Weed*, 1:573; ZT to Jefferson Davis, 16 Aug. 1847, p. 10, ZT MSS.

25. ZT to Henry Clay, 4 Nov. 1847, Clay MSS; ZT to Dr. A. P. Merrill, 29 May 1847, quoted in *NYT*, 1 Feb. 1931, ZT to Jefferson Davis, 16 Feb. 1848, quoted in *Boston Advertiser*, 1 Oct. 1863, both in ZT MSS.

26. Barnes, *Life of Weed*, 1:572–573; ZT to J[ohn] J. Crittenden, 15 Sept. 1847, p. 8, Crittenden MSS; Letter to Henry Clay, 24 Aug. 1847, pp. 2–4, Clay MSS; Weed in Rayback, *Free Soil*, pp. 162, 53; Clay in Merrill D. Peterson, *The Great Triumvirate* (New York, 1987), p. 434.

27. ZT to John S. Allison, 22 Apr. 1848, in Rayback, *Free Soil*, pp. 154–155; ZT to Joseph Taylor, 15 May 1848, p. 5, ZT MSS.

28. ZT to J[efferson] Davis, 10 July 1848, p. 2, ZT MSS.

29. Henry Clay to Worsely et al., 28 June 1848, p. 1, Clay MSS; *JoWh*, 21 June 1848, p. 2.

30. Rayback, *Free Soil*, pp. 270–271.

31. *WasU*, 17 June 1848, p. 2; *WasU*, 1 Oct. 1848, p. 2; *WasU*, 17 Oct. 1848, p. 3.

32. Howell Cobb in Brock, *Parties and Political Conscience*, p. 23.

33. *WasU*, 18 June 1848, pp. 2–3; *WasU*, 2 Nov. 1848, p. 2.

34. ZT to J[ohn] S. Allison, 4 Sept. 1848 in Barnes, *Life of Weed* 1:579–582.

35. Monroe (PA) *Democrat* quoted in *WasU*, 18 Oct. 1848, p. 3; Barnes, *Life of Weed*, 1:579; Seward quoted in Joel Silbey, *A Respectable Minority* (New York, 1977), p. 10.

36. Barnes, *Life of Weed*, 1:583; Greeley, *Recollections*, pp. 214–215.

37. The Free Soilers opposed extending slavery into the Western territories. Throughout this period, third-party movements freed the most disgruntled voters from the two-party straitjacket. The Liberty party in 1844, the Free Soil party in 1848 and 1852, and the American (Know-Nothing) party in 1856, attracted ideologues and played the role of spoiler.

38. Greeley in James G. Blaine, *Twenty Years of Congress*, 2 vols. (Norwich, CT: 1884–1886), 1:104–105.

39. A. W. Bradford to Hamilton Fish, 24 June 1852, Fish MSS.

40. Letter to the [New York?] *Tribune*, quoted in *WasU*, 28 Mar. 1852, p. 3; *LouD*, 29 Sept. 1852, p. 3.

41. *WasU*, 7 Oct. 1852, p. 2; John M. Bradford to [William H. Seward], 5 Aug. 1852, p. 2, Seward MSS.

42. Dudley P. Phelps to W[illia]m H. Seward, 29 Sept. 1852, Seward MSS.

43. *Natl*, 26 Oct. 1852, p. 1; *Sunday* (New York?) *Mercury* in *NYM*, 12 Oct. 1852, p. 1.

44. *LouD*, 9 Oct. 1852, p. 3; Telegram from Baltimore, MD, 16 Sept. 1852, in *LouD*, 30 Sept. 1852, p. 3; *NYTr*, 27 Sept. 1852, p. 4.

45. Kenneth Cmiel, *Democratic Eloquence* (New York, 1990), pp. 25, 61; Daniel J. Boorstin, *The Americans: The National Experience* (New York, 1965), p. 310; *WasU*, 5 Oct. 1852, p. 2.

46. *NYM*, 22 Oct. 1852, p. 3. See James W. Ceaser et al., "The Rise of the Rhetorical Presidency," chap. 18 in Thomas E. Cronin, ed., *Rethinking the Presidency* (Boston, 1982), p. 234.

47. *National Democrat* quoted in *NYM*, 16 Oct. 1852, p. 1; *WasU*, 28 Sept. 1852, p. 3.

48. *NasU*, 23 Oct. 1852, p. 2; *WasU*, 16 Oct. 1852, p. 2; *WasU*, 16 Oct. 1852, p. 2; *WasU*, 21 Oct. 1852, p. 2.

49. For a Whig example see *Natl*, 23 Sept. 1852, p. 1. For a Democratic example see *WasU*, 28 Sept. 1852, p. 2.

50. *WasU*, 16 Oct. 1852, p. 2; *NasU*, 23 Oct. 1852, p. 2.

51. Weed, of course, admitted that Scott went "to see and be seen of the people." For Whigs who broke party ranks and criticized Scott see *NYM*, 22 Oct. 1852, p. 3. Barnes, *Life of Weed* 2:218. Thurlow Weed to [William H. Seward], 25 Sept. 1852, Seward MSS; Wayne Cullen Williams, *A Rail Splitter for President* (Denver, 1951), p. 24; *NYTr*, 22 Sept. 1852, p. 6.

52. 20 Oct. 1852, Allan Nevins and Milton Halsey Thomas, eds., *The Diary of George Templeton Strong*, 4 vols. (New York, 1952), 2:106.

53. One account from 1840 described how volunteers relayed Harrison through Ohio on his way to a mass meeting. In Loudonville, a Mr. Haskell was drafted to convey the General to Wooster, because Haskell's little one-horse wagon, without any springs, had "the most aristocratic 'turn out' in the neighborhood." Twelve years later, railroad mileage had quadrupled from 2,818 miles of track in 1840 to 12,908 miles. *Loudonville* (OH) *Advocate*, 27 July 1905, WHH MSS; Henry V. Poor, *Manual of the Railroads of the United States*, 3rd ser. (New York, 1870), p. xlvi.

54. Pierce resigned from the U.S. Senate in 1842 and from his commission as Brigadier General; he refused nominations as New Hampshire Governor and Attorney General. He was usually motivated by his lucrative law practice, not his modest farm. In 1842 a bout with alcoholism prompted his retirement. *WasU*, 6 June 1852, p. 2, hails Pierce's modesty.

55. Gideon Welles to FP, 5 June 1852, p. 1, FP to Edmund Burke, 14 June 1852, p. 3, both in FP MSS; *NYM*, 22 Oct. 1852, p. 3.

56. Joseph J. Bradford to FP, 3 July 1852, FP MSS.

57. 20 Oct. 1852, Nevins, *Strong Diary*, 2:106; Heale, *Presidential Quest*, p. 103; FP to Edwin De Leon, 23 July 1852, quoted in (Little Rock) *Arkansas Whig*, 2 Sept. 1852, p. 1.

58. *Detroit Advertiser*, 14 Oct. 1852, in Wilmer C. Harris, *Public Life of Zachariah Chandler* (Lansing, MI, 1917), p. 16; R. P. Letcher in Allan Nevins, *Ordeal of the Union*, 2 vols. (New York, 1947), 2:35; *NYM*, 23 Oct. 1852, p. 1; *NYTr*, 25 Aug. 1852, p. 4.

59. Greeley quoted in Pamela Herr, *Jessie Benton Frémont* (New York, 1987), p. 252.

60. Longfellow quoted in Nevins, *Ordeal*, 2:487; George W. Julian, *Political Recollections, 1840 to 1872* (Chicago, 1884), p. 152; Rollo Ogden, ed., *Life and Letters of Edwin Lawrence Godkin*, 2 vols. (New York, 1907), 1:116, 112.

61. Acceptance Letter of J. C. Frémont, 8 July 1856, in Benjamin F. Hall, *The Republican Party and Its Present Candidates* (New York, 1856), pp. 465–469; Frémont quoted in Nevins, *Ordeal*, 2:503.

62. JB to Harriet Lane, 9 Nov. 1855, in John Bassett Moore, ed., *The Works of James Buchanan*, 12 vols. (Philadelphia, 1908–1911), 9:458.

63. Though lengthy, Buchanan's acceptance was less pugnacious than Frémont's, and called for harmony. JB to John E. Ward et al., 16 June 1856, p. 2, JB to Henry A. Wise, 28 June 1856, p. 1, John Slidell to JB, 18 July 1856, pp. 1, 4, all in JB MSS.

64. Millard Fillmore, running on the Know-Nothing (American) party ticket, also observed the proprieties: "I never gave a pledge in my life," he explained. "The constitution is my guide and my character the only pledge. Those who believe me honest will require nothing more; those who do not, should not rely on my pledges." Millard Fillmore to W. C. Rives, 23 July 1856, p. 1, Fillmore MSS. Stevens quoted in Richard N. Current, *Old Thad Stevens* (Madison, 1942), p. 106; (Washington, D.C.), *National Era*, 21 Aug. 1856, p. 2.

65. Lyman Trumbull to [AL], 15 June [18]56, p. 3, Trumbull MSS.

66. Godkin, 22 Mar. 1859, quoted in Ogden, *Godkin*, 1:258; HG to Charles A. Dana, 20 Mar. 1856, quoted in Jeter Allen Isely, *Horace Greeley and the Republican Party, 1853–1861* (Princeton, 1947; reprint ed. New York, 1965), p. 162.

CHAPTER FOUR. *Passive Winners and Active Losers*

1. W. C. Bryant to AL, 16 June 1860, AL to [William Cullen Bryant], 28 June 1860,

both in Parke Godwin, *A Biography of William Cullen Bryant*, 2 vols. (New York, 1883), 2:142–143.

2. Oliver H. P. Parker to AL, Sept. 1860, p. 1, Tho[mas] T. Swann to AL, 15 June 1860, pp. 2–3, both in AL MSS.

3. Bell remained passive throughout the campaign. Breckinridge made one well-publicized stump speech refuting the charge of disunion. Even the Republican *Tribune* praised Breckinridge's speech, despite his departure from the "dignified and proper" course "for a Presidential candidate." *NYTr*, 7 Sept. 1860, p. 4. Letter of John Bell, 23 July 1860, p. 2, in Bell MSS; Breckinridge quoted in *NYTr*, 6 Sept. 1860, p. 5; Robert W. Johannsen, *Stephen A. Douglas* (New York, 1973), p. 777.

4. It is difficult to quantify the spread of democracy, and the term itself is not well defined. This generational notion may help. Clearly, the Jacksonian era witnessed a "democratization," evidenced by a host of institutional novelties and homages to the common man. But these innovations did not take root overnight. The resistance to the democratization of the campaign reveals the delayed nature of the change. See Lawrence A. Cremin, *American Education: The National Experience, 1783–1876* (New York, 1980), pp. 179, 490–491; Chilton Williamson, *American Suffrage* (Princeton, 1960), pp. 281–293; David Donald, *Lincoln Reconsidered*, rev. 2nd ed. (New York, 1961), pp. 228–229; Merle Curti, *Growth of American Thought* (New York, 1943), pp. 304, 295–300, 344, 360. Malcolm Cowley, ed., *Walt Whitman's Leaves of Grass* (New York, 1959), pp. 5–6.

5. America had not become a democratic paradise. Southerners were particularly resistant to these liberal-democratic notions. But Curtis and most of his contemporaries believed that the common man had triumphed, and behaved accordingly. For resistance see Drew G. Faust, *James Henry Hammond and the Old South* (Baton Rouge, 1982), pp. 40–43, 54, 288. On the "problem of the middle class" see Sean Wilentz, *Chants Democratic* (New York, 1984), p. 11, passim. "The American Doctrine of Liberty," 17 July 1862, in Charles Eliot Norton, ed., *Orations and Addresses of George William Curtis*, 2 vols. (New York, 1894), 1:111.

6. The President still virtually represented women, blacks, children, and his opponents. And the Electoral College kept the election theoretically indirect. But the Electoral College had not been a factor in an election since 1828. On the liberal-democratic thrust to this popular presidency see Robert Kelley, *The Transatlantic Persuasion* (New York, 1969), p. 410. Cowley, ed., *Leaves of Grass*, p. 92; W[illia]m K. DeGraffenreid to SAD, 16 July 1860, p. 3, SAD MSS.

7. A. R. Brown et al., to SAD, 27 July 1860, in SAD MSS. See Jean H. Baker, "The Ceremonies of Politics," in William F. Cooper, Jr., et al., *A Master's Due: Essays in Honor of David Herbert Donald* (Baton Rouge, 1985), pp. 173–178.

8. Democrats in Georgia, New York, Virginia, Wisconsin, Maine, and Louisiana promised Douglas that if he came he could win their state. He reached all these states—and lost them all. DeGraffenreid to SAD, p. 1, Gordon Tanner to SAD, 16 Aug. 1860, pp. 1–2, Erskine Douglas to SAD, 25 June 1860, pp. 2–3, all in SAD MSS.

9. H. B. Tebbetts to SAD, 19 Aug. [18]60, p. 1, J. J. Seibels to SAD, 14 Aug. 1860, p. 3, both in SAD MSS.

10. Reid Sanders to SAD, 10 Aug. 1860, p. 4, in SAD MSS.

11. SAD quoted in *ChiT*, 26 June 1860, p. 4.

12. *DetFP*, 6 July 1860, p. 4; Johannsen, *Douglas*, pp. 778–779.

13. Up to Boston, out to Albany, through to Vermont, and back across to Newport, Douglas stumped. E. K. Smart to SAD, 4 Aug. 1860, p. 1, SAD MSS.

14. Reprinted from the *Minnesotan* in *CharM*, 10 Sept. 1860, p. 4.

15. *Charleston Courier* in Washington (D.C.) *Constitution*, 25 Aug. 1860, in Milton MSS; *Illinois State Journal* in Wayne Cullen Williams, *A Rail Splitter for President* (Denver, 1951), pp. 30–31.

16. Speech of SAD, 5 Oct. 1860, in *NatI*, 12 Oct. 1860, p. 2.

17. Ibid.

18. This proto-rear platform campaign predated William Jennings Bryan by four decades. *DetFP*, 11 Oct. 1860, p. 2; David Davis to [George Perrin Davis], 30 Sept. 1860, p. 2, in D. Davis MSS; David Davis to E. D. Morgan, 22 Sept. 1860, p. 8, Morgan MSS.

19. While at Harvard in mid-July, Douglas had predicted a Republican victory and revealed his plans to go South "to urge the duty of all to submit to the verdict of the people." Charles C. Patton, *Glory to God and the Sucker Democracy* (n.p., 1973), p. 122. Johannsen, *Douglas*, pp. 797–798.

20. Speech of Isaac Hazelhurst, Esq., quoted in *PhI*, 21 Sept. [1860], enclosed in Simon Cameron to AL, 21 Sept. 1860, AL MSS.

21. Mrs. Mary Todd Lincoln expected to serve champagne at the notification ceremony. Fearful of offending the temperance people, her husband insisted on ice water. William E. Baringer, "The Republican Triumph," in Norman A. Graebner, *Politics and the Crisis of 1860* (Urbana, 1961), pp. 316–317. Reinhard H. Luthin, *The First Lincoln Campaign* (Cambridge, 1944; reprint ed., Gloucester, MA, 1964), p. 224; Reply to Notification, Acceptance Letter, in Roy P. Basler, ed., *The Collected Works of Abraham Lincoln*, 9 vols. (New Brunswick, 1953–1955), 4:51–53; AL quoted in George C. Fogg to AL, 18 Aug. 1860, p. 3, AL MSS.

22. For attacks see *IlSR*, 8 Oct. 1860, in Milton MSS. For dissuading see Fogg to AL, 18 Aug. 1860, pp. 3–4. W[illiam] H. Herndon to [Lyman] Trumbull, 19 June 1860, p. 2, Trumbull MSS.

23. For example, William DeGraffenreid told Douglas that Herschel Johnson, the Democratic vice-presidential nominee, "consulted me as to the propriety of taking the stump and I advised him to go wherever he was invited but to publish no speeches." The context suggests that Johnson was concerned with tactics, not taste, and that DeGraffenreid responded in kind. DeGraffenreid to SAD, p. 2.

24. President Jefferson Davis of the Confederate States of America was elected to a single six-year term in November, 1861. Robert Hardy Smith of Alabama considered "the retention of the old mode of electing the President. . . . the chief defect" of the Confederate Constitution. The delegates could not agree on an alternative. J. G. Randall and David Donald, *The Civil War and Reconstruction*, rev. ed. (Boston, 1969), pp. 156–157. Adams in Harold M. Hyman, "Election of 1864," Arthur M. Schlesinger, Jr., and Fred Israel, eds., *History of American Presidential Elections*, 4 vols. (New York, 1971), 2:1155; David Herbert Donald. "The Republican Party, 1864–1876," in Arthur M. Schlesinger, Jr., ed., *History of U.S. Political Parties*, 4 vols. (New York, 1973), 2:1286.

25. Isaac J. Wistar to GMc, 3 Sept. 1864, pp. 1–2, GMc MSS.

26. GMc to Horatio Seymour et al., 8 Sept. [1864], in *DNC 1864*, pp. 60–61; *Daily News* in Irving Katz, *August Belmont* (New York, 1968), p. 135.

27. Dewar Barnes to GMc, 5 Sept. 1864, pp. 2–3, GMc MSS; *NYTr*, 13 Aug. 1864, p. 4.

28. Edwin D. Morgan and William E. Chandler dominated the Republican National Committee from the 1860s through the 1880s. Both kept extensive records, yet neither collection features many communications with nominees, nor did many correspondents pay much attention to a nominee's behavior. "Plan of Democratic Campaign for October 1864," Marble MSS; Manton Marble to GMc, 12 Sept. [1864], p. 2, James Braden et al., to GMc, 25 Oct. 1864, p. 2, both in GMc MSS.

29. William Safire, *Safire's Political Dictionary*, rev. ed. (New York, 1978), p. 181; Fessenden, Aug. 1864, quoted in Edward Chase Kirkland, *The Peacemakers of 1864* (New York, 1927), p. 97.

30. Lincoln drew up plans for the period between the election and the new president's inauguration. See Memorandum of AL, 23 Aug. 1864, Basler, ed., *Lincoln*, 7:514–515. AL quoted in Donald, *Lincoln Reconsidered*, p. 79.

31. Benjamin Wade quoted in M[ichael] J. Cramer, *Ulysses S. Grant: Conversations and Unpublished Letters* (New York, 1897), p. 68.

32. William S. McFeely, *Grant: A Biography* (New York, 1981), p. 279; USG quoted in Adam Badeau, *Grant in Peace* (Hartford, 1887), p. 144; Geo[rge] L. Miller to HS, 18 Aug. 1868, HS MSS.

33. USG to J[ohn] M. Schofield, 25 Sept. 1868, pp. 1–2, Badeau MSS; USG quoted in Badeau, *Grant in Peace*, p. 148; USG to Elihu B. Washburne, 23 Sept. 1868, in James Grant Wilson, *General Grant's Letters to a Friend* (New York, 1897), p. 57.

34. "When a man is forced into a position against his will should his friends rejoice or condole with him?" a cousin asked. Morris Miller to HS, 1 Aug. 1868, HS MSS. HS at Tammany Hall, 10 July 1868, quoted in Stewart Mitchell, *Horatio Seymour of New York* (Cambridge, 1938), p. 461.

35. Frank Blair, Jr., to James O. Broadhead, 23 June 1868, in Katz, *August Belmont*, p. 180; Henry C. Bach to HS, 9 Sept. 1868, pp. 2–3, HS MSS.

36. NYW, 21 Oct. 1868, p. 6; William Cassidy to [HS], 25 Sept. [18]68, pp. 1–2, HS MSS.

37. NYW, 23 Oct. 1868, p. 3; Seymour at Erie, 23 Oct. 1868, clipping from NYW, Scrapbook, HS MSS.

38. Andrew Johnson to HS, quoted in NYW, [c. 22 Oct. 1868], clipping, Scrapbook, HS MSS.

39. *Baltimore American* reprinted in (Washington, D.C.) *National Republican*, 23 Oct. 1868, p. 2; *Cincinnati Daily Gazette*, 31 Oct. 1868, p. 2; 31 Oct. 1868, Allan Nevins and Milton Halsey Thomas, eds., *The Diary of George Templeton Strong*, 4 vols. (New York, 1952), 4:230; "Seymour, The Visit of the Great Statesman to the West," NYW, n.d., clipping, Scrapbook, HS MSS.

40. USG to J. R. Hawley, 29 May 1868, RNC 1868, p. 141.

41. NYTr, 1 June 1868, p. 4.

42. These reservations about unchecked majority rule eventually helped stop the Radicals' "constitutional revolution." W. R. Brock, *An American Crisis* (New York, 1963), p. 265. NYW, 15 June 1868, p. 4; NYW, 1 June 1868, p. 4.

43. These bonds of unity continued to grow after the 1860s. Although the Civil War marked a great leap forward for national government in America, its effect, especially on industrialization, should not be exaggerated. O[restes] A. Brownson, *The American Republic* (New York, 1866), p. 370.

44. Grant and his immediate successors did not exercise as much power as Lincoln had. Still, the presidency in the 1870s and 1880s was more relevant to most Americans, and more powerful, than it had been in the 1850s.

314 Notes

45. Edwards Pierrepont, 2 Oct. 1872, quoted in William B. Hesseltine, *Ulysses S. Grant, Politician* (New York, 1935), p. 288; William E. Chandler, 4 July 1872, quoted in Leon Burr Richardson, *William E. Chandler, Republican* (New York, 1940), p. 137; Geo[rge] H. Boker to E. B. Washburne, 19 Aug. 1872, p. 3, Washburne MSS.
46. For example, Grant told one reporter that his opponent, Horace Greeley, surrounded himself with "disreputable characters" and wanted to put them into "important" offices. "Can any of our readers recall any previous President or Presidential Candidate who would not speak in personal and respectful terms of his opponents?" the *Cincinnati Enquirer* sniffed. *CinE*, 20 July 1872, p. 4. Hesseltine, *Grant*, p. 288; USG to Roscoe Conkling, 15 July 1872, p. 2, Conkling MSS.
47. Matthew T. Downey, "Horace Greeley and the Politicians in the Liberal Republican Convention in 1872," *JAH* 53 (Mar. 1967):727-750, argues that Greeley was the most popular candidate, refuting the claim that the nomination was obviously suicidal. John G. Sproat, *The Best Men* (New York, 1968), pp. 11-44, 74-88; George W. Julian, *Political Recollections, 1840 to 1872* (Chicago, 1884), p. 335.
48. *NYW* quoted in Katz, *August Belmont*, p. 200.
49. A "Straight" Democratic convention met at Louisville in September, rejected Greeley, and nominated Charles O'Conor. Turnout in 1868 was 78.1 percent, in 1876 81.8 percent. *Historical Statistics of the United States*, 2 vols. (Washington, D.C., 1975), 2:1071-1072. Richardson, *Chandler*, pp. 141, 140; *NYW*, 27 May 1872, p. 4; Henry Lee, 8 Sept. 1872, quoted in Sarah Forbes Hughes, ed., *Reminiscences of John Murray Forbes*, 3 vols. (Boston, 1902), 3:98.
50. HG to [Whitelaw] Reid, 13 [July?] 1872; Reid to Alfred Cowles, 14 July [1872], Letterbook, p. 68; Horace White to Reid, 27 June 1872, p. 2, all in Reid MSS; Alfred Cowles to Reid, quoted in Joseph Logsdon, *Horace White* (Westport, CT, 1971), p. 245; Reid to James F. Rhodes, n.d., Letterbook, pp. 737-738, Reid to HG, [10 or 11 Aug. 1872], both in Reid MSS.
51. *NYTr*, 9 Aug. 1872, p. 5; *NYTr*, 13 Aug. 1872, p. 1.
52. *Nat*, 8 Aug. 1872, p. 83; HG to Mason W. Tappan, 8 Nov. 1872, in HG MSS.
53. *NYTr*, 16 Aug. 1872, p. 1.
54. A[lfred] Pleasanton to [Carl Schurz], 1 Sept. 1872, p. 2, in Schurz MSS; M. C. Kerr to [Lyman Trumbull], 1 Sept. [18]72, p. 4, Trumbull MSS.
55. *NYS*, 30 Nov. 1872, p. 1.
56. *NYTr*, 30 Sept. 1872, p. 2; *NYTr*, 24 Sept. 1872, p. 1; *NYTr*, 28 Sept. 1872, p. 5.
57. Watterson quoted in Richardson, *Chandler*, p. 148; Reid to Henry Watterson, [1 Oct. 1872], Reid to Bayard Taylor, 7 Oct. [18]72, Letterbook, pp. 749, 792, Reid MSS; *NYTr*, 25 Sept. 1872, p. 4; Hesseltine, *Grant*, p. 289.
58. *HarC*, 21 Sept. 1872, p. 2; *Cincinnati Daily Gazette*, 18 Sept. 1872, p. 2.
59. *NYW*, 16 Aug. 1872, p. 4.
60. *NYW*, 10 Oct. 1872, p. 4; *CinE*, 20 July 1872, p. 4; D. H. Wheeler, "President Making," *Lakeside Monthly* (Mar. 1872), p. 242, in Earle Dudley Ross, *The Liberal Republican Movement* (New York, 1919), p. 151.
61. *Cleveland Herald, AlEJ*, both quoted in *NYTr*, 26 Sept. 1872, p. 2; *HarC*, 26 Sept. 1872, p. 2; *CinE*, 18 Sept. 1872, p. 4.
62. *HarC*, 2 Nov. 1872, p. 2.
63. *NYW*, 24 Sept. 1872, p. 4; *NYW*, 26 Oct. 1868, p. 6; M. L. Weems, *The Life of George Washington* (Philadelphia, 1858), pp. 6-7.
64. HG to [Charles] Lanman, 27 June 1872, HG MSS.

65. *NYS*, 30 Nov. 1872, p. 1; HG to Tappan, 8 Nov. 1872; *NYT*, 30 Nov. 1872, p. 4.

66. RBH quoted in Hesseltine, *Grant*, pp. 274–275; "A Queer Campaign," *New York Evening Post*, clipping, Scrapbook, USG MSS.

67. Hayes did not work closely with the National Committee. Stalwarts like Zachariah Chandler would not surrender control of the party machinery. This struggle between the nominee and the party committee persisted throughout the 1880s and 1890s. Marie Chatham, "The Role of the National Party Chairman" (Ph.D. diss., University of Maryland, 1953), p. 12. James G. Blaine, *Twenty Years of Congress*, 2 vols. (Norwich, CT: 1884–1886), 2:572; 22 Oct. 1876, T. Harry Williams, ed., *Hayes: The Diary of a President* (New York, 1964), p. 44; RBH to E[dwin] D. Morgan, 10 July 1876, Morgan MSS; RBH to W[illia]m D[ean] Howells, 24 Aug. 1876, copy, RBH MSS.

68. Grant's 1868 letter had 221 words, his 1872 letter 249. Hayes's letter had nearly 1,500 words. RBH to Edward McPherson et al., 8 July 1876, *RNC 1876*, pp. 115–118. 8 July 1876, 29 Oct. 1876, Williams, *Hayes Diary* pp. 27, 45.

69. On Election Day Tilden won 250,000 more popular votes than Hayes, but his electoral vote total of 184 was one short of a majority. After months of crisis the disputed electoral votes of Florida, Louisiana, and South Carolina were cast for Hayes, swinging the election to him in March 1877. *Nat*, 1 Feb. 1877, p. 69; *NYTr*, 8 Nov. 1876, p. 4.

70. Tilden's prenomination campaign inspired one of the first complaints about political advertising in American history: "[The] American people . . . can never be persuaded to reduce the Presidency of the United States to the level of a White Pine extract or a recipe for Stomach Bitters." *CinE*, 22 June 1876, p. 4.

71. This contrast is reflected in the historiography. Such contemporaries as James G. Blaine portray Tilden as "Skillfully and quietly direct[ing] all the movements of the canvass," as do some historians like Alexander Flick. Allan Nevins, however, considers Tilden "tardy, vacillating, and excessively conservative," an analysis Keith Polakoff echoes, arguing that "Tilden took . . . [the traditional] injunction seriously, even more so than Hayes." See Blaine, *Twenty Years*, 2:579; Alexander Clarence Flick, *Samuel Jones Tilden* (New York, 1939), p. 299; Allan Nevins, *Abram S. Hewitt* (New York, 1935; reprint ed., New York, 1967), p. 312; Keith Ian Polakoff, *The Politics of Inertia* (Baton Rouge, 1973), p. 113. Gore Vidal, *1876: A Novel* (New York, 1976), p. 134; *HarpW*, 25 Nov. 1876, p. 947.

72. One editor told Tilden that his nearly 4,400-word letter was "able but too long for people to read." Tilden sneered "It was not intended for *people* to read." Flick, *Tilden*, pp. 297, 299; Samuel J. Tilden to John A. McClernand et al., 11 July 1876, *DNC 1876*, pp. 181–192. Sidney Webster to Samuel J. Tilden, 12 Aug. 1876, John Bigelow, ed., *Letters and Literary Memorials of Samuel J. Tilden*, 2 vols. (n.p., 1908; reprint ed., Freeport, NY, 1971), 2:450; *NYTr*, 19 Sept. 1876, p. 4.

73. *HarC*, 17 July 1876, p. 2; *NYTr*, 3 Aug. 1876, p. 4; Alfred D. Chandler, Jr., *The Visible Hand* (Cambridge, 1977), p. 1; Nevins, *Abram Hewitt*, pp. 307–311; Michael E. McGerr, *The Decline of Popular Politics* (New York, 1986), pp. 71–75.

74. "An Over Anxious Candidate Warned," New York *Graphic*, clipping, Scrapbook, RBH MSS; W[illia]m C. Whitney to S[amuel] J. Tilden, 5 Sept. 1876, pp. 2–3, Tilden MSS; Bigelow Diary Entries, 29 Aug. 1876, p. 133, 15 Sept. 1876, p. 143, Bigelow MSS; Webb C. Hayes to Russel Hastings, 18 Sept. 1876, p. 2, RBH MSS.

75. *CinE*, 23 June 1876, p. 4.

76. *HarpW*, 18 Nov. 1876, p. 927; *HarC*, 5 Sept. 1876, p. 2.
77. *NYTr*, 26 Oct. 1876, p. 4; *NYT*, 16 Nov. 1876, clipping, Scrapbook, RBH MSS; Thurlow Weed to [JGB], 8 June 1876, p. 2, JGB MSS.

CHAPTER FIVE. *The Front Porch or the Stump? 1880–1896*

1. "The Two Rival Political Huckster Shops," (NY) *Irish World*, 30 Oct. 1880, Scrapbook, JAG MSS.
2. *Nat*, 21 Oct. 1880, p. 283.
3. From 1876 through 1896, 78.5 percent of those eligible voted, 85 percent excluding the South. Morton Keller, *Affairs of State* (Cambridge, 1977), pp. 545, 533.
4. Julian S. Rammelkamp, *Pulitzer's Post-Dispatch* (Princeton, 1967), p. 41; Robert A. Rutland, *The Newsmongers* (New York, 1973), p. 281; Charles C. Clayton, *Little Mack: Joseph B. McCullagh of the St. Louis Globe-Democrat* (Carbondale, 1969), p. 147.
5. Alfred McClung Lee, *The Daily Newspaper in America* (New York, 1937), p. 182.
6. Draft, Speech of James S. Clarkson to the National League of Republican Clubs, [c. 1890s], p. 6, Clarkson MSS. On the educational campaign see Michael E. McGerr, *The Decline of Popular Politics* (New York, 1986), pp. 69–107.
7. C. A. Boutelle in M[att] S. Quay et al., "The Man, or the Platform?" *NAR* 154 (May 1892):522.
8. Richard Croker, "Tammany Hall and the Democracy," *NAR* 154 (Feb. 1892):225.
9. The "best men," known as Mugwumps after 1884, were the most prominent exponents of this renewed republican critique. But these doubts about the American voter also appeared in election-day sermons, campaign speeches, and the popular press. The lack of a sustained attack against the critique as "undemocratic," and the fact that the Mugwumps were not defensive about these views, proves that the doubts were widespread. *HarpW*, 3 Nov. 1888, p. 826; James G. Blaine, "The Presidential Election of 1892," *NAR* 155 (Nov. 1892):525; D. H. Wheeler, "President Making," *Lakeside Monthly* (Mar. 1872), p. 242, in Earle Dudley Ross, *The Liberal Republican Movement* (New York, 1919), p. 151; J. L. Spalding, "The Basis of Popular Government," *NAR* 139 (Sept. 1884):203–204.
10. *NYT*, 10 July 1888, p. 4; *NYT*, 3 Aug. 1884, p. 6.
11. *NYTr*, 25 June 1880, p. 4; *NYW*, 13 July 1880, p. 4; C[arl] Schurz to JAG, 9 July 1880, Schurz MSS.
12. Daniel Dougherty quoted in [Almira Russell Hancock], *Reminiscences of Winfield Scott Hancock. By His Wife* (New York, 1887), pp. 170–171; Winfield S. Hancock, 5 Sept. 1880, quoted in Herbert J. Clancy, *The Presidential Election of 1880* (Chicago, 1958), p. 210; *AlEJ*, 9 Aug. 1880, p. 2.
13. *Cincinnati Daily Gazette*, 14 Sept. 1880, p. 4; *HarpW*, 10 July 1880, p. 434; Glenn Tucker, *Hancock the Superb* (Indianapolis, 1960), p. 301; *AlEJ*, 9 Aug. 1880, p. 2; "Mr. Nasby Details the Trouble that Ensued by Defective Machinery at Hancock's Headquarters," clipping, Scrapbook, 16:446, JAG MSS.
14. *NYTr*, 6 Oct. 1880, p. 4; Speech, 29 Sept. 1880, in Sherman Evarts, ed., *Arguments and Speeches of William Maxwell Evarts*, 3 vols. (New York, 1919), 2:638.
15. Clancy, *Election of 1880*, pp. 218–221.
16. The close election seemingly confirmed the Democratic perceptions. Barnum quoted in *AtlC*, 21 Aug. 1892, in Whitney MSS; [Hancock], *Reminiscences*, p. 172.

17. In fact, a major party would not nominate a military figurehead until the Republicans nominated Dwight D. Eisenhower in 1952.

18. Joseph B. McCullagh, the editor of the St. Louis *Globe-Democrat*, introduced the term "boom" to American politics in connection with the push for Grant. When a river overflowed, Mississippi riverboat pilots would shout "By jove, but she's booming." Jim Allee Hart, *A History of the St. Louis Globe-Democrat* (Columbia, 1961), p. 149.

19. JAG to Whitelaw Reid, 21 July [18]80, p. 3, Reid MSS; W[illiam] E. Chandler to JAG, 24 July 1880, p. 3, JAG MSS.

20. JAG to Reid, 21 July [18]80, p. 2, Marshall Jewell to JAG, 29 July 1880, p. 7, Anson G. McCook to JAG, 31 July 1880, p. 2, all in JAG MSS.

21. JAG Diary, 4 Aug. 1880, JAG MSS; "Ohio," (n.p.) *Times*, 16 Oct. [1880], clipping, Scrapbook, 15:5, JAG MSS; *HarpW*, 28 Aug. 1880, p. 546.

22. [Thomas M.] Nichol to JAG, 18 Aug. 1880, p. 2, JAG Diary, 26 Sept. 1880, 10 Aug. 1880, p. 2, Marshall Jewell to JAG, 7 Sept. 1880, p. 3, RBH to JAG, 22 Aug. 1880, p. 2, all in JAG MSS.

23. Even Roscoe Conkling eventually showed up. After speaking in Warren, Ohio (and barely acknowledging Garfield's candidacy), Conkling papered over his differences with Garfield in the "Treaty of Mentor." George H. Mayer, *The Republican Party, 1854–1964* (New York, 1964), p. 203.

24. JAG to [Harry Garfield and James Garfield, Jr.], 31 Oct. 1880, p. 4, in JAG MSS; CinE in Theodore Clarke Smith, *The Life and Letters of James Abram Garfield*, 2 vols. (New Haven, 1925), 2:1041.

25. *NYTr*, 14 Aug. 1880, p. 4.

26. *NYS*, 7 Aug. 1884, reprinted in "Malice v. Merit," clipping, Scrapbook, JGB MSS.

27. H. Wayne Morgan, "The Republican Party, 1876–1893," in Arthur M. Schlesinger, Jr., ed., *History of U.S. Political Parties*, 4 vols. (New York, 1973), 2:1413.

28. *NYW*, 22 Sept. 1884, p. 4.

29. To their credit, neither nominee propagated these scandals and each one, unbeknown to the other, quashed additional allegations about his opponent. Mark D. Hirsch, "Election of 1884," in Arthur M. Schlesinger, Jr., and Fred Israel, eds., *History of American Presidential Elections*, 4 vols. (New York, 1971), 2:1574–1575.

30. "Malice v. Merit," clipping; Claude Moore Fuess, *Carl Schurz: Reformer (1829–1906)* (New York, 1932), p. 294.

31. Hirsch, "Election of 1884," 2:1564–1565, 1573–1574.

32. JGB, 6 Sept. 1884, in "Letter to William Walter Phelps Explaining His Marriage," clipping, Scrapbook, JGB MSS; JGB to Whitelaw Reid, 27 July [18]84, p. 2, Reid MSS.

33. R. W. Patterson to James S. Clarkson, 20 Sept. 1884, in McGerr, *Decline of Popular Politics*, p. 36; *NYT*, 4 Nov. 1884, p. 2.

34. John Hay to JGB, 5 Nov. 1884, p. 3, JGB MSS.

35. *NYT*, 25 Sept. 1884, p. 4; "A Champion Vote Beggar," clipping, Scrapbook, JGB MSS; *Nat*, 13 Nov. 1884, p. 407.

36. The Democrats won New York by 1,149 votes, out of 1,125,000 cast. Lee Benson disagrees with Allan Nevins and others that Burchard affected the outcome. Benson argues that Blaine reversed the Republican decline in six states and, given the long-term voting trends, personalities were insignificant. Blaine, however, insisted he would have "carried New York by 10,000 if the weather had been clear on

election day and Dr. Burchard had been doing missionary work in Asia Minor."
Lee Benson, "Research Problems in American Political Historiography," in Mirra
Komarovsky, ed., *Common Frontiers of the Social Sciences* (Glencoe, IL, 1957),
pp. 123–141; JGB to Francis Fessenden, 17 Nov. 1884, in Mayer, *Republican Party*,
p. 534, n. 80. John R. Lambert, *Arthur Pue Gorman* (Baton Rouge, 1953), p. 106.

37. *AtlC*, 21 Aug. 1892, Whitney MSS.
38. RBH to JAG, 5 Aug. 1880, pp. 1–2, JAG MSS; *Buffalo Commercial Advertiser*, clipping, Scrapbook, JGB MSS.
39. *WasP*, 27 June 1888, quoted in H. Wayne Morgan, *From Hayes to McKinley* (Syracuse, 1969), p. 302.
40. "Cleveland in a Tight Box," *Newport Observer*, 9 Oct. 1888, clipping, Scrapbook, Whitney MSS; Allan Nevins, *Grover Cleveland* (New York, 1933), p. 377.
41. GC to Chauncey F. Black, 14 Sept. 1888, in Allan Nevins, ed., *Letters of Grover Cleveland, 1850–1908* (Boston, 1933), p. 189.
42. Louis J. Lang, ed., *The Autobiography of Thomas Collier Platt* (New York, 1910), p. 211; *BosG*, 13 Aug. 1888, clipping, Scrapbook, 6:79, BH MSS.
43. Morgan, *Hayes to McKinley*, p. 306.
44. "Benjamin Harrison's Presidential Campaign of 1888, Michener's Report: Harrison's Speeches in 1888," Louis T. Michener, "Benjamin Harrison: An Appreciation," p. 7, both in Michener MSS.
45. "Mr. Harrison, Personally," clipping, Scrapbook, vol. 6, BH MSS. See Harry J. Sievers, *Benjamin Harrison*, 2 vols. (New York, 1959), 2:372, 358–359.
46. *BosG*, 13 Aug. 1888, 6:79; James N. Tyner to Louis T. Michener, 21 Sept. 1888, p. 4, Michener MSS.
47. Morgan, *Hayes to McKinley*, p. 308; *HarpW*, 1 Sept. 1888, p. 647.
48. For years, visitors had paraded through candidates' homes to consult, to pitch in, to impress, or to pay homage. But the Garfield and Harrison efforts were unprecedented in their scale, and in their elaborate response, which attracted more visitors than ever before. Railroad operators were thrilled. One even offered to run trains out to Garfield's farm, but neighbors who profited from ferrying visitors back and forth objected. *BosG*, 13 Aug. 1888, 6:79.
49. "Cleveland *lost* the election just as surely as Harrison won," H. Wayne Morgan contends. "Only a bold, personal campaign could have counteracted the brilliant Republican effort." Richard Jensen, however, finds the campaigns irrelevant. Party loyalty was stable; the voting patterns were the same as in 1886. Richard Jensen, *The Winning of the Midwest* (Chicago, 1971), p. 33. NYS, 13 Nov. 1888, p. 4; Morgan, *Hayes to McKinley*, p. 318.
50. Morgan, *Hayes to McKinley*, p. 319.
51. *Evening Post*, 12 Aug. 1892, clipping, Scrapbook, BH MSS; Lang, *Platt Autobiography*, p. 215; Jensen *Winning the Midwest*, p. 163; George Harmon Knoles, *The Presidential Campaign and Election of 1892* (Stanford, 1942), p. 44 n.56; *NYT*, 25 July 1892, p. 5.
52. Dorman B. Eaton, "The Perils of Reelecting Presidents," *NAR* 154 (June 1892):691; *NYT*, 13 July 1892, p. 4; *NYT*, 20 July 1892, p. 9; BH to Whitelaw Reid, 15 Aug. 1892, p. 2, Reid MSS.
53. *NYT*, 3 July 1892, p. 16.
54. BH, 3 Oct. 1892, quoted in R. A. Alger to J[ames] S. Clarkson, 6 Oct. 1892, in Clarkson MSS; *NYT*, 13 Sept. 1892, p. 9.

55. Ernest Samuels, ed., *The Education of Henry Adams* (Boston, 1973), p. 320; George F. Parker to GC, 22 Sept. 1892, p. 2, GC MSS.

56. GC quoted in Morgan, *From Hayes to McKinley,* p. 405.

57. Although the New York *World* claimed that it first suggested the idea, most people credited Whitney. *NYW,* 13 July 1892, p. 9.

58. GC to W[illia]m C. Whitney, 13 July 1892, p. 2, Whitney MSS; Vance in *New York Telegram,* 13 July 1892, clipping, Scrapbook, Whitney MSS.

59. Harrity quoted in *NYT,* 25 July 1892, p. 9; Harrity quoted in *NYH,* 25 July 1892, clipping, Scrapbook, Whitney MSS; *Indianapolis News* quoted in "The Notification Meeting," (n.p.) [Standard-Union], clipping, Scrapbook, BH MSS.

60. *Brooklyn Standard Union,* 21 July 1892, *Washington* (D.C.) *Sentinel,* 23 July 1892, both clippings, Scrapbooks, Whitney MSS; (n.p.) *Commercial Advertiser,* 21 July 1892, clipping, Scrapbook, BH MSS; Murat Halstead, "Is Whitney a Great General and Cleveland a Great Man?" *Brooklyn Standard Union,* n.d., clipping, Scrapbook, Whitney MSS.

61. *Brooklyn Standard Union,* 21 July 1892, *NYTr* quoted in *Saginaw* (MI) *Courier Herald,* 21 July 1892, "That Official Notification," *Cleveland Leader,* n.d., *New Haven Palladium,* 22 July 1892, all clippings, Scrapbook, Whitney MSS.

62. W[illia]m C. Whitney to GC, 9 Aug. 1892, pp. 2, 4, GC MSS; Whitney to GC, 30 Aug. 1892, p. 2, Whitney MSS; Whitney to GC, 10 July 1892, p. 4, GC MSS.

63. *Life,* 10 Nov. 1892, p. 262, in Morgan, *Hayes to McKinley,* p. 427; *NYH,* 26 Oct. 1892, p. 10; G. G. Vest, William L. Wilson, in Quay, "Man, or Platform?" pp. 517, 529.

64. B. L. Wade to GC, 21 Sept, 1892, F. H. Busbee to GC, 23 Sept. 1892, GC to R. W. Gilder, 25 Sept. 1892, p. 5, all in GC MSS.

65. Lodge, Wall, quoted in Stanley L. Jones, *The Presidential Election of 1896* (Madison, 1964), pp. 293, 338; J[ohn] H[ay] to [Whitelaw] Reid, 31 Aug. [18]96, p. 1, Reid MSS.

66. *NYT,* 27 July 1896, p. 5; [Whitelaw Reid] to Mr. Brown, 1 Sept. 1896, p. 1, Reid MSS.

67. Gilbert C. Fite, "Election of 1896," Schlesinger, *History of Elections,* 2:1808–1810; *Nat,* 5 Nov. 1896, p. 337.

68. William Jennings Bryan and Mary Baird Bryan, *The Memoirs of William Jennings Bryan* (Chicago, 1925), p. 263.

69. James K. Jones to W[illiam] J. Bryan, 21 July [1896], in Bryan MSS; Hill quoted in Morgan, *Hayes to McKinley,* p. 511; Bryan quoted in *NYT,* 30 Sept. 1896, p. 3.

70. *NYT,* 3 Nov. 1896, p. 4; *NYT,* 21 July 1896, p. 3.

71. *NYT,* 14 Aug. 1896, p. 4; William J. Bryan, *The First Battle* (Chicago, 1896), p. 299.

72. Paxton Hibben, *The Peerless Leader: William Jennings Bryan* (New York, 1967), p. 198; *SLPD,* 3 Nov. 1896, p. 4. See Bryan, *First Battle,* p. 619.

73. *LouCJ,* 21 Sept. 1896, p. 4; Paolo E. Coletta, *William Jennings Bryan,* 3 vols. (Lincoln, 1964–1969) 1:204–205.

74. John Hay to [Whitelaw] Reid, 23 Sept. [18]96, Reid MSS; *NYT,* 29 Oct. 1896, p. 4; *BalS,* 22 Sept. 1896, p. 4; *NOP,* 1 Nov. 1896, p. 4; *NYT,* 25 Sept. 1896, p. 4.

75. McKinley "didn't like to be called a politician," Dick added, "but he was ready to resent it if somebody said he wasn't a politician." McKinley's political acumen was underestimated because of his reliance on Mark Hanna and his own pretensions to statesmanship. "Dictated Statement of Senator Charles Dick, of Akron, Ohio," 10

Feb. 1906, p. 19, Hanna–McCormick MSS. Reed in James McGurrin, *Bourke Cockran* (New York, 1948), p. 147.

76. The ease with which the money was collected and the ultimate sum were exaggerated. After the election, Bryan asked the Republican Charles Dawes, "How much did you fellows spend to beat me?" Dawes replied: "We spent $3,562,325.59." Bryan was amazed: "Why, Tom Lawson told me he saw Pierpont Morgan give Hanna a check for five million dollars." Bascom N. Timmons, *Portrait of an American: Charles G. Dawes* (New York, 1953), p. 63. Hanna quoted in Paul W. Glad, *McKinley, Bryan, and the People* (Philadelphia, 1964), p. 195.

77. McKinley was right. When Bryan was offered a private Pullman car, a supporter objected. "You are the great commoner, the people's candidate, and it would not do to accept favors from the great railroad corporations." The name stuck; the policy did not. By October, Bryan had a private railroad car, inaptly named "The Idler." It was, however, a day coach, not a more comfortable and elitist Pullman. Coletta, *Bryan*, 1:152. Timmons, *Dawes*, pp. 40, 56; Morgan, *Hayes to McKinley*, p. 516.

78. Champ Clark, *My Quarter Century of American Politics*, 2 vols. (New York, 1920), 1:428. See also "Statement of Dick," pp. 23–25.

79. Bryan, too, was overwhelmed with gifts. Francis B. Loomis to Whitelaw Reid, 29 Oct. 1896, p. 2, Reid MSS; Morgan, *Hayes to McKinley*, p. 517; Timmons, *Dawes*, pp. 59–60.

80. [Whitelaw Reid] to Francis B. Loomis, 26 Aug. 1896, p. 1, in Reid MSS; SLPD, 3 Nov. 1896, p. 4.

81. TR quoted in Margaret Leech, *In the Days of McKinley* (New York, 1959), p. 69.

CHAPTER SIX. *The "Old-Fashioned" Campaign Trail*

1. Bryan set the stage, while Taft and Wilson echoed Roosevelt, though often unconsciously or unwillingly.

2. McKinley in Marvin Weisbord, *Campaigning for President* (Washington, D.C., 1964), p. 78; *Boston Herald* in "The Importance of the Ohio Elections," *Public Opinion* 27 (26 Oct. 1899):519.

3. J. Rogers Hollingsworth, *The Whirligig of Politics* (Chicago, 1963), pp. 178–179.

4. OSJ, [7 Nov. 1900], clipping, Scrapbook, 8:92, McKinley MSS.

5. Henry Cabot Lodge to TR, 29 June 1900, in Henry Cabot Lodge, ed., *Selections from the Correspondence of Theodore Roosevelt and Henry Cabot Lodge*, 2 vols. (New York, 1925), 1:467; Edmund Morris, *The Rise of Theodore Roosevelt* (New York, 1979), p. 724.

6. TR to Mark Hanna, 25 June 1900, *TR-Lett*, 2:1339–1340; Louis J. Lang, ed., *The Autobiography of Thomas Collier Platt* (New York, 1910), p. 396; TR Speech, 8 Oct. 1900, in *NYT*, 9 Oct. 1900, p. 3; Mr. Dooley in Morris, *Rise of TR*, p. 731.

7. Kenneth Cmiel, *Democratic Eloquence* (New York, 1990), pp. 248–250; "President William McKinley," 21 June 1900, n.p., *Brooklyn Daily Eagle*, 3 Nov. 1900, both clippings, Scrapbooks, 6:61, 8:74, McKinley MSS; *NYH*, 22 July 1900, 4:1.

8. *NYT*, 25 Oct. 1900, p. 6.

9. *SLPD*, 6 Nov. 1900, p. 6. See for example *NYT*, 7 Oct. 1900, p. 2.

10. TR to Cecil Arthur Spring Rice, 19 Nov. 1900, *TR-Lett*, 2:1423; *New Orleans Times-Democrat*, reprinted in "Cartoons of the Month," *RoR* 22 (Aug. 1900):160; Paolo E. Coletta, *William Jennings Bryan*, 3 vols. (Lincoln, 1964–1969), 1:278.

11. McKinley was born in 1843, Roosevelt in 1858, and Bryan in 1860. Roosevelt would be the first postbellum Republican president not to have fought in the Civil War.

12. John Hay to [Whitelaw Reid], 22 July 1902, p. 1, Reid MSS.

13. Root in James Ford Rhodes, *The McKinley and Roosevelt Administrations* (New York, 1922), p. 292; Robert H. Wiebe, *The Search for Order* (New York, 1967), p. xiii.

14. John Morton Blum, *The Republican Roosevelt* (Cambridge, 1954; reprint ed., New York, 1962), p. 63; TR in Paul George Goodwin, "Theodore Roosevelt: The Politics of His Candidacy, 1904, 1912," (Ph.D. diss., Syracuse University, 1961), p. 170.

15. William Allen White, *Masks in a Pageant* (New York, 1928), pp. 313–314.

16. TR to Kermit Roosevelt, 26 Oct. 1904, *TR-Lett*, 4:993.

17. *RNC 1904*, pp. 11–22, 143–151, 157–160; *The Campaign Text Book of the Democratic Party of the United States, 1904* (New York, 1904), pp. 22, 31–32, 48, 50–52, 40.

18. In a 12,000-word acceptance letter, Roosevelt mentioned Congress only four times, totaling less than one hundred words. This ratio of "one hundred and twenty to one is about the President's estimate of his own performance as compared with that of the people's representatives," the *New York Times* remarked, attesting to the controversy surrounding Roosevelt's expansion of the presidency. *NYT*, 14 Sept. 1904, p. 8. TR to Henry Cabot Lodge, 25 June 1904, Henry Cabot Lodge to TR, 29 June 1904, both in *Roosevelt and Lodge*, 2:84, 86; TR to George Bruce Cortelyou, 1 Oct. 1904, *TR-Lett*, 4:964. See also Boxes 34, 35 in Cortelyou MSS.

19. J. J. Dickinson, "Theodore Roosevelt: Press-Agent, And What His Newspaper 'Cuckoos' Have Done for Him," *HarpW*, 28 Sept. 1907, p. 1410. See also George Juergens, *News from the White House* (Chicago, 1981), pp. 5–9, 267–268.

20. [Whitelaw Reid] to [Donald] Nicholson, 16 July 1904, in Reid MSS.

21. See Henry Laurent, *Personality: How to Build It*, quoted in Warren Susman, *Culture as History* (New York, 1984), p. 277.

22. TR to K. Roosevelt, 26 Oct. 1904, 4:993; Oswald Garrison Villard, *Fighting Years* (New York, 1939), pp. 178–181.

23. In 1912 Oswald G. Villard charged that Roosevelt made peace with leading industrialists during a secret 7 A.M. White House meeting in 1904. Agreeing to restrain his antitrust crusade, the President asked for at least a quarter of a million dollars. Years later, the steel man Henry Clay Frick bitterly recalled Theodore Roosevelt's empty promises: "He got down on his knees to us. We bought the son of a bitch and he did not stay bought." The records of the 1912 Senate commission investigating contributions refer occasionally to a White House "luncheon or dinner" involving Frick and the industrialist Hamilton McK. Twombly, among others, in exchange for campaign contributions. This "Clapp commission," and the 1905 investigation of life-insurance companies in New York State, documented many examples of contributions ranging from $25,000 to $50,000 to the Republican campaign. Roosevelt denied the charges: "I asked no man to contribute to the campaign fund when I was elected President of the United States," he testified. Villard, *Fighting Years*, pp. 178–181; U.S., Congress, Senate, *Testimony Before a Subcommittee of the Committee on Privileges and Elections, pursuant to S. Res. 79*, 62nd Cong., 2nd sess., 1912, 1:488, 614, 899–900.

24. This unprecedented involvement in fund-raising by a candidate highlighted one benefit of the republican taboo. Insulation from organizational activities protected the candidate from impropriety. Involvement in these often disreputable enterprises further degraded both the candidate and the presidency.

25. Amelia Campbell Parker, "Alton Brooks Parker," pp. 13, 17, ABP MSS.

26. NYS, 6 July 1904, clipping, Scrapbook, vol. 23, ABP MSS; NYT, 16 July 1904, p. 2; NYS, 27 July 1904, p. 4.

27. AlAr, 27 Mar. 1840, p. 4.

28. NYS, 11 July 1904, p. 4.

29. (n.p.) *Globe*, 8 Aug. 1904, clipping, Scrapbook, 24:86, ABP MSS; Hollingsworth, *Whirligig of Politics*, p. 230.

30. *Norfolk* (VA) *Landmark*, *Boston Advertiser*, quoted in (n.p.) *Globe*, 30 Aug. 1904, *Brooklyn Daily Eagle*, 24 Aug. 1904, both clippings, Scrapbook, 25:75, 39, ABP MSS.

31. [New York] *Evening Mail*, 22 Aug. 1904, NYTr, 15 Aug. 1904, *New York Press*, 30 July 1904, all clippings, Scrapbooks, 25:26, 24:134, 25, ABP MSS.

32. Only Calvin Coolidge in 1924 would avoid the stump completely. He took advantage of incumbency and his characteristic insouciance.

33. NYT, 10 Sept. 1904, p. 1; "The Progress of the World," *RoR* 30 (Nov. 1904):522.

34. SLPD, 1 Nov. 1904, p. 10.

35. ABP, "Notes for Memoirs," ABP MSS.

36. A. C. Parker, "A. B. Parker," p. 17; ABP, 31 Oct. 1904, in ABP, "Biographical Ex[c]erpts," p. 4, ABP MSS; (n.p.) *Globe*, 1 Nov. 1904, clipping, Scrapbook, 26:100, ABP MSS.

37. TR to George Bruce Cortelyou, 2 Nov. 1904, TR Letter, 4 Nov. 1904, both in *TR-Lett*, 4:1012, 7:606–607.

38. Will Irwin, ed., *Letters to Kermit from Theodore Roosevelt* (New York, 1946), pp. 84, 68.

39. TR to K. Roosevelt, 26 Oct. 1904, 4:993; Theodore Roosevelt, *An Autobiography* (New York, 1913; reprint ed., New York, 1985), p. 402.

40. TR to George Otto Trevelyan, 19 June 1908, in Rhodes, *McKinley and Roosevelt Administrations*, pp. 382–386.

41. A story circulated that Roosevelt demonstrated his "clairvoyant powers" to Mr. and Mrs. Taft. "I see a man before me weighing 350 pounds," Roosevelt predicted. "There is something hanging over his head. I cannot make out what it is. . . . At one time it looks like the presidency—then again, it looks like the chief justiceship." "Make it the presidency!" yelled Mrs. Taft. "Make it the chief justiceship!" her husband pleaded. Francis Russell, *The President Makers* (Boston, 1976), p. 87. Rhodes, *McKinley and Roosevelt Administrations*, p. 378; Lodge quoted in NYT, 19 June 1908; Henry F. Pringle, *The Life and Times of William Howard Taft*, 2 vols. (New York, 1939), 1:261, 264.

42. Judith Icke Anderson, *William Howard Taft: An Intimate History* (New York, 1981), p. 109; William Henry Harbaugh, *Power & Responsibility* (New York, 1961), p. 357; Pringle, *Taft*, 1:358.

43. NYT, 21 Aug. 1908, p. 3; Pringle, *Taft*, 1:358; Russell, *President Makers*, pp. 107–108.

44. William Jennings Bryan to Henry Watterson, 4 Aug. 1908, Watterson MSS.

45. NYT, 22 Sept. 1908, p. 3; Coletta, *Bryan*, 1:437–438.

46. George H. Mayer, *The Republican Party, 1854–1964* (New York, 1964), p. 304; *Nat*, 10 Sept. 1908, p. 223; *Washington Times*, 23 Aug. 1908, clipping, Scrapbook, 26:30, TR MSS.

47. NYT, 7 Sept. 1908, p. 3; *Nat*, 10 Sept. 1908, p. 223.

48. Coletta, *Bryan*, 1:417; *NYT*, 7 Sept. 1908, pp. 1–2.
49. On August 6, Taft was characteristically abstruse about the federal courts. He said: "While we may properly felicitate ourselves on this widened function of our courts, enabling us to avoid less peaceable methods of settling important politico–legal questions, have we the right to say that our present administration of justice generally insures continued popular satisfaction with its results?" Speech at Hot Springs, VA, 6 Aug. 1908, Speech at Athens, OH, 20 Aug. 1908, both in William H. Taft, *Political Issues and Outlooks* (New York, 1909), pp. 5, 36.
50. Henry Pringle, *Theodore Roosevelt*, rev. ed. (New York, 1956), p. 355; TR quoted in Lawrence F. Abbott, ed., *The Letters of Archie Butt* (Garden City, NY, 1924), pp. 143–144. On Dale Carnegie see Daniel J. Boorstin, *The Americans: The Democratic Experience* (New York, 1973), p. 469.
51. Jeffrey K. Tulis, *Rhetorical Presidency* (Princeton, 1987), p. 4; Speech at Newark, 19 Oct. 1908, Taft, *Political Issues*, pp. 188, 193; TR quoted in Abbott, *Butt Letters*, p. 144.
52. "William Howard Taft," *RNC 1908*, p. 18, passim.
53. Literary Bureau, Republican National Committee, "Mr. Taft on the Stump," n.d., clippings, Scrapbook, 15:96, 87, Taft MSS.
54. *SLPD*, 1 Nov. 1908, 3B.
55. *NYT*, 24 Sept. 1908, p. 2; "President Roosevelt's Masterly Tactics, n.p., 24 July 1908, clipping, Scrapbook, 25:172, TR MSS; Pringle, *TR*, p. 356; *NYH*, 26 Sept. 1908, clipping, Scrapbook, 26:59, TR MSS.
56. Henry Litchfield West, "The President and the Campaign," *The Forum* 40 (Nov. 1908):415.
57. William Manners, *TR and Will* (New York, 1969), p. 59; Letter of Archie Butt, 5 Nov. [1908], Abbott, *Butt Letters*, p. 153; Russell, *President Makers*, p. 104.
58. "Nominating Speech of Mr. Henry S. Boutell, of Illinois," *RNC 1908*, p. 144.
59. "To Make Issues of Men," clippings, Scrapbook, 15:155, Taft MSS; Dunne, *NYT*, 6 Nov. 1904, 3:1; Ostrogorski in *NYTM*, 12 July 1908, 5:7.
60. "A New Era in Political Campaigning," *National Magazine*, Sept. 1908, pp. 601, 605, in Hitchcock MSS; *NYT*, 12 Oct. 1908, p. 4.
61. *NYT*, 2 Oct. 1908, p. 8; *SLPD*, 8 Nov. 1904, p. 10.
62. *Nat*, 15 Feb. 1912, p. 150.
63. TR, "What a Progressive Is," Address at Louisville, KY, 3 Apr. 1912, in Elmer H. Youngman, ed., *Progressive Principles by Theodore Roosevelt* (New York, 1913), p. 6.
64. La Follette, Child, in Edward R. Lewis, *A History of American Political Thought* (New York, 1937), pp. 448–449, 489; Arthur George Sedgwick, *The Democratic Mistake* (New York, 1912), p. 91.
65. TR, "The Right of the People to Rule," Address at New York, 20 Mar. 1912, Youngman, *Progressive Principles*, p. 19.
66. *Harper's Weekly* claimed that Roosevelt's "Hate, not hat, is in the ring." TR, *HarpW*, in William Safire, *Safire's Political Dictionary*, rev. ed. (New York, 1978), p. 293. *NYT*, 17 Mar. 1912, p. 12; Taft in John Milton Cooper, Jr., *The Warrior and the Priest* (Cambridge, 1983), p. 156.
67. TR, "What a Progressive Is," p. 6; Cooper, *Warrior and Priest*, p. 157; *NYT*, 24 May 1912, pp. 1–2.
68. *NYT*, 28 Apr. 1912, p. 16; *WasP*, 28 Apr. 1912, p. 4.
69. *Philadelphia American*, 9 Apr. 1912, clipping, Scrapbook, WW MSS.

70. W. H. Taft to Helen H. Taft, 22 July 1908, Pringle, *Taft*, 2:817.

71. *NYT*, 14 July 1912, 2:2; Pringle, *Taft*, 2:823, 818, 834.

72. Republican National Committee, "The Real Taft," Taft Broadsides, Proof, [1912], Hilles MSS.

73. *Trenton* (NJ) *Evening Times*, 22 Oct. 1912, *WW-Link*, 25:451; Ray Stannard Baker, *Woodrow Wilson: Life and Letters*, vol. 3: *Governor, 1910–1913* (Garden City, NY, 1931), p. 374; *NYT*, 4 Aug. 1912, p. 5; "Men Pygmies as Compared with Issues in This Campaign," Circular, Woolley MSS.

74. *NYT*, 19 May 1912, 6:5.

75. WW to Mary Allen Hulbert, 1 Sept. 1912, WW to Henry Beach, 24 Aug. 1912, both in *WW-Link*, 25:67, 54.

76. Wilson's pallid image helped quiet rumors about an adulterous affair he may have had with Mrs. Mary Allen Hulbert. Roosevelt scoffed that some allegedly incriminating letters "would be entirely unconvincing. Nothing, no evidence, would ever make the American people believe that a man like Woodrow Wilson, cast so perfectly as the apothecary's clerk, could ever play Romeo!" TR in Manners, *TR and Will*, p. 278. WW to Mary Allen Hulbert, 25 Aug. 1912, Frank K. Kelley, *The Fight for the White House* (New York, 1961), p. 215; Robert Woolley, Autobiography, "Politics Is Hell," chap. 24, p. 16, Woolley MSS.

77. Josephus Daniels, *The Life of Woodrow Wilson, 1856–1924* (Philadelphia, 1924), pp. 118–119.

78. Elmer E. Cornwell, Jr., *Presidential Leadership of Public Opinion* (Bloomington, 1965; reprint ed., Westport, Ct, 1979), p. 34; WW to Mary Allen Hulbert, 17 Aug. 1912, 25 Aug. 1912, both in *WW-Link*, 25:46, 55.

79. Baker, *Wilson: Governor*, 3:369; John M. Blum, *Joe Tumulty and the Wilson Era* (Boston, 1951), p. 47.

80. Cornwell, *Presidential Leadership*, p. 35; Robert W. Woolley, "Putting A Candidate Over," [1924?], p. 4, Woolley MSS.

81. *HarpW*, 14 Sept. 1912, p. 4.

82. "Remarks from the Rear Platform in Union City, Indiana," 16 Sept. 1912, in *WW-Link*, 25:148.

83. *SLPD*, 8 Nov. 1904, p. 10; *NYT*, 26 Oct. 1912, p. 10.

84. "Remarks in Michigan City, Indiana, from a Rear Platform," 19 Sept. 1912, in *WW-Link*, 25:184.

85. "Ridiculous Campaigning," n.p., 9 Oct. 1912, clipping, Scrapbook, WW MSS.

86. Baker, *Wilson: Governor*, 3:375; *NYT*, 8 Oct. 1912, p. 12.

87. "The Secret of Wilson's Leadership," n.p., 14 Oct. [1912], clipping, Scrapbook, WW MSS; William H. Richardson, *Theodore Roosevelt: One Day of His Life* (Jersey City, 1921), p. 26.

88. Cooper, *Warrior and Priest*, pp. 191, 195, 196.

89. TR to E. R. Grey, 15 Nov. 1912, *TR-Lett*, 7:649.

90. The split in Republican ranks was the true key to Wilson's victory. *NYT*, 1 Nov. 1912, quoted in Baker, *Wilson: Governor*, 3:404; William G. McAdoo, *Crowded Years* (Boston, 1931), p. 170.

91. *NYT*, 14 July 1912, 5:6; *NYT*, 19 May 1912, 6:5; *Nat*, 15 Feb. 1912, p. 150.

CHAPTER SEVEN. *Reluctant Runners, 1916–1928*

1. Walter Lippmann, *Drift and Mastery* (New York, 1914), pp. 152, 211, 153, 326.

2. Woodrow Wilson, *Constitutional Government in the United States* (New York, 1908; paperback ed., 1961), p. 68; Alfred McClung Lee, *The Daily Newspaper in America* (New York, 1937), pp. 66, 323.

3. Homer Cummings, "Memorandum," 7 Aug. 1916, in *WW-Link*, 38:8.

4. This reluctance to campaign disproves the claim that Wilson was the founder of the modern presidential campaign. See James W. Ceaser et al., "The Rise of the Rhetorical Presidency," chap. 18 in Thomas E. Cronin, ed., *Rethinking the Presidency* (Boston, 1982), p. 243. PConf, 29 Sept. 1916, in *WW-Link*, 38:287.

5. WW to J. Campbell Cantrill, quoted in *NYT*, 5 Aug. 1916, p. 4.

6. PConf, 29 Sept. 1916, in *WW-Link*, 38:289, 288.

7. Edward M. House, *The Intimate Papers of Colonel House*, Charles Seymour, ed., 4 vols. (Boston, 1926–1928), 2:353, 357–358.

8. The growth of specialization and the spread of leisure and informality, though seemingly contradictory, were very much related, according to Kenneth Cmiel in *Democratic Eloquence* (New York, 1990), p. 251. On advertising see Stephen Fox, *The Mirror Makers* (New York, 1984), chap. 1 and 2 passim.

9. [Robert W. Woolley] to E. M. House, 6 Sept. 1916, p. 2, Woolley MSS.

10. Vachel Lindsay in Warren I. Susman, *Culture as History* (New York, 1984), p. 109; Talcott Williams in Edward M. Sait, *American Parties and Elections* (New York, 1927), p. 492.

11. CEH in Seymour, *House*, 2:345; *Charleston News and Courier* quoted in "Effect of Hughes's Candidacy on the Supreme Court," *Current Opinion*, July 1916, p. 4.

12. [George Harvey], "'Vox Populi,' On the Eve of the National Conventions," *NAR* 203 (June 1916): 801; Beerits Memoranda, "The Presidential Campaign of 1916," pp. 7, 9, CEH to William R. Day, Bridgehampton, 7 July [19]16, both in CEH MSS.

13. TR in S. D. Lovell, *Presidential Election of 1916* (Carbondale, 1980), p. 124; CEH in *ChiT*, 9 Aug. 1916, p. 1; Frederick M. Davenport, "Across the Continent with Hughes," *Out*, 13 Sept. 1916, p. 88; "Mr. Hughes and His Campaign," *Out*, 16 Aug. 1916, p. 881; Howard D. Hadley, "Coast to Coast Campaign with Hughes," Galley Proofs, p. 2, in CEH MSS.

14. *NYT*, 14 Sept. 1916, p. 1; Davenport, "Across the Continent with Hughes," p. 91; *New York Evening Post* correspondent in Jacob Gould Schurman, "Mr. Hughes's Trip," *Ind*, 4 Sept. 1916, p. 342.

15. Frederic H. Parkhurst to CEH, 21 Sept. 1916, pp. 2–3, in CEH MSS.

16. *NYTM*, 27 Aug. 1916, 5:13; *NYT*, 21 Aug. 1916, p. 10.

17. F. A. Vanderlip et al. to CEH, 18 Oct. 1916, pp. 1–2, CEH MSS.

18. William Allen White to TR, 27 Dec. 1916, in Walter Johnson, *William Allen White's America* (New York, 1947), p. 173; Woolley to House, 6 Sept. 1916, p. 1.

19. CEH in *ChiT*, 9 Aug. 1916, p. 1; *Nat*, 19 Oct. 1916, p. 367.

20. PConf, 29 Sept. 1916, *WW-Link*, 38:292; Seymour, *House*, 2: 377; William J. Stone to Joseph P. Tumulty, 1 Oct. 1916, in *WW-Link*, 38:318.

21. WW Telegram, 29 Sept. 1916, in *WW-Link*, 38:286.

22. PConf, 29 Sept. 1916, *WW-Link*, 38:293; *NYT*, 5 Oct. 1916, p. 1.

23. *WW-Link*, 38: 475, 302.

24. CEH, "Autobiographical Notes," "1916," pp. 233–234, 236, CEH MSS.

25. Randolph C. Downes, *The Rise of Warren Gamaliel Harding, 1865–1920* ([Columbus], 1970), p. 248.

26. "A Close Season," *TNR*, 1 Sept. 1920, pp. 5–6; Bertrand Russell, *Free Thought and Official Propaganda* (New York, 1922), p. 37.

27. "Money to Nominate," *TNR*, 14 Apr. 1920, p. 198; Richard Boeckel, "The Man With the Best Story Wins," *Ind*, 22 May 1920, pp. 245, 244.
28. Francis Russell, *Shadow of Blooming Grove: Warren G. Harding in His Times* (New York, 1968), p. 383; *NYT*, 19 July 1920, p. 2.
29. *NYT*, 28 July 1920, p. 1; Herbert Parsons to Will H. Hays, 15 June 1920, Hays MSS.
30. Will H. Hays to Mrs. Leonard G. Woods, 23 June 1920, Robert G. Tucker to Will H. Hays, 14 June [1920], pp. 2, 4, both in Hays MSS.
31. Will H. Hays, *Memoirs of Will H. Hays* (Garden City, NY, 1955), p. 255; Robert K. Murray, *Harding Era* (Minneapolis, 1969), p. 50.
32. Lodge and Penrose quoted in Downes, *Rise of Harding*, p. 428; *NYT*, 19 July 1920, p. 2.
33. Lasker in Downes, *Rise of Harding*, pp. 472, 491.
34. Roger Lewis, "The Two Ohio Editors Again," *Col*, 16 Oct. 1920, p. 6.
35. *NYT*, 11 July 1920, p. 1; Wesley M. Bagby, *The Road to Normalcy* (Baltimore, 1962), p. 131.
36. Lewis, "Two Editors," p. 5; Franklin K. Lane to James M. Cox, 25 July 1920, pp. 1–2, Cox MSS; *ChiT*, 21 Oct. 1920, p. 8.
37. James M. Cox, "The Way to Peace and Progress," *Ind*, 2 Oct. 1920, p. 28; FDR quoted in *NYT*, 21 July 1920, p. 5.
38. Richard Washburn Child to Will Hays, 2 Sept. 1920, pp. 1–2, 8 Sept. 1920, p. 1, both in Hays MSS.
39. *NYT*, 19 July 1920, p. 2; Murray, *Harding Era*, p. 53.
40. *NYT*, 8 Sept. 1920, p. 10.
41. Marvin Weisbord, *Campaigning for President* (Washington, D.C., 1964), p. 27.
42. Oswald Garrison Villard, *Fighting Years* (New York, 1939), p. 474; William Allen White, *Puritan in Babylon* (New York, 1938), p. v.
43. Donald R. McCoy, *Calvin Coolidge, the Quiet President* (New York, 1967), p. 255; Calvin Coolidge, *The Autobiography of Calvin Coolidge* (New York, 1929), pp. 190, 189.
44. "Coolidge," *Nat*, 18 June 1924, p. 696.
45. Edward L. Bernays, *Propaganda* (New York, 1928), p. 9.
46. [Edward T.] Clark to M[atthew] C. Bush, 4 Apr. 1924, Clark MSS.
47. Daniel J. Boorstin, *The Americans: The Democratic Experience* (New York, 1973), p. 467; "Three Essentials of Good Copy," clipping, 27 Nov. 1924, [BB] to Frank W. Stearns, 19 May 1924, both in BB MSS.
48. Not everyone was that welcoming. When a microphone was thrust in front of the Republican war-horse Elihu Root, he cried: "Take that away. I can talk to a Democrat, but I cannot speak into a dead thing." Elihu Root in *NYT*, 4 Oct. 1936, 4:8. Gleason L. Archer, *History of Radio to 1926* (New York, 1938), p. 3; George Baker in Edward W. Chester, *Radio, Television and American Politics* (New York, 1969), p. 283.
49. Daniel J. Czitrom, *Media and the American Mind* (Chapel Hill, 1982), p. 187. See also John F. Kasson, *Civilizing the Machine* (New York, 1977), pp. vii, 233.
50. BB to George Barr Baker, 7 July 1924, p. 2, BB MSS.
51. [Edward T. Clark] to William N. Butler, 18 Apr. 1924, Clark MSS.
52. Mencken quoted in McCoy, *Coolidge*, p. 260.
53. John W. Davis to John L. Shuff, 4 Aug. 1924, in Davis MSS; Robert Woolley, "Autobiography," chap. 45, p. 12, Woolley MSS.

54. "Some Points to Consider in Making Plan of Battle," p. 2, in Box 146, Davis MSS; Woolley, "Autiobiography," 45:15. For complaint see *New York Telegram and Mail*, 14 Aug. 1924, clipping, Davis MSS.

55. Pittman in "Bad Breaks May Hurt Davis," clipping, Davis MSS; William N. Butler to E[dward] T. Clark, 26 July 1924, Clark MSS; John Hiram McKee, *Coolidge, Wit & Wisdom* (New York, 1933), p. 43.

56. See "Sport Is Elected," *Nat*, 17 Sept. 1924, p. 278.

57. Arthur M. Schlesinger and Eric McKinley Erikkson, "The Vanishing Voter," *TNR*, 15 Oct. 1924, p. 162.

58. Samuel G. Blythe, "Why Not Pick a Good One?" *SatEP*, 24 Dec. 1927, p. 6.

59. Joan Hoff Wilson, *Herbert Hoover: Forgotten Progressive* (Boston, 1975), pp. 121, 79; Herbert Hoover, *The Memoirs of Herbert Hoover*, 3 vols. (New York, 1951-1952), 2:198, 197.

60. *NYT*, 22 June 1928, p. 22; [BB] to Merle Thorpe, 18 June 1928, p. 2, BB MSS; *NYT*, 2 Aug. 1928, p. 20; William Allen White, "The Education of Herbert Hoover," *Col*, 9 June 1928, p. 45.

61. Bernard M. Baruch, *Baruch: the Public Years* (New York, 1960), pp. 211-212.

62. Alfred E. Smith, *Up to Now* (New York, 1929), p. 384; Richard O'Connor, *The First Hurrah* (New York, 1970), p. 206; Geoffrey Perrett, *America in the Twenties* (New York, 1982), p. 313.

63. Alfred E. Smith, Draft of "Electioneering 'Old and New'," *SatEP* [1930], pp. 1, 18, Alfred E. Smith, "The Lighter Side of Electioneering," *SatEP*, original mss. p. 2, both in Smith MSS; John K. Winkler, "Al Smith Tells How He Gets a Crowd," *Col*, 31 Oct. 1925, p. 20.

64. *NYT*, 14 Oct. 1928, 11:1; Smith, "Lighter Side," pp. 4, 2; Smith, *Up to Now*, p. 395.

65. Ray T. Tucker, "The Personalities Have It," *Outlook and Independent*, 7 Nov. 1928, p. 1123; *NYT*, 16 Sept. 1928, p. 3; *NYT*, 29 Sept. 1928, p. 18.

66. David Burner, *Herbert Hoover, A Public Life* (New York, 1978), p. 204.

67. "Catholic and Patriot: Governor Smith Replies," *AtMo*, May 1927, p. 722. See also Charles C. Marshall, "An Open Letter to the Honorable Alfred E. Smith," *AtMo*, Apr. 1927, pp. 540-549.

68. Edmund A. Moore, *A Catholic Runs for President* (New York, 1956), pp. 179-182.

69. Ibid., pp. 179, 186; "Static," *SatEP*, 27 Oct. 1928, p. 28.

70. Samuel G. Blythe, "Alarums and Excursions," *SatEP*, 20 Oct. 1928, p. 33.

71. *NYT*, 16 Sept. 1928, 12:4; "Radio 'Debunking' the Campaigns," *LitD*, 1 Dec. 1928, p. 13. For Smith see *NYT*, 8 July 1928, 9:12.

72. *NYT*, 19 Aug. 1928, 8:13.

73. Smith, *Up to Now*, pp. 391-392.

74. Tucker, "The Personalities Have It," p. 1141.

75. Ibid., p. 1123.

76. *NYT*, 22 Oct. 1928, p. 7; "Governor Smith's Speech at Madison Square Garden, New York City, on Saturday Night, November 3rd, 1928," p. 1, Smith MSS; *NYW* quoted in *LouCJ*, 4 Nov. 1928, p. 4.

77. *ChiT*, 24 Oct. 1928, p. 12; Katharine Dayton, "What's The Matter With Hoover?" *SatEP*, 11 Aug. 1928, p. 102.

78. PConf, 29 Sept. 1916, *WW-Link*, 38:286.

79. Hoover, *Memoirs*, 2:199; John W. Davis to A. Mitchell Palmer, 29 Sept. 1924, Davis MSS.

80. CEH, "Additiona[l]," "Speeches, Methods," pp. 4–5, CEH MSS; William Safire, *Safire's Political Dictionary*, rev. ed. (New York, 1978), p. 350.

81. Smith, "The Lighter Side of Electioneering," p. 4; Boorstin, *Democratic Experience*, p. 472.

82. [Edward T. Clark] to F. Stuart Crawford, 30 July 1928, in Clark MSS; Ernest Hamlin Abbott, "A Contest of Personalities," *Out*, 24 Oct. 1928, p. 1013.

CHAPTER EIGHT. *The President as Campaigner*

1. *NYT*, 21 Oct. 1936, p. 26.

2. Edward W. Chester, *Radio, Television and American Politics* (New York, 1969), p. 46; "Campaign Paradox," *LitD*, 21 Nov. 1936, p. 8; Raymond Gram Swing, "Will Radio Kill Democracy?" *Vital Speeches of the Day*, 15 Aug. 1936, p. 723.

3. *NYT*, 19 June 1932, p. 1; *NYT*, 13 July 1932, p. 4.

4. BB to Lawrence Richey, 21 Jan. 1932, BB MSS.

5. "Acceptance Address of Governor Franklin D. Roosevelt, Nominee for President of the United States," *DNC 1932*, pp. 375, 383.

6. Ibid., p. 376.

7. U.S. Air Services, Aug. 1932, Buffalo, NY, pp. 17–18, clipping, FDR Personal Book, Vol. 2, Scrapbook 12–2, FDR-Gov; Lela Stiles, *The Man Behind Roosevelt* (Cleveland, 1954), p. 191; "Roosevelt Air Dash Typical, Daniels Avers," *Washington Herald*, FDR Personal Convention Book, Scrapbook 12–4, FDR-Gov; Samuel I. Rosenman, *Working with Roosevelt* (New York, 1952), p. 74.

8. R. G. Tugwell, *The Brains Trust* (New York, 1968), p. 347.

9. James A. Farley, *Behind the Ballots* (New York, 1938), pp. 163–164; Entry, 29 July 1932, p. 49, Cummings Diaries; Tugwell, *Brains Trust*, p. 279.

10. Experiments at Harvard revealed near "uniformity of opinion regarding the personality of a radio speaker" from the sound of his voice. Hadley Cantril and Gordon W. Allport, *The Psychology of Radio*, 2nd ed. (New York, 1935), pp. 109, 121–125. Frank Freidel, *Franklin D. Roosevelt: The Triumph* (Boston, 1956), p. 182.

11. G. W. Davis to FDR, 27 Sept. 1944, Box 122, FDR-PPF 200B.

12. FDR Speech in *NYT*, 31 July 1932, p. 2.

13. Flamboyant radio speakers like Huey Long, Adolph Hitler, and Father Coughlin proved that Roosevelt's "cool" style was not the only path to radio success. Still, all cultivated the "human" touch. Charles Coughlin quoted in Alan Brinkley, *Voices of Protest* (New York, 1982), p. 97; Charles W. Smith, Jr., *Public Opinion in a Democracy* (New York, 1939), p. 98.

14. Stiles, *Man Behind Roosevelt*, p. 166; Sidney M. Milkis, "Franklin D. Roosevelt and the Transcendence of Partisan Politics," *PSQ* 100 (Fall 1985):479–504. See also Box 54 in Howe MSS.

15. *NYT*, 12 Sept. 1932, p. 2; FDR Speech in Los Angeles, *NYT*, 25 Sept. 1932, p. 32; Eleanor Roosevelt, *This I Remember* (New York, 1949), p. 72; *Brooklyn Daily Eagle*, 25 Sept. 1932, clipping, Scrapbook 12–5, FDR-Gov.

16. FDR in *SLPD*, 1 Nov. 1932, 2B; Paul Y. Anderson, "Mourning Becomes Herbert," *Nat*, 29 Sept. 1932, p. 281; *NYS*, 9 July 1932, p. 10.

17. Clark quoted in Gene Smith, *The Shattered Dream* (New York, 1970), p. 190; "President Herbert Hoover's Address of Acceptance," *RNC 1932*, p. 261; *New York [?] Post*, 12 Aug. 1932, clipping, Smith MSS.

18. *NYT*, 16 Sept. 1932, p. 2; *SLPD*, 21 Sept. 1932, 2C.

19. Hoover Speech in *SLPD*, 5 Oct. 1932, 1C; *DenP*, 5 Oct. 1932, p. 2; *SLPD*, 6 Oct. 1932, p. 1.

20. Hoover quoted in *Cleveland Press*, 29 Oct. 1932, pp. 1–2.

21. *SFX*, 1 Nov. 1932, p. 1; *SLPD*, 2 Nov. 1932, 2B.

22. David G. Clark, "Radio in Presidential Campaigns: The Early Years, 1924–1932," *Journal of Broadcasting* 6 (Summer 1962):236–237; "The Fortune Quarterly Survey: IV," *Fortune*, Apr. 1936, p. 104.

23. "Candidates on the Stump," *SatEP*, 26 Nov. 1932, p. 20; *Los Angeles Evening Herald and Express*, 1 Nov. 1932, clipping, FDR Scrapbook 1932, 12–50, FDR-Gov.

24. A survey in June 1949 concluded that Americans, "in reacting to a national leader, put great emphasis on his personal warmth." Of the respondents who considered Roosevelt a good leader, 37.3 percent pointed to some personal characteristic; 19.5 percent specifically mentioned a "warm" trait. Fillmore Sanford, "Public Orientation to Roosevelt," *POQ* 15 (Summer 1951):198, 192–193. Walter Lippmann in *NYHTr*, 7 Oct. 1932, p. 21.

25. Farley, *Behind the Ballots*, pp. 317–318.

26. On origin of "Fireside Chats" see Robert West, *The Rape of Radio* (New York, 1941), pp. 421–422. See also Graham J. White, *FDR and the Press* (Chicago, 1979).

27. On radio's often paradoxical impact see Brinkley, *Voices of Protest*, p. 159. Clinton Rossiter, *The American Presidency*, 2nd ed. (New York, 1960), pp. 42–43; Mrs. Leon M. Aldrich to FDR, 29 Sept. 1944, p. 2, Box 122, FDR-PPF, 200B.

28. Robert Westbrook, "Politics as Consumption," chap. 5 in Richard Wightman Fox and T. J. Jackson Lears, *Culture of Consumption* (New York, 1983), pp. 148–149; Kristi Anderson, *Creation of a Democratic Majority* (Chicago, 1979), p. 82; James MacGregor Burns, *Roosevelt: The Lion and the Fox* (New York, 1956), pp. 198–199.

29. Raymond Moley, *After Seven Years* (New York, 1939), p. 342; Arthur M. Schlesinger, Jr., *Age of Roosevelt: The Politics of Upheaval* (Boston, 1960), 3:574; Milkis, "FDR and Partisan Politics," p. 487; PConf #301, 16 June 1936, FDR-press 7:285.

30. FDR to Josephus Daniels, 19 July 1936, in Elliott Roosevelt, ed., *FDR: His Personal Letters, 1928–1945* (New York, 1950), 1:604; Rosenman, *Working with Roosevelt*, p. 107; James A. Farley, *Jim Farley's Story* (New York, 1948), pp. 61–62.

31. PConf #306, 7 July 1936, PConf #312, 4 Aug. 1936, PConf #313, 7 Aug. 1936, 8:9, 48, 56, FDR-press.

32. Raymond Clapper in *Washington Daily News*, 13 Aug. 1936, p. 2, Scrapbook, p. 62, Early MSS; *LAT*, 3 Aug. 1936, p. 4; *NYT*, 4 Oct. 1936, 4:3; *SLPD*, 18 Sept. 1936, 1D.

33. *SFX*, 15 Sept. 1936, p. 20; FDR to James M. Cox, 11 Sept. 1936, Cox MSS.

34. PConf #318, 8 Sept. 1936, 8:104, FDR-press; *NYTM*, 4 Oct. 1936, 4:3.

35. *Boston Evening Transcript*, 22 Oct. 1936, p. 14; *ChiT*, 2 Nov. 1936, p. 12; *ChiT*, 17 Oct. 1936, p. 14; *LAT*, 1 Nov. 1936, p. 1.

36. Gustave Le Bon, *The Crowd* (London, 1922), p. 36; *SFX*, 15 Sept. 1936, p. 20; *SFX*, 2 Nov. 1936, p. 10. See also Michael Schudson, *Discovering the News* (New York, 1978), pp. 122–134.

37. *NYTM*, 13 Sept. 1936, 7:8; Schlesinger, *Upheaval*, p. 602.

38. Historians like Robert McElvane, along with Arthur Schlesinger, Jr., consider 1936 "the first time the methods used to sell soap and soft drinks were tried on a large scale in marketing a presidential candidate." Robert S. McElvane, *The Great Depres-

sion (New York, 1984), p. 280; Schlesinger, *Upheaval*, pp. 616–618. *NYTM*, 13 Sept. 1936, 7:8; "G.O.P. Puts All Political Eggs in One Basket," clipping, Fort Wayne, IN, 24 Aug. 1936, BB MSS; Erik Barnouw, *History of Broadcasting in the United States*, 3 vols. (New York, 1966–1971), 2:51.

39. Donald R. McCoy, *Landon of Kansas* (Lincoln, 1966), pp. 297, 268.

40. Pinchot quoted in Schlesinger, *Upheaval*, p. 602; *SFX*, 2 Nov. 1936, p. 10; Landon quoted in West, *Rape of Radio*, pp. 416–417.

41. Marquis W. Childs, *I Write from Washington* (New York, 1942), p. 118.

42. Harold L. Ickes, *The Secret Diary of Harold L. Ickes: The First Thousand Days, 1933–1936* (New York, 1953), p. 702.

43. Entry, 13 Nov. to 15 Nov. 1936, p. 164, Cummings Diaries; Emil Hurja, "Discussion of Presidential Polls," *National Inquirer*, 1936, p. 2 in FDR-OF 300.

44. *NYT*, 23 Oct. 1932, 8:2.

45. Theodore Roosevelt quoted in *NYT*, 25 Sept. 1932, 8:8.

46. Two social psychologists, Gordon Allport and Hadley Cantril, compared listening to a radio speech to being temporarily "blinded"; radio reduced the visual and social "cues for judging the personality of a speaker and for comprehending his meaning." Alternatively, a live speaker established "a more normal and satisfying social relationship." Compensating for the sensory deprivations, stumping fleshed out this "skeletonized" interaction: Blinded men could see. Cantril and Allport, *Psychology of Radio*, pp. 262–263, 234–236, 9. *SLPD*, 15 Oct. 1936, 2C; *NYTM*, 9 Feb. 1936, 7:3; *NYT*, 4 Oct. 1936, 4:8; *SFX*, 2 Nov. 1936, p. 10.

47. J[ames] H. R[owe], Jr., to [Edwin P.] Watson, 19 May 1939, Box 27, Rowe MSS; Herbert S. Parmet and Marie B. Hecht, *Never Again: A President Runs for a Third Term* (New York, 1968), p. 13.

48. Charles W. Stein, *The Third-Term Tradition* (New York, 1943), p. 322; Jean Henri Clos to Margaret LeHand, 1 July 1940, Box 20, FDR-OF 2526.

49. Robert H. Jackson, "Will Roosevelt Run in 1939?" pp. 13, 19, FDR-PPF 5304; Stein, *Third Term*, p. 322; Henry I. Harriman to FDR, 17 Oct. 1940, FDR-PPF 3572.

50. "Acceptance Address by Honorable Franklin D. Roosevelt, President of the United States," *DNC 1940*, p. 255.

51. Rosenman, *Working with Roosevelt*, p. 244; Arthur Krock in *NYT*, 5 Sept. 1940, p. 22.

52. *NYT*, 1 Sept. 1940, 4:8; PConf #689, 15 Oct. 1940, PConf #679, 10 Sept. 1940, PConf #934, 8 Feb. 1944, 16:267, 200, 23:39, FDR-press.

53. *LouCJ*, 11 Sept. 1940, p. 7; *Lynchburg* (VA) *News*, 6 Oct. 1940, clipping, Scrapbook, 1 Aug. 1940 to 20 Jan. 1941, Early MSS.

54. *SFChr*, 17 Sept. 1940, clipping, Scrapbook, 1 Aug. 1940 to 20 Jan. 1941, "Mr. Early's Press Conference, Poughkeepsie, NY, 10 Sept. 1940," Box 40, "Non-Political," *Hutchinson* (KS) *Herald*, 7 Oct. 1940, clipping, Scrapbook, 1 Aug. 1940 to 20 Jan. 1941, all in Early MSS; PConf #675, 27 Aug. 1940, 16:157, FDR-press.

55. Frances Perkins, *The Roosevelt I Knew* (New York, 1946), p. 115; Richard Norton Smith, *Thomas E. Dewey and His Times* (New York, 1982), p. 328.

56. Ellsworth Barnard, *Wendell Willkie: Fighter for Freedom* (Marquette, MI, 1966), pp. 149, 155; Henry O. Evjen, "An Analysis of Some of the Propaganda Features of the Campaign of 1940," *Southwestern Social Science Quarterly* 27 (Dec. 1946):256.

57. Parmet, *Third Term*, p. 122.

58. "Address of Wendell L. Willkie Accepting the Nomination for President of the United States," 17 Aug. 1940, *RNC 1940*, p. 380.

59. J. D. Ferguson to Mrs. Wendell L. Willkie, 10 Jan. 1945, pp. 1–2, WLW-IN.
60. "Willkie Acceptance," p. 392; *LouCJ*, 29 Aug. 1940, 7A; Donald Bruce Johnson, *The Republican Party and Wendell Willkie* (Urbana, 1960), p. 125.
61. "Transcript of Remarks of Wendell Willkie, Upon Leaving Joliet, Saturday, September 14," Box 1, WLW-Yale; "This Was Foretold," *SatEP*, 24 Aug. 1940, p. 28; *ChiT*, 19 Oct. 1940, p. 12.
62. Moley, *After Seven Years*, pp. 48, 51.
63. Charles Michelson, *The Ghost Talks* (New York, 1944), p. 193.
64. *NYT*, 19 Oct. 1940, p. 19; "He Insists on Being Himself," *World-Telegram*, clipping, WLW-Yale; *NYHTr*, 29 July 1940, p. 14; [New York] *Daily News*, 11 July 1940, clipping, WLW-IN.
65. Warren Moscow, *Roosevelt and Willkie* (Englewood Cliffs, NJ, 1968), p. 142; *NYT*, 19 Oct. 1940, p. 19; *ChiT*, 16 Oct. 1940, p. 1.
66. Thompson quoted in Fox, *Mirror Makers*, pp. 308–309.
67. Parmet, *Third Term*, pp. 230–231, 246; *NYT*, 25 Aug. 1940, 9:10.
68. Evjen, "The Willkie Campaign," p. 248; Perkins, *Roosevelt I Knew*, p. 116; Willkie Speech, Newark, NJ, in *NYT*, 8 Oct. 1940, p. 17; FDR in *LouCJ*, 29 Aug. 1940, 7A.
69. Ickes, *Secret Diary*, p. 352; Oren Root, *Persons and Persuasions* (New York, 1974), p. 48.
70. PConf #690, 18 Oct. 1940, 16:276, FDR-press; [FDR] to Oscar R. Ewing, 22 Oct. 1940, in President's Secretary's File, Box 122, FDR MSS; Rosenman, *Working with Roosevelt*, pp. 222–223.
71. On the origin of the two famous phrases see Rosenman, *Working with Roosevelt*, pp. 238, 240. Raymond Clapper, "Willkie Trend," 9 Sept. [1940], clipping, WLW-IN.
72. PConf #957, 13 June 1944, PConf #961, 11 July 1944, 23:257, 24:24, 23, FDR-press.
73. Bricker quoted in *NYT*, 29 July 1944, p. 11.
74. "Acceptance Speech by President Franklin D. Roosevelt," 20 July 1944, in Arthur M. Schlesinger, Jr., and Fred Israel, eds., *History of American Presidential Elections*, 4 vols. (New York, 1971), 4:3062.
75. See James MacGregor Burns, *Roosevelt: The Soldier of Freedom* (New York, 1970), p. 508.
76. Westbrook, "Politics as Consumption," pp. 160–162; George Gallup and Saul Forbes Rae, *The Pulse of Democracy* (New York, 1940), pp. 261, 289; O. R. McGuire, "The Republican Form of Government and the Straw Ballot," *United States Law Review* 73 (Oct.–Nov. 1939):500–504.
77. Smith, *Dewey*, pp. 417, 299; C[arl] B[yoir] Memorandum, [1944], box 57, BB MSS; *NYT*, 12 Sept. 1944, p. 18.
78. Smith, *Dewey*, p. 420; Herbert Brownell interview, p. 216, Dewey MSS.
79. "Radio's Election Bonanza," n.d., clipping, Box 57, BB MSS.
80. The Gallup Poll of 6 September 1944 gave Dewey 51 percent to Roosevelt's 49 percent. George H. Gallup, *The Gallup Poll*, 2 vols. (New York, 1972), 1:460. *DetN*, 8 Sept. 1944, p. 18.
81. Smith, *Dewey*, p. 407; Perkins, *Roosevelt I Knew*, p. 120.
82. Burns, *Soldier of Freedom*, pp. 521–524. On origins of defense of Fala see Rosenman, *Working with Roosevelt*, p. 473.
83. Rosenman, *Working with Roosevelt*, pp. 473, 478; *Time*, 2 Oct. 1944, p. 21.

84. Smith, *Dewey*, p. 422; Dewey Speech in *NYT*, 26 Sept. 1944, p. 15.
85. *SLPD*, 25 Sept. 1944, 2B; *DetN*, 27 Sept. 1944, p. 18.
86. *CharO*, 1 Oct. 1944, p. 12.
87. This survey includes letters to the editor published in thirteen newspapers from September 25 through October 3, 1944. The sample was skewed to reflect Roosevelt supporters disproportionately. Six of these newspapers supported the fourth term, although the *Editor and Publisher* of November 4, 1944 estimated that only 22 percent of the daily press supported the President's reelection. The pro-Roosevelt papers were the *Atlanta Constitution*, *Birmingham Age-Herald*, *Charlotte Observer*, *Louisville Courier-Journal*, *Philadelphia Evening Bulletin*, and *St. Louis Post-Dispatch*. The pro-Dewey papers were the *Baltimore Sun*, *Chicago Tribune*, *Detroit News*, *Los Angeles Times*, *New York Times*, *San Francisco Examiner*, and *Washington Post*. In all, sixty-seven letters about the Fala speech and Dewey's Oklahoma City response were published in these newspapers. Thirty-five condemned Roosevelt's speech and only nine approved of it, while thirteen assailed Dewey's speech, with only eight applauding. Two letters condemned both candidates. In the pro-Roosevelt press, fourteen letter-writers denounced the Fala speech; only five approved. Although the similarities in the language used are striking, there is no evidence that either the letters to the editor or the letters written to the White House were anything but spontaneous expressions.
88. *DetN*, 28 Sept. 1944, p. 24.
89. T. M. Madden to FDR, 30 Sept. 1944, Box 123, Mrs. S. S. Watkins to FDR, 25 Sept. 1944, Box 124, C. S. Bootheby to FDR, 26 Sept. 1944, Box 124, all in FDR-PPF 200B.
90. Arthur Krock in *NYT*, 26 Sept. 1944, p. 22 and *NYT*, 28 Sept. 1944, p. 18; Ed Ainsworth, *LAT*, 1 Oct. 1944, 2:4.
91. Smith, *Dewey*, pp. 425, 421.
92. Burns, *Soldier of Freedom*, p. 529.
93. PConf #972, 13 Oct. 1944, 24:160, FDR-press.
94. FDR Speech, *NYT*, 3 Nov. 1944, p. 14.
95. *NYT*, 29 Oct. 1944, 4:10; FDR Speech, Boston, MA, *NYT*, 5 Nov. 1944, p. 38; Burns, *Soldier of Freedom*, p. 530.
96. *CharO*, 2 Nov. 1944, p. 10; "A Bad Campaign," *TNR*, 30 Oct. 1944, p. 549.
97. See Burns, *Soldier of Freedom*, p. 524; Smith, *Dewey*, p. 421.
98. *DetN*, 4 Aug. 1944, p. 14; *NYTM*, 9 Feb. 1936, 7:3.
99. Harold J. Gallagher, "Hollywood Bowl Appearance," Memorandum, [1940], WLW-IN; Daniel Boorstin, *The Image* (New York, 1961), p. 9.
100. Pendleton Herring, *Politics of Democracy* (New York, 1940), p. 23; Clinton Rossiter, *American Presidency*, p. 34.
101. Herring quoted in Westbrook, "Politics as Consumption," p. 153.

CHAPTER NINE. *Televising the President, 1948–1964*

1. Metro-Goldwyn-Mayer, *State of the Union*, 1948.
2. James A. Farley, *Behind the Ballots* (New York, 1938), pp. 315–316; George H. Gallup, "They Want to Be Good Citizens," *National Municipal Review*, Jan. 1947, p. 29. See Paul F. Lazarsfeld et al., *The People's Choice*, 2nd ed. (New York, 1948), pp. 101–104.

3. HST to Dr. H. H. Brummall, 24 May 1948, mentioned in Official File, Box 947, HST MSS.

4. Drafted by the political operative James Rowe, the memorandum was signed by the White House aide Clark Clifford, supposedly because Truman disliked Rowe's law partner, Tommy Corcoran. Clark Clifford to HST, 19 Nov. 1947, pp. 7, 25, 29, "Campaign Material, 1948," both in Political Files, Clifford MSS. On authorship see James Rowe to Ken Hechler, 22 Apr. 1981, Hechler MSS.

5. Truman claimed that the idea of a tour "was entirely my own." But in November 1947 the Clifford memorandum proposed such a trip. The idea's many fathers attests to its success and to its wide acceptance after Roosevelt's campaigns. Harry S. Truman, *Memoirs*, 2 vols. (Garden City, NY, 1955–1956), p. 178; Clifford to HST, p. 29. See Irwin Ross, *The Loneliest Campaign* (New York, 1968), p. 78. HST quoted in "The Shape of Things," *Nat*, 19 June 1948, p. 673; *Time*, 21 June 1948, p. 24; *Life*, 21 June 1948, p. 43.

6. Senator Kenneth S. Wherry quoted in *WasP*, 8 May 1948, p. 2; *Kansas City Times*, 1 June 1948, Roll #19, White House Scrapbooks, HST MSS; *WasP*, 8 May 1948, p. 6.

7. *NYT*, 18 June 1948, p. 5; William Safire, *Safire's Political Dictionary*, rev. ed. (New York, 1978), pp. 790–791.

8. *Nwswk*, 31 May 1948, pp. 21–22.

9. Dewey in "Issues and Platitudes," *Nat*, 9 Oct. 1948, p. 387; Elmo Roper, *NYHTr*, 9 Sept. 1948, p. 1.

10. Ross, *Loneliest Campaign*, p. 177; "Remarks of the President at City Hall, Providence, RI, 28 Oct. 1948," Box 7, HST-PSF; *Nwswk*, 27 Sept. 1948, p. 17.

11. *SLPD*, 19 Sept. 1948, 1B; Richard Rovere, "Letter from a Campaign Train," *NYer*, 9 Oct. 1948, pp. 63–64.

12. *NYHTr*, 29 Oct. 1948, p. 21; "Remarks of the President at South Park, Fall River, MA, 28 Oct. 1948," "President at Providence," 28 Oct. 1948, both in Box 7, HST-PSF.

13. Truman received some complaints about his coarse language. See Official File, Boxes 947–948, HST MSS. Jhan Robbins, *Bess and Harry* (New York, 1980), p. 123; Joseph and Stewart Alsop, *The Reporter's Trade* (New York, 1958), p. 121; *New York Star*, 18 Oct. 1948, clipping, White House Scrapbooks, Roll #22, HST MSS.

14. Tallulah Bankhead in *Nwswk*, 1 Nov. 1948, p. 18; Herbert Brownell interview, p. 321, Dewey MSS. See also *Kansas City Star*, 29 Sept. 1948, White House Scrapbooks, HST MSS.

15. Robert J. Donovan, *Conflict and Crisis* (New York, 1977), p. 437.

16. Elliot E. Cohen, "Citizen's Victory," *Commentary*, Dec. 1948, p. 511; "Polling," 13 Nov. 1948, in E. B. White, *Writings from the New Yorker*, Rebecca M. Dale, ed. (New York, 1990), p. 160; *St. Louis Star-Times*, 4 Nov. 1948, p. 18, Box 19, Clifford MSS.

17. Charles G. Ross, "How Truman Did It," *Col*, 25 Dec. 1948, p. 87.

18. Eisenhower in *NYT*, 15 June 1952, p. 50; *NYT*, 16 June 1952, p. 16.

19. George H. Gallup, *The Gallup Poll*, 2 vols. (New York, 1972), 2:1056, 1054; John Bartlow Martin, *Adlai Stevenson of Illinois* (Garden City, NY, 1976), p. 578; *Major Campaign Speeches of Adlai E. Stevenson, 1952* (New York, 1953), pp. xxiv–xxvi.

20. "The March of the News," *USNWR*, 19 Sept. 1952, p. 2.

21. *Stevenson Speeches*, p. xii; John Kenneth Galbraith, *A Life in Our Times* (Boston, 1981), p. 303.
22. *Nwswk*, 22 Sept. 1952, p. 64; Kathleen Hall Jamieson, *Packaging the Presidency* (New York, 1984), p. 44; Joseph Siebert, *The Influence of Television on the Election of 1952* (Oxford, OH, n.d.), p. 227.
23. AES in *NYT*, 11 Sept. 1952, p. 1; AES, Detroit, MI, 7 Oct. 1952, *Stevenson Speeches*, p. 213.
24. Dwight D. Eisenhower, *White House Years*, 2 vols. (Garden City, NY, 1963–1965), 1:54; *Nwswk*, 20 Oct. 1952, p. 132; *NYT*, 19 Oct. 1952, 6:10.
25. Eric Sevareid to Carl [McGowan], 2 Oct. 1952, p. 5, AES MSS; TRB, "Washington Wire," *TNR*, 13 Oct. 1952, p. 3; Eisenhower, *White House Years*, 1:52.
26. Beverly Smith, "Here's What's Behind Ike's Grin," *SatEP*, 27 Sept. 1952, p. 33; AES to T. S. Matthews, 11 Aug. 1952, in Walter Johnson et al., eds., *The Papers of Adlai Stevenson*, 8 vols. (Boston, 1972–1979), 4:41; Galbraith, *A Life*, p. 290; Eisenhower, *White House Years*, 1:60; Martin, *Stevenson of Illinois*, p. 637.
27. Kingsland, Commissioner of Patents v. Dorsey, 338 U.S. 318, p. 324 (1949) (Jackson, J., Dissenting).
28. Stephen E. Ambrose, *Nixon: The Education of a Politician* (New York, 1987), pp. 276–295.
29. *NYT*, 28 Sept. 1952, 2:13; *Gallup Poll*, 2:1085.
30. Lazarsfeld, *The People's Choice*, pp. 121–122; Jamieson, *Packaging the Presidency*, p. 44; [Rosser Reeves] to Joe McConnell, [Jan. 1954], pp. 3–4, 7–8, Box 19, Reeves MSS.
31. Reeves to McConnell, pp. 3–4, 8, 5, Rosser Reeves to William S. Cutchins, 15 Sept. 1952, "Eisenhower TV Spot Campaign, Report, August, 1952," p. 4, all in Box 19, Reeves MSS; Jamieson, *Packaging the Presidency*, p. 85.
32. AES in *NYT*, 4 Oct. 1952, p. 10; *NYT*, 3 Oct. 1952, p. 15.
33. Richard Jensen, "Armies, Admen and Crusaders, Types of Presidential Campaigns," *History Teacher* 2 (Jan. 1969): 35; *New York Post*, 21 July 1956, clipping, Box 24, Reeves MSS; Sig Mickelson, *From Whistle Stop to Sound Bite* (New York, 1989), p. 71. See also Robert Westbrook, "Politics as Consumption," in Richard Wightman Fox and T. J. Jackson Lears, eds., *The Culture of Consumption* (New York, 1983), pp. 143–174 passim.
34. "Senator Lodge on Eisenhower and the Presidential Campaign," *American Mercury*, July 1952, p. 95; [Alman J.] Taranton to [Rosser] Reeves, 27 Jan. 1953, Box 19, Reeves MSS; George Ball in Edward P. Doyle, *As We Knew Adlai* (New York, 1966), p. 149; Theodore H. White, *The Making of the President 1960* (New York, 1961), p. 56.
35. *USNWR*, 2 Sept. 1955, p. 36; Siebert, *TV in 1952*, p. 313; Leo Bogart, *The Age of Television* (New York, 1956), pp. viii, 10, 65, 210; Dewey, Taft quoted in Mickelson, *Whistle Stop to Sound Bite*, p. 168; Walter Cronkite, "Government by Hooper Rating?" *Theatre Arts*, Nov. 1952, pp. 31, 30.
36. *NYTM*, 29 April 1956, 6:13, 30; Stewart Alsop, "Barnum of the G.O.P.," *SatEP*, 26 May 1956, pp. 27, 119.
37. *Gallup Poll*, 2:1386, 1384; Eisenhower, *White House Years*, 1:4–5; *SLPD*, 7 Oct. 1956, 1B; *NYT*, 14 May 1956, p. 1.
38. Estes Kefauver and Sidney Shallett, "Why Not Let the People Elect Our President?" *Col*, 31 Jan. 1953, p. 34; Theodore H. White, *America in Search of Itself* (New York, 1982), p. 76.

39. *NYT*, 19 Aug. 1956, 4:1; George W. Ball, *The Past Has Another Pattern* (New York, 1982), p. 135; Harry Ashmore in Doyle, *Adlai as We Knew Him*, p. 229.

40. *NYTM*, 27 May 1956, 6:11; Ball, *Past*, p. 135; John Bartlow Martin, *Adlai Stevenson and the World* (Garden City, NY, 1977), p. 327.

41. [AES] to Roger Kent, 21 June 1956, AES MSS; AES to Archibald MacLeish, 23 Aug. 1956, Johnson, *Letters*, 6:201.

42. AES to Dean Acheson, 26 Aug. 1956, Johnson, *Letters*, 6:205; *NYT*, 2 Sept. 1956, 4:7; Brightman in Westbrook, "Consumption," p. 156; *Time*, 17 Sept. 1956, p. 56.

43. *Time*, 8 Oct. 1956, p. 20.

44. *Nwswk*, 10 Sept. 1956, pp. 32–33; Bill Rivkin to Arthur Schlesinger, Jr., quoted in Martin, *Stevenson and the World*, pp. 356–357; AES, New Haven, CT, in *NYT*, 6 Oct. 1956, p. 14.

45. Thirty percent predicted another heart attack; only 11 percent expected another stomach operation. Democrats were three to four times more likely to be pessimistic than Republicans. *Gallup Poll*, 2:1437. *USNWR*, 24 Aug. 1956, p. 29; *NYT*, 16 Sept. 1956, 4:2.

46. Eisenhower PConf, *NYT*, 28 Sept. 1956, p. 14; Eisenhower PConf, *NYT*, 1 Sept. 1956, p. 8; Herblock, "Who's Whistle-stopping?" *WasP*, 26 Sept. 1956, p. 12; *Life*, 15 Oct. 1956, p. 33.

47. *Louisville Times*, 20 Oct. 1956, p. 3; *SLPD*, 7 Oct. 1956, 2B; *Washington Star*, 25 Sept. 1956, A:15.

48. *CIPD*, 2 Nov. 1956, p. 45; *Gallup Poll*, 2:1457; AES to Albert M. Greenfield, 16 Nov. 1956, Johnson, *Letters*, 6:346.

49. *Sponsor* quoted in Charles A. H. Thomson, *Television and Presidential Politics* (Washington, D.C., 1956), p. 62; *NYT*, 20 Sept. 1956, p. 32; *NYT*, 4 Oct. 1956, p. 19.

50. "Town Meeting by Oscillation," *SatR*, 9 Aug. 1952, p. 20; Mickelson, *Whistle Stop to Sound Bite*, p. 167; *Gallup Poll*, 2:1644, 1660–1661; *WasP*, 11 Mar. 1960, D:11.

51. Public Law 86-274, *United States Code Annotated*, Title 47, Section 315, p. 226; Nicolas Zapple, "Historical Evolution of Section 315," in Austin Ranney, ed., *The Past and Future of Presidential Debates* (Washington, D.C., 1979), pp. 56–60.

52. Stevenson explained that he did not challenge Eisenhower to debate in 1952, because he feared appearing to be trading on the General's good name, and in 1956, because he feared insulting the President with what might be "misunderstood" as a "gimmick." Statement of Hon. Adlai E. Stevenson in U.S. Congress, Senate, Committee on Interstate and Foreign Commerce, *Presidential Campaign Broadcasting Act, Hearings Before the Communications Subcommittee of the Committee on Interstate and Foreign Commerce on S. 3171.* 86th Cong., 2nd sess., 1960, pp. 4, 8.

53. Ibid., pp. 8–9; "Free Time for Television Candidates," U.S. Congress, Senate, Senator Mike Monroney speaking for S. 3171, 86th Cong. 2nd sess., 10 March 1960, *Congressional Record* 106:5147.

54. John Fischer, "The Choice," *Harper's*, Oct. 1960, p. 16.

55. "Only Kennedy . . . ," Box 33, RFK-pre.

56. Kennedy's Catholicism remained an issue throughout the campaign, and scholars still debate its impact on the outcome. See Herbert B. Asher, *Presidential Elections and American Politics*, 4th ed. (Chicago, 1988), p. 130.

57. Ambrose, *Nixon*, pp. 297, 411; *Time*, 5 Nov. 1956, p. 26.

58. CBS, "Presidential Countdown. Mr. Nixon: A Profile," 12 Sept. 1960, in U.S. Congress, Senate, Committee on Commerce, *Freedom of Communications, Final Report*

of the Committee on Commerce, United States Senate; Prepared by Its Subcommittee of the Subcommittee on Communications, Pursuant to S.Res. 305, 86th Congress, Report 994, 87th Cong., 1st sess., 1961, 3:20; White, *1960,* pp. 318–319, 374; Richard Nixon, *RN* (New York, 1978), 1:267.

59. Kennedy also dismayed party bosses by being independent. *RNC 1960,* p. 347; White, *1960,* p. 376.

60. William Atwood, "Memo on the 1960 Campaign," June 1960, p. 11; Ken Galbraith to Ted.[Sorenson], "Confidential Memorandum: Campaign Strategy, 1960," pp. 2–3, both in Goodwin Files, Box 996, JFK-pre.

61. Ambrose, *Nixon,* p. 559; Douglass Cater, "Notes from Backstage," chap. 6 in Sidney Kraus, *The Great Debates* (Bloomington, 1962), p. 129.

62. CBS, "Eyewitness to History," with Charles Kuralt, 14 Oct. 1960, in *Report 994,* 3: 222; *CSM,* 27 Sept. 1960, p. 1; "First Debate, September 26, 1960," Samuel Lubell, "Personalities vs. Issues," both in Kraus, *Great Debates,* pp. 351, 367, 152; *ChiT,* 9 Oct. 1960, p. 12; MBS-Radio, "The Top of the News with Fulton Lewis, Jr.," 29 Sept. 1960, *Report 994,* 4:125.

63. White, *1960,* pp. 346–347; Ambrose, *Nixon,* p. 575; Richard M. Nixon, "L.B.J. Should Debate on TV," *SatEP,* 27 June 1964, p. 14.

64. Marshall McLuhan, *Understanding Media,* 2nd ed. (New York, 1964), p. 102.

65. Herbert A. Seltz and Richard D. Yoakam, "Production Diary of the Debates," in Kraus, *Great Debates,* pp. 92, 95; Ambrose, *Nixon,* p. 575.

66. *ChiST,* 7 Sept. 1960, 2:6; Erik Barnouw, *Tube of Plenty,* rev. ed. (New York, 1982), p. 277.

67. Robert W. Sarnoff, "An NBC View," chap. 3 in Kraus, *Great Debates,* p. 62; Walter Lippmann in *WasP,* 29 Sept. 1960, A:23; Richard Nixon, *Six Crises* (Garden City, NY, 1962), p. 358; Talk by Frank Stanton, Sigma Delta Chi Luncheon, 3 Dec. 1960, p. 10, Box 1051, JFK-pre; Henry Steele Commager in *NYTM,* 30 Oct. 1960, 6:80.

68. *CSM,* 28 Sept. 1960, p. 1; White, *1960,* pp. 395–396; *Time,* 7 Nov. 1960, p. 26.

69. The networks devoted a record seventeen hours and thirty-two minutes to the presidential campaign in 1960; four years later, when the Equal Time Rule was not suspended, the figure dropped to one hour and eighteen minutes. Samuel L. Becker and Elmer W. Lower, "Broadcasting in Presidential Campaigns," chap. 2 in Sidney Kraus, ed., *The Great Debates: Carter vs. Ford, 1976* (Bloomington, 1979), pp. 13, 18. CBS, "Nixon: A Profile," 3:19; CBS, "Person to Person with Charles Collingwood," 27 Oct. 1960, *Report 994,* 3:304; CBS-TV, "Presidential Countdown. Mr. Kennedy: A Profile," 19 Sept. 1960, p. 4, Box 1027, JFK-pre.

70. Letter to Robert F. Kennedy, 4 Oct. 1960, Box 33, RFK-pre; *SFCh,* 21 June 1960, p. 23; NBC, The Jack Paar Show, "Tonight," 25 Aug. 1960, *Report 994,* 3:5.

71. *NYT,* 2 Nov. 1960, p. 1; Theodore Sorenson, *Kennedy* (New York, 1965), p. 179.

72. White, *1960,* p. 373; "Speech of the Vice President," Anchorage, AS, 6 Nov. 1960, *Report 994,* 2:1065.

73. Diana Hirsch to Bob Kennedy, "Proposed Text for JFK on Republic Steel Film," 27 Sept. 1960, RFK-pre; White, *1960,* p. 353.

74. Nixon, *Six Crises,* p. 422.

75. "The Honorable Barry M. Goldwater Accepts the Nomination for President of the United States," *RNC 1964,* p. 413; Stephen Fox, *The Mirror Makers* (New York, 1984), pp. 311–312.

76. Harold Faber, ed., *The Road to the White House* (New York, 1965), p. 82; Barry M. Goldwater, *With No Apologies* (New York, 1979), p. 199.

77. NBC, "The Campaign and the Candidates," 12 Sept. 1964, 475 CBU, Box 5, LBJ-64; Faber, *Road to White House*, p. 147.

78. John Kenneth Galbraith to LBJ, 3 Aug. 1964, CF PL 2, Box 77, LBJ MSS; Lyndon B. Johnson, *The Vantage Point* (New York, 1971), p. 103; CBS, "World News Roundup with Dan Rather," 7 Sept. 1964, 238 CBU, Box 5, LBJ-64.

79. LBJ PConf, 5 Sept. 1964, p. 228, Box 1, LBJ-64; *Time*, 30 Oct. 1964, p. 27. See also *USNWR*, 28 Sept. 1964, p. 47.

80. LBJ PConf, 24 July 1964, pp. 38, 41, LBJ Speech, Scranton, PA, 14 Oct. 1964, p. 563, both in Box 1, LBJ-64; James MacGregor Burns, *Presidential Government* (Boston, 1966), p. 167.

81. CBS, "World News Roundup," 29 Sept. 1964, with Roger Mudd, 75 GPR, Box 5, LBJ-64; *Nwswk*, 12 Oct. 1964, p. 33; Barry M. Goldwater with Jack Casserly, *Goldwater* (New York, 1988), pp. 192–193; *Nwswk*, 19 Oct. 1964, p. 32; Theodore H. White, *The Making of the President 1964* (New York, 1965), p. 339.

82. MBS, Cedric Foster, 25 Sept. 1964, 457 WBP, Box 5, LBJ-64.

83. MBS, "Top of the News with Fulton Lewis, Jr.," 18 Sept. 1964, 207 WBP, Box 5, LBJ-64.

84. Jamieson, *Packaging the Presidency*, pp. 213–214; *Time*, 30 Oct. 1964, p. 27.

85. *Time*, 11 Sept. 1964, p. 98; CBS, "The World This Week," 19 Sept. 1964, with Charles Kuralt, WBP 233, Box 5, LBJ-1964.

86. *Nwswk*, 21 Sept. 1964, p. 76; Fox, *Mirror Makers*, p. 312.

87. George Gallup, frag., Series 13, Box 1, Dewey MSS.

88. *Time*, 30 Oct. 1964, p. 27; *Time*, 2 Oct. 1964, p. 41; *Gallup Poll*, 2:1908.

89. Dean Burch, "Presidential Campaigns Are a Sham," *SatEP*, 27 Mar. 1965, p. 12.

90. Eisenhower, *White House Years*, 1:45.

91. Arthur M. Schlesinger, Jr., *A Thousand Days* (Boston, 1965), p. 74. See Taylor Branch, *Parting the Waters* (New York, 1988), pp. 351–378.

92. For an opposite view see V. O. Key, Jr., *The Responsible Electorate* (Cambridge, 1966), p. 7. Angus Campbell et al., *The American Voter* (New York, 1960), p. 253.

CHAPTER TEN. *A Cross-Country Marathon*

1. Joseph Napolitan, *The Election Game and How to Win It* (Garden City, NY, 1972), p. 65.

2. Robert Montgomery, *Open Letter from a Television Viewer* (New York, 1968), p. 14; Steven B. Greenberg, "Marshall McLuhan and the Presidential Election of 1968," seminar paper, Annenberg School of Communications, University of Pennsylvania, Dec. 1985; Marshall McLuhan, *Understanding Media*, 2nd ed. (New York, 1964), p. viii; Marshall McLuhan, "All of the Candidates Are Asleep," *SatEP*, 10 Aug. 1968, p. 34.

3. Richard Nixon, *RN*, 2 vols. (New York, 1978), 1:376.

4. *PhB*, 20 Sept. 1968, p. 42; Joe McGinniss, *The Selling of the President 1968* (New York, 1969), pp. 66–67.

5. McGinniss, *Selling the President*, p. 58; Theodore White, *The Making of the President 1968* (New York, 1969), pp. 128, 132.

6. Lewis Chester, Godfrey Hodgson, Bruce Page, *An American Melodrama* (New York, 1969), p. 751; McGinniss, *Selling the President*, pp. 70, 174–175.

7. *CharO*, 5 Nov. 1968, 2B; Carl Solberg, *Hubert Humphrey* (New York, 1984), p. 354.

8. White, *1968*, p. 340.

9. White, *1968*, p. 341; Ernest R. May, "Introduction," in Ernest R. May and Janet Fraser, eds., *Campaign '72* (Cambridge, 1973), p. 7.

10. *NYT*, 29 Sept. 1968, p. 75; May, "Introduction," p. 7.

11. "TV Debates," *TNR*, 2 Nov. 1968, p. 9; Edward W. Knappman, *Presidential Election 1968* (New York, 1970), pp. 195, 203; *NYT*, 26 Oct. 1972, p. 42.

12. White, *1968*, p. 352. See also Kathleen Hall Jamieson, *Packaging the Presidency* (New York, 1984), p. 239.

13. *Cleveland Press*, 16 Oct. 1968, B:5.

14. McGinniss, *Selling the President*, pp. 32, 160; Napolitan, *Election Game*, p. 106.

15. Nixon, *RN*, 2:161; Theodore H. White, *Making of the President 1972* (New York, 1973), p. 299; Timothy Crouse, *The Boys on the Bus* (New York, 1972), p. 257.

16. Jamieson, *Packaging the Presidency*, p. 284.

17. Richard Nixon to H. R. Haldeman, 9 May 1971, in Bruce Oudes, ed., *From: The President* (New York, 1989), p. 252.

18. Michael Schudson, *Discovering the News* (New York, 1978), chap. 5, pp. 160–194.

19. Anthony Smith, *Goodbye Gutenberg* (New York, 1980), pp. 45–47; White, *1972*, pp. 332 n. 2, 292.

20. Robert Teeter to Clark MacGregor, 15 July 1972, p. 3, in Box 1, Teeter MSS; *MilJ*, 21 May 1972, 5:2. For opposing views see Edward W. Knappman et al., *Campaign '72* (New York, 1973), p. 77.

21. *Harris Survey Yearbook of Public Opinon, 1972* (New York, 1976), pp. 37, 36; Arthur Schlesinger, Jr., in *NYT*, 17 Mar. 1972, p. 41. For attack see Robert H. Finch in *NYT*, 30 Apr. 1972, 4:13.

22. *The State* (Columbia, SC), 14 July 1972, in Knappman, *Campaign '72*, p. 119; Ben Wattenberg in May and Fraser, *Campaign '72*, p. 182; *NYT*, 9 Nov. 1972, p. 24.

23. Christopher Lasch, *The Culture of Narcissism* (New York, 1978), p. 13; Frankel quoted in Stephen Hess, *The Presidential Campaign*, 3rd ed. (Washington, D.C., 1988), p. 16.

24. *NYT*, 19 Oct. 1972, p. 46; *PhI*, 15 Oct. 1972, 4H.

25. Gary Hart, *Right from the Start* (New York, 1973), p. 289; *NYT*, 9 Sept. 1972, p. 10.

26. *NYT*, 9 Sept. 1972, p. 10; George McGovern, *Grassroots* (New York, 1977), pp. 228–229; *NYT*, 23 July 1972, p. 30.

27. Richard Nixon to H. R. Haldeman, 12 Aug. 1972, in Oudes, *From: The President*, p. 537; *NYT*, 15 Sept. 1972, p. 1; *NYT*, 24 Oct. 1972, p. 30; *NYT*, 11 Aug. 1972, p. 28.

28. NOP, 1 Oct. 1972, p. 16; *NYT*, 4 Oct. 1972, p. 47; *Syracuse Herald-Journal*, 15 Oct. 1972, Knappman, *Campaign '72*, p. 243.

29. Oudes, *RN: From the President*, p. 570; PConf, 5 Oct. 1972, *Nixon: The Fourth Year of his Presidency* (Washington, D.C., 1973), p. 139-A.

30. Richard Nixon, *In the Arena* (New York, 1990), p. 202.

31. Haynes Johnson, *MilJ*, 23 Oct. 1972, 3:2; Norman H. Nie, Sidney Verba, John R. Petrocik, *The Changing American Voter: Enlarged Edition* (Cambridge, 1979), p. 46.

32. Herbert B. Asher, *Presidential Elections and American Politics*, 4th ed. (Chicago, 1988), p. 20.

33. Jimmy Carter, "Formal Announcement," 12 Dec. 1974, in *The Presidential Campaign 1976*, vol. 1, part 1, *Jimmy Carter* (Washington, D.C., 1978), p. 3; Jimmy Carter, *"Why Not the Best?"* (Nashville, TN, 1975), p. 11.

34. Jimmy Carter, 4 Dec. 1974, in *Jimmy Carter*, 1:1, p. 1; *AtlC*, 2 Nov. 1976, 6A.

35. Martin P. Wattenberg, *The Decline of American Political Parties, 1952-1980* (Cambridge, 1984); Thomas E. Patterson and Richard Davis, "The Media Campaign," chap. 4 in Michael Nelson, ed., *The Elections of 1984* (Washington, D.C., 1985), p. 112.

36. *LAT*, 19 Feb. 1984, p. 29; Hugh Winebrenner, *The Iowa Precinct Caucuses: The Making of a Media Event* (Ames, 1987), p. vii.

37. *Jimmy Carter*, 1:1, pp. 2, 209.

38. Jules Witcover, *Marathon* (New York, 1977), p. 564; Bill Rhatican to Dave Gergen, 25 Aug. 1976, Box 3, Office of the Press Secretary, GF MSS; Richard B. Cheney, "The 1976 Presidential Debates: a Republican Perspective," Oct. 1977, p. 20, Box 62, Teeter MSS; "Campaign Plan—Final Copy, 4 of 4," pp. 50, 64, 72 Box 13, Dave Gergen to Mike Duval, 21 June 1976, Box 14, Mike Duval and Foster Chanock to [Richard B.] Cheney, 11 June 1976, p. 3, Box 13, all in Duval MSS.

39. Charles M. Firestone, "Legal Issues Surrounding Televised Presidential Debates," chap. 2 in Joel Swerdlow, ed., *Presidential Debates* (Washington, D.C., 1987), pp. 20-22.

40. Ruth C. Clusen et al., to the President, Telegram, 19 Aug. 1976, in White House Central File, Box PL 85, GF MSS; *AtlC*, 21 Aug. 1976, 4A; "Gallup Polls on Presidential Debates, 1960-1987," in Swerdlow, *Debates*, p. 168. For a more skeptical view see *WasP*, 6 July 1976, A17.

41. Napolitan, *Election Game*, p. 102; Garry Trudeau, "Doonesbury," *AtlC*, 23 Sept. 1976, 5:A.

42. Sander Vanocur, in *WasP*, 8 Sept. 1976, D1. See also Gerald M. Pomper, "The Presidential Election," chap. 3 in Marlene M. Pomper, ed., *The Election of 1976* (New York, 1977), p. 69.

43. Robert Scheer, "Jimmy Carter," in G. Barry Golson, ed., *The Playboy Interview* (New York, 1981), pp. 486-488.

44. *AtlC*, 21 Sept. 1976, 4A; Congressman Joel Pritchard, p. 1, Special Files, First Debate, 9/23/76, Papers of GF Staff Secretary, GF MSS; *AtlC*, 19 Sept. 1976, 12A; Bill Carruthers to Mike Duval, 20 Sept. 1976, p. 3, Box 29, Duval MSS.

45. Joseph Kraft, *WasP*, 26 Sept. 1976, C7; "The First Ford-Carter Debate," Philadelphia, PA, 23 Sept. 1976, in Sidney Kraus, ed., *The Great Debates: Carter vs. Ford, 1976* (Bloomington, 1979), p. 473; Herbert A. Seltz and Richard D. Yoakam, "Production Diary of the Debates," chap. 8 in Kraus, *1976 Debates*, pp. 132-136.

46. Teeter correlated the news reports with the drop in the polls. "The media perception of the event clearly influenced, more than the event itself, the final result," he concluded. "Post Election Analysis—Speeches and Reports," p. 13 in Box 62, Teeter MSS. "The Second Debate," San Francisco, CA, 6 Oct. 1976, in Kraus, *1976 Debates*, pp. 481-482; Witcover, *Marathon*, p. 638.

47. Ford did not believe he erred. In preparing to defend the controversial Helsinki Accords, he had scribbled "No Soviet sphere of influence in Eastern Europe." "Second Debate: Ford Notes on Briefing Material," in "Special Files, Second Debate, 10/6/76," Papers of GF Staff Secretary, GF MSS.

48. See President's Daily News Summary, 5 Oct. 1976, p. 1, in GF MSS.

49. *WasP*, 20 Oct. 1976, A15.

50. Witcover, *Marathon*, p. 667; *WasP*, 29 Oct. 1976, A4.

51. McGovern in *WasP*, 4 Nov. 1976, A16; "Teeter, Bob—Notes," p. 2, in box 24, Duval MSS.

52. Jimmy Carter, PConf, 13 Feb. 1980, in *President Carter, 1980* (Washington, D.C., 1981), p. 162.
53. Martin Schram, "Carter," in Richard Harwood, ed., *The Pursuit of the Presidency 1980* (New York, 1980), p. 114.
54. *LAT*, 28 March 1980, p. 20; *NYT*, 2 May 1980, B:6.
55. Herblock Cartoon, *LAT*, 10 May 1980, 2:4.
56. *DesMR*, 18 Jan. 1980, 1A; *WasP*, 18 Jan. 1980, A4.
57. Lou Cannon and William Peterson, "GOP," in Harwood, ed., *Pursuit*, p. 138; *NYT*, 4 May 1980, p. 24.
58. "John Anderson Interview," *Playboy*, June 1980, p. 82.
59. *WasP*, 28 Aug. 1980, A27.
60. *NYT*, 23 Sept. 1980, B9.
61. *NYT*, 15 Sept. 1980, B12.
62. Albert R. Hunt, "The Campaign and the Issues," chap. 5 in Austin Ranney, ed., *The American Elections of 1980* (Washington, D.C., 1981), p. 165; Richard Harwood, "Labor Day 1980," in Harwood, ed., *Pursuit*, p. 284.
63. *NYT*, 24 Oct. 1980, p. 18.
64. "'80 Presidential Debates," 28 Oct. 1980, in Harwood, *Pursuit*, pp. 363, 397. For origin of "There you go again," see Lou Cannon, *Reagan* (New York, 1982), p. 297.
65. Commager, *LAT*, 2 Nov. 1980, 6:3; Cater, *WasP*, 4 Nov. 1980, A21.
66. Asher, *Elections*, p. 183; *NYT*, 9 Nov. 1980, p. 36.
67. Tony Schwartz, *The Responsive Chord* (Garden City, NY, 1973), p. 18; T. Schwartz, *Media: The Second God* (Garden City, NY, 1983); Mark Hertsgaard, *On Bended Knee*, paperback ed. (New York, 1989), p. 17. Larry J. Sabato offers a less benign view of consultants in *The Rise of Political Consultants* (New York, 1981).
68. Jane Mayer and Doyle McManus, *Landslide* (Boston, 1988), p. 7.
69. Peggy Noonan, *What I Saw at the Revolution* (New York, 1990), p. 121.
70. Austin Ranney, *Channels of Power* (New York, 1983), pp. 17–19; Edward Jay Epstein, *News from Nowhere* (New York, 1973), chap. 9, pp. 258–273.
71. Hertsgaard, *On Bended Knee*, p. 35; Ranney, *Channels of Power*, p. 42; *LAT*, 20 Aug. 1984, p. 18.
72. *LAT*, 20 Aug. 1984, pp. 1, 18.
73. *LAT*, 19 Feb. 1984, p. 1.
74. *ChiT*, 26 Feb. 1976, 2:2; Harris Survey, *Houston Post*, 15 July 1976, 2C; David Broder, *WasP*, 19 Feb. 1984, C8.
75. *CIPD*, 6 May 1984, *Newsbank*, POL 1984, 40:A6.
76. *DMN*, 16 Sept. 1984, p. 1.
77. Broder, *WasP*, 19 Feb. 1984, C8.
78. *LouCJ*, 16 Aug. 1984, p. 1; Richard Darman, Maxine Isaacs in Jonathan Moore, ed., *Campaigning for President: The Managers Look at '84* (Dover, MA, 1986), pp. 193–194.
79. James A. Johnson in Moore, ed., *Campaign '84*, p. 193; Keith Blume, *The Presidential Election Show* (South Hadley, MA, 1985), pp. 69, 73; Walter Mondale, *WasP*, 27 Sept. 1984, A19.
80. Martin Diamond, quoted in *Los Angeles Herald Examiner*, 2 Sept. 1984, *Newsbank*, POL, 92:A3.
81. *PhI*, 22 July 1984, 1F; David Broder, *WasP*, 8 July 1984, D7; Richard Darman in Moore, ed., *Campaign '84*, p. 175; Ronald Reagan in *Nwswk*, 6 Feb. 1984, p. 19; *WasP*, 12 Mar. 1984, A3.

82. Rollins in Moore, ed., *Campaign '84*, p. 42.
83. Ridings quoted in *DMN*, 2 May 1984, 12A; *LouCJ*, 7 Oct. 1984, *Supplement*, p. 2; *LAT*, 5 Oct. 1984, 6:1; *Syracuse Herald American*, 7 Oct. 1984, *Newsbank*, 1984 POL 108:G2.
84. Rollins in Moore, ed., *Campaign '84*, p. 196.
85. *WasP*, 9 Oct. 1984, A19; *Wall Street Journal*, 9 Oct. 1984, p. 1; *MinST*, 14 Oct. 1984, p. 1.
86. *DMN*, 12 Oct. 1984, p. 1; *WasP*, 12 Oct. 1984, A22.
87. *BalS*, 22 Oct. 1984, p. 1.
88. *WasP*, 11 Nov. 1984, A3; *WasP*, 14 Nov. 1984, A19.
89. 13 Nov. 1984, in Ben J. Wattenberg, *The First Universal Nation* (New York, 1991), p. 322; Carl Rowan, *WasP*, 14 Nov. 1984, A19.
90. Hertsgaard, *On Bended Knee*, p. 38.

CHAPTER ELEVEN. *The Search for Virtue in the Presidential Campaign*

1. "Presidential Debate," 15 Oct. 1992, Richmond, Virginia, transcript by News Transcripts, Inc., Washington, D.C., pp. 7–8.
2. New York Times, CBS News Poll of 21–24 Oct., *NYT*, 30 Oct. 1988, 4:1; Alexander Heard and Michael Nelson, *Presidential Selection* (Durham, 1987), p. 301. For other attacks on issue vagueness see Robert Westbrook, "Politics as Consumption," chap. 5 in Richard Wightman Fox and T. J. Jackson Lears, *Culture of Consumption* (New York, 1983), p. 168; Benjamin I. Page, *Choices and Echoes in Presidential Elections* (Chicago, 1979), pp. 10–61, 152–153.
3. "Presidential Debate," 15 Oct. 1992, p. 5; Stephen Hess, *The Presidential Campaign*, 3rd ed. (Washington, D.C., 1988), pp. 16, 46.
4. October 4, *The Gallup Poll: Public Opinion 1992* (Wilmington, 1993), pp. 176, 175; *NYT*, 1 Nov. 1992, 4:1.
5. Dukakis in *Nwswk*, 21 Nov. 1988, p. 114; Jim Wooten, "One Campaign Too Much," in Arthur Grace, *Choose Me* (Hanover, 1989), p. 25; Martin Peretz, "Why Dukakis Lost," *TNR*, 28 Nov. 1988, p. 16.
6. Nelson W. Polsby and Aaron Wildavsky, *Presidential Elections*, 8th ed. (New York, 1991), p. 228.
7. *Nwswk*, 21 Nov. 1988, p. 47.
8. Michael Dukakis, "Acceptance Speech," 21 July 1988, DNC, 1988, p. 474; Jack W. Germond and Jules Witcover, *Whose Broad Stripes and Bright Stars?* (New York, 1989), p. 447; Richard Ben Cramer, *What It Takes* (New York, 1992), p. 1028.
9. Germond and Witcover, *Broad Stripes and Bright Stars*, pp. 450, 411; Ed McCabe, "The Campaign You Never Saw," *New York*, 12 Dec. 1988, p. 48.
10. Germond and Witcover, *Broad Stripes and Bright Stars*, p. 452.
11. Peggy Noonan, *What I Saw at the Revolution* (New York, 1990), p. 305.
12. *WasP*, 10 July 1988, C1; Germond and Witcover, *Broad Stripes and Bright Stars*, p. 157.
13. Sidney Blumenthal, *Pledging Allegiance* (New York, 1990), p. 265; Cramer, *What It Takes*, p. 999.
14. Kathleen Hall Jamieson, *Dirty Politics* (New York, 1992), p. 17; Barbara Bush, *A Memoir* (New York, 1994), p. 243.
15. Fitzhugh Green, *George Bush* (New York, 1991), p. 228; Germond and Witcover, *Broad Stripes and Bright Stars*, p. 163; Blumenthal, *Pledging Allegiance*, p. 266.

16. In 1988, three-quarters of those surveyed believed that candidates "mostly just say . . . what they need to say in order to get elected." In fact, twentieth-century presidents "kept approximately three-fourths of the issues positions taken in their campaigns." See Michael Krukones, "Predicting Presidential Performance through Political Campaigns," *Presidential Studies Quarterly* 10 (Fall 1980):527. Survey, 2 Nov. 1988, *Gallup Poll 1988* (Wilmington, Del., 1989), p. 218. Bush in Peter Goldman, Tom Mathews et al., *The Quest for the Presidency* (New York, 1990), p. 398.

17. William Greider, *Who Will Tell the People: The Betrayal of American Democracy* (New York, 1992), p. 11; Jamieson, *Dirty Politics*, p. 16. See also E. J. Dionne, *Why Americans Hate Politics* (New York, 1991), p. 10.

18. Germond and Witcover, *Broad Stripes and Bright Stars*, p. 464.

19. *The Economist*, 19 Sept. 1992, p. 26. See also Joe Klein, "The Year of the Voter," *Nwswk*, Nov./Dec. 1992, p. 15.

20. *NYT*, 6 May 1992, A26.

21. Perot in *NYT*, 2 Oct. 1992, A12; Perot in Peter Goldman and Tom Mathews, "The Inside Story: America Changes the Guard," *Nwswk*, Nov./Dec. 1992, p. 75.

22. The sign, written by James Carville, read: "Change vs. more of the same/The economy, stupid/Don't forget health care." See Mary Matalin and James Carville, *All's Fair* (New York, 1994), p. 244.

23. The Clintons appeared at one of the *Christian Science Monitor* columnist Godfrey Sperling's weekly Washington "power" breakfasts. "Sex and the Candidate," *TNR*, 3 Feb. 1992, p. 7.

24. For a plaintive argument that "voters are not fools," see V. O. Key, Jr., *The Responsible Electorate* (Cambridge, 1966), p. 7. Samuel L. Popkin, *The Reasoning Voter* (Chicago, 1991), p. 7. See also Jamieson, *Dirty Politics*, p. 17. Bill Clinton, Speech, University of Pittsburgh branch at Johnstown, PA, 22 April 1992, in *NYT*, 26 April 1992, 1:24.

25. Henry Muller and John F. Stacks, "An Interview with Bill Clinton," *Time*, 20 July 1992, p. 19.

26. Bush in *NYT*, 12 Oct. 1988, A24; Max Weber, *Economy and Society*, ed. Gunther Roth and Claus Wittich (New York, 1968), 3:1140; Russ Hodge, "White Men Can't Jump," *New York*, 30 Nov. 1992, p. 43.

27. "Presidential Debate," 15 Oct. 1992, p. 5; Michael Duffy and Dan Goodgame, *Marching in Place* (New York, 1992), pp. 259, 263; "Text of Quayle Speech Accepting Nomination," Houston, TX, 20 Aug. 1992, in *NYT*, 21 Aug. 1992, A14.

28. "Nominating Speech of Hon. J. B. Foraker of Ohio," *RNC* (Philadelphia, 1900), p. 117.

29. "Remarks by Republican Presidential Candidate Pat Buchanan," Republican National Convention, Houston, TX, 17 Aug. 1992, pp. 7, 5, 4. Transcript provided by Republican National Committee. To place this appeal in a political context, see Thomas Byrne Edsall with Mary D. Edsall, *Chain Reaction* (New York, 1991, 1992), pp. 289–292. For a historical context see T. J. Jackson Lears, *No Place of Grace* (New York, 1981), p. 7; Christopher Lasch, *The True and Only Heaven* (New York, 1991), p. 505.

30. *WasP*, 16 Sept. 1992, A12.

31. "Presidential Debate," 15 Oct. 1992, p. 7.

32. M. S. Quay et al., "The Man, or the Platform?" *North American Review* 154 (May 1892):513.

33. By Election Day, 64 percent of voters surveyed considered the economy, jobs, or the budget deficit the number-one issue, but only 24 percent believed Perot "could be trusted to deal with all the problems a President has to deal with." He received 19 percent of the popular vote. "Exit Poll Results 1992," in *Newswk*, Nov./Dec. 1992, p. 10; *NYT*, 1 Nov. 1992, 4:1.

34. *Gen. Harrison's Speech at the Dayton Convention, September 10, 1840* (Boston, [1840]), p. 2, in WHH MSS.

35. This confusing of intellectual achievement and upper-class breeding underscores the class tensions that Richard Hofstadter neglected in *Anti-Intellectualism in American Life* (New York, 1963), pp. 155–156. Elizabeth Kolbert, "Test-Marketing a President," *NYTM*, 30 Aug. 1992, 6:68.

36. *Time*, 2 Nov. 1992, p. 37; Vice Presidential Debate, 13 Oct. 1992, Atlanta, transcript by News Transcripts, Washington, D.C., p. 10.

37. Goldman and Mathews, "America Changes the Guard," p. 55.

38. See Richard Jensen, "Armies, Admen, and Crusaders: Types of Presidential Election Campaigns," *History Teacher* 2 (1969): 34–37; Westbrook, "Politics as Consumption," pp. 145–173. Matalin and Carville, *All's Fair*, p. 212; Grunwald in Larry King, *On the Line* (New York, 1993), p. 32.

39. Walter Mondale in *NYT*, 3 Nov. 1992, A16; James Carville and Paul Begala, "It's the Candidate, Stupid!" *NYT*, 4 Dec. 1992, A31.

40. *The New Republic* soon felt compelled to replace its regular column of "Bushisms of the Week" with a "Clinton Suck-up Watch." See, for example, Garry Wills, "Clinton's Forgotten Childhood," *Time*, 8 June 1992, pp. 37–38. William Burlie Brown, *The People's Choice* (Baton Rouge, 1960), analyzes humble origins as a recurring theme in campaigning. Edward Pessen, *The Log Cabin Myth* (New Haven, 1984), questions the claims to humble birth of most presidents.

41. Muller and Stacks, "Interview," p. 20; Judith Warner, *Hillary Clinton* (New York, 1993), p. 164; Bill Clinton and Al Gore, *Putting People First* (New York, 1992), pp. 213, 210, 218–219.

42. "Remarks by President George Bush," Republican National Convention, Houston, TX, 20 Aug. 1992, p. 16. Transcript provided by Republican National Committee.

43. Bush claimed this incident was a typical media distortion; he was impressed by the newest scanners. Whether or not the story was true, the sentiment was clear: the president cannot be so out of touch. *NYT*, 13 Feb. 1992, A23. See Matalin and Carville, *All's Fair*, p. 130.

44. George Bush, press conference, 10 April 1992, in Duffy and Goodgame, *Marching in Place*, p. 269.

45. The president did veto attacks on Clinton's sexual conduct. And ads contrasting pictures of Clinton as a bearded antiwar activist and Bush as a fighter pilot were vetoed as well. Goldman and Mathews, "America Changes the Guard," p. 94. *NYT*, 30 Oct. 1992, A1; Michael Kinsley, "Stay Mad," *TNR*, 16 Nov. 1992, p. 6.

46. Heartland Poll, the University of Iowa Social Science Institute, *ChiT*, 29 Oct. 1992, 1:5; Goldman and Mathews, "America Changes the Guard," p. 84.

47. The link between popular culture and political culture has been more effectively explored for the nineteenth century than for the twentieth century. See, for example, Michael McGerr's *The Decline of Popular Politics* (New York, 1986). For a look at this contemporary relationship in slightly different terms, see Westbrook, "Politics as Consumption."

48. Presidential Debate, 11 Oct. 1992, St. Louis, transcript by News Transcripts, Inc.,

Washington, D.C., p. 8; "Presidential Debate," 15 Oct. 1992, p. 11.

49. *NYT*, 11 Feb. 1992, A22; *NYT*, 2 Feb. 1992, 4:1.

50. *NYT*, 2 Apr. 1992, A10; Ken Auletta, "Loathe the Media," *Esquire*, Nov. 1992, p. 179.

51. Goldman and Mathews, "America Changes the Guard," p. 91; *NYT*, 18 Oct. 1992, p. 24.

52. "Clinton for President," *TNR*, 9 Nov. 1992, p. 9.

53. *Time*, 19 Oct. 1992, p. 42.

54. Hodge, "White Men," p. 44; Quayle in *NYT*, 4 Nov. 1992, B6.

55. The distinction between republicanism and liberal democracy is paralleled somewhat in Christopher Lasch's distinction between populism and progressivism. Lasch, *The True and Only Heaven*.

56. An ABC poll showed that the candidate qualities that mattered most to Bush voters were experience (31 percent) and an ability to handle crises (26 percent). "Representing Issues and Candidate Qualities," Voter Research & Surveys, ABC, *Montreal Gazette*, 5 Nov. 1992, A11; *Time*, 2 Nov. 1992, p. 29.

57. Tom Rosenstiel, *Strange Bedfellows* (New York, 1993), p. 345; Elizabeth Drew, *On the Edge* (New York, 1994), p. 395.

58. *Rolling Stone*, 9 Dec. 1993, p. 81.

59. Joe Klein, "The Politics of Promiscuity," *Nwswk*, 9 May 1994, pp. 19, 16.

60. *NYTM*, 6 May 1990, p. 58. See *Time*, 3 Oct. 1988.

61. Matalin and Carville, *All's Fair*, p. 131.

62. Hendrik Hertzberg, "A Prig or a Fool," *TNR*, 17 Oct. 1988, p. 12; Estrich in *Time*, 3 Oct. 1988, pp. 19–20; *NYT*, 6 Nov. 1988, p. 43.

63. Alexander Hamilton [Publius], "No. 68," Edward Mead Earle, ed., *The Federalist* (New York, n.d.), pp. 441–444; "Speech of General Harrison Delivered at the Old Hamilton Convention," 1 Oct. 1840, p. 6, MVB MSS; SFX, 2 Nov. 1936, p. 10; BosG, 13 Nov. 1988, B:1.

64. Richard Nixon, *In the Arena* (New York, 1990), p. 198; Lance Morrow, "Of Myth and Memory," *Time*, 24 Oct. 1988, p. 21; Matalin and Carville, *All's Fair*, p. 188.

65. Kathleen Hall Jamieson, *Packaging the Presidency* (New York, 1984), pp. 451–453; Thomas E. Patterson and Robert D. McClure, *Political Advertising* (Princeton, N.J., n.d.), p. 21.

66. Polsby and Wildavsky, *Elections*, p. 1; Andy Hiller, WBZ-TV, in BosG, 9 Nov. 1988, p. 89; *NYT*, 22 Nov. 1988, B:6.

67. On the fear of power, see "Power and Liberty: A Theory of Politics," chap. 3 in Bernard Bailyn, *The Ideological Origins of the American Revolution* (Cambridge, 1967), pp. 55–93.

68. Alan Ehrenhalt distinguishes between Democratic party "careerists" who "believe in government" and Republican "amateurs" who are more skeptical of government in *The United States of Ambition* (New York, 1991, 1992), pp. 224, 214. "Cato's Letters," no. 61, 13 Jan. 1721, p. 239 in Leonard W. Levy, ed., *Cato's Letters*, 2 vols. (New York, 1971), 2:239.

69. A New York Times/CBS exit poll showed that of those whose family's financial situation was worse in 1992 than it had been in 1988, 61 percent voted for Clinton, 14 percent voted for Bush. *NYT*, 5 Nov. 1992, B9. On Harding's appeal as a respite from the "age of the Titans," see Mark Sullivan, *Our Times* (New York, 1935), 6:125.

70. This fear of decline stemmed from republicanism and Puritanism. See John Patrick

Diggins, *The Lost Soul of American Politics* (New York, 1984), p. 10. James K. Glassman, "The Solipsistic Campaign," *TNR*, 28 Nov. 1988, p. 46; *Time*, 24 Oct. 1988; John Chancellor, *Peril and Promise* (New York, 1990), p. 141.

71. King, *On the Line*, pp. 81, 2, 96, 6.
72. JFK Interview, Chet Huntley and David Brinkley, 30 Sept. 1960, NBC, "The Campaign and the Candidates," 1 Oct. 1960; Richard Rendell, MBS, "News," 27 Sept. 1960, both in U.S. Congress, Senate, Committee on Commerce, *Freedom of Communications, Final Report of the Committee on Commerce, United States Senate; Prepared by Its Subcommittee of the Subcommittee on Communications, Pursuant to S.Res. 305, 86th Congress,* Report 994, 87th Cong., 1st sess., 1961, 3:119; 4:55.
73. Ursula R. Culver in Jonathan Cottin, "Advance Men," chap. 4 in Robert Agranoff, *The New Style in Election Campaigns,* 2nd ed. (Boston, 1976), p. 106; Sununu in King, *On the Line*, p. 131.
74. King, *On the Line*, p. 176.
75. Paul F. Lazarsfeld et al., *The People's Choice,* 2nd ed. (New York, 1948), pp. 121–122, 101–104; *BosG*, 7 Nov. 1988, p. 18.
76. Sidney Blumenthal, *The Permanent Campaign* (New York, 1980).
77. Daniel T. Rodgers and others have justifiably criticized the use of republicanism as an explanatory catchall. Still, just because republicanism and liberalism do not stand up as paradigms to explain everything, we should not rush to the opposite extreme and assume they explain nothing. Even republicanism's "birth announcement"—Robert Shalhope's 1972 article "Toward a Republican Synthesis"—acknowledged that during the Revolution "republicanism represented a general consensus solely because it rested on such vague premises." Words such as "republicanism," "virtue," "personality," and "character" are "tools" that capture certain ideas developed over time. Just as Rodgers recognizes in his book *Contested Truths* that political terms can be fluid yet still useful, historians can use broad terms like republicanism and liberal democracy as symbols of continuity. Daniel T. Rodgers, "Republicanism: The Career of a Concept," *JAH* 79 (June 1992): 37, 23; Robert E. Shalhope, "Toward a Republican Synthesis," *William and Mary Quarterly* 29 (Jan. 72): 72; Daniel T. Rodgers, *Contested Truths* (New York, 1987).
78. George F. Will, *The New Season* (New York, 1988), p. 176.
79. John Dewey quoted in Diggins, *Lost Soul,* p. 162.

An Essay on Sources

Accounts of elections glut American political scholarship. While few facts remain to be discovered, much synthesis and analysis needs to be done. Many social scientists, for example, fail to place the campaign in proper historical perspective. A work like Kathleen Hall Jamieson's *Packaging the Presidency: A History and Criticism of Presidential Campaign Advertising* (New York, 1984) stands out, because it begins with an historical overview, albeit a brief one. Historians tend to concentrate on the issues, incidents, and personalities of a particular election, to the exclusion of long-term trends. The many studies of individual elections rarely place candidates' actions in the context of their careers, while discussions in biographies often view the campaign itself as stagnant, rather than evolving. In the 1970s, various statistical studies by Walter Dean Burnham, Richard Jensen, and Joel Silbey, among others, revolutionized our understanding of electoral politics. The works, however, focused on parties and voting, overlooking the candidates themselves.

Eugene H. Roseboom's *A History of Presidential Elections* (New York, 1957), typifies works that place the campaign in a broader perspective, using the campaigns as building blocks to construct a "history of national politics." Roseboom's summary thus ignores changing attitudes and tactics. Robert J. Dinkin, *Campaigning in America: A History of Election Practices* (New York, 1989) offers valuable tidbits and highlights some trends, but also shies away from an overall interpretation of the campaign itself. Charles S. Sydnor's superior *American Revolutionaries in the Making: Political Practices in Washington's Virginia* (New York, 1965) stops after the colonial period. Arthur Schlesinger, Jr., and Fred Israel, *History of American Presidential Elections, 1789–1968*, 4 vols. (New York, 1971) is encyclopedic but uneven.

Recently, some historians have begun to explore what Jean Baker calls the campaign's "latent function," not its "purposive goals." Baker deftly blends anthropology and history in *Affairs of Party: The Political Culture of Northern Democrats in the Mid–Nineteenth Century* (Ithaca, 1983). Michael E. McGerr's *The Decline of Popular Politics: The American North, 1865–1928* (New York, 1986) explores the impact of changes in political "style" on voting. M. J. Heale's *The Presidential Quest: Candi-*

dates and Images in American Political Culture, 1781–1852 (New York, 1982) uses campaign literature to trace the candidates' developing role in the early republic. Richard P. McCormick's *The Presidential Game: The Origins of American Presidential Politics* (New York, 1982) probes the gap between republican rhetoric and electoral realities, concentrating on the electoral process through the 1840s. Richard Jensen's article "Armies, Admen and Crusaders, Types of Presidential Campaigns," *History Teacher* 2 (Jan. 1969):33–50, offers a useful framework. Jeffrey K. Tulis highlights changes in the presidency and the campaign in *The Rhetorical Presidency* (Princeton, 1987). But the book is overly concerned with changing theories, and neglects the time lag between a conceptual change and its eventual implementation.

In examining attitudes about campaigning, *See How They Ran* explores some of the common myths that unite and confuse the American polity, what Edmund S. Morgan in *Inventing the People: The Rise of Popular Sovereignty in England and America* (New York, 1988), calls the sustaining "fictions" underlying any political culture. Focusing on these common myths obscures America's much-vaunted pluralism. But, as Robert H. Wiebe insists in *The Segmented Society: An Introduction to the Meaning of America* (New York, 1975), to "ignore the areas of agreement is to deny the existence of an American society." When arguing about how candidates should behave, Americans usually acted as Americans. This concern with mainstream public opinion parallels the concerns of Michael Kammen in his excellent book *A Machine That Would Go of Itself: The Constitution in American Culture* (New York, 1986).

Focusing on the candidate's role highlights the continuing obsession with republican ideas of virtue. On republicanism, Bernard Bailyn's *Ideological Origins of the American Revolution* (Cambridge, 1967) remains definitive, supplemented by Gordon Wood's *The Creation of the American Republic, 1776–1787* (New York, 1969). J. G. A. Pocock's *The Machiavellian Moment: Florentine Political Thought and the Atlantic Republican Tradition* (Princeton, 1975) is useful on republicanism's European origins. Robert E. Shalhope offers a good overview in *The Roots of Democracy: American Thought and Culture, 1760–1800* (Boston, 1990). He borrows the anthropological concept of a "liminal" or marginal state of transition to explain that in the absence of new "cultural steadfasts," some Americans clung to republicanism long after it was "outmoded." This continuing allegiance to republicanism, and the resulting "struggle for predominance between competing cultural forces," can be seen in the century-long tug-of-war over the candidate's role.

Attacks on the so-called Bailyn school are also illuminating. Forrest

McDonald and Ellen Shapiro McDonald in *Requiem: Variations on Eighteenth-Century Themes* (Lawrence, 1988), reject the republican synthesis but confirm the importance of "character" to the Framers. Similarly, John Patrick Diggins, *The Lost Soul of American Politics: Virtue, Self-Interest, and the Foundations of Liberalism* (New York, 1984) champions liberalism as the dominant American ideology. Yet in arguing that nineteenth-century Americans lacked "virtue," Diggins implicitly confirms the continuing desire for it, if only in rhetoric.

Surprisingly, the literature on liberal democracy is less satisfying. Still, Robert Kelley has two fine books, *The Transatlantic Persuasion: The Liberal-Democratic Mind in the Age of Gladstone* (New York, 1969) and *The Cultural Pattern in American Politics: The First Century* (New York, 1979). On origins see "Historians and the Problem of Early American Democracy," chapter 9 in J. R. Pole, *Paths to the American Past* (New York, 1979) and Morgan's book on popular sovereignty. The "consensus" historians of the 1950s remain the best chroniclers of American democracy, especially Louis Hartz, *The Liberal Tradition in America* (New York, 1955) and Richard Hofstadter, *The American Political Tradition and the Men Who Made It* (New York, 1973).

Recently, much of the historiographical ferment about democracy in America has focused on culture, not politics. Daniel Boorstin's *The Americans*, 3 vols. (New York, 1958-1973), is majestic. Robert Westbrook's essay on "Politics as Consumption: Managing the Modern American Election," chapter 5 in Richard Wightman Fox and T. J. Jackson Lears, eds., *The Culture of Consumption: Critical Essays in American History* (New York, 1983), analyzes the relationship between campaigning and the emerging consumer culture, while Kenneth Cmiel, *Democratic Eloquence: The Fight Over Popular Speech in Nineteenth-Century America* (New York, 1990), links the evolution of speaking styles with changes in politics and culture. Warren Susman, "'Personality' and the Making of Twentieth Century Culture," chapter 14 in *Culture as History: The Transformation of American Society in the Twentieth Century* (New York, 1984), distinguishes "personality" from "character."

For works on modern American culture's most potent vehicle, advertising, see Stephen Fox, *The Mirror Makers: A History of American Advertising and Its Creators* (New York, 1984) and Roland Marchand's *Advertising the American Dream: Making Way for Modernity, 1920-1940* (Berkeley, 1985). In assessing whether advertising mirrors American culture, Marchand speaks of a "Zerrspiegel," a "distorting mirror that would enhance certain images." This metaphor aptly describes the evolution of political style, for candidates and the public successively distorted perceptions of each other, as often occurs in a funhouse filled with mirrors reflecting images back and forth.

Scholars have long debated whether political change "mirrors" broader, external forces, as Frank Sorauf argues in "Political Parties and Political Analysis," chapter 2 in William Nisbet Chambers and Walter Dean Burnham, eds., *The American Party System: Stages of Political Development*, 2nd ed. (New York, 1975). While the campaign changed in line with broader political forces like parties as well as with such social forces as technology, stumping appeared long after it "should" have, and persists long after it became "obsolete." As Daniel Czitrom's *Media and the American Mind: From Morse to McLuhan* (Chapel Hill, 1982), and John Kasson's *Civilizing the Machine: Technology and Republican Values in America, 1776–1900* (New York, 1977) have shown in different contexts, America's "Go-Getter" culture was surprisingly resistant to change. Far too many scholars are satisfied with a deterministic model, wherein politics changes in lockstep with technology. See, for example, Richard Rubin, *Press, Party, and Presidency* (New York, 1981). A more sophisticated approach can be found in Allan R. Pred, *Urban Growth and the Circulation of Information: the United States Systems of Cities, 1790–1840* (Cambridge, 1973). On political change see also Richard L. McCormick, *The Party Period and Public Policy: American Politics from the Age of Jackson to the Progressive Era* (New York, 1986).

Alan Brinkley explores the impact of one technology, radio, on politics in *Voices of Protest: Huey Long, Father Coughlin & the Great Depression* (New York, 1982). Michael Schudson's *Discovering the News: A Social History of American Newspapers* (New York, 1978) links the rise of objectivity with the growth of the American marketplace. Useful studies of journalism during particular periods include George Juergens, *News from the White House: The Presidential–Press Relationship in the Progressive Era* (Chicago, 1981); Graham J. White, *FDR and the Press* (Chicago, 1979); and Mark Hertsgaard, *On Bended Knee: The Press and the Reagan Presidency* (New York, 1988). On TV see Erik Barnouw, *Tube of Plenty: the Evolution of American Television*, rev. ed. (New York, 1982) and Austin Ranney, *Channels of Power: The Impact of Television on American Politics* (New York, 1983).

The literature on the presidency is vast. See the collections by Aaron Wildavsky, ed., *The Presidency* (Boston, 1969) and Thomas E. Cronin, ed., *Rethinking the Presidency* (Boston, 1982). Wilfred E. Binkley, "The President as a National Symbol," *Annals of the American Academy of Politics and Social Science* 283 (Sept. 1952):86–93, emphasizes the president's roles as both king and prime minister. Ralph Ketchum, *Presidents*

Above Party: The First American Presidency, 1789–1829 (Chapel Hill, 1984), explores the early presidency.

On parties and politics in general, see the books by Chambers and Burnham, McGerr, Baker, and the McCormicks already cited. Richard Hofstadter, *The Idea of a Party System: The Rise of Legitimate Opposition in the United States, 1780–1840* (Berkeley, 1970) examines the gradual acceptance of the first party system. On the Jacksonian period see Ronald Formisano, *Transformation of Political Culture: Massachusetts Parties, 1790s–1840s* (New York, 1983) and Richard P. McCormick, *The Second American Party System: Party Formation in the Jacksonian Era* (New York, 1973). For the Civil War see William E. Gienapp, *The Origins of the Republican Party, 1852–1856* (New York, 1987), J. G. Randall and David Donald, *The Civil War and Reconstruction*, rev. ed. (Boston, 1969), and the illuminating essays in David Donald, *Lincoln Reconsidered: Essays on the Civil War Era*, rev. 2nd ed. (New York, 1961). For a good summary of the postbellum era see H. Wayne Morgan, *From Hayes to McKinley: National Party Politics, 1877–1896* (Syracuse, NY, 1969). Franklin Roosevelt's relation to the Democratic party is illuminated in Kristi Anderson, *The Creation of a Democratic Majority* (Chicago, 1979) and Sidney M. Milkis, "Franklin D. Roosevelt and the Transcendence of Partisan Politics," *Political Science Quarterly* 100 (Fall 1985):479–504. On party "dealignment" in the modern era see Martin Wattenberg, *The Decline of American Political Parties, 1952–1980* (Cambridge, 1984). Arthur M. Schlesinger, Jr., reminds us not to get too nostalgic about parties in "The Short Happy Life of American Political Parties," *The Cycles of American History* (Boston, 1986).

The post–World War II boom in political science and polling created a new genre of voter studies. Paul F. Lazarsfeld, Bernard Berelson, and Hazel Gaudet set the pace with *The People's Choice: How the Voter Makes Up His Mind in a Presidential Campaign*, 2nd ed. (New York, 1948). Since 1952 the University of Michigan's Survey Research Center has tracked voter attitudes, leading to Angus Campbell, Philip E. Converse, Warren E. Miller, and Donald E. Stokes, *The American Voter* (New York, 1960) and Norman H. Nie, Sidney Verba, and John R. Petrocik, *The Changing American Voter: Enlarged Edition* (Cambridge, 1979). In *The Responsible Electorate: Rationality in Presidential Voting, 1936–1960* (Cambridge, 1966), V. O. Key argues that voters are "not fools."

For the study of recent campaigns, Theodore White remains the great hero *and* villain. His *Making of the President* series, from 1960 through 1980, inspired a generation of journalists and scholars. Yet too many of White's successors simply catalogue campaign trivia. Among

the few who inherited White's historical sense are Timothy Crouse in
The Boys on the Bus (New York, 1972); Jules Witcover in *Marathon:
the Pursuit of the Presidency, 1972–1976* (New York, 1977); and Sidney
Blumenthal in *Pledging Allegiance: The Last Campaign of the Cold War*
(New York, 1990). Joe McGinniss's *The Selling of the President 1968* (New
York, 1969) has much to offer, if viewed somewhat skeptically, while
Larry J. Sabato, *The Rise of Political Consultants: New Ways of Winning
Elections* (New York, 1981) is valuable, if overly pessimistic. Finally, stud-
ies of modern elections benefit from the published proceedings of a "de-
briefing" of rival campaign managers held at Harvard's John F. Kennedy
School of Government since 1972. The first (and arguably the best) one
is Ernest R. May and Janet Fraser, eds., *Campaign '72: the Managers
Speak* (Cambridge, 1973). Subsequent editors and publishers have
varied.

These secondary sources guided the search through primary sources.
This study relies on the available personal papers of major party presidential nominees from 1840 through 1988 and their advisers. I paid closest attention to the period from just before the nominating conventions
until a month after the elections. The papers of each victorious candidate until Herbert Hoover are available in microfilm as part of the Library of Congress Presidential Papers Microfilm Series. The papers of
each President since Hoover are housed in particular presidential libraries scattered throughout the country.

Unfortunately, the most valuable items in these collections—copies
of letters written by the candidates themselves—are the hardest to find.
The incoming correspondence in each collection did, however, provide
a sense of the pressures on the candidate from the public, and offered a
glimpse of some of the discussions taking place among advisers. Especially for candidates after 1868, the Scrapbooks offered a wide sampling
of newspaper reaction to the activities of the nominee.

To see the candidates' actions as the public saw them, I sampled
newspapers in each election from the period before the convention
through December of the election year. These "bibles of democracy," as
Walter Lippmann called them, are the best repositories of contemporary
political wisdom [Walter Lippmann, *Liberty and the News* (New York,
1920), p. 57]. Alternating between Whig or Republican journals and
Democratic ones, I surveyed newspapers within an election year until
the reactions became repetitious. American newspapers always reprinted items from other journals. These recycled articles, and the subsequent wire-service reports, allow the historian to generalize about Whig,
Republican, and Democratic reactions to events. This news flow also

partially mitigates regional variations. The *New York Tribune* in the mid–nineteenth century and the *New York Times* thereafter offered thorough daily coverage of the campaigns.

Most of the more obscure journals cited in notes are housed in state portfolios in the Newspaper and Periodical Collections of the Library of Congress.

Index

Paar, Jack, 213, 265
Parker, Alton B., 113–119, 128, 132
Parties, political; *see also* Character;
    Issues; Personality
  decline of, 2–4, 81, 83–86, 97,
    100–102, 109, 134, 167–168,
    191–192, 209, 222, 229–230,
    234, 238–239, 241, 274,
    277–278, 281
  dictating propriety, 18, 36–38,
    41–42, 278
  growth of, 12–14, 20–21, 41–45, 49,
    57, 61, 83–85, 107
  inverse relation with candidate
    strength, 30, 36, 45, 68, 81, 86,
    101, 102, 106–107, 109,
    111–112, 167–168, 218, 277
  questionable legitimacy of, 12–14,
    21, 38, 53, 135
  organization of, 41–45, 73, 79–80,
    105, 135, 167–168, 179, 229
  reinforcing republican taboo, 30,
    36–38, 41–42, 50, 51, 56–60
  relative importance of, 2–3, 12–14,
    41–42, 45, 49, 57, 59–60, 76–77,
    109, 111–112, 131–132, 143,
    148, 209, 263, 277
Paterson Daily Guardian, 87
Patronage, 15, 42, 73, 84, 97, 120
Pendleton, George, 67, 68
Penrose, Boies, 143
Pentagon Papers, 228
Perkins, Frances, 178
Perot, Ross, 255, 261, 264–265, 267–
    268, 270
Personality; *see also* Issues
  as distinct from "character," 107,
    114, 131, 255, 279
  importance of, relative to parties,
    2–3, 76–77, 84, 109, 111–112,
    143, 158
  increasingly important, 78, 84, 94,
    95, 101, 107, 114, 116, 121, 122,
    124, 128–132, 133, 136, 137,

    146, 150, 162, 164, 166, 167,
    182, 191, 203–204, 208, 213,
    220, 230, 251, 255, 257–258,
    262, 265, 267, 271–275, 279–280
  questionable legitimacy of, 2, 77,
    115, 118, 124–125, 128, 146, 196,
    197, 209, 217, 258, 259, 269, 273
Photography, 114–116, 119, 136, 145,
    149, 151, 152, 156, 159, 164, 171,
    172, 177, 188
Physical appearance of candidate, 25,
    146, 202, 274
Pierce, Franklin, 51, 55–57, 98
Pinchot, Amos, 171
Pinkerton, James, 258
Pittman, Key, 150
Platforms, party, 18, 39, 41, 45, 86
Platt, Thomas, 95, 110
Playboy, Jimmy Carter's interview
    with, 238, 280
Political memory, 216, 221, 277
Polk, James K., 21, 30–32, 34–35, 37,
    41, 46, 253
Polls and polling, 2, 167, 172, 182, 189,
    191, 193–196, 199, 205, 207, 221,
    233, 235, 237–238, 242, 245, 247,
    264, 274
  pros and cons of, 181, 194, 195,
    241, 280
Polsby, Nelson W., 257, 274
Popkin, Samuel, 262
Popular politics, 20, 57, 84–86
Popular presidential campaign, 4, 6, 10,
    20, 57
Popularity, as distinguished from elect-
    ability, 68, 99–100, 104, 112,
    121, 131, 154, 194–195
Populism, 102, 103, 126
Powell, Jody, 241
Power, fear of, 8, 9, 17, 119, 173, 201,
    274–275; *see also* Republicanism
Powers, Dave, 214
Presence of campaigner, valued, 25,
    45, 64, 75, 101, 107, 258